C000145309

ALL-ASIA GUIDE

SOUTH ASIA

VOLUME I

FarEasternEconomic
REVIEW

Published by

Review Publishing Co. Ltd,
G.P.O. Box 160,
Hongkong

Distributed by

Roger Lascelles, Cartographic and Travel Publisher
47 York Road, Brentford, Middlesex TW8 0QP.   Tel: 081-847 0935

ISBN 962-7010-40-5

Published by

Review Publishing Co. Ltd.
G.P.O. Box 160,
Hongkong

Printed by
DAI NIPPON PRINTING CO. (HK) LTD
Tsuen Wan Industrial Centre, 2-5/F., 220-224 Texaco Road,
Tsuen Wan, N.T., Hongkong

ISBN 962-7010-40-5

WRITTEN AND COMPILED BY

Salamat Ali (*Pakistan*)

Carmen Jones Clad (*India*)

S. Kamaluddin (*Bangladesh*)

Bertil Lintner (*Burma*)

James Pringle (*Maldives*)

Mohan Samarasinghe (*Sri Lanka*)

Brian Shaw (*Bhutan*)

Kedar Man Singh (*Nepal*)

Editor: Michael Malik

Assistant Editor: Ron Knowles

Production Editor: Paul Lee
Henry Chiu (*Deputy*)
Winnie Law (*Assistant*)

Design Consultant: John Hull

Cover Picture: Derek A. C. Davies

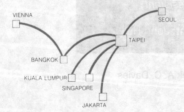

CONTENTS

SYMBOLS

Accommodation

Banks

Business hours

Climate

Currency

Customs

Dining

Dress

Entertainment

Entry

Government

Health

History

Holidays

Immigration

Language

Shopping

Sports

Tourist information

Tours

Transport

Swimming pool

Western food

Asian food

INTRODUCTION

Guide books are almost by definition out of date before they reach the reader — imagine having attempted to produce a guide to Eastern Europe or the Soviet Union in 1989. As a minor example, since the section of this book on Indonesia was printed, Jakarta telephone numbers starting with the figures 34 have all been changed to 384, while numbers which were previously started 578 now start 571 and those which used to start 5801 now start 5715. In other parts of Indonesia numbers have been completely changed, and the best advice, if looking for a hotel number, for example, is to check with the international exchange.

Prices, of course, are constantly changing and while we have endeavoured to make the prices quoted in this book as up-to-date as possible, we do not claim to be infallible. As supply and demand change constantly, some travellers might be pleasantly surprised to find there are heavy discounts available, while in other places prices may have increased. Never be afraid to ask for a discount, however, even at the most exclusive hotels. Discount fares are, of course, also available, and only those travelling on company expenses should buy an air ticket direct from an airline, since most travel agents can get you a better deal — even including their commission.

Currency rates of exchange also are unpredictable and while we quote hotel prices in US dollars, their equivalent in other currencies will change.

While we are aiming mainly at the business traveller, we have not neglected to include advice and accommodation for the budget traveller as well.

Although this is in no way a back-packer's guide, there is some advice which applies to all travellers — one of the most important is to travel light. Many travellers, even the most experienced, burden themselves with far more luggage than they really need, and there is nothing worse than having to struggle with three suitcases — even if you can find a trolley — through an airport when one would probably be quite enough if your luggage is carefully selected.

The ideal, if it can be managed, is to limit yourself to one bag which conforms to airline specifications for cabin luggage. The advantage of this is to be able to walk straight off a plane and to beat the crush at the immigration counter, while others are waiting for their luggage to arrive on the carousel.

This book will tell you the temperature range of your destination, and do not neglect to check it. In New Delhi, for instance, the range can be extreme — from more than 37°C (100°F) in summer to near 0°C (32°F) in winter, while in southern India or the Maldives, it is more or less tropical all year round. If you are going from southern India to Kashmir in winter, you will need two sets of clothes. Obviously in tropical climates where temperatures can exceed 35°F (95°C), and humidity is often high, you are going to need to change your clothes possibly several times a day, so drip-dry garments — and thin cotton underwear which you can wash yourself and wear the next day — are useful to avoid not only bulk in your luggage but what can be exorbitant hotel laundry charges.

One, or even better two, changes of shoes are recommended for the tropical areas, where sudden rain can land you in ankle-deep floods even in central city areas. Always pack a few coat-hangers since few hotels provide enough.

Conforming to local customs is also a very important point, especially for those not familiar with Asia. Not removing your shoes on entering a mosque in Muslim countries and Buddhist or Hindu temples, for instance, is greatly insulting. It is also the custom to take your shoes off at the door when entering private houses in many parts of Asia. Just follow your host's example.

While it is quite acceptable for women to bathe or sunbathe topless in places such as Bali in Indonesia, and on private hotel beaches in many Thai resorts, it is not acceptable in most Muslim countries which include Indonesia (apart from Bali which is basically Hindu), Malaysia or Singapore. It is always a good idea to ask local advice on this.

Do not carry political literature or leaflets of any kind — Left, Right or even Centre — it is not worth the problems you may encounter.

And remember that carrying drugs, not only heroin and cocaine, but cannabis — even for your own use — can not only land you in prison, but is subject to the death penalty in Thailand, Malaysia and Singapore.

In most Asian countries it is advisable to avoid drinking water that has not come out of a sealed bottle or been boiled. If you do not drink beer or other alcohol, stick to tea.

Each chapter in this book will tell you of the minimal health certificates needed for entering a country, but you would be advised, if coming from outside Asia, to seek advice from a doctor on such requirements as anti-malaria medication — which should start before arriving in malarial regions — and other prophylactics such as any diarrhoea medicine, which can be very important for those unfamiliar with Asian food.

If travelling outside major cities, take your own soap and suntan cream. Women should carry a good supply of tampons or sanitary towels, which are often not available. Reading matter in your own language should be added to your luggage for those long flights and television-less evenings in many places.

Carry several copies of a list of dutiable goods you have with you and intend to take home, such as cameras, tape recorders or disc players, including the maker's name and any identification number — for body and lens in the case of cameras. Most countries will not require it, but those which do (such as India) can keep you for hours at the airport filling in forms. It is also always useful to have with you a supply of passport photographs of yourself for unexpected visas or passes.

Do not assume that you can take duty-free alcohol into every country just because you are a tourist. Pakistan, for instance, confiscates it on entry and though theoretically it should be returned to you on leaving the country, this is easier said than done — unless you want to spend half a day at the airport before your flight.

Finally, while several Asian countries have a deserved reputation for cheap and easily available sex, remember that AIDS is spreading fast in the region and take appropriate precautions.

This 15th edition of the All-Asia Guide comes in a new format. While there is still a complete compendium edition, it is also being printed in three sections, covering Southeast Asia, Northeast Asia and South Asia, for the convenience of those travellers only interested in one region. It is also fully colour-illustrated for the first time and the binding — a problem with some previous editions — has been improved. Another new feature is a chapter on Soviet Asia and Siberia, now becoming much more open to visitors.

The book has been re-organised so that each chapter is self-contained, including a section on local food and shopping (including precious stones) instead of one chapter on these subjects as in previous editions. The Hotel Guide also has been rearranged so that each country's hotels are listed at the end of individual chapters, instead of them all appearing at the back of the book.

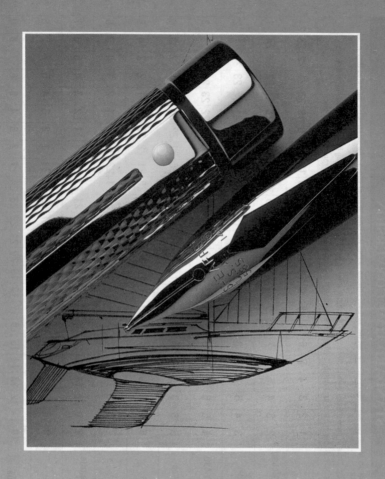

SHEAFFER.

STANDARD TIME CONVERSION

Find your location, move across columns to current hour. Move up or down the vertical column to find the time in other zones. An asterisk (*) indicates that 30 minutes must be added to the hour.

Time in blue shaded area is tomorrow. Time in grey shaded area is yesterday. (Example: when it is 10 am Tuesday in Hongkong its is 9 pm Monday in New York.)

The chart below lists Standard times only: Summer Time or Daylight Saving Time is observed in many countries, some with regional variations.

Location																								
Tokyo, Fukuoka, Osaka, Seoul, Darwin*, Adelaide*	1	2	3	4	5	6	7	8	9	10	11	12	13	14	15	16	17	18	19	20	21	22	23	24
Sydney, Melbourne, Brisbane, Hobart, Port Moresby, Vladivostock	2	3	4	5	6	7	8	9	10	11	12	13	14	15	16	17	18	19	20	21	22	23	24	1
New Caledonia, Solomon Islands, New Hebrides	3	4	5	6	7	8	9	10	11	12	13	14	15	16	17	18	19	20	21	22	23	24	1	2
Auckland, Fiji, Wake Island, Kiribati	4	5	6	7	8	9	10	11	12	13	14	15	16	17	18	19	20	21	22	23	24	1	2	3
American Samoa, Western Samoa	5	6	7	8	9	10	11	12	13	14	15	16	17	18	19	20	21	22	23	24	1	2	3	4
Hawaiian Islands, Cook Islands	6	7	8	9	10	11	12	13	14	15	16	17	18	19	20	21	22	23	24	1	2	3	4	5
Anchorage, Tahiti	7	8	9	10	11	12	13	14	15	16	17	18	19	20	21	22	23	24	1	2	3	4	5	6
Los Angeles, San Francisco, Seattle, San Diego, Vancouver	8	9	10	11	12	13	14	15	16	17	18	19	20	21	22	23	24	1	2	3	4	5	6	7
Edmonton, Calgary, Denver, Salt Lake City, Albuquerque	9	10	11	12	13	14	15	16	17	18	19	20	21	22	23	24	1	2	3	4	5	6	7	8
Chicago, Detroit, Houston, Mexico City, San Jose, Managua	10	11	12	13	14	15	16	17	18	19	20	21	22	23	24	1	2	3	4	5	6	7	8	9

La Paz, Santiago

Location																								
Buenos Aires, Rio de Janeiro, San Paulo, Montevideo	13	14	15	16	17	18	19	20	21	22	23	24	1	2	3	4	5	6	7	8	9	10	11	12
Part of Greenland, South Georgia	14	15	16	17	18	19	20	21	22	23	24	1	2	3	4	5	6	7	8	9	10	11	12	13
The Azores, Cape Verde	15	16	17	18	19	20	21	22	23	24	1	2	3	4	5	6	7	8	9	10	11	12	13	14
London, Dublin, Iceland, Dakar, Accra	16	17	18	19	20	21	22	23	24	1	2	3	4	5	6	7	8	9	10	11	12	13	14	15
Stockholm, Amsterdam, Paris, Rome, Frankfurt, Zurich, Lagos	17	18	19	20	21	22	23	24	1	2	3	4	5	6	7	8	9	10	11	12	13	14	15	16
Helsinki, Athens, Bucharest, Cairo, Johannesburg	18	19	20	21	22	23	24	1	2	3	4	5	6	7	8	9	10	11	12	13	14	15	16	17
Moscow, Leningrad, Bahrain, Riyadh, Nairobi, Madagascar	19	20	21	22	23	24	1	2	3	4	5	6	7	8	9	10	11	12	13	14	15	16	17	18
Gorki, Baku, Dubai, Muscat, Seychelles Islands, Mauritius	20	21	22	23	24	1	2	3	4	5	6	7	8	9	10	11	12	13	14	15	16	17	18	19
Karachi, Bombay*, Delhi*, Calcutta*, Colombo	21	22	23	24	1	2	3	4	5	6	7	8	9	10	11	12	13	14	15	16	17	18	19	20
Rangoon*, Tashkent	22	23	24	1	2	3	4	5	6	7	8	9	10	11	12	13	14	15	16	17	18	19	20	21
Bangkok, Jakarta, Hanoi, Medan	23	24	1	2	3	4	5	6	7	8	9	10	11	12	13	14	15	16	17	18	19	20	21	22
Hongkong, China, Taipei, Manila, Singapore, Brunei, Malaysia, Perth	24	1	2	3	4	5	6	7	8	9	10	11	12	13	14	15	16	17	18	19	20	21	22	23

THE WINGED CHARIOT

Fly Biman. It's like you are on a winged chariot.

The dream-world emerges on board: visions come and go all the way. You'll find there are sari-clad fairies at your service. Ask for your palate. Just wait, and have it. A motion picture is on the screen. It's fantastic! Dive into it. Are you tired? Use the head set and drink sweet notes of the classic music to the lees. Now it's time to relax.

Biman
BANGLADESH AIRLINES
Your home in the air

BANGLADESH

A bitter and often bloody nine-month war of independence in 1971 resulted in the birth of Bangladesh, one of Asia's youngest nations. Originally part of Pakistan, the Bengali-speaking people, now numbering about 100 million, rose in revolt following the Pakistani army crackdown at midnight on March 25-26, 1971 and became independent on December 16. Independence, however, failed to resolve most of the country's major problems. About a seventh of the country's 55,000 m^2 is under water. Floods, occurring at regular intervals, and other natural calamities like cyclones and drought, wipe out crops and livestock. Although foreign aid has been pumped into Bangladesh at a very high rate, it has not yet managed to compensate for the terrible damage wrought by the war of independence.

For nearly four years after independence, Bangladesh had a stable though indifferent political life. In August 1975, though, a coup saw the end of Awami League rule and the assassination of the young nation's leader, Sheikh Mujibur Rahman. Khandker Mushtaq Ahmed, a member of Mujib's cabinet, took over, but only for 11 weeks. Another coup removed Mushtaq on November 4, 1975. Again, three days later, Maj.-Gen. Ziaur Rahman was installed in office as a result of a popular upsurge. Although Justice A. M. Sayem took over nominally as president, the country was being ruled by a three-man martial-law administration made up of armed-forces chiefs.

In late 1976 Zia became the chief martial-law administrator, and in April 1977 he also took over the presidency from Sayem, who retired on health grounds. In May 1977 Zia held a referendum on his appointment as president and promised to hold a general election by the end of 1978. Zia was elected president in June 1978 for a five-year term under a free election, defeating retired general M. A. G. Osmany, the C-in-C of the Bangladesh liberation forces in 1971, by a huge margin. He also kept his promise by holding a general election for a 300-seat parliament in February 1979. He subsequently withdrew martial-law rule after the first session of the newly elected parliament in March 1979.

However, once again a group of army officers attempted a coup while Zia was over-nighting in Chittagong on May 30, 1981 and killed him. The coup attempt ended in a failure with the rebel leader himself being killed by a loyal officer.

Vice-president Abdus Sattar immediately took over and was duly elected as president in November 1981 for a five-year term. But his presidency ended on March 24, 1982 when the chief of army staff, Lieut.-Gen. Hossain Mohammad Ershad seized power in a bloodless coup.

Ershad, in keeping with his promise to hold national elections, held parliamentary polls to elect a 300-seat house on May 7, 1986. The government-backed Jatiya Party managed to win a simple majority in the parliament.

Ershad resigned from the army on August 31 and was elected president on October 15, 1986. Following a prolonged and violent anti-government agitation in November 1987 by the mainstream opposition parties, a state of emergency was proclaimed at the end of November and the parliament was dissolved soon after-

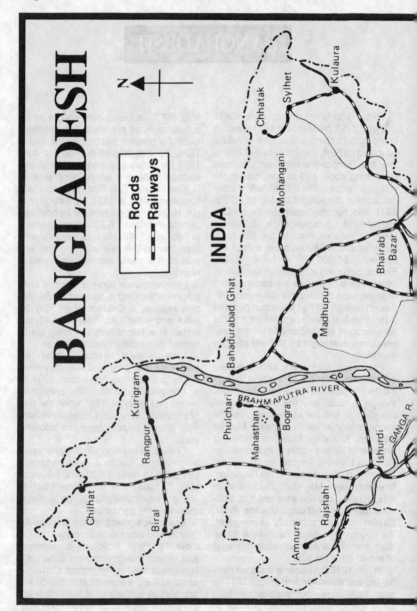

BANGLADESH

N

INDIA

Roads

Railways

BRAHMAPUTRA RIVER

GANGA R.

Kulaura

Sylhet

Chhatak

Mohangani

Bhairab Bazar

Madhupur

Bahadurabad Ghat

Kurigram

Rangpur

Chilhat

Biral

Phulchari

Bogra

Mahasthan

Ishurdi

Rajshahi

Amnura

Chapai

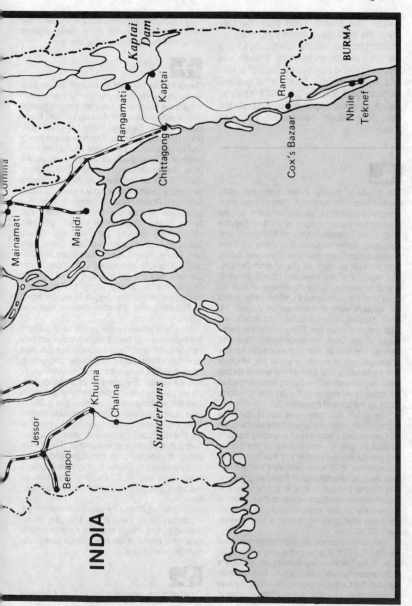

wards. The March 1988 parliamentary elections were boycotted by the main opposition parties and the ruling Jatiya Party gained a two-thirds majority. Ershad was forced to stand down in the face of unrest and rioting in late 1990. In a general election on February 27, 1991 Khaleda Zia, a zealous opponent of Ershad, led her Bangladesh Nationalist Party to power.

The region's history dates from the early Gupta Period (4th century AD) when there were already established kingdoms such as the Samatata in the delta region of the Brahmaputra River. Two important sites of Mainamati and Paharpur, where excavation is going on, have revealed significant Buddhist structures dating from at least as early as the seventh century. The region's affairs were tied up with those of the other Bengali-speaking people of eastern India from the 18th century until the setting up of the eastern wing of Pakistan on August 14, 1947. Muslim influence dates from around the 13th century when the Turks under the suzerainty of the Delhi emperor, Ghori, captured Bengal. The Muslim faith of the eastern reaches of Bengal was to continue under the Moghuls and the British and to provide the reason for this ethnically distinct people joining the strangers of the Indus River region on the far side of India to make up the state of Pakistan.

The union, however, was not to last. The economically neglected people of East Pakistan had demanded a measure of autonomy from the earliest stages. Events leading to the bloody and painful dismemberment of Pakistan began in December 1970 when president Yahya Khan held the first free election in Pakistan's history. The Awami League won a landslide victory in East Pakistan and thanks partly to the numerical supremacy of the eastern over the western wing, became qualified to form a new government of Pakistan.

Bangladesh dates its independence from March 26, 1971. This was the day when Maj.-Gen. Ziaur Rahman announced the country's independence over a clandestine radio operating from the Chittagong area. Ironically, he was assassinated by rebel army officers, also in Chittagong on May 30, 1981.

In February 1991, Khaleda Zia, leader of the Bangladesh Nationalist Party, was elected prime minister in a free general election.

Dhaka can be reached by air from almost anywhere in the world. In addition to Bangladesh Biman, the national flag carrier, which connects Dhaka with Amsterdam, Athens, London, Paris, Rome, Tripoli, Bangkok, Kuala Lumpur, Singapore, Bombay, Calcutta, Kathmandu and nearly one dozen cities in the Middle East, other international airlines such as British Airways, Air India, Indian Airlines, Aeroflot, Thai International, Pakistan International Airlines, Burma Airways, Kuwait Airways, Iraqi Airways, Saudia, Gulf Air, Royal Nepal Airlines, Dragon Air, Singapore Airlines and Emirate Airlines also fly to Dhaka. Calcutta, Rangoon, Bombay, Kathmandu, Karachi, Bangkok, Abu Dhabi, Dubai, Kuwait, Riyadh, Baghdad, Doha, Bahrain, Rome, Athens, Amsterdam, Paris and London are directly connected with Dhaka. From Calcutta, one can get two daily direct flights to Dhaka and six weekly flights to Chittagong. Bangladesh Biman has begun its regular flights to Frankfurt and will soon resume flights to Tokyo.

Overland you can enter by road and rail from the Indian state of West Bengal and by road only from Assam and Tripura states, but the land route from Assam is not considered convenient. From the West Bengal border town of Bongaon, you can enter Bangladesh at Benapol from where you can travel to the nearby large town of Jessore in Bangladesh, which is just a 26-minute flight from Dhaka. It is also possible to go to Dhaka by train or by coach services (considerably cheaper), but the route is rather circuitous owing to a plethora of waterways. There is no overland route to Burma from Bangladesh.

By sea you can enter through the country's major port city of Chittagong and through the other port town of Chalna near the Sundarbans.

On leaving Dhaka by an international flight, an airport tax of Taka 200 is charged. Those leaving by sea should apply for a road permit to reach the docks at the Immigration and Passport Office in Dhaka.

Passports are required of all visitors. Nationals of India must have their passports specially en-

The Baitul Mokarram Dhaka.

Photo: Noazesh Ahmed

dorsed for Bangladesh at any Indian regional passport office.

A visa is required for all countries except the nationals of the following countries: Bhutan, Barbados, Cyprus, New Zealand, Western Samoa, Canada, Singapore, Tonga, Leone, Lesotho, Zambia, Tanzania, Malta, Nigeria, Kenya, Somalia, Nauru, Bahamas, Grenada, Papua New Guinea, Seychelles, Trinidad, Tobago, Ghana, Sri Lanka (stay not exceeding one month), Ireland, Tunisia, Vatican, Gabon, Spain, Mauritius, Malaysia, Malawi, Gambia, Swaziland, Botswana, Jamaica, Guyana and Sierra Leone. No entry permit/visa will be needed for a period up to 15 days by the foreign nationals of the following countries arriving in or transitting through Bangladesh provided they hold return or onward air tickets: the US, Norway, Sweden, Denmark, Finland, the Netherlands, France, Portugal, Spain, Italy, Germany, Luxembourg, Belgium, Australia, Indonesia, Thailand, Nepal, Austria, Maldives, the Philippines, Switzerland and Greece. However, those arriving without a visa are generally given three-day visas on arrival. No registration and exit permit is required by any foreigner except for Pakistani nationals. Visas are issued by Bangladesh diplomatic missions abroad, including the trade commissions where there is no full embassy or consulate. Nationals of Yugoslavia, Japan and South Korea do not require any visa if their stay does not exceed three months (only for tourists).

International travellers coming from infected areas of yellow fever must possess a certificate showing inoculation against the disease.

Visitors are allowed to bring into Bangladesh duty-free 200 cigarettes, 50 cigars or half-a-pound of tobacco, one small bottle of perfume, two bottles of liquor or wine and reasonable quantities of personal belongings. Items such as cameras, portable typewriters and radios will usually be recorded to ensure their re-export. Those wishing to bring in motor vehicles via India, should be in possession of the usual international carnet de passage.

The taka is the unit of currency. In April 1991 the official exchange rate was Taka 35.8:US$1. However, tourists get a better rate at more than Taka 36. The taka is divided into 100 poisha. Notes of 1, 5, 10, 20, 50, 100 and 500 taka and coins of 1, 5, 10, 25 and 50 poisha are in circulation.

19

Bangladesh

Any amount of foreign currency may be brought into the country, but local currency is restricted to Taka 100 only. Foreign currency not exceeding US$1,000 is not required to be declared. Foreign currency not in excess of that imported and declared may be taken out again.

Currency declaration forms will be collected on departure and should tally with the amount of cash you have in hand. When leaving the country you may reconvert up to Taka 500 or 25% of the total amount in foreign exchange you have changed into convertible currency.

While Bangla (Bengali) is the official language, English is still used widely in official work and an English-speaking visitor will have no problem finding someone speaking English, even in the villages.

The climate is semi-tropical, with an average annual rainfall in Dhaka of 75 ins, most of which falls during the monsoon season from mid-May until the first week of October. Temperatures are not extreme — reaching an average of 90°F (32°C) — but humidity is high. April and September are the hottest months, when the temperatures may go over 100°F (38°C). From November through March the weather is quite pleasant with daytime temperature maximums ranging from 70-80°F (20-26°C). Evenings are cold in this period and temperatures may fall to 50°F (10°C) or even below. However, some variations in weather conditions have been noticed in the past few years.

Except for the winter months — November to March — easily laundered clothing is suitable throughout Bangladesh. Light woollens are required for the winter, especially for evenings.

Government offices operate Saturday to Thursday from 9 am to 4 pm with half-an-hour lunch break. They are closed on Fridays, as are the offices of international firms and embassies — most of which remain closed on Saturdays as well.

Commercial offices open from 9 am and work until 5 pm with an hour's lunch break between 1 pm and 2 pm. All firms are closed on Fridays. Most firms work half-day on Thursdays to 1 pm.

From Saturday to Wednesday banks are open from 9 am to 1 pm and up to 11 am on Thursdays. Post offices work government office hours but major post offices also work in the evenings up to 8 pm and certain telegraph offices in Dhaka and Chittagong are open 24 hours.

Most shops in Dhaka and the main towns operate between 9 am and 8 pm Shops work half-day on Thursdays and remain closed on Fridays. However, some markets, such as Dhaka Government New Market, are open on Fridays and closed on Tuesdays.

Restaurants, with the exceptions of larger hotels, are closed by 9 pm. The few bars are open from 11 am to 3 pm and from 6 pm to 11 pm. All bars are closed on Fridays, but residents of hotels can order their drinks inside their rooms.

Transport facilities, both surface and air, have improved tremendously in Bangladesh over the past few years. One can now travel from Dhaka to any part of the country by car, which is in itself an achievement considering the country's topography. Biman Bangladesh Airlines, the national flag-carrier, which began operations in January 1972, now has a fleet of two F-28s, three ATPs and four DC-10-30s. Biman provides air services from Dhaka to the major port city of Chittagong (28 flights a week each way), Sylhet (21 weekly flights), Jessore (14 flights), Saidpur (nine flights), Rajshahi (nine flights) and Cox's Bazar (three flights).

There are two daily flights between Dhaka and Calcutta, one each operated by Biman and Indian Airlines, and two flights a week between Chittagong and Calcutta. Biman's international network includes four flights a week to London, two each to Rome, Athens, Amsterdam, Paris, Bombay, Tripoli, Rangoon, Kuala Lumpur and Karachi, four flights to Singapore, six flights to Bangkok, three flights to Kathmandu, 13 flights to Dubai, two flights to Sharjah and one flight to Frankfurt. Biman goes to Japan (Narita and Nagoya) operating two flights a week. More international points, including Peking, Manila and New York, are expected to be opened in the near future when at least two more wide-bodied and one short haul aircraft to service Calcutta, Rangoon and Kathmandu are added to the fleet.

DHAKA

TRANSPORT FROM THE AIRPORT: A taxi is the usual means of transportation from the airport, though mini-buses are also available. Taxis normally charge Taka 250 from the new Zia International Airport to the city hotels. However, Bangladesh Parjatan Corp. (BPC — government tourist organisation) runs pick-up services between the city's main hotels and the airport which is much cheaper.

TAXIS: A limited number of taxis are available in Dhaka and taxi stands are located in Dhaka Sheraton, Sonargaon, Purbani and Sundarbans hotels and the airport. Check the fare for the journey you intend making with your hotel reception desk and bargain with the taxi driver before setting out. It is better to keep the same taxi if you want to use one more than once and tell the taxi driver when you need him. They are fairly reliable.

HIRE CARS: BPC runs regular rent-a-car services including transfers from airport to hotels. The charge is Taka 85 (air-conditioned) and Taka 65 (non–air-conditioned) per hour plus Taka 10 and Taka 7 per km with a minimum charge of Taka 450 and Taka 350 respectively. BPC's microbus (air-conditioned and non–air-conditioned) charge Taka 120 and Taka 90 per hour and Taka 20 per km and Taka 12 per km.

RICKSHAWS: Pedal rickshaws (trishaws) are perhaps the convenient way to travel in the city for short distances and are readily available. Fares are Taka 4-5 per mile, to be negotiated before the journey to avoid bitter controversy at the end. It is always better to ask your hotel reception desk for advice on such fares. In any case, rickshaws are not very expensive, even when you are overcharged.

MOTOR RICKSHAWS (SCOOTERS/BABY TAXIS): Fares are about Taka 6 per mile and should be negotiated beforehand. Although these are a faster means of transport than pedal rickshaws, motor rickshaws are not easily available and very noisy. Besides, the scooter drivers mostly will not agree to take passengers for a short distance.

BUSES: Buses and mini-buses operate all over the city and other parts of the country. There are not enough buses and they are therefore always crowded. However, mini-buses have eased the situation somewhat. They are available frequently and you can get a seat if you avoid the rush hours. The bus fare is 75 poisha per mile while mini-buses charge a little more.

RIVER BOATS: Oar-driven boats and sail boats can be hired at about Taka 30-35 per hour, but motor boats are not easily available for hire except through the BPC at Dhaka and Rangamati under BPC's rent-a-boat scheme. A three-seater speed boat can be hired at Taka 260 per hour, Taka 130 for half-an-hour, Taka 20 for an hour's halt and Taka 50 for an overnight halt. A luxury speed boat for six will cost Taka 600 for an hour, Taka 310 for half-an-hour, Taka 25 for an hour's halt and Taka 100 for an overnight halt. These rates may be changed upward at short notice.

UPCOUNTRY

Although Bangladesh is criss-crossed with numerous waterways, one can now travel either by rail or road from Dhaka to any part of the country. Despite a number of ferry crossings on certain routes, no place in the country is more than 12 hours by car from Dhaka. Only during the height of the monsoon season, because of sudden floods, are road links disrupted.

BUSES: The government-owned Bangladesh Road Transport Corp. (BRTC) runs regular bus services between the main cities and towns and into outlying village areas. These buses are quite comfortable and give the visitor a chance to see more of the countryside. Fares are very low, but in some cases seats must be booked in advance. A large number of private operators also run bus services between Dhaka and major cities and district headquarters and are quite dependable. Express buses, some of them air-conditioned, are even better, since they do not carry more passengers than seats available.

TRAINS: A fairly well-organised railway system in Bangladesh provides the visitor with a cheap and conventional mode of transport. Railway authorities have recently opened several express train services between Dhaka and other major cities. They are fast and comfortable. Air-conditioned coaches are available during the summer season and are a bit more expensive (comparable to air fares). Air fares in Bangladesh are still the cheapest in the world.

WATER TRANSPORT: Boats of all kinds operate throughout the country and local inquiries are necessary for routes and prices. Of special note is the Rocket steamer service which runs daily between Dhaka and the southern Sunderbans town of Khulna in 18 hours. The food available on board is excellent. All first-class bookings have to be in advance. The Dhaka-Khulna-Dhaka round trip first-class ticket costs about Taka 1,200.

AIR: Bangladesh Biman, the national airline, flies Fokker Friendships — both 41-seat F-27s and 85-seat F-28s — on its domestic routes and fares are very low.

BPC offers sightseeing tours around Dhaka and Chittagong every day for tourists. Prices are subject to frequent revision. However, they are still quite inexpensive compared with other Asian cities. Upcountry tours can be arranged by BPC, which also provides bilingual or trilingual guides for tourist groups. BPC has offices which will arrange these tours in Chittagong, Cox's Bazar, Kaptai, Rangamati, Bogra, Sylhet, Rajshahi and Khulna.

The **Sheraton**, **Sonargaon** and **Purbani** hotels in Dhaka and the hotel **Agrabad** in Chittagong, offer international-class accommodation. One more medium-range hotel is now under construction near the Zia International Airport at Kurmitola, 20 km out of the city centre.

A number of new, inexpensive but clean hotels have been built in Dhaka to meet the increased number of budget-conscious tourists and government and semi-government corporation rest houses all over Bangladesh offer reasonable living accommodation minus the trappings of luxury. BPC-owned motels at Cox's Bazar, Rangamati, Chittagong, Khulna, Bogra and Rajshahi are comfortable, efficient and modern. Some of them also offer air-conditioned rooms and suites. Bookings can be made in advance in Dhaka. The YMCA on New Eskaton Rd in Dhaka offers low-cost accommodation.

Western food is available in all major hotels and most of the big restaurants in the important cities. But local dishes are normally far better and more exotic. Curries of many kinds abound, cooked with proper spices and hot curry powders, including korma, rezala, bhoona and masala gosht, done with chicken, mutton, beef, fish and prawns. Chicken afghani, chicken baghdadi, chicken kashmiri, chicken tikka, boti kebab, shutli kebab and a variety of fish curries should be tried. Rice in the form of pullao, biriyani — with rice and mutton or chicken — and khichri are commonly available in any reasonable restaurants. Those who do not care for rice dishes can try mughlai paratha, plain paratha or naan, which go very well with curries. Seafood and sweet-water fish are available in most of the towns. Fish-lovers should not miss smoked hilsa and fresh bhetki, chingri (lobster/king prawns) and malaikari. Prawn dopiyaza is also one of the delicacies and is highly recommended.

In Dhaka, a number of good restaurants provide local and Western food, among them: the **Balaka**, Zia International Airport (Tel: 600111); **Karwan Sarai**, Sonargaon Hotel (Tel: 315001); **Kafe Aram**, Hotel Sheraton (Tel: 252911); **Cafe Firdous**, Hotel Purbani International (Tel: 254081); **Kari House Restaurant**, North South Rd; **The Chalet**, Green Rd (near Gree supermarket); **Mary Anderson Floating Restaurant** (Tel: 71288); **The Ramna**, Ramna Green at Ramna Park (Tel: 256644); **Red Button**, Old Airport Rd (Tel: 317717); **Ruchita**, Bangabandhu Ave (Tel: 254446), and **Sakura**, Dit Supermarket, opposite the Sheraton.

Chinese restaurants in Dhaka are numerous and new ones seem to open each month. Recommended Chinese restaurants include **King's Kitchen**, on the Airport Rd near Gulshan; **Far East Chinese Restaurant**, Airport Rd near Gulshan; **Chung Wah**, North South Rd (Tel: 251044); **Golden Dragon**, near Mahakhali railway crossing (Tel: 603460); **Golden Inn** and **King Hwa**, Lake Circus, Kalabagan; **La Diplomat**, Gulshan (Tel: 602282) and **Shanghai** (Tel: 314373). Imported alcoholic beverages are expensive. Scotch whisky, for example, will cost around US$2.50 for a small measure and a can of imported beer (any brand) almost the same in big hotels. They are marginally cheaper elsewhere. There is no local beer made, but Bangladesh produces good-quality gin and vodka and the rum and whisky are very drinkable, though a little stronger than average Scotch whisky.

There is very little in terms of regular nightlife in Bangladesh. Several top hotels have a band and vocalists in the bar and in the dining room. They also put on special weekly or bi-weekly shows. A few dozen theatrical groups perform in Dhaka daily. If you are lucky you may see a rare English-language drama staged by one of several amateur drama groups. There are more than 300 cinemas throughout the country showing mostly Bengali films, but some English-language films are also shown. Sometimes Japanese and Soviet films, dubbed in English, are

Paharpur 8th century AD Buddhist monastery.

Photo: Noazesh Ahmed

also shown. December and January are good months for entertainment with folk music, dances, and country fairs. In Dhaka a month-long national theatre festival is held from the middle of January each year. Similar festivals are also organised in most important cities and towns.

Browsing in the bazaars for local items is the best way of shopping in Bangladesh, though foreign goods are plentiful. The famous Dhaka muslin, though in short supply, is worth looking for. Rajshahi silk, or home-spun khadi-cotton textiles are good buys. They are good materials for dresses, jackets and safari suits. Khadi is especially suitable for hot weather. Those who are prepared to spend a little more can purchase pink pearls. Unusual jute goods, cottage industry and handicraft products, also attract visitors. Prices are very low. Ready-made shirts and kurtas of raw silk and khadi products are available in many shops in Dhaka and elsewhere in the country.

Among the more interesting art galleries are the **Bangladesh Shilpakala Academy**, Segunbagicha; the **Bangladesh College of Arts and Crafts**, Mymensigh Rd; the **Contemporary Arts Ensemble**, 48/1 Commercial Bldg, South Ave, Gulshan and the **Jiraj Art Gallery**, Shahbagh Shopping Arcade.

In addition, well-known painter Quamrul Hasan, who specialises in folk art, runs his own gallery (Tel: 318496).

Big-game hunting is strictly prohibited but a trip through the dense forest in the Sundarbans is most enjoyable. You can see from the safety of your anchored launch, the famous Royal Bengal Tigers, spotted deer and crocodiles. Small-game hunting in some areas is still possible, but special arrangements have to be made in advance. Fishing in the lakes and rivers can provide good sport. For golfers, there is the **Dhaka Club's** golf course (only nine holes) and the **Kurmitola Golf Club** (18 holes). A new golf club — **Bhatiary Golf Club** — in Chittagong can be used by visitors by appointment.

Swimming is another popular pastime. Soccer, hockey and cricket are the most popular spectator sports. Cricket is played mostly in the winter. For tennis, contact the **Bangladesh Lawn Tennis Federation**, about 100 yd from Dhaka's Sheraton Hotel. The Dhaka Club, next to the Lawn Tennis Federation, also pro-

23

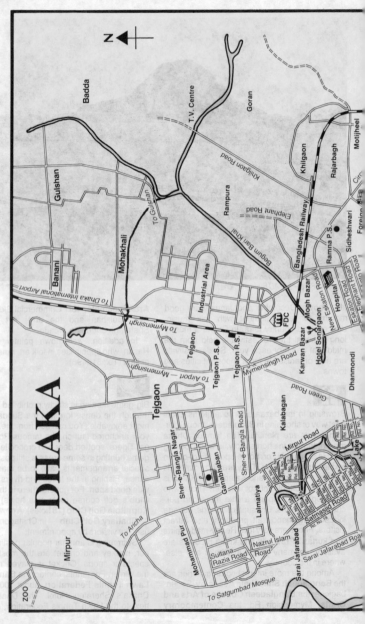

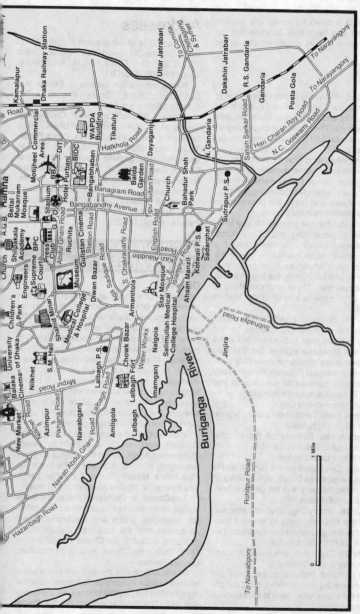

25

vides playing facilities for tennis and squash. Most hotels also have their facilities. For details, interested visitors should enquire at the hotel.

Festivals and holidays combine observance of religious occasions and significant events in the nation's history and the struggle which resulted in independence. The former are dependent on the lunar calendar and vary, while the latter fall on fixed dates.

The most interesting time for visitors to observe festivals which show aspects of Bengali culture, is from the end of November to the end of February, when fairs, dancing, singing, music, art shows and plays are presented in Dhaka and elsewhere in the country.

Variables: Eidul Fitr, the greatest Muslim festival, follows a month-long fast. Eidul Azha, another Muslim festival, commemorates the sacrifice of the Prophet Ibrahim — one of the prophets of Islam, known as Abraham among Christians — and falls during the last month of the Islamic calendar. Those who can afford it, make the pilgrimage to Mecca at the time of Eidul Azha.

February 21: Shaheed (Martyr's) Day commemorates the death of five students (in fact more died, but five were known) in 1952 when the Bengalis protested against the Pakistan central government decision to have only Urdu as the state language of Pakistan, though nearly 56% of Pakistan's population lived in what was then East Pakistan and spoke Bengali.

March 26: Independence Day.

Bengali New Year: Variable but usually around April 15 or 16 (public holiday).

Eid-i-Miladunnabi: Birthday of the Prophet Mohammad (public holiday), variable.

May Day: May 1 (public holiday).

Durga Puja: Celebrated by the Hindus as the birthday of the goddess Durga, wife of Shiva, in October (public holiday). It is the greatest festival of the Bengali Hindus.

December 16: Victory Day, celebrating the surrender of the Pakistan Army to the joint command of the Bangladesh-Indian forces on December 16, 1971 (public holiday).

December 25: Christmas, celebrated throughout the country (public holiday).

Some Buddhist festivals spread over the year are interesting and colourful, most are observed on the nights when there is a full moon in autumn and spring.

Addresses

The head office of Bangladesh Parjatan Corp. (BPC) is at the Old Airport Bldg, Tejgaon, Dhaka 15, Tel. 325155-9; Cable: PARJATAN, DHAKA; Telex: 642206 TOUR BJ.

Tourist information centres in **Dhaka**: Airport, Tel: 609416. Dhaka Sheraton, Tel: 509479, 252911/ext. 566.

Regional BPC offices are at **Chittagong**: Tourist Information Centre, Motel Shaikat Bldg, Station Rd, Tel: 209845, 209514. **Cox's Bazar**: Tourist Information Centre, Motel Rd, Tel: 246 and 258. **Rangamati**: Tourist Information Centre, Deer Park, Tel: 366 and 236. **Moulvi Bazar (Sylhet)**: Tourist Information Centre, Tourist Rest House, Tel: 350. **Khulna**: Tourist Information Centre, Tourist Motel, Banani, Tel: 5044. **Rajshahi**: Tourist Information Centre, Parjatan Motel, Tel: 2392.

DISCOVERING BANGLADESH

DHAKA

Although what is known as the city of Dhaka was founded in 1608 by the Moghuls, there are records suggesting that even as early as the 11th century a thriving township existed in the same place and it is claimed that around the late 11th century Dhaka was the most populated city in the world. Nothing of that period has survived, it is said, because of a great fire. However, many interesting and historic structures built by the Moghul rulers have survived and these are interesting tourist attractions. By far the most interesting area is the **Old City** clustered along the north bank of the Buriganga river.

In the west of the old city is the **Lalbagh (Red Garden) Fort**, which was built by Prince Mohammad Azam, son of the Moghul Emperor Aurangzeb in 1678. Adjacent to the fort is the **Pari Bibi's Mazar** (Tomb of the Fair Lady), daughter of the Moghul governor at that time.

The **Chawk**, or Old Market Place, is a larger square from which four bazaars lead off in different directions. Shops and residences crowd all around and the area has a good many mosques, including the **Chawk Masjid** built in 1676. Today, the Chawk remains an important business centre.

Dhaka is probably the only city in the world where there are as many as 700 mosques and is rightly called the City of Mosques. All are in regular use. The most significant are the **Baitul**

Mokarram, the **University Mosque**, the **Kar Talab** (built in 1709), the **Star Mosque** and the **Saat Gambuz** (Seven Domes) **Mosque**. Before setting out to visit one, it is wise to obtain the services of a guide or to have someone in the hotel explain to your taxi or rickshaw driver in detail where you wish to go.

At Dhaka University, the **Curzon Hall**, an interesting blend of Western and Moghul architecture, is worth a visit, as is the nearby **Dhaka Museum** with its collection of stone, metal and wood sculptures, paintings and coins. The museum at Baldha Garden has been closed.

UPCOUNTRY

About 16 km south of Dhaka on the banks of the river Sitalakhya is the town of **Narayanganj**, the largest inland river port in the country whose harbour swarms with hundreds of small boats bringing jute to the town's mills, including **Adamjee Jute Mills**, the world's largest jute mill. Just a few miles away is the ancient town of **Sonargaon**, the seat of the first Pala dynasty, which ruled from the seventh to 10th centuries. A number of monuments and shrines from that time are still intact. Bangladesh's only **Museum of Folk Art and Culture** has been set up at Sonargaon.

Approximately 80 km to the east is the township of **Comilla**, lying almost on the eastern border with India (which can be reached by air and railway connecting Dhaka and Chittagong as well as by numerous bus and coach services). Eight kilometres out of the town are the important archaeological sites of **Mainamati** and **Lalmai**. Considered as remains of the once political and cultural centre of the region which has now become Bangladesh, the structures are spread along a ridge for a distance of some 17 km. Most are unexcavated, but the sites known as **Salban Vihara**, with a museum (closed on Thursdays), are fully accessible. **Kota Mura** and **Charpetra Mura** have been excavated but are in a military zone. The structures are Buddhist monasteries and stupas, often inset with characteristic terra-cotta plaques. They date from as early as the seventh century.

Located on the shores of the Bay of Bengal in the southeastern section of Bangladesh is the country's biggest port and second-largest city, **Chittagong**. Of interest in the city are the **Chandanpura, Shaid Jame** and **Kadam Mubarak** mosques. Kadam Mubarak contains a slab bearing what is claimed to be the footprint of the Prophet Mohammad. The tomb of **Hazrat**

Bayazid Bostami, with very old turtles in the adjacent pond, is also a favourite visiting place.

From Chittagong you can venture further north to the region known as the **Chittagong Hilltracts**. **Kaptai** (approx. 56 km from Chittagong) and **Rangamati** (72 km) are both located on the shores of the 663 km^2 **Kaptai Lake**. A dam on the reaches of the **Karnaphuly River** has created the largest man-made lake in the Subcontinent. There are modern air-conditioned resthouses and bungalows, and yachting, boating, fishing and water skiing on the lake are pleasant diversions. Inquire in Chittagong at the tourist office for information regarding the renting of accommodation. Several hill tribes, some of whom are Buddhists, live in this area. The **Murong** and **Mogh** people are especially worth visiting.

About 150 km south along the coast from Chittagong is **Cox's Bazar** with its natural beach over 100 km long. You can go by land, sea or air from Chittagong. The inhabitants of the area are a mixture of Muslims, Hindus, and Buddhists, the latter immigrants of Burmese and Arakanese origin. Colourful and architecturally interesting Buddhist temples, known as kyangs of the Mogh tribe, are found in Cox's Bazar and in the villages of **Ramu, Teknaf** and **Nhila** to the south. Cox's Bazar has a modern complex of hotels and motels run by BPC. Resthouses, scattered throughout the area, also provide reasonable accommodation. Booking inquiries should be directed to the Tourist Office at Cox's Bazar or BPC offices in Chittagong or Dhaka. Rates are still quite cheap.

In the northeast is the town of **Sylhet**, resting among the tea estates in the picturesque **Surma Valley**. Accommodation is easily available in an area where you can hunt for small game. Access is most convenient by air or rail. About 130 km northwest of Dhaka is the **National Park and Forest Area** known as **Modhupur**. There are hunting lodges and resthouses in the forest for overnight stays.

The **Sundarbans**, tropical jungles and marshes lying deep in the delta areas of the Ganga and Brahmaputra rivers, were once famous for hunting. Boats are available for hire at about Taka 250-300 per hour. You can also hire guides. **Khulna** is the principal town of the region.

In the northwest, not far from the town of **Rajshahi**, is another important Buddhist archaeological site, **Paharpur**, with its massive central Vihara (monastery) measuring about 320 m in diameter.

HOTEL GUIDE

Hotel address	Phone	Fax	Telex	Cable	〰	🍴	🍲
A (US$80 and above) **B** (US$50-80) **C** (US$30-50) **D** (US$30 or below)							
BOGRA **D**							
Parjatan Motel Banani, Bogra	6753			PARJATAN		▲	▲
Youth Inn Mahasthangarh							
CHITTAGONG **B**							
Agrabad Agrabad Comm. Area **D**	500112-20		66237 ALIO BJ	ALIOTEL	▲	▲	▲
Saikat Station Rd, Chittagong	209514, 209845			TOURISM		▲	▲
Shahjahan Sadarghat Rd, Chittagong	203446			SHAHJAHAN		▲	▲
Hotel Hawal Agrabad Comm. Area	500671-5			HOTELHAWAI		▲	▲
Safina 50 Jubilee Rd, Chittagong	204317			SAFINA		▲	▲
Miska Station Rd, Chittagong	204017-9, 203623			MISKA		▲	▲
COX'S BAZAR **C**							
Hotel Sharkit Cox's Bazar, Sea Beach **D**	274, 275			PARJATAN	▲	▲	▲
Motel Upal Cox's Bazar, Sea Beach	246, 258			PARJATAN		▲	▲
Prabal Cox's Bazar, Sea Beach	211			PARJATAN		▲	▲

Hotel address	Phone	Fax	Telex	Cable	〰	🍽	🍷
COX'S BAZAR – *Cont'd* **D**							
Youth Inn Motel Rd, Cox's Bazar				PARJATAN		▲	▲
Hotel Sayeman Cox's Bazar	231, 233			SAYEMAN		▲	▲
DHAKA **A**							
Sonargaon Kawran Bazar, Dhaka	315001-9		642426 SNHT BJ	STAROTELS	▲	▲	▲
Dhaka Sheraton Shahbagh Ave, Dhaka **C**	252911-19, 505061		642401 HID BJ	INHOTELCOR	▲	▲	▲
Purbani International 1, Dilkusha St, dha-2 **D**	254081-5 256081-9		642460 BHL BJ	PURBANI		▲	▲
Park International 46 Kakrail	405791-2					▲	▲
Tourist Hotel Mahakhali	600796, 605398			PARJATAN DHAKA		▲	▲
Hotel Sundarban Kawran Bazar	505055-59		642928 A/B SUN HIT BJ	SUNDARBAN		▲	▲
Park International 46 Kakrail	405791-2					▲	▲
The Blue Nile 36 New Elephant Rd	326400					▲	▲
Hotel Brighton 163 Elephant Rd	312619, 326182					▲	▲
Hotel Rajdoot 24 Outer Circular Rd	405030					▲	▲
Zakaria International Gulshan Ave, Dhaka	601172, 601334			ZAKARIAHOTEL		▲	▲
Golden Gate 28 Mirpur Rd	310321-5			GOLDENGATE		▲	▲
Green Shahbagh Ave				GREEN		▲	▲

Hotel address	Phone	Fax	Telex	Cable	〰	🍴	🍽
DHAKA – *Cont'd* **D**							
Purborag 3, Dilkusha St	252177, 255801					▲	▲
Metropolitan North-South Rd	257357					▲	▲
Al-Helal Motijheel Circular Rd	406533					▲	▲
De Palace Outer Circular Rd	402536					▲	▲
Thote Rpt Hotel Abakash Mahakali	607085-9		642206	PARATAN TOURSR BJ		▲	▲
KHULNA **D**							
Hotel Rupsa International Jessore Rd	61563			KHULNA		▲	▲
RAJSHAHI **D**							
Parjatan Motel Abdul Majid Rd (near the church)	5442					▲	▲
RANGAMATI **D**							
Parjatan Motel, Deer Park Rangamati	3126, 3196			PARJATAN RANGAMATI			▲
SYLHET **D**							
Hotel Anurag Dhupadighi North, Sylhet	6718						▲
Hotel Hilton Telehaor, Sylhet	8262-64			HILTON		▲	▲

Hotel address	Phone	Fax	Telex	Cable	≋	🍴	🍽
BAGERHAT **D**							
Youth Inn Bagerhat				PARJATAN			▲

BHUTAN

The small, sovereign state of Bhutan has strong economic ties with its large and friendly southern neighbour, India. It maintains embassies at substantial expense in Dhaka and New Delhi, and permanent missions to the UN in New York and Geneva. Diplomatic relations have also been established with Denmark, the EC, Finland, Japan, the Maldives, Nepal, the Netherlands, Norway, Pakistan, South Korea, Sri Lanka, Sweden, Switzerland, and Thailand. Honorary consuls have been appointed in Hongkong, Macau, Osaka, Singapore and Seoul.

Further expansion of diplomatic ties will be gradual, as both resources and trained staff are so far limited. The country for most of this century generally pursued an isolationist policy and discouraged foreign visitors. Travel is in any case, time-consuming and difficult in the absence of roads.

The Bhutanese have always traded extensively with Tibet in the north (both directly and through Kalimpong) and with Assam and Bengal in the south. However, the father of the present king, Jigme Singye Wanchuck, began cautiously opening up the country, with extensive aid from India. From the late 1950s, a beginning was made on the construction of roads to link Bhutan's valleys both east to west, and south to India. The coronation of the present king in June 1974 was the occasion for the greatest assemblage of foreign dignitaries in Bhutan this century.

Controlled entry of foreign tourists dates from this time (1974-75 arrivals were 287; the 1986-87 target was 4,720; actual 1989, 1,480, down from a 1986 high of 2,486). These numbers are not kept low by government quota but are regulated by the substantial daily tariff (from US$130 a head for trekking to US$200 a head for peak festival times) and by the limited facilities available at peak times (e.g. at the Paro festival in March-April).

The country has joined many international organisations in recent years, including the Economic and Social Council for Asia and the Pacific, the World Bank, the Asian Development Bank and Unesco. In October 1988, Bhutan joined the International Telecommunications Union. As its domestic modernisation proceeds, Bhutan is projecting a stronger international identity, both regionally and globally. At present, Bhutanese officials are working with their counterparts in India and the Tibet region of China respectively formally to delineate and demarcate the kingdom's entire borders.

The ordinary Bhutanese are known for their kindliness, hospitality and generosity of spirit. Like many highland-dwelling people, they are also shrewd and canny in their judgments. Most as yet are little touched by change, which is most noticeable in the market towns in the plains adjacent to the duars (literally doors — valleys which give access to the elevated central part of the country) and in the capital, Thimphu.

In the rural areas, the families are still largely self-sufficient, living in large, square, white-washed houses built of compressed mud walls, stone, wood and clay, and adorned with colourful motifs. The shingled roofs of slate are held in place by heavy stones to prevent them from being carried away by the strong winds that sometimes sweep down from the mountains. The rural economy is largely based on barter, though some

◁ *Archery: Bhutan's national sport.*
Photo: Nancy Nash

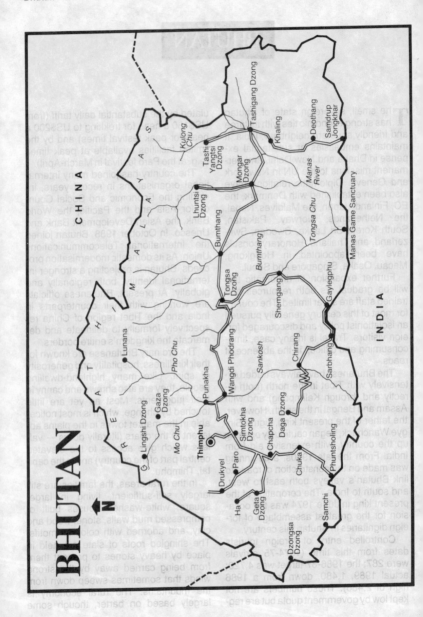

34

cash crops are being developed, mainly in the south.

A quarter of the permanent dwellers in Bhutan trace their origins to settlers from Nepal late last century. They speak Nepali and follow Hindu rites; these are the Southern Bhutanese. Other Bhutanese include the Sharchops of the eastern part of the country around Tashigang (believed to have been the earliest inhabitants, and having close affinities with the peoples of the hills in northeastern India), and the Ngalops in the west (descendants of Tibetan immigrants from the eighth century onwards).

The state religion is the Drukpa subsect of the Kagyud school of Mahayana Buddhism. The ideas and practices of this form of Buddhism still play a vital role in the life of Bhutanese and in the development of their national institutions. The combination of striking mountain and forest scenery, the colour and pageantry of the religious festivals, the beauty of the architecture of monasteries and homes, the unrivalled abundance of bird-life and flowers, and the gracious people themselves, are bound to leave a lasting impression on all who are fortunate enough to spend time in the kingdom.

Little is known for certain about the peoples of Bhutan before the introduction of Buddhism in the seventh century AD. The Tibetan Buddhist king Srongtsen Gampo is recorded as having built the first lhakhangs (shrines) in old Bhutan, that of Jampe in Bumthang (central Bhutan) and of Kyichu in Paro. At the end of the eighth century, the Indian Buddhist saint Padmasambhava (Guru Rimpoche) came from Tibet to Bumthang and had monasteries built in various places (including the Taktsang, or Tiger's Nest, in Paro valley).

The Kagyud school came from the 11th century, but the Drukpa sub-sect was not established as orthodoxy until the time of the scholar Padmalingpa (1450-1521). This laid the basis for the independent theocracy of Druk-yul (land of the thunder-dragon), firmly institutionalised by Shabdrung Ngawang Namgyal who came to Bhutan from Tibet in 1616.

The Shabdrung is widely venerated today as the unifier of the country, as a law-giver and builder of most of the remarkable administrative temple-fortresses known as dzongs. He also established a dual system of spiritual and temporal rulers (respectively styled Je Khenpo and Desi) which continued — uneasily at times — until the election of Sir Ugyen Wangchuck (governor of Tongsa from 1883) as the first hereditary king of Bhutan.

In 1910 the Indian Government moved to pre-empt any Chinese movement southward beyond Tibet by concluding a treaty with Bhutan which provided, among other things, that Bhutan would "be guided by the advice" of the Indian Government in external relations, while the latter would refrain from any interference in Bhutan's internal affairs.

The era of the modern Bhutanese state dates from this time, and acceptance of the principle of an hereditary monarchy has been the base from which has evolved the present "proto-constitutional monarchy" form of rule. Sir Ugyen ruled until he was succeeded in 1926 by his son, Jigme Wangchuck, who in turn, ruled until March 1952. The third monarch, Jigme Dorji Wangchuck, ruled until his sudden death in July 1972 at the age of 43.

Major developments occurred during his reign, and he is venerated as "the father of modern Bhutan." His son, the present king, Jigme Singye Wangchuck, formally became the fourth monarch in 1974.

In 1949 independent India renewed the 1910 agreement that Bhutan would be "guided by the advice" of India in foreign affairs, while India would refrain from interference in Bhutan's internal affairs. In the wake of events in Tibet from 1959, when China annexed the area, Thimphu aligned itself with India and commenced a process of modernisation (primarily funded by India) to escape Tibet's fate.

The kingdom joined the UN in 1971 with India's sponsorship. Following the relaxation of many policies in China since 1978, Bhutan has moved cautiously to assert a position on regional and world affairs that takes account of (but is not always identical with) that of India. The Indian leaders acknowledge Bhutan's right to do so, and have acted in many ways (for example, by amending maps which previously showed Bhutan as administratively attached to India) to strengthen Bhutan's assertion of its sovereignty.

By agreement with Bhutan, the Indian Dantak task force (under the paramilitary Border Roads Organisation) at present has responsibility for recruiting some 60,000 labourers from Nepali-speaking communities in Sikkim and elsewhere on short-term contracts for road repair work in Bhutan. An Indian military training and assistance team (Imtrat) has for many years assisted the training of the 5,000-strong Royal Bhutan Army.

India's defence interest in Bhutan stems from the fact that the Chumbi valley of Tibet abuts the narrow Siliguri neck of West Bengal, which if blocked would cut off the entire northeast of India from the rest of that country. The Bhutanese have also not forgotten that Tibetans made a number of aggressive but unsuccessful forays into western Bhutan in the early 17th century.

The National Assembly (Tshogdu) was instituted in 1953, and at present has 151 members of whom 106 are directly or indirectly elected representatives of the people, 12 elected by the Monk Body, and 33 nominated officials. The assembly usually meets twice a year, and in principle it is the supreme authority for law within the country.

A Royal Advisory Council of 10 members (six elected by the assembly) meets in permanent session, virtually as a government department. The cabinet, chaired by the king, consists of ministers, secretaries of departments, members of the Advisory Council and others, but it meets infrequently. In practice, the king is supreme, though he accepted that, in the last analysis, he is accountable to the assembly and people.

The area of Bhutan is 46,500 km² and the last official estimate of population in mid-1987, was 1.3 million (the actual figure is almost certainly much higher and a new census was to be completed by the end of 1990). The population is concentrated in pockets in the south and in the east, though the farming community lives in the broad fertile valleys of the inner Himalaya, at altitudes of 1,200-3,500 m. Rice, wheat, maize, buck-wheat and other crops, as well as fruit, are grown. Along the southern foothills, many of the population are relatively new arrivals from Nepal or India.

Religious sentiment is strong in Bhutan, especially in the centre and the east of the country. Because of the absorption of other former areas of Tibetan culture into China, India or Nepal, it remains — as has been written by one expert — "the one resolute and self-contained representative of a fast disappearing civilisation."

To travel to Bhutan other than as an invited guest, you must be a member of a tour group, though may arrive as an individual traveller to participate in one of three special arrangements involving tours of four or seven nights. Travellers also need Bhutan Government visa clearances before seeking to enter, and applications take at least one month to process (individual travellers should allow two months). Transit permits issued by the government of India are required in order to travel overland from Bagdogra to Bhutan via Phuntsholing, and the appropriate application forms should be submitted at least six weeks (preferably two or three months) ahead of the proposed dates of travel (which may not then be varied by more than one day either side). Citizens of India require permits, and those of Nepal require visas, to proceed north of Phuntsholing.

Until 1988, most travellers arrived at Bagdogra airport (near Siliguri) from either New Delhi or Calcutta. After meeting representatives of the Bhutan Tourism Corp., they then travelled by car or minibus to Phuntsholing, where they stayed overnight (the journey from Bagdogra to the border — about 175 km — took about three hours by car). From Phuntsholing it is 180 km (about six hours' drive) to Thimphu. For local people, there are several buses of the Royal Government's Transport Service travelling daily from Siliguri to Phuntsholing and vice versa, and buses also ply the Kalimpong to Phuntsholing route. Although the overland route to Thimphu is rather long and may be tiring, it provides an unrivalled way of seeing the changing living conditions at different altitudes.

The present most-used approach to Bhutan is to fly from either Bangkok, Calcutta, New Delhi, Dhaka or Kathmandu to Paro airport by Druk Air. The service to Calcutta was inaugurated in February 1983 with a single 18-seater Dornier 228-100 aircraft (a second was commissioned in September 1983): that to Dhaka began in November 1986. A 78-seater BAe146-100 was purchased at the end of 1987 and came into service in November 1988, enabling twice-weekly direct Paro–New Delhi flights. A weekly Paro-Kathmandu service commenced in February 1989 (using Dorniers), and Paro-Bangkok (using the BAe) in March 1989.

Scheduled services are provided to/from Calcutta on Mondays, Tuesdays, Wednesdays, Fridays, and Saturdays, but extra flights are made to meet demand (for example to accommodate groups of 15 or 16). Monday to Saturday daily flights are scheduled for March-May and September-November, the peak tourist seasons. Paro-Dhaka flights are once a week (Thursday) in each direction. The fare from Paro to either Calcutta or to Dhaka is US$150 (local people pay Ngultrum 1,200) each way. In the 1990s, a second major airstrip is to be constructed in Phuntsholing, on the left bank of the river Torsa, and additional landing areas for domestic flights are being considered at Bumthang and elsewhere.

There are a number of helipads, for example at the entrance to Thimphu valley, for VIP use in connecting to/from the Indian Air Force field at Hashimara. A concrete runway was constructed at the beginning of the 1960s at Yangphulla (near Tashigang), but is now only used by helicopters as high winds pose wind-shear problems for fixed-wing craft.

Other overland entry points from India are Sarbhang and Gaylegphug (in the central region) and (using Gauhati airfield) Samdrup Jongkhar (in the eastern region), but travellers through these places must be in possession of the appropriate Indian permit. Few foreigners come this way at present. It is possible to travel from Calcutta to Phuntsholing by deluxe coach service, offered three times a week by a subsidiary of the Royal Bhutan Insurance Corp.; foreigners must have the required Indian transit permits — in addition to normal visas — in advance of travel.

Bhutan Standard Time is six hours ahead of GMT, and 30 minutes ahead of Indian Standard Time.

Travellers to Bhutan must have a valid passport visaed for Bhutan, or the appropriate entry permit. Those travellers transitting India to reach Bhutan, whether by land or by air, must initially comply with Indian visa and other immigration requirements. Applications for permission to proceed to Bhutan can be made at least one month (preferably two months) in advance, to any of the following:

Bhutan Tourism Corp., Royal Government of Bhutan, P. O. Box 159, Thimphu, Bhutan (Tel: 22647, 22570, 22666, 22854; Cable: BHUTRISM THIMPHU; Telex: 890-217 BTCTPU BT);

The Royal Bhutan Embassy, Chandragupta Marg, Chanakyepuri, New Delhi 110021, India (Tel: 699227, 699228; Telex: 081-31-62263 DRUK IN);

Druk Air Corp., 48 Tivoli Court, 1A Ballygunj Circular Rd, Calcutta 700 019, India (Tel: 441301, 441302);

The Permanent Mission of the Kingdom of Bhutan to the United Nations, 866 Second Ave, New York NY 10017, US (Tel: 212-371-6235);

The Royal Bhutan Embassy, House No. 58, Rd, No. 3A, Dhanmondi R. A., Dhaka, Bangladesh (Tel: 505418);

The Honorary Consul for the Kingdom of Bhutan, Kowloon Centre, 2nd Fl., 29-43 Ashley Rd, Kowloon, Hongkong (P. O. Box 95106 Kowloon) (Tel: 369-2112, 721-8844);

The Permanent Mission of the Kingdom of Bhutan to the UN in Geneva, 17-19 Chemin du-Champ d'Amier, 1209 Geneva, Switzerland (Tel: [022] 98-7971);

The Royal Bhutanese Embassy, Post Box 1510, Safat, Kuwait (Tel: 2564825).

Visas will normally be stamped into passports on arrival at either Phuntsholing or at Paro Airport, as appropriate. The normal visa fee of US$20 per person is paid at the entry point directly to the representative of the Ministry of Foreign Affairs (visa section): note that this fee is additional to the daily tourist rate. For non-tourist guests, visas will normally be granted for only one week in the first instance, extendable according to circumstances.

Individual travellers in particular should note that you will not be allowed to board the Druk Air aircraft at foreign airports, even if you hold a ticket purchased by another person for the flight concerned, unless notification of your visa clearance has already been received from Thimphu's Ministry of Foreign Affairs in advance of the flight.

In addition to the entry requirements, all foreigners within Bhutan require permits from the Department of Immigration and Census, Thimphu, in order to travel outside of Paro, Thimphu, and Tashigang.

Since April 1, 1988, passengers departing Bhutan by Druk Air have been charged airport departure tax (from July 1, 1990, Nu 100 a head).

Health certificates are not required, except for travellers coming directly from a notified affected area. It is advisable, especially in the summer and at lower altitudes, to take precautions against malaria, which is endemic in southern Bhutan. The main illnesses among the local population are of the respiratory tract, influenza, diarrhoea and dysentery. Travellers would find it prudent to carry appropriate remedies. Rabies is endemic in some areas; hepatitis is not uncommon and meningitis has flared up during recent winters. Those making an extended trek should take prior medical advice. In the spring especially, lip salve is helpful against the very dry air.

There are no private medical practitioners in Bhutan. The government provides free medical service to all Bhutanese, and adequate medical facilities are available in the main towns and civil administrative centres except for serious or complex illnesses. Most of the common patent drugs are dispensed by pharmacists in the towns. In Thimphu, the Druk Medical House is a well-stocked pharmacy opposite the Lugar cinema on the main street, and it is open from 8 am to 8 pm every day of the year. Elsewhere, some dispensaries close on Tuesdays. The usual vaccinations and inoculations (but not yellow fever vaccination) can be given at Thimphu general hospital.

On arrival by air, if you feel short of breath, you may need a day or so to acclimatise properly, so take it easy to begin with and avoid both alcohol and over-exertion. Remember that even the most fit person can display symptoms of altitude sickness; if you sleep badly after arrival in Paro or in Thimphu, carefully assess whether you should travel to Taktsang monastery if this is on your itinerary, as it is at 3,000 m.

Although most non-trekking travellers will rarely travel higher than 3,500 m, those with heart conditions should have a thorough medical check-up before departure for Bhutan. Don't forget mosquito repellent — useful even in Thimphu, especially during summer nights.

As Bhutan and India by agreement constitute a single free-trade area, travellers coming from outside India to visit Bhutan are first subjected to Indian Customs formalities. The 1989 Indian baggage rules explicitly state: "Passengers coming from Nepal or Bhutan are not entitled to

any free allowance." For the same reason, persons departing Calcutta or New Delhi by air for Bhutan are not permitted to purchase duty-free items though they are charged a Foreign Travel Tax of Rs 50.

Under Bhutan's own rules, the following items may be brought in free of duties: used personal articles, alcoholic liquor up to two bottles, up to 600 cigarettes (or up to 150 cigars, or up to 500 grams of tobacco), professional apparatus, cameras "and other equipment required for tourism purposes." All passengers must declare foreign exchange over US$2,000 or its equivalent in other currencies, as well as high-value personal articles or gifts.

It is forbidden to bring into Bhutan any unlicensed firearms, explosives, dangerous weapons, narcotics, goods subject to quarantine, indecent or obscene works or articles. Gold ingots or biscuits "other than gold jewellery" are also banned. Restrictions on exports have been vigorously enforced since early 1983, and departing travellers are invited to make oral declarations before their baggage is thoroughly checked.

Export of the following is forbidden: antiques, icons, idols, musk, and bear bile; firearms, ammunition, military stores and explosives; all kinds of narcotics; gold ingots, bars and biscuits. Since the definition of antique is not yet clarified, any item which appears to be a cultural artifact is liable to be confiscated, unless the traveller has made the purchase at the Government Emporium at Thimphu and can produce a receipt.

A certificate from the Department of Antiques Preservation (offices at Tashi-chhodzong) under the Ministry of Home Affairs is required for the exportation of artifacts, idols and statues purchased. Allow at least three full working days for this.

Arriving at Calcutta airport from Bhutan, passengers are (from January 1988) subject to baggage checks by Indian Customs.

The Bhutanese currency unit is the Ngultrum (Nu), at par with the Indian rupee at around Nu 17.12:US$1 in March 1990. The Nu is divided into 100 chetrum (the current coins spell this chhertum). There is also — to add further confusion — a unit called the sertum (Nu 100), but this gold coin issue is primarily for foreign collectors. As in India, it is usually very unusual to come across small change, but Bhutan is to mint its own coins by late 1991. The paper issue (formerly by the Bank of Bhutan, now wholly by the Royal Monetary Authority of Bhutan) is in denominations of 1, 2, 5, 10, 20, 50, and 100 ngultrum; there are coins of 5, 10, 25 and 50 chetrum and of 1 ngultrum. It is planned to withdraw the Indian rupee from issue by the Bank of Bhutan in due course, though rupees would still be interchangeable for purposes of trade inside and outside the country.

The Bank of Bhutan has 25 branches throughout the country, and its main offices will readily exchange US dollars, Swiss francs, British pounds sterling, Deutschemarks and yen for ngultrum. Travellers' cheques are preferred and obtain a better rate. In Thimphu, the bank will not encash travellers' cheques on weekdays after its normal closing time of 1 pm, though the Royal Monetary Authority (upstairs, entrance from the left side of the Bank of Bhutan building) will do so during weekdays up to 4.30 pm.

From February 1, 1986 all foreign nationals were required to pay all expenses in Bhutan in local currency only; conversion from foreign currencies can be made at Motithang, Bhutan, Jumolhari and Druk hotels (Thimphu), Olathang (Paro), or Druk and Kharbandi (Phuntsholing); or at Bank of Bhutan offices in Phuntsholing, Paro or Thimphu. However, direct payments in convertible foreign exchange can be accepted in settlement of bills by the above hotels, and also by Bhutan Tourism Corp., Druk Air Corp., and the Handicrafts Emporium. A foreign exchange counter has also been opened at the Paro airport terminal building.

The Thimphu American Express agent is Chhundu Travels, 39/40 Norzin Lam, Thimphu, and they can arrange card-member services (travellers' cheque refunds, emergency cheque cashing, emergency card replacement). Other credit cards are expected to become valid in Bhutan soon, but were not in late 1990.

The American Express credit card can be used at the following service establishments in Thimphu, Paro and Phuntsholing:

Thimphu: Hotel Druk, Hotel Jumolhari, Motithang Hotel, Etho Metho Tshongkhang, Pel Jorkhang Tshongkhang, Gyeltshen Tshongkhang, Dolkar Tshongkhang, Handicrafts Development Corp., Yu Druk Travels, Chhundu Travels. Paro: Olathang Hotel. Phuntsholing: Hotel Druk.

Departing travellers should note that it will be virtually impossible to change unused ngultrum outside Bhutan. The Bank of Bhutan counter at the Motithang Hotel (open 7-8 am, 5-7 pm) will convert unused Nus to rupees on production of the original exchange receipt.

Bhutan's official language is Dzongkha, or the language of the dzongs, which is a dialect similar to Tibetan but with many distinctive national characteristics (especially in pronunciation). Choekay (pronounced chokey) is the written form used in traditional and monastic schools. Different dialects are to be found even in adjoining valleys, testifying to the great difficulties of communications until recent times. Sharchopkha is an important dialect of the area around Tashigang in the east. Nepali is spoken in the south. Since the early 1960s, English has been the medium of instruction in the schools and it is widely understood by all those who have regular dealings with visitors.

There is no phrase-book widely available, though you may be lucky to find an old copy of *Introduction to Dzongkha*, a school text-book from 1977. A smaller, pocket-sized booklet, *Dzongkha Handbook* by Dorji Choden (1986) may be obtainable at Etho-Metho ("Chrysanthemum") in the BTC complex near the Lugar cinema.

In the southern foothills the climate is tropical, with an average rainfall of around 250 cm a year. Misty, cold hills — some up to 4,000 m — enclose hot, sultry valleys. Sudden brief showers occur frequently in Phuntsholing during July and August.

In the higher, temperate regions of the Paro and Thimphu valleys, the winters are cold with mild springs and autumns, and warm summers; rainfall is light, most days are sunny and clear, and nights are cool. The somewhat lower regions of Punakha and Wangdiphodrang have mild winters and warm summers.

On the whole, there are four distinct seasons in Bhutan: spring (between March and May, though there can be glorious days in February and bone-chilling rain and wind in mid-March), summer (June, July and August, with most of the country's rain falling from around early June to late August), autumn (from early September until mid-December), and winter (late December, January, and early February). Winter is the ideal time to visit Manas game sanctuary in the south.

A Bhutanese farmhouse.

Photo: Bob Watson

For tourists, only casual clothing is required; foreign officials, experts or businessmen who are to meet with their counterparts should wear formal clothes. Bhutanese (both men and women) are very smartly dressed in their national dress for formal events, but are also very much at ease in informal situations. During most of the year, light woollens (or cottons in the summer: it is usually quite humid) are sufficient for day wear (around 30°C in the sun; about 10°C cooler in the shade). Warmer clothes are needed for the evenings. Heavy woollen clothing or down jackets are required during the winter months along with adequate headgear and warm gloves to protect against the icy winter wind.

In the mountain regions, temperatures can differ greatly between night and day and at varying altitudes (−10°C to +30°C); here clothing should be layered to adapt easily to changing conditions. Slip-on shoes are convenient if your schedule involves several visits to religious places, since you are usually required to leave your footwear at the entrance to the prayer rooms. On the other hand, since a fair amount of walking will be required in most circumstances, pack a comfortable pair of sturdy walking shoes (preferably boots for ankle support on slopes). Trekkers should bring their own sleeping bags and warm clothes; the rest will be provided by the Bhutan Tourism Corp.

The official summer working hours for the 11,000-strong civil service (based mainly at Thimphu) are 9 am to 5 pm, Mondays to Fridays; during winter months (November 1 to March 31) 9 am to 4 pm. Most government offices are closed on Saturdays. Branches of the Bank of Bhutan open from 9 am to 1 pm on weekdays and from 9 am to 11 am on Saturdays; closed on Sundays and public holidays. The General Post Office is open daily from 9 am to 5 pm during the week, 9 am to 1 pm on Saturdays (*see* **Shopping**). Microwave links through India, inaugurated in November 1984, improved international communications from the Thimphu terminal, with New Delhi the gateway exchange.

A temporary telex facility was established in May 1985, and by late 1986 Bhutan had its permanent telex facility (initially 20 lines in each of Thimphu and Phuntsholing), also using the New Delhi gateway. A further important development was the inauguration in Thimphu in March 1990 of a satellite earth station and switching system built by Japanese companies for Bhutan Telecom. The facility cost US$5.5 million and was financed by the Bhutan Government with technical assistance from the International Telecommunications Union (ITU) through UNDP, and by August 1990, Bhutan had two-way IDD links with 14 countries. Outward calls from Thimphu are now either direct dial or operator-assisted in

Thimphu, connecting through leased circuits in an Intelsat relay satellite over the Indian Ocean to England, whence they are switched to their destinations. The international country access code for Bhutan — a member of the ITU since 1988 — is 975. Further agreements are being discussed.

The whole of the main highway between Phuntsholing and Bumthang, and Mongar to Tashigang, has been asphalted, excepting only a few brief patches where the road is still settling down. The side roads to Paro, Thimphu and Punakha are also asphalt, so that the Bhutan Tourism Corp. is now able to get tourists easily to places of interest.

Horses can be hired from local farmers to carry travellers up to (but not down from) the cliff-side Taktsang monastery (in accordance with an old proverb that "a horse is not a horse if it cannot carry a man up a mountain; a man is not a man if he cannot descend a mountain without a horse"). Yaks can also be hired from local herdsmen to accompany trekking parties in the higher places. Both horses and yaks are pack animals, however, not riding animals, as their imperviousness to commands makes clear.

Buses run most frequently from Phuntsholing to Thimphu and are usually crowded. There are also irregular bus services from Thimphu to Bumthang, from Bumthang to Tashigang (via Mongar, whence there is a feeder service to Lhuntshi), from Tashigang to Samdrup Jongkhar, and between Tongsa and Gaylegphug. But these are not for the tourist. Four-wheel-drive vehicles are used on newly paved roads and subsidiary tracks.

For the most popular religious festivals attended by foreign tourists, private vehicles may be hired (with their owners driving) by the tourism authorities to convoy smaller groups: this form of transport can be an adventure in itself.

TRAVEL AGENTS

A number of agencies have come up in recent years, operating with varying degrees of efficiency. The **Bhutan Tourism Corp**. is Bhutan's general sales agent for Lufthansa Airlines. **Chhundu Travels**, 39/40 Norzin Lam, Thimphu, handles bookings for air travel. **Yangphel Travels** (established in April 1989), Gatoen Lam (opposite Benez) Tel: 22897; Telex: 224; Cable: YANENTTPU BT; offers air ticketing and reservations out of Bangkok.

At its session in July 1987, the national assembly resolved that access by tourists (other than religious devotees) to temples, monasteries, meditation centres, centres of Buddhist studies and other places of worship, as well as the climbing of sacred mountains, should be banned from 1988. The move was not unexpected: the Special Commission for Cultural Affairs had for some time foreshadowed limiting the activities of tourists as part of a policy designed to strengthen respect for traditional religion and culture. The assembly argued that these places should not be commercialised.

In practice, trekking has not been greatly affected, though cultural tours have relied on access to religious art in monasteries for much of their appeal. Some argue that the commercialisation of religion and culture is largely the responsibility of the growing number of foreign experts and volunteers residing in Bhutan, who since early 1985 have been allowed to invite friends and relatives to visit the country. The Bhutan Tourism Corp. (BTC) has allowed selected groups to mountaineer, also other groups (mostly of Buddhist devotees) to visit holy places such as Taktsang which would otherwise be off limits to foreigners. Cases are decided on their merits.

For financial and administrative reasons, Bhutan tourism offices in New York and Calcutta were closed with effect from mid-July 1987, leaving an officer attached to the embassy at New Delhi as the principal liaison with foreign groups and the Indian Government.

BTC at present offers two main types of tours, package and trekking, for groups with a minimum of six and a maximum of 30 people. All tours are escorted by BTC guides. Each member of the group is charged US$130 a night (for those attending Paro tschhu, US$200 a night in hotels, US$150 a night in private homes, and US$130 a night in tented accommodation) during the season March to June and September to December. Charges are reduced to US$90 a night during the off-season. Package tours cover sightseeing programmes for eight to 12 days. The daily rates cover board, lodging, sightseeing, transport, guide charges, entertainment and all local taxes (excluding laundry and bar charges).

Diplomats receive a concessionary rate of US$90 a head per night in all seasons; it is not mandatory for them to form a group. The rates in part reflect the fact that tourism is virtually the only independent source of hard currency for the Bhutan Government. For all tours, visa fees of US$20 a head are added.

The package tours (which include cultural treks) cover the main points of interest in Paro, Thimphu, Punakha, Tongsa, and Bumthang valleys and surrounding countryside (and Phuntsholing for those entering by road). They also include scenic excursions across high mountain passes from which the perpetual snow of the north may be seen. Cultural tours involving mini-treks to Kurte (Lhuntshi) and Mongar, both in eastern Bhutan, were introduced from 1984 on a trial basis.

A popular and interesting programme is the central Bhutan (Bumthang) cultural trek, coming in through Phuntsholing and out by air from Paro; this is offered from September to May with a variable duration from 19 to 21 days, at a cost of US$90 a night.

Independent travel by individuals within the country is neither feasible nor allowed. However, individual tourists now have the opportunity of joining one of three conducted tours arranged by BTC, and offered internationally by **Thai International Airways** as part of their **Royal Orchid Holidays** programme. These are:

1. "Seven Days — Bhutan." Royal Orchid, departure: from Bangkok Wednesday only.

2. "Three Kingdoms tour (Westbound). Royal Orchid Bhutan Extension 5 days/4 nights. Departure: from Bangkok Wednesday only.

3. "Three Kingdoms tour (Eastbound). Royal Orchid Extension 4 days/3 nights. Departure: from Kathmandu and Nepal, only.

Druk Air, the state carrier, will organise various trekking tours, ranging from 13 to 30 days' duration. There are two 13-day cultural treks to **Dagala** in the mid-Himalayan range, or Samtegang; a 17-day trek to **Chomolhari** (7,316 m) though the group only goes to the base camp; an 18-day **Phubjikha** cultural trek; and (only for the very fit) a 26-day trek through **Lunana**, crossing high passes and reaching 5,140 m. The basic charge for trekking tours is US$90 a night, plus US$130 for each night in a hotel.

Mountaineering expeditions have been allowed from April 1983, commencing with the opening of the 7,000 m peak **Jitchu Drake** in the Lingshi area. The 7,200 m **Mount Masagang** was opened in 1985, and further peaks are to be opened at the rate of one every two years.

All tourists, trekkers and mountaineers can extend their stay in Bhutan at the all-inclusive rate of US$150 a night (including guide and transport). All international tourists booked through BTC will be charged for a shared double room; if a visitor asks for a room with single occupancy, there is an additional payment of US$15 a night.

Visitors are accommodated in comfortable hotels, cottages and guesthouses, many of which were constructed for the present king's coronation in 1974 and have since been extended. They are decorated inside and out in Bhutanese style, and rooms are furnished with elaborately carved wooden couches, cushions of locally woven wool, and handwoven bed covers of local silk or cotton. Local people and tourists from neighbouring countries can stay in a number of private hotels and guesthouses for a relatively modest charge in keeping with the facilities.

Electricity is 220/240V, in western Bhutan.

PHUNTSHOLING: The Hotel Druk (formerly the Motel Druk, now completely renovated), Tel: 308. It is operated by the Welcom Group. Located in the middle of town, right next to the upcountry bus station which springs noisily to life at a remarkably early hour, this hotel has 32 double rooms. It is well managed and offers good European, Indian, Chinese and Bhutanese food.

PARO: The Olathang Hotel (Tel: 58 and 99) is 3 km from the market and is pleasantly situated among pine trees on a hill slope. The main building consists of 18 twin rooms and six suites, with central heating; a further 32 twin rooms are available in 20 detached or semi-detached cottages in the grounds.

THIMPHU: The main accommodation for tourists, the **Motithang Hotel** (Tel: 22445, 22434, 22435), is an imposing hillside building, formerly a royal guesthouse but extended by an annex in 1974. It is 3 km from the town. Including a new wing opened in 1985, the hotel has 36 twin rooms. It has efficient central heating and reasonably good food if you are with a tourist group (buffets are usually provided, and the kitchen staff has been trained in Hongkong and Singapore), but service for individuals leaves much to be desired in timeliness and quality.

Businessmen will do better in the town centre at the **Chomolhari**, the **Druk**, or the **Druk Sherig**. The **Taktsang Hotel** (Tel: 22101, 22102) is privately owned, and is located in the middle of town, near the Swiss Bakery; one single room, eight twins and one suite. **Jumolhari Hotel** (Tel: 22747, 22787; Telex: 890-210, answerback JUMOTPU BT) is also privately owned and opened its doors in March 1983. Centrally located, it has 18 twin rooms, three deluxe rooms, three small suites and three large suites. The **Hotel Druk** (Tel: 22966; Telex: 890-207, answerback DRUKTPU BT). The **Druk Sherig Guesthouse** (Tel: 22714) in the centre of Thimphu's main street, opened in mid-1988 and has 12 well-appointed rooms (two suites) with telephones in each room; breakfast is included in the tariff.

WANGDIPHODRANG: The **PWD Guesthouse** (Tel: 214). Six double rooms (one of which has a lavatory attached).

TONGSA: The **Sherubling Tourist Lodge** (Tel: 26), formerly the Tongsa Guesthouse, was handed over to Bhutan Tourism Corp. at the end of 1983 by the PWD. It is pleasantly situated on the hillside about 30 minutes' walk from the dzong, and offers good views of the dzong and the watchtower above it. Locally generated electricity is usually available in the evenings. The supply of hot water from the kitchen attached sometimes fails. The main building has four double rooms and two suites; there are four double rooms in the nearest annex, and five double rooms in a second annex.

BUMTHANG: The **Chhokhar Guesthouse** has five rooms and two suites; but most groups have since late 1984 been accommodated in Bhutan Tourism Corp.'s **Wangdichholing Tourist Lodge**, a newly built complex of four separate buildings each with four double rooms, together with a dining hall. Staff for Tongsa and Wangdichholing Tourist Lodges have been trained at Bhutan Hotels in Thimphu, and their number now includes several charming girls from different parts of the kingdom trained as housekeepers. Both the Chhokhar and the Tongsa Guest lodges operate smokeless stoves (chullas) in their kitchens, a great improvement on the traditional stoves.

Elsewhere in Bhutan, there are government guesthouses in the main towns. The standard bed-only rate for non-tourists at the Olathang and Motithang hotels is Nu 165 single, Nu 230 twin and Nu 410-450 for suites. Tourists at Wangdichholing, Tongsa, and Manas Tourist Lodges are charged Nu 130 single, Nu 200 double.

Taktsang charges Nu 65 single, Nu 85 double, Nu 350 for a suite. Jumolhari charges Nu 200 single, Nu 390 double, Nu 550 for suites (all

prices include 10% service). Hotel Druk at Phuntsholing charges Nu 215 single, Nu 300 double for air-conditioned rooms; deduct Nu 25 for rooms without air-conditioning. The Hotel Druk in Thimphu charges Nu 215 single, Nu 300 double, Nu 550 for suite (single deluxe Nu 350; double deluxe Nu 435). Druk Sherig Guesthouse charges Nu 450 for a suite, Nu 350 double, and Nu 250 single. All of the above tariffs draw an additional 10% service charge for food and drinks.

Tourists will usually be restricted by circumstances to food in the hotels, generally of the buffet variety — mainly vegetarian, but often with pungent cow's-milk cheese (*dartsi*) dressings on the salads. Bhutanese soup is a nutritious mixture of gruel (*thukpa*) and rice; other dishes may include beef dumpling, mushroom cheese with sliced chillies and onions used as a condiment, roast pig's head, a dish made of potatoes and cheese, roast pork with leafy greens chicken curry. The *dartsi* is not usually eaten on its own but added in pieces to cooked vegetables, to make a sauce. Red chillies cooked in melted cheese is a popular dish. *Nake*, or "poor man's asparagus," grows wild and is highly appreciated (the season is April-June).

Souza is Bhutanese tea, with a pinch of soda, some butter and salt to taste, is refreshing but not immediately to everyone's taste. You may also care to try sweetened or saffron rice, but the local red rice is by far the preferred staple dish. Outside the hotels and private homes, the quality of food is quite depressing and the presentation uninteresting. The local red chillies are quite hot and can be provided on request at hotels; they are liberally used by the local people. It is also worth making an effort to sample the large Bhutanese apples, during the season.

Fresh yak cheese is agreeable, and there is also *Tilsitter* cheese made in Bumthang by the Department of Agriculture, which consists of cubes of dried yak cheese strung like beads on a string or a yak hair, and is useful to have on a trek. Millet is the staple in the Bumthang area, and the local millet noodles are tasty.

In general, the standard of preparation and presentation of food served to tourists has improved greatly in the past few years and should continue to do so; a number of chefs and apprentices go each year to Hongkong, Singapore and Germany for training. **The Jumolhari Hotel** is well regarded for its Chinese dishes. **Hotel Druk** in Thimphu has a good menu, with north and south Indian, European and Chinese dishes.

Bhutan has distilleries at Samchi and Gaylegphug, and produces a variety of liquors which are all sweet and tend to taste the same. Although Bhutan Mist (a malt whisky) is perhaps the most famous, Bhutanese consider that Special Courier (a blended whisky) is the best local product: a 750-cc bottle costs Nu 80 in the market. Golden Eagle beer from India costs Nu 11 or 12 a bottle (15-17 in hotels); the stronger Black Label (also from India) is more expensive. Apple brandy from Bumthang is a fine brew and is well priced at Nu 20 a 375-cc bottle. *Chang*, made from fermented wheat and tasting like a thin, rough cider, can be sampled at the many liquor shops in towns, or at Thimphu's Sunday market. Another local drink, *tomba*, is made from millet, but its public sale was stopped in 1985 for "reasons of hygiene."

There is no public nightlife in Bhutan to speak of; during the working week, people go to bed early and get up early. Bhutanese like to party in their homes on holiday eves, and put on splendid provisions of drinks, along with cooked foods and condiments.

Indian films (mostly in Hindi) show regularly to packed houses at two rather scruffy cinemas in Thimphu. All the hotels have bars which are reasonably well stocked with local and some imported drinks.

The greatest entertainment for visitors are the spectacular ancient dance and music performances, preserved so faithfully in Bhutan. Most of these dances and the associated pageantry can be seen during the local festivals. Between festivals, The Royal Bhutan Dance Troupe may give short open-air performances of both southern and western Bhutanese dances and songs in the grounds of one of the hotels, but there is no substitute for the real communal gatherings.

There are small bazaars in the towns where some interesting local items may be found, including antique silverware and old Tibetan or Bhutanese coins. But you will need a certificate to be allowed to export the antiques. There is a

small settlement of silver and goldsmiths at Dechenchholing in Thimphu who will make to order with reasonable advance notice. The *chukar*, betel and areca nut container is a typical example of the art. The **Handicrafts Emporium** in the centre of Thimphu is open from 9 am to 12 pm, and 1 pm to 4 pm, Mondays to Fridays (9 am to 1 pm on Saturdays), and offers a growing range of Bhutanese handicrafts at prices somewhat higher than in the market for comparable items. However, here you can obtain papiermache masks (in miniature sizes to suit air travellers), woven cloth of wool or silk, prayer wheels, silkscreen decorative motifs on handmade paper, rings and ornaments for clothing.

The natural-dye hand-woven cloth (of wool or silk) used for making up the national dress is of excellent quality, though chemical dyes are now being used by some, rather than natural colouring. The long robe worn by men is known as the *kho*, tied at the waist and pouched over the belt to form a huge pocket over the chest into which an amazing variety of items can be put. All senior officials must wear a sword for ceremonial occasions. Women wear an ankle-length robe called a *kira*, tied at the waist with a wide sash and fastened at the shoulders with two silver brooches. Women also wear a richly embroidered strip of cloth over their left shoulders for formal occasions.

In the larger towns, most shopkeepers speak some English. Shop-stalls close around 7 pm.

Bhutan produces attractive postage stamps on both international and local themes; the latter make lightweight souvenirs, but they are not always available at hotels, but the Thimphu General Post Office (opened in late 1988) is open to 3 pm daily, and incorporates the Philatelic Division of the Bhutan Post Office.

Fossil coral beads from Tibet can be bought, but are very expensive. Turquoise is also sold: the smooth, polished bright blue stones brought from Iran through India are very cheap, while Himalayan fossil stones are of a blotchy greenish-blue hue, and are much more expensive. All other stones are brought in from India: tiny fresh-water pearls are beginning to appear, but are somewhat over-priced in relation to their size. The best selection is probably to be seen at Dolkar's shop in the BTC complex in Thimphu.

Archery is the national sport and the Sunday practice session is well worth seeing to appreciate the keen eyes and sturdy hands of the archers, and the victory dance performed on a successful hit. US-made aluminium-frame competition bows are now very popular, and have largely replaced the traditional hunting bows. A national team was coached for the 1984 Olympics and Asian regional competitions in 1985. Soccer, volleyball, golf, badminton, basketball, tennis and table tennis are other popular sports, and the king is a vigorous participant in — as well as patron of — most of these. A swimming pool complex in Thimphu is open during summer months: temporary membership is available for visitors.

The majority of national public holidays in the Bhutanese year are of religious significance, with the remainder relating to civil institutions of monarchy and state. The religious holidays are variable, according to the Bhutanese calendar which is similar to the Chinese Lunar arrangements calendar.

May-June: Buddha's Birthday.
June-July: First sermon of Buddha.
September-October: Blessed Rainy Day, Thimphu Domchey, Thimphu Tsechhu (three days holiday for the latter).
December-January: Nine Evils' Day.
   The secular holidays (fixed and movable) are:
January-February: Bhutanese New Year, (two days).
May 2: Birthday of the late king.
June 2: Anniversary of the coronation (in 1974) of the fourth hereditary king.
June-July: Summer solstice.
July 21: Anniversary of the death of the late king.
October-November: Dussehra (Southern Bhutanese New Year).
November 11, 12 and 13: King's Birthday;
December 17: National Day.
December-January: Winter Solstice.
   In addition, each locality celebrates its own religious festivals. Of these, the *tsechhu* (literally, 10th day) is the most popular and colourful. During the festival different religious dances — with or without masks — are performed by the monks and lay people. In some places folk dances are also performed by the villagers.
   The Bhutan Tourism Corp. lists the major festivals annually that foreign groups may attend.

Addresses

The Bhutan Tourism Corp. (BTC), formed as Bhutan Travel Agency in 1974 when tourist activity was started, is a division of the Ministry of Communications in Thimphu (P.O. Box 159, Thimphu; Tel: 22647, 22570, 22666, 22854; Tlx: (890) 217 BTCTPU BT).

Publications

The BTC arranges all foreign tourism activities in-country (and sub-contracts tour arrangements for Indian clients while providing its own guides), and does not itself sell guidebooks, though it has published a booklet, *Trekking and Mountaineering* (giving details of standard trekking tours) and a list of rules governing mountaineering expeditions. It also publishes a few publicity posters and brochures of a general nature.

Few books on Bhutan can yet be purchased within the country itself. The Oxford Bookshop in Connaught Circus, New Delhi, usually has a good selection, as does its branch at 17 Park St, Calcutta 700016. In Darjeeling, another Oxford Bookshop on the Mall has a good stock. All three will post books overseas.

An informative — but now dated — 48-page colour brochure, *Bhutan: Himalayan Kingdom*, is available for US$5 from the Permanent Mission of Bhutan to the United Nations.

EMBASSIES AND CONSULATES
Embassies in Bhutan
Bangladesh, P. O. Box 178, Thorilam, Thimphu: Tel: 22539.
India, India House, Lungtenzampa, Thimphu. Tel: 22162; Tlx: (890) 211 INDE-MBTPU BT.
UN Development Programme, Samten Lam (off Norzin Lam), Thimphu. P. O. Box 162, Thimphu. Tel: 22315, 22498, 22424, 22443, 22605; Tlx: (890) 205 UNDPTPU BT or 81-31-62411.
Honorary Consulates
   Republic of South Korea: c/o Tashi Enterprises, Thimphu.

CHAMBER OF COMMERCE
Bhutan Chamber of Commerce and Industry, Thimphu. Cable: BHUCHAMB Thimphu. P. O. Box 147. Tel: 22506, 22742.

The Royal Monetary Authority (RMA), P. O. Box 154, Thimphu. Tel: 22540, 22847; Cable: ROMA; Tlx: (890) 206 RMATPU BT. Established in 1982, the RMA operates virtually as a Central Bank, dealing with foreign exchange, currency and coordination of financial institutions and implementation of a unified monetary policy.

Bank of Bhutan, head office, Phuntsholing, P. O. Box 75. Tel: 300, 402, 225, 268; Cable: BHUTANBANK; Tlx: (890) 304 BANKPLG BT, (890) 218 BANKTPU BT (Thimphu). No foreign banks operate in Bhutan.

DISCOVERING BHUTAN

THIMPHU

Thimphu, capital of Bhutan since 1960, lies in a broad west-central river valley at an altitude of 2,435 m. The town has about 20,000 inhabitants

and is dominated by **Tashichho dzong** ("fortress of the glorious religion"). The fortress retains the central keep of the original structure built in 1641, but otherwise was entirely reconstructed in 1961-62.

Today it houses the main government departments (others have temporary offices outside the fortress building or in the town), the government assembly room, the throne room of the king, and the summer headquarters of the Central Monastic Body (headed by the Je Khempo). Women are forbidden to remain in the building after sunset, under a rule dating back several centuries.

A new National Library (opened for readers' services in May 1985), the High Court, and the Royal Bhutan Golf Club links premises are a little way uphill from the *dzong*, while the king's cottage is below it, near the river. The bazaar consists of several lines of shops in the traditional style, run by Bhutanese and Tibetans.

A memorial to the present king's father, and to world peace , can be seen prominently as one

Tiger's Nest monastery.

Photo: Bob Watson

enters the valley: it contains wall paintings and religious representations of high quality, and there will nearly always be the sight of devout pilgrims walking round the building clockwise as they tell their beads.

The Tibetan-style **Changgangkha lhakhang** is only a few minutes from the bazaar. It has interesting frescoes and old wooden masks.

The queen mother resides at the Royal Palace at Dechenchholing, about 15 minutes by car up the valley from the centre of town.

On the western slopes of the valley near the large Indian Embassy compound is **Dechenphodrang lhakhang**. From here one can walk up or around the ridge to **Wangditse**, with fine examples of sculptured stupas. Further up the ridge is Chukortse lhakhang, where a market every Wednesday and Sunday, offers fruits, vegetables, meat, fish and household articles, plus the opportunity to sample the local spirt, *chang*.

One may also see one or two people chanting prayers with their portable shrines with exquisite miniature paintings and gilded images.

The entrance to Thimphu valley, about 8 km from the town, is guarded by Bhutan's oldest fort, **Simtokha**, build it 1627. The frescoes and slate carvings here are of a fine standard. From here, a track climbs a further 700 m to Phajoding monastery, with fine views overlooking the town, and dating from 1748. One may continue on this path to reach Paro valley. Many other monasteries and forts have been built on the hilltops surrounding the valley.

UPCOUNTRY

Tourists see much of the countryside during the drive from **Phuntsholing** (270m), the main town for entry by land, about 220 km from Thimphu. The black-topped road was built by recruits under national service in the early 1960s. It rises sharply from the plains to around 1,800 m, remains at this level for some distance, and eventually climbs to 2,526 m at the Chapcha pass, before descending to Paro, Thimphu and the east. Traces of the old track used before the highway was constructed (when it took an arduous five or six days to travel by pony or mule from Thimphu to Phuntsholing) are often visible. Before Chapcha, a little more than three hours after leaving Phuntsholing, one comes to the enormous Chukha hydroelectric scheme, begun in 1976 as a goodwill project by India on very favourable terms to Bhutan.

A further 45 minutes on, Khujoog Jakhang (BTC's cafeteria at Bunakha) comes into view for a welcome meal halt. From here it is 40 minutes to Chapcha pass from where you can get an excellent view of some of the road you have travelled. After a further 30 minutes or so, the Paro and Wang rivers meet at an altitude of 2,102 m. Branch roads to the left go to the Ha valley and to Paro (23 km distant). Thimphu is one-and-a-half to two hours further on along the main road.

The Paro river meanders gently through a patchwork of rice paddies and wheat fields and this is considered by many to be the most beautiful of Bhutan's valleys, especially in spring when peach and apple trees blossom. On a hillside above the river, a little distance from the airfield, stands Rimpung fort, (popularly known as Paro fort) built on foundations dating back to 1645. Burnt down in 1907, it was rebuilt and today houses the administrative headquarters for Paro district and a state monastery.

The inner court is brilliantly carved and painted; the towering central keep is an impressive example of Bhutanese architecture and form. It also contains a collection of sacred masks, ritual objects and ornaments, some dating back several centuries.

On a steep ridge above the fort is an ancient watchtower where the National Museum has been housed since 1967 (groups are admitted free; individuals pay Nu 1 and photography is not permitted).

Coming down from the museum by road, the distinctive "hat" shape of Duntse lhakhang appears, originally constructed by the "iron-bridge builder" from Tibet, Thangton Gyalpo, in the 15th century.

About 8 km west of Paro, **Kyichu lhakhang** lies on the left. This is one of the holiest temples of Bhutan and, like Jampe lhakhang of Bumthang, its original construction is dated to the seventh century.

Continuing west, the **Taktsang (Tiger's Nest)** monastery can be seen clinging to the sheer cliffside at 3,000 m. It is a place of pilgrimage that all Bhutanese seek to visit once in their lifetime. Even higher than Taktsang, 15 minutes further on up the mountain, is the **Santog Pelri Monastery (Monastery of Heaven)**, a 300-year-old retreat.

From Thimphu, a three-hour drive east brings you to Punakha (at 1,200 m), former capital of the kingdom, an outstanding example of Bhutanese architecture. The climate of this valley is temperate and the Central Monk Body goes there to spend the winter.

BURMA

Burma is a land of almost unparalleled scenic variety and ethnic diversity. The Burman-dominated ricelands in the central plains are surrounded by a horse-shoe-shaped ring of wild and remote mountain ranges and high plateaux where an abundance of ethnic minorities live. But all peoples of Burma are naturally friendly and hospitable, English is widely spoken and a foreign visitor will encounter few problems when dealing with the ordinary people in the street or in the countryside.

The Burmese capital, Rangoon, is devoid of tall residential blocks, fuming industrial complexes and noisy traffic jams. Towering above Rangoon is the famous Shwe Dagon Pagoda, magnificently gilded and symbolic of a country rich in religion and resources. Seen from the height of the pagoda precincts, the city presents a view of broad expanses of green woodland and parks interspersed with little white villas.

The city centre is still dominated by colonial-style buildings and tree-lined streets which run east to west and north to south. Government offices, law courts, commercial houses, shopping centres, hotels, restaurants and cinemas are mostly concentrated in this area. There is, however, a total absence of the garish night-life that is to be found elsewhere in Southeast Asia.

Since the present military regime assumed power in September 1988, many neighbourhoods have been relocated on the outskirts of Rangoon, roads have been widened and an abundance of parks have been built. While done in the name of "beautifying" the city, this forced relocation of hundreds of thousands of people has also been criticised internationally; property has been confiscated without compensation and the residents have even had to pay for the demolition of their own houses as well as the construction of new homes in these "satellite towns." A 10 pm to 4 am curfew has been in force since the military crushed a popular uprising in 1988 against the regime that had been in power since 1962.

Outside the confines of Rangoon, Burma is a country of enchanting scenic beauty, pleasant towns and historical sites which are unique even in an Asian context. The northern city of Mandalay, the royal capital prior to the British conquest in 1885, is well worth a visit, as is nearby Pagan, though some of its famous ruins were damaged by an earthquake in 1975. The more important edifices have since been restored, to become once again marvels of ancient architecture and a source of fascination for visitors. The hill stations of Maymyo and Taunggyi enjoy a purity of air rarely found anywhere else in Asia.

Burma is a place in which to meet friendly and sophisticated people, to relax and absorb the atmosphere without having to go out and chase it. It is ideal for those who want to shake off the concerns of life for a while and escape from familiar surroundings. So long as you do not expect all the modern conveniences of Western life, a holiday in Burma can provide a rewarding experience.

On May 27, 1989, it was decided to use the traditional Burmese name for Burma, Myanmar, also in English text. Shortly afterwards, the military government decided to Burmanise local place names as

◁ *Shwedagon Pagoda.*
Photo: Paisal Sricharatchanya

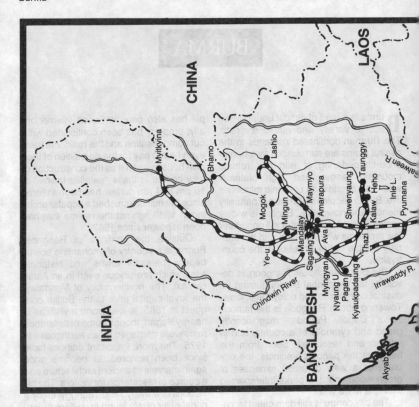

well. Thus, Rangoon has officially become *Fangon*, Moulmein is now referred to as *Mawlamyine* and the Irrawaddy river has become the *Ayeyarwady*. However, for reasons of simplicity, the *All-Asia Guide* will continue to use the English

names since even English-speaking Burmese use these in daily conversations and place names are found in the old version on most maps. Whenever deemed necessary, the new spellings will be added ed in brackets.

Burmese history begins with Tagaung, says a Burmese aphorism. It refers to the historical fact that by about the 5th Century BC, a Burmese kingdom had already been in existence at Tagaung, a place about 160 km up the Irrawaddy River from the present site of Mandalay. A dynasty of 50 kings ruled Tagaung until it fell

to Tartar invaders from the north. A scion of the last king then fled south and founded a new dynasty at Sri Khettara (near the present site of Prome, 320 km north of Rangoon), which was peopled by the Pyus, the forefathers of the modern Burmese.

By about this time, a Mon-Khmer group of early immigrants from India had also settled in the Irrawaddy delta and south Burma. Called

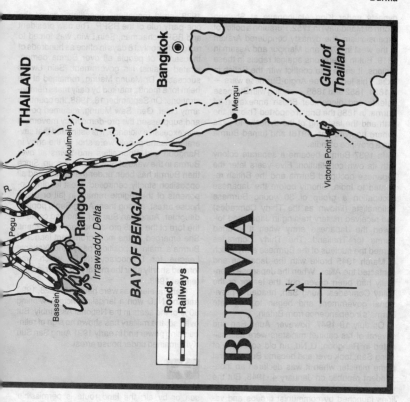

Mons or Talaings (derived from the Indian word Telegana), these immigrants were the first to come under the influence of Buddhism spreading from India.

In about the 1st century AD, the Pyu kingdom of Sri Khettara fell apart, wrecked by internal dissension and threats from the Mons in the south. A nephew of the 27th and the last Pyu king regrouped his scattered countrymen and led them in a 12-year long march to the Pagan site in central Burma where another group of Pyus had settled. There, he founded the famous Pagan dynasty, of which Anawrahta, the 42nd and most noted king in Burmese history, inaugurated, in the 11th century, the country's first golden age.

But the Pagan dynasty ended with its 50th king following a Mongol invasion in the 13th century. The kingdom broke up into small principalities until national unity was restored under the Ava dynasty (1364-1555), with the imperial capital at Ava (near the present site of Mandalay). After about 200 years the dynasty was succeeded by another, the Toungoo dynasty (1486-1752). The most eminent member of this dynasty was King Bayinnaung who forged Burma into a strong, united and respected nation in Southeast Asia. The dynasty did not get on well with neighbouring Thailand and wars between the two nations culminated in the Burmese sacking of the Thai capital of Ayudhia (Ayuthaya) in 1767.

Meanwhile, the Mons of south Burma had restored their kingdom at Pegu. Their revolt ended the Toungoo dynasty, but Burmese supremacy was re-established with the coming of a new dynasty under King Alaungpaya at Shwebo (north of Mandalay) in 1752. Pursuing a policy of expansionism, the dynasty conquered Arakan in the west in 1785 and Manipur and Assam in 1819. But in operations against rebels in these regions, it came into conflict with the British in India. This led to three Anglo-Burmese wars — in 1824, 1852 and 1885 — ending with Burmese defeats and piecemeal British annexation of Burma. In 1886 the British deported Thibaw, the 11th and the last king of the dynasty, to India (where he lived until 1916) and turned Burma into a province of India.

In 1937 Burma became a separate colony with its own constitution. Five years later the Japanese occupied Burma and the British retreated to India. Shortly before the Japanese occupation a group of 30 young Burmese nationalists (known as the Thirty Comrades) had received military training in Japan and followed the Japanese army when it invaded Burma for Thailand. The Thirty Comrades formed the nucleus of the Burmese army which in March 1945 broke with the Japanese and contacted the Allies. When the Japanese eventually had been driven out, the leader of the Thirty Comrades, Aung San, headed a provisional government and began to negotiate Burma's independence from Britain.

On July 19 1947, however, Aung San and several of his cabinet ministers were assassinated in Rangoon. U Nu, an old colleague of Aung San, took over and became Burma's first prime minister when it was declared an independent republic on January 4, 1948. But the young nation almost immediately faced rebellions launched by communist groups and various ethnic minorities. The insurgency was brought under control after a few years but even so, the military, led by general Ne Win, seized power on March 2, 1962 on the excuse that rebels were threatening to break up the country.

Ne Win's coup ended Burma's 14-year-long experiment with parliamentary democracy. The ideology of the military government was "the Burmese Way to Socialism" and the Burma Socialist Programme Party (BSPP) became the country's only legally permitted political organisation. The economy declined, the insurgencies flared anew and Burma went into a state of self-imposed isolation.

Ne Win resigned as president in 1981 but remained chairman of the BSPP. He was succeeded as head of state by one of his most trusted proteges, San Yu. Both Ne Win and San Yu resigned from their respective posts in July

1988, amid mounting opposition against the one-party rule of the BSPP. The new president and BSPP chairman, Sein Lwin, was forced to resign after only 18 days in office as hundreds of thousands of people all over Burma demonstrated against his government. Sein Lwin's successor, Dr Maung Maung, remained at the helm for a month, marked by daily mass demonstrations. On September 18, 1988, the country's army chief, Gen. Saw Maung, assumed power and suppressed the pro-democracy movement with excessive violence. It is estimated that several thousand people were shot by the army in Rangoon and other cities and towns all over Burma in the wake of Saw Maung's coup. Since then Burma has been under martial law and all opposition strictly controlled. Most leading opponents of the regime remain in jail or under house arrest, among them Aung San's popular daughter, Aung San Suu Kyi, who had come to the fore of the 1988 pro-democracy movement. She emerged as the most prominent leader of Burma's main opposition party, the National League for Democracy (NLD) which was formed shortly after the military takeover in September 1988.

General elections were held on May 28, 1990 and the NLD won a landslide victory, winning 80% of the seats in the National Assembly. But even so, the military has shown no sign of relinquishing power and in early 1991 Aung San Suu Kyi remained under house arrest.

Most foreign visitors can enter Burma only by sea or by air; the land route is permissible solely for Thai nationals crossing the border on one-day visits at a few approved points, notably Ranong/Kawthaung in the south, Three Pagodas Pass and Mae Sot/Myawadi in the central region, and Mae Sai/Tachilek in the north. Indian nationals can usually visit the border town of Moreh opposite Tamu in Manipur under a similar agreement, as can Chinese citizens at some points along the Sino-Burmese frontier.

The following airlines fly to Rangoon:

Myanmar Airways, the national flag carrier, flies from Bangkok every day (twice on Thursdays) and from Singapore via Penang on Thursdays.

Thai International flies from Bangkok on Mondays, Thurdays and Saturdays.

Bangladesh Biman flies from Dhaka to Rangoon and on to Bangkok on Tuedays and from Bangkok to Rangoon and on to Dhaka on Thurdays.

CAAC operates a weekly flight from Kunming, China, to Rangoon.

Aeroflot flies from Vientiane to Rangoon and on to Bombay and Moscow once a week.

Passports and visas are required for visits to Burma. Tourists are given visas according to the duration of their organised tour, or a maximum of 15 days (14 nights). The visa fee is Baht 800 in Bangkok or the equivalent at other places. Business visas can be extended easily but extensions of tourist visas are usually not granted. Tourists are required to join tours organised by authorised travel agents. Individual visits are usually not approved other than for businessmen and official visitors. Tourists usually have their visas arranged through the travel agency that organises their visits. Business visitors may apply for visas at any of the Burmese (Myanmar) embassies or consulates listed below:

Australia, 85 Mugga Way, Red Hill, Canberra, ACT 2600. Tel: 95-0045

Bangladesh, Plot No. 38, Rd No. 11, Banani Model Town, Dhaka. Tel: 30-1915, 30-1461.

Britain, 19A Charles St, Berkeley Square, London W 1X 8ER. Tel: 499-8841, 493-9494.

Canada, 85 Range Rd, Apt 907, Ottawa.

China, No. 6, Tung Chih Men Wai St, Chaoyang District, Beijing. Tel: 52-1488, 52-1425.

Czechoslavakia, Romania Rollanda 3, Bubenec 6, Praha. Tel: 38-1140, 38-1149.

Egypt, 24 Mohamed Mazhar Zamalek, Cairo. Tel: 80-9154, 80-9176.

Germany, Schumannstrasse 112, 5300 Bonn. Tel: (0228)21-0191.

Hongkong, Rm 2424, Sun Hung Kai Centre, 24th Fl, 30 Harbour Rd, Wanchai. Tel: 891-3329.

India, No 3/5OF, Shanti-path, Chanakyapuri, New Delhi. Tel: 70251.

Indonesia, 109 Jalan Haji Angus Salim, Jakarta. Tel: 40440. 47204.

Israel, 12 Mattei Aharon St, Ramt Gun, Tel Aviv. Tel: 78-3151.

Italy, Via Vincenzo Bellini, 20 Interno, 10098 Rome. Tel: 85-9374, 85-6863.

Japan, 8-26, 4-chome, Kita Shinagawa, Shinagawa-ku, Tokyo. Tel: 441-9291.

Pakistan, 386, Shalimar 6/3, Islamabad. Tel: 22460, 20123.

Philippines, Ground Fl., ADC Bldg, 6805 Ayala Ave, Makati, Rizal, Manila. Tel: 87-2373.

Malaysia, 7 Jalan Taman V Thant, Kuala Lumpur. Tel: 25798.

Nepal, Thapathali, Kathmandu. Tel: 13146, 14083.

Singapore, 15 St. Martin's Drive, Singapore 10. Tel: 235-8763.

Soviet Union, 141 Gertsena St, Moscow. Tel: 291-0534.

Sri Lanka, 53 Rosmead Place, Colombo 7. Tel: 91964.

Switzerland 3, Giacomettistrasse, 3006 Bern. Tel: 43-3024.

Thailand, 132 North Sathorn Rd, Bangkok. Tel: 233-2237, 234-0278.

United Nations, Permanent Mission of the Union of Myanmar (Burma) to the UN, 10 East 77th St, New York, NY 10021. Tel: (212) 535-1310.

US, 2300 "S" Street NW, Washington D.C. 20008. Tel: (202) 302-9044/6.

Vietnam, Hotel Thong nhat, Hanoi. Tel: 52784, ext. 368.

Yugoslavia, 72 Kneza Milosa, Belgrade. Tel: 645-420, 645-128.

Yellow fever certification is required if arriving within nine days after leaving or transiting affected areas. Other vaccinations are not needed although doctors recommend travellers to Burma to be inoculated against cholera. Malaria is rampant in all forested areas of Burma and prophylactic medicine is recommended.

Visitors are allowed duty-free import of 200 cigarettes, 50 cigars or a quarter-pound of tobacco; one quart bottle of alcoholic spirit and one pint bottle of perfume or eau de cologne. Personal effects in reasonable quantities are allowed, as also are jewellery and professional instruments such as typewriters, still and movie cameras, radios and tape-recorders on condition that they are re-exported. Motor vehicles are not allowed to be brought in. Baggage is usually examined on entry and departure.

There is no restriction on export of articles of genuine tourist interest, but export permits may be required for certain items and one should inquire on purchasing expensive souvenirs whether such a permit is required. Export of Burmese antiques is prohibited. Jewellery and gems, unless bought from the government diplomatic shop in central Rangoon or the duty-free store at the airport, cannot be exported.

The currency unit is the kyat (pronounced "chat") which is divided into 100 pyas. In April 1991, the official exchange rate was Kyats 6.30:US$1. Notes in denominations of Kyats 1, 5, 10, 15, 45, 90 and 200 (market with Arabic and Burmese numerals) and coins in denominations of Kyat 1, 5, 10, 25 and 50 pyas (in different shapes and sizes but marked only with Burmese numerals) are in circulation. There is a flourishing black market in Burma and private money changers offer up to 10 times as much as the government's banks. These transactions, however, are against the law.

All kinds of foreign currencies, cash and cheques, can be brought in without limit but must be declared on arrival. The declared sum is entered on a currency conversion form which must be presented whenever money is converted and the amount entered by the officer making the conversion. This form has to be presented to customs officials on leaving the country, and a check may be made to see that the amount of the foreign currency remaining in your possession tallies with the balance shown in the form. Loss of this document may entail a good deal of trouble on leaving the country. Foreign currency changed into kyats and left unspent will be re-converted into foreign currency at the airport on departure, provided the currency conversion form is presented. Import and export of Burmese currency is prohibited.

Foreign currency can be exchanged only at the Foreign Trade Bank in Rangoon, the Inya Lake Hotel, Strand Hotel, Thamada (President) Hotel and the airport exchange counter. As authorised currency conversion centres are rare upcountry, you are advised to change sufficient money in Rangoon to see you through your journey. Hotel bills at the better hotels, which are owned by the state, can be paid only in foreign currency. American Express credit cards are accepted at some hotels and the Myanmar Travels and Tours, the government-run tour operator.

The main language of Burma is Burmese, which is also the official language. But there are also regional tongues of minority races spoken in their respective areas, the most important being Arakanese (in Arakan State, west Burma), Shan (in Shan State, east Burma), Kachin (in Kachin State, north Burma) and Karen and Mon (in Karen and Mon States, south Burma). Hindi, Bengali and several Chinese dialects are also spoken among Indian, Bangladeshi and Chinese communities, found mostly in the large towns and border areas adjoining India, Bangladesh and China.

Signboards of shops, restaurants, banks, government offices etc., are written in Burmese though some are written in English as well. Written Burmese is based on a modified version of the old Mon alphabet which, in turn, is derived from South Indian alphabets. Street names are written only in Burmese, as are the names of railway stations. But a visitor will have no difficulty in finding someone who understands English and is willing to help him find places.

The Tropic of Cancer lies about 160 km north of Mandalay in central Burma. The greater part of Burma therefore lies in the tropical zone.

There are three general seasons: winter from November-February; the hot seasons from March to May and the rainy seasons from the end of May to the end of October. Climatic conditions, however, vary with the regions. The heat of the hot season, for instance, will not be as intense in the mountain regions of the Shan State (where the hill stations of **Maymyo** and **Taunggyi** are situated) as in what is known as the dry zone in central Burma (which contains **Mandalay**) where temperatures may rise above 100°F (38°C). In the rainy season the annual rainfall may vary from 86 cm in the dry zone to around 250 cm in the Rangoon delta region and 500 cm in the Arakan and Tennasserim coastal regions and the hilly areas of the far north. This is because the monsoon winds sweeping northeast from the Indian Ocean are first intercepted by high mountains in the Arakan and Tennasserim regions, and as they are forced higher up they lose temperature and drop much of their rain. They go through the same process when they are forced up by the Pegu Hills near Rangoon and the mountains in the far north. But in central Burma, which stretches northwards from Prome (320 km north of Rangoon) and lies on the leeward side of the Arakan and Pegu hills, these winds have no mountain barrier to pass over. Hence the scanty rainfall in this region.

The arrival of the monsoons in May usually means welcome relief from the intense heat, though it results in rather humid conditions. Rain falls mostly in the afternoon and evenings. But it is wise to carry an umbrella at all times, as, according to an ancient Burmese saying, rain is as wayward as a bull.

Winter is the most pleasant time of the year in which to visit Burma. The temperature in Rangoon and Mandalay can fall to as low as 60°F (16°C). It is much cooler in the hill areas such as Maymyo and Taunggyi where temperatures hover around 40°F (4.5 °C).

Tourists are asked to dress respectably to conform with local customs. To be properly dressed for women means to avoid bra-less T-shirts or singlets, shorts, mini-skirts or anything too revealing. Wearing shoes, slippers, footwear or socks in the precincts of pagodas, temples and monasteries is strictly forbidden.

Light tropical clothing is enough for most of the year in Burma, though heavier or warmer clothing is needed if you plan to visit the hill stations of Maymyo and Taunggyi.

Government offices open from 9:30 am to 4:30 pm without a break. Usual working hours for the military are 8 am to 3 pm. Saturdays and Sundays are holidays for all offices.

The Post Office also keeps government hours though the Central Telegraph Office remains open from 8 am to 9 pm on weekdays and from 8 am to 8 pm on Saturdays and Sundays and other holidays. Banks are open to the public from 10 am to 2:30 pm on weekdays.

Government and cooperative shops follow government hours, though on certain occasions such as the approach of an important anniversary or a religious festival, they may run extra hours. They close on Saturdays and Sundays but shops dealing in medicines and drugs have their respective weekend holidays on different days of the week, so that some of them are open on Saturdays and Sundays.

Small private shops keep longer hours than government ones. Private restaurants stay open until around 9:30 pm. A 10 pm to 4 am curfew has been in force since the State Law and Order Restoration Council (SLORC) assumed power in September 1988.

From the airport: if travelling in a group, transfer from the airport to your hotel is arranged by your travel agent. Individual travellers may hire government or private taxis at the taxi-stand outside the airport. The fare has to be negotiated; it varies between Kyats 100 and 150.

RANGOON

TAXIS: The government provides a taxi service with a small fleet of Mazda pickups which are distinguished by a red stripe over a blue-painted body. A far larger number of private Mazda, Toyota and Nissan pickups of various colours, with red number-plates, cruise around the city's main streets as taxis seeking custom. Both government and private taxis are unmetered and fares are a matter of negotiation between passenger and driver. Normally, the minimum charge is Kyats 15 for short runs of up to a mile, irrespective of whether the number of passengers is one, two, three or four. For longer rides, fares may range from Kyats 15 upwards.

Starting from May 1986, private cars registered with the newly-formed Regional Tourism Committees, were also available for hire by tourists both in Rangoon and other tourist centres. These vehicles can be identified by a sticker on the left side of the windscreen. Payment of fares to these cars will have to be made in "transfer service coupons" available at all Tourist Burma (now renamed Myanmar Travel and Tours) offices and at the counters of government hotels.

Old-model cars and a few newer ones are also available for hire at the central hotels. They are distinguished from other cars by their red number-plates and windscreen stickers. They are not usually available at the Inya Lake Hotel, 7 miles out of town, but reasonably good private saloon cars are available for hire there most of the time.

The rates are Kyats 80 per hour for trips around the inner city or journeys into the suburbs (and Kyats 50-60 per subsequent hour; negotiable). Full-day rates for trips out of town range from Kyats 250 to Kyats 350 and can be negotiated. Most drivers of these cars speak English but in case you meet one who does not, it is advisable to have a note from your hotel with directions in Burmese. Myanmar Travel and Tours offers Mazda limousines for US$35 for a 10-hour day or otherwise US$5 an hour, with a 50% surcharge if the trip is out of town.

BUSES: Privately owned buses operate over most roads in Burma though most of them are in the Rangoon area. The fares are reasonable — 50 pyas on slower and older buses and up to Kyats 3.5 on newer and faster buses, depending on the distance and type of bus. Government buses are 30 or 60-seat Hinos and some converted trucks. Old private buses are primitive World War II machines kept going only by the amazing ingenuity of Burmese mechanics. New private buses are Nissan and Toyota Hilux vans brought in by Burmese seamen on return home from service abroad. All the buses are crowded throughout the day and a good deal of pushing and pulling will be necessary to get in and out of them.

TRISHAWS: These tricycles can be found everywhere in town except in a few busy streets where they are banned for reasons of road safety. Usual charges are Kyats 5-15 depending on the distance — much higher rates than a few years ago as a result of an acute shortage of spare parts and tyres. In Burmese, trishaws are called "sidecars" since the passenger's seat is beside the bicycle. Trishawmen are usually polite and obliging, but to guard against inflated charges you should check with your hotel as to what is a fair price.

TRAINS: Commuter trains run shuttle services between Rangoon town and the suburbs in the north, east and west. Trains leave the central Rangoon station every half hour or so in the mornings and evening, and about hourly at other times of the day. There are also circular-line trains running from Rangoon station between 5 am and 8 pm, returning about three hours later. Ten of these trains run in a clockwise and 13 in an anti-clockwise direction. The round fare is Kyats 1.80 per head. Passing through the town area and the countryside, the trains provide one with a chance to see the ordinary lifestyle of the Burmese people. However, the trains tend to be overcrowded, especially in the morning and evening rush hours around 9 am and 4 pm and provide little by way of luxury.

RIVER BOATS: Triple-decked catamarans and double-decker motor launches ply between Rangoon and Syriam town on the opposite side of the river. Leaving every half hour from the jetty about a mile to the east of the Strand Hotel, they take about half-an-hour for the crossing. The fare is Kyats 1-2 per person. There are also river sampans for hire at the riverfront below the Strand which can be taken out for a mid-river cruise. Some of them are fitted with outboard motors. The charges range from Kyats 5 upwards and can be negotiated with the operator. Boatmen speak no English but a word or two of English plus gestures can make them understand your requirements.

UPCOUNTRY

TRAINS: Rangoon is the hub of a railway network linking the Burmese capital with towns in the north, northeast, west, the south and southwest, traversing wide areas of the Burmese countryside with its kaleidoscopic scenery. One line runs for 620 km to the old royal capital of **Mandalay**.

Some 410 km from Rangoon on this line is **Pyinmana** town, from where a branch line runs northwest 225 km to **Kyaukpadaung** which is about 53 km by road from **Pagan**, an important tourist attraction. About 480 km north from Rangoon on the main Rangoon-Mandalay line is **Thazi** town, from where a branch line runs eastward up the Shan hills to **Shewnyaung**. It is 18 km by road to **Taunggyi**, another tourist centre. From Mandalay, a line runs further north to **Myitkyina** (520 km) in the Kachin state and another to the northeast up the Shan hills to **Lashio** 275 km via Maymyo (70 km).

From Rangoon another line runs north to **Prome**, about 320 km away on the east bank of the Irrawaddy. Another line runs northeast to **Pegu** (83 km), and from there to **Moulmein** in the south and beyond to **Thanbyuzayat**, the Burmese terminal of the notorious Thailand-Burma "death railway" of World War II.

There are only two classes for passengers — upper and ordinary. Upper-class fares are roughly three times those of the ordinary. Fares vary and are usually included in the price of a package tour. Other travellers have to pay for train fares in foreign exchange, which also varies, so it is impossible to state what current fares are.

On the **Mandalay** line the best train to take is the 6 am express. Its neat and clean carriages imported from Japan carry well-disciplined and courteous railway attendants recruited from among retired military personnel to look after the needs of passengers throughout the journey. Tickets are available 24 hours in advance and there are two classes, ordinary and upper. The train takes just 11 hours for the trip, making brief stops only at four intermediate stations. As separate luggage vans are provided and seats in carriages are numbered and reserved for each passenger, there is no congestion as in other trains. Another express train which leaves Rangoon at 6:15 pm, reaching Mandalay the

Horse-drawn carriage in Syrium.

Photo: Paisal Sricharatchanya

next morning, provides sleeping berths.

To get to **Pagan**, it is best to go to **Thazi** by train and from there take the bus. Myanmar Travel and Tours now operates a shuttle bus service between the two towns and bookings can be made at the office in Rangoon.

There is a scheduled private bus service between Pagan and **Taunggyi**. If you are interested, inquiries may be made at the Travel and Tours office in either Pagan or Taunggyi.

If you prefer a train journey up the beautiful Shan hills to Taunggyi, take the Rangoon-Mandalay train, changing at Thazi station from where you proceed by train to **Shwenyaung**, the terminal town. From there you take a bus, if you like, or, taxi for the 18-km road journey up a steep hill to Taunggyi (which in Burmese means big hill).

For those bound for Shwenyaung on their way to Taunggyi, a special train leaves Rangoon at 6:15 pm running only up to Thazi. It has special carriages marked Shwenyaung so that passengers going to that town can take the carriages concerned and need not change at Thazi, where it arrives at 5:30 am the next day. There are sleeping berths.

Information about train times, connections, etc., can easily be obtained from the English-speaking duty officer at the inquiry counter of the Rangoon railway station.

The trains have no restaurant car and only light refreshments and soft drinks are obtainable, so it is advisable to take your own food and drink. Burmese food (rice and chicken, beef or pork curry, as well as fruits such as bananas, pineapples, guavas, oranges, watermelons, mangoes according to season) can be had from vendors at the stations at each stop. But if your stomach is particularly sensitive to unaccustomed foods, carry tablets for diarrhoea or other intestinal ailments. A container of tea or water is also recommended for journeys during the hot months (March, April and May).

TAXIS: Jeep taxis are often a most convenient way of travel in Burma. A good number of them, as well as Nissan and Toyota pickups, can be found in Mandalay and can be hired for visits to places of interest in and out of town. The charges are negotiable but it is wise to inquire from your hotel about standard rates. There are no fixed rates for taxis but everything is negotiable in Burma these days.

The 67-km trip from Mandalay to the hill station of **Maymyo** is cheaper if you are prepared to share the taxi with other passengers with their baggage. But you can hire the whole vehicle for yourself (and your companions).

PONY CARTS: These horse-drawn conveyances

57

can be found in most upcountry towns and provide a leisurely means of transport for short-distance travel. Kyats 5-10 is the going rate depending on the length of the trip.

BUSES: Privately owned buses operate over most roads in Burma though most of them are not of a high standard. Lately, the state-owned Road Transport Corp. and some cooperative societies have also introduced long-distance bus services using 30-passenger buses between Rangoon and some main towns such as **Meiktila**, **Magwe** (in central Burma) and **Prome** (at the northern tip of the Irrawaddy delta). You can travel comfortably without fear of breakdown on these buses. Routes include Rangoon-Pegu, Rangoon-Meiktila, Rangoon-Magwe and Rangoon-Prome. The bus for Magwe leaves Rangoon at 3 am and reaches Magwe in the evening. This service can be used for trips to Pagan or nearby **Nyaung-U**.

But in general, long-distance buses in Burma are uncomfortable and unreliable and it is better to travel by train or air.

SHIPPING: Government, cooperative and privately owned ships of various sizes ply the rivers and you can pick and choose from among them to suit your convenience. Fares are generally higher if you travel in boats of the government-run Inland Water Transport Corp., but they are comparatively more reliable for safety and punctuality. The delta town of Bassein is best reached by one of these boats. If you want a cruise down the placid Irrawaddy, you might take the boat from Mandalay to Nyaung-U near Pagan — 190 km with ordinary and upper class accommodation. The double-decker boat sails from Mandalay at dawn and reaches Nyaung-U at about 7 am or 8 am the next day.

You may spend the night on board before sailing at no extra charge, but to get sleeping space you must spread out your own bedding or buy a woven sleeping mat. The same applies even if you are travelling upper class. All that is provided for upper-class passengers is a cabin on the upper deck at the bow of the vessel separated from the much more crowded lower and upper decks. Buddhist monks often travel in this cabin and as their religion forbids physical contact with women, you should take care to observe this rule. There is no rule preventing them from talking with women or accepting alms or food offered by women. As only poor-quality Burmese rice and curry, tea and soft drinks are available on board, you would do well to take your own food. The boat formerly touched at Pagan, 18 km down river, the next morning, but

has stopped doing so now. Visitors to Pagan should therefore disembark at Nyaung-U and take the horsecart or bus from there to Pagan. But do not go in March, April or May, when low water levels in the river cause navigation hazards.

Burma's coastal and overseas shipping is run by the state-owned Burma Five Star Corp. (132-136, Theinbyu St, Rangoon). The corporation is the agent for all foreign shipping lines calling at Burmese ports.

There may be restrictions on foreigners taking certain river trips, but these will be clear when one applies for tickets.

AIR: The state-owned Burma Airways Corp., the only domestic airline, operates internal services linking many towns. There are daily scheduled flights from Rangoon to most places of interest such as Mandalay, Pagan, Taunggyi and **Sandoway** (noted for its beautiful beach). You may also take flights from Mandalay to northern towns such as Myitkyina and Lashio.

Prop-driven Fokker Friendships are used on most trips, though for short shuttle flights between Mandalay and northern towns 20-passenger turboprop de Havilland Twin Otters are used.

Air tickets must be purchased in foreign currency or exchange certificates produced to prove legal exchange if you are paying in local currency. The fares are cheaper if the flight is booked in advance and paid for overseas because of the favourable exchange rates given by some government agencies. Internal air fares are included in the price of most package tours. There is a US$4 departure tax from Burma but no taxes for internal flights. There is a surcharge for taking the Fokker F-28 jet flights from Rangoon to Mandalay Nyaung-U rather than the slower Friendship.

Tourists have to visit Burma in groups organised by authorised travel agents. Several travel agencies in Thailand offer tours to Burma with two of them being able to offer better service and facilities than the others: **Diethelm Travel**, 140/1 Wireless Rd, Bangkok. Tel: 255-9150-70, 255-9115; Fax: 256-0248, 256-0249; and **Mandalay Myanmar Tours** which is a joint venture between the state-owned Myanmar Hotels and Tourism Services and Skyline Travel Service, IFB Bldg, 23/13-14 Saladaeng Soi 1, off Rama IV Rd, Bangkok 10500. Tel: 235-9780-1, 236-6583-4, 236-6586, 235-5903; Fax: (662) 236-

6585; Telex: 82243 SKYLIPS TH.

A typical 15 days, 14 nights programme including Rangoon, Mandalay, Maymyo, Pagan, Taunggyi and Pegu costs US$1,350 with full board, US$900 room and breakfast. The price includes accommodation and internal travel in Burma — but not the Bangkok-Rangoon-Bangkok airfare (US$180 with Myanmar Airways and US$210 with Thai International), visa fee US$17 and departure tax US$6.

In Burma, the state-owned **Myanmar Travels and Tours** has a virtual monopoly on tourism. Train and air tickets can be bought at its head office opposite Sule Pagoda in central Rangoon. It has its deficiencies and foreign tour operators always emphasise that they have no control over Burmese Government departments. These tour operators are "therefore not liable for, nor accept claims for expenses due to changes, delays, accidents, injury, loss, political actions or unrest which shall be carried by the passengers."

The hotels in Burma are of modest standards compared to those in some neighbouring countries though they are equally expensive. Count on US$20-100 for a single, double or suite, with or without air-conditioning, plus 10% service charge.

RANGOON

Currently, there are five hotels in Rangoon which cater to foreign visitors:

The Strand Hotel, Strand Rd. Tel: 81533. Tlx: 21220 STANHO BM.

Thamada (President) Hotel, Signal Pagoda Rd. Tel: 71499. Tlx: 21339 TAMHO BM.

Inya Lake Hotel, Kaba Aye Pagoda Rd. Tel: 50644. Tlx: 21502 INYAHO BM.

Dagon Hotel, 256/260 Sule Pagoda Rd. Tel: 71140.

Kandawgyi (Royal Lake) Hotel on Kennedy Rd. Tel: 82255, 82327.

The Strand, facing the Rangoon port, is a relic of pre–World War II British days and was once rated one of the the best in Asia. It still retains a tradition of homely service with a hint of the artistocratic atmosphere of the old days. The Thamada which overlooks the central railway station, has less atmosphere but its service is better. The Inya Lake is the biggest, built by the Soviets as a gift to Burma in the early 1950s. It is located 11 km north of the actual city centre. The

Kandawgyi is a converted boat-club building on the southern shore of the Royal Lake near the zoological gardens. The Dagon is in the midst of the city's cinemas and is the least expensive of the state-run hotels.

The standard of Burma's hotels may soon be upgraded as experienced Hongkong-based hotelier Adrian Zecha's Hale Corporation Ltd has taken over the Strand, the Thamada and the Inya Lake. All three hotels have been earmarked for renovation.

UPCOUNTRY

Accommodation is available in both state and privately owned hotels in Mandalay, Taunggyi, Kalaw, Maymyo, Pagan and Sandoway. Recently private hotels have also opened in Bassein, Prome and other smaller towns. The standard is adequate and prices are reasonable.

Among the better upcountry hotels are:

The Mandalay Hotel, Corner of 26th and 68th St, Mandalay. Tel: 22499.

Thiripyitsayar Hotel, Pagan. Tel: 28.

Kalaw Hotel at the small hill station of Kalaw between Thazi and Taunggyi. Tel: 47.

Taunggyi Hotel, Taunggyi. Tel: 21302.

The classic, Victorian red-brick building, **Maymyo Hotel** in the hills north of Mandalay is also called the Candacraig. Tel: 2047.

The Strand at the beach resort of Sandoway in Arakan State is an old-fashioned, British-style beach hotel. It is open from October to May only. Tel: 27.

The staple Burmese food is boiled rice which is eaten with dishes of curry, fish, beef, mutton, chicken or pork, cooked with potatoes or green vegetables. The most favoured dish is *sibyan*, in which the fish or meat is stewed in a generous dose of groundnut oil mixed with condiments to give it a soft, sweet and soothing taste. Burmese food is usually accompanied by *ngapi*, a kind of fish sauce mixed with ground baked chillies. It is eaten with fresh vegetables such as slices of cucumber, green mango, cabbage or lettuce, or with boiled vegetables or bamboo shoots. A side dish called *npagigyaw* or *balachaung* is also often taken with the main dishes. The former is rather hot and is made of salted fish or shrimp paste fried in groundnut oil with chilli, garlic and onions. The latter is much milder, as it contains less chilli and the strong taste of the paste is softened by a mixture of sweet dry

59

prawns. It is less liable to upset your stomach.

The hotels offer a limited choice of local dishes among their Western, Indian and Chinese food. But Burmese food is readily available at foodstalls scattered throughout the city, especially near market places. Stalls selling *mohinga* — a popular soup of rice noodles, fish, eggs, onion and tender banana — can be found in virtually every market in Burma. The soup is served sprinkled with coriander leaves and leeks. *Khaoswes* is another popular soup. It is based on a Shan dish (*khao soi*) and contains rice noodles and meat boiled in a thick gravy of coconut milk.

There are several Chinese restaurants in Rangoon. The most famous are the **Yankin Restaurant**, No.1 (Kanbe Rd, Yankin township. Tel: 50545. **Mya Kan Tha**, 70 Natmauk Lanthwe. Tel: 52712. **Nagani** in Koemaing and the **Yin Swe** at 137 University Ave. There is a new Japanese restaurant on Shwegondaing Rd, called **Furusato**, which serves mediocre Japanese dishes but excellent sake.

Indian food can be found in the area west of the Sule Pagoda. **The Karaweik Restaurant** (Tel: 52352) on the royal lakes (a copy of a royal barge of the ancient Burmese kings) serves good Burmese, Chinese and Western food.

Nan Yu, 81, Pansodan St in central Rangoon is clean and offers enormous servings of delicious noodles at reasonable prices. For Western food the **Inya Lake** and **The Strand** hotels are the best. Most restaurants serve imported beer from Europe and China, as well as the local brew, called Mandalay, when available.

Rangoon is without nightlife, and but for a few teashops everything is closed by about 9 pm. But Burma is a land of festivals (each month having a particular festival) and Rangoon has a hefty share of them. In the cool dry season (November to April) — which is in fact the most pleasant period in which to visit Burma — you will find these festivals being held in the open air at night at one or more places in the city. The festivals are carnival-like affairs with rows of brilliantly lit shops and cafes and amusement centres. But the main attraction is the *pwe*, a concert of dance and music given on a mobile stage and lasting from about 9 pm to midnight. After that the *pwe* resumes with classical and dramatic performances called *zat*, with themes drawn from Buddhist lore or the life stories of ancient kings.

The performance opens with the famous Burmese duet dance in which the actor and actress sing and dance together in resplendent costumes to the accompaniment of exotic music. The theme of the drama is tagged on to the duet performance and then developed until they end at about dawn.

These festivals will give you a chance to look at Burmese life and culture at close quarters. The music may sound strange as it is on the septitonic scale and has no chromatic scale. But modern Burmese music is beginning to show evidence of its contacts with Western music. A good many musical pieces are adaptations of Western tunes, and Western musical instruments such as the piano, saxophone, guitar, clarinet and electronic organ now form part of the musical equipment of the better-known *pwe* troupes. You should ask at your hotel for information about these festivals.

If you are a movie fan, there are Burmese, Western, Indian and often Japanese films showing at the cinemas in Rangoon, Mandalay and other towns. Despite the language barrier, Burmese movies give a good insight into Burmese life and culture at various levels.

Although Burma does not offer as wide a range of goods as in the past, it still has many things you might want to buy. In Rangoon, the **Bogyoke** market (formerly known as Scott Market), is one of the best shopping centres where Burmese handicrafts may be bought: Mandalay silk longyis (skirt-like pieces of cloth) of distinctive designs, beautiful Shan woven bags, Burmese slippers, wood and ivory carvings, lacquerware, silverware, Bassein parasols (women's sunshades made in the delta town of Bassein), paintings, Burmese cigarettes and cheroots etc., can be bought here. Some curio and antiques dealers have lately set up shop here, providing opportunities for bargain-hunters.

As trade in gems, rubies, sapphires, jade, pearls etc. — for which Burma is famous is officially a government monopoly, they are best bought at the government-run **Diplomatic Shop** on Sule Pagoda Rd. There are good selections of stones set in jewellery of attractive local designs. It is safer to make gem and jewellery purchases here as their quality is guaranteed officially and export permitted. Silverware, lacquerware and mother-of-pearl items are also

The Pointing Buddha.   Photo: Rodney Tasker

available here. All payments in this shop have to be in US dollars.

There are now two foreign-owned department stores in Rangoon: one operated by SKS of Singapore and the other by the South Korean giant Daewoo. They offer imported consumer goods of little interest to tourists and businessmen.

The entrance to the Shwedagon Pagoda is another big shopping centre. There you will find Burmese drums of different sizes, wooden puppets and horses for children, papier mache toys and masks, metal and brassware, Burmese swords and wood and ivory carvings. For lovers of curios and antiques, the place to go is **Curio da City** at 35 Bahan Rd on the eastern environs of the Shwedagon Pagoda.

For book lovers there is the government-run special bookshop at 221 Sule Pagoda Rd and the Sarpay Beikman bookshop at 529-531 Merchant St.

At the latter shop you can buy books on Burma such as the *Pagan Guide* and *Historic Sites of Burma*. Those with a fascination for old or rare English-language books on a wide variety of subjects should find it rewarding to visit the well-stocked Pagan Book Shop in 31st St.

If you are an art lover, the places to visit are

the **Burma Art Centre** at 187 Bogyoke market and **Lokanath Art Shop** at Phayre St.

In Mandalay the **Zegyo bazaar** (main market) offers a wide variety of Shan bags, jewellery, lacquerware, slippers, parasols, pottery and other handicraft items. Mandalay night bazaar, which opens at sundown near the railway station, is an excellent place to visit. Brilliantly lit with electric lights and lanterns and thronged with shoppers, it has the lively atmosphere of a carnival.

Soccer is the most popular sport, and **Aung San Stadium** in Rangoon near the Thamada Hotel is the venue of the major soccer events of the season which runs from June to February. Tennis, hockey, cricket, golf, volleyball and basketball are also played in the larger towns. Boxing, both Western and Burmese style, is popular. The Burmese style is not governed by the Queensberry rules and allows the use of legs, elbows and head, and the bout ends as soon as one of the fighters gets a bleeding wound, however slight. The fight takes place to the accompaniment of Burmese martial music which rises to a crescendo as the tempo of the fight increases.

The most widely played national sport is the game of **chin-lone** or cane-ball. Similar to other variations played in most of Southeast Asia, it consists of keeping a small ball woven of thin strips of cane up in the air with the use only of the feet, head or shoulder, but not the hands. Played alone, or by a team of two to seven players of either sex, standing in a circle of about 3.5 m in diameter, the game is most interesting to watch. It needs no special arena or field in which to play, so you may find the game being played in parks or even in the streets.

There are festivals and celebrations throughout the year in Burma. Many of these are centred on famous pagodas in cities such as Rangoon and Mandalay, but some are associated with pagodas which, though in jungles far outside the cities, are highly revered for their romantic legends. Other festivals are national affairs derived from Buddhist practices or related to the varying seasons. All these are linked to the lunar calendar and so vary in date from one year to the next. But there are also political events. These are pegged to the Western Gregorian calendar and occur on the same dates each year. Regional festivals are superimposed on the national programme in the territories of the various ethnic groups.

January 4: Independence Day — marking the attainment of Burma's independence from the British on January 4, 1948 — is celebrated with public sports and festivities nationwide. Theatrical plays and dancing are presented in the evenings for free public entertainment.

February 12: Union Day — in honour of Bogyoke Aung San achieving the union of the country's racial groups on February 12, 1947, which led up to the eventual independence of the country — is the biggest political festival. It features a grand, week-long government exhibition and carnival in Rangoon and fairs, dancing and theatrical performances in other towns.

February-March: The Full Moon of Tabaung Lunar Month marks the occasion of the rice harvest and also the enshrinement of eight sacred hair-relics of Buddha in the Shwedagon Pagoda of Rangoon more than 2,500 years ago. Offerings are placed before Buddhist images and presented to monks. Among the offerings is the special food made of glutinous rice known as *htamane* which is shared by all.

March 2: Peasants' Day (public holiday).

March 27: Defence Services' Day. This marks the occasion in 1945 when the Burmese began organised resistance against the Japanese. There are military parades and an evening fireworks display (public holiday).

April: Thingyan (the Water Festival) welcomes the Burmese New Year. It lasts three to four days — the period being determined by astrological requirements varying from year to year — and begins with ceremonial washing of Buddhist images in scented water and offering of a morning meal to monks. Then follows a period of rowdy merry-making for all; the throwing of water over one another is the most notable part of the fun and is the customary way of wishing good luck in the new year. Young men and women wearing colourful (often outlandish) costumes enjoy themselves a great deal, dancing and singing and attending the many shows in town. This period of revelry is followed by the calm solemnity of the New Year Day, which is observed by performing charitable deeds at pagodas and monasteries (public holiday, four days).

April-May: The Full Moon of Kason Lunar Month is in triple celebration of the Buddha's birth, enlightenment and attainment of Nirvana (on his death). The sacred banyan trees are blessed with holy water and rituals are enacted at the Shwedagon and other pagodas (public holiday).

May 1: May Day (World Workers' Day — public holiday).

June-July: The Waso Festival marks the beginning of the three-month period of the Buddhist Lent and monks are presented with robes and gifts of everyday necessities. Over the Lenten period, monks observe a period of spiritual retreat and stricter religious duties, and it is the most common period for young men to enter the monkhood temporarily. The general populace is also expected to heighten its religious observances during the period. Weddings are banned during Lent as are festivities of most kinds (public holiday).

July 19: Martyrs' Day commemorates the assassination on July 19, 1947, of Bogyoke Aung San and members of his cabinet. Religious customs are observed and wreaths laid at the Martyrs' Mausoleum near the north entrance to the Shwedagon Pagoda (public holiday).

August-September: The festival of Nats (spirits) — held at Taungbyone village near Mandalay.

October: The Festival of Thadingyut (also called the Festival of Lights) occurs on the full moon in Thadingyut Lunar Month and marks the end of Lent. During a three-day period, myriad lights — candles, oil lamps and electric lights — illuminate the night, especially at the pagodas, and masses of fire-balloons are sent aloft. There is dancing and other entertainment. The occasion commemorates the Buddha's return from a non-human world when angel-like beings illuminated his way (public holiday, one day).

November: The Tazaungdaing Festival is another occasion for lights, again on the full-moon. There are celebrations in the towns with dancing and shows, and at the Shwedagon Pagoda there is an all-night robe-weaving competition, the results of which are donated to the monks (public holiday).

December 25: Christmas Day (public holiday).

DISCOVERING BURMA

RANGOON

Occupying an area of about 130 km^2 in the midst of lush delta rice fields, this city of 3.3 million people was originally described as a small "village of peace where all strife ends." As it grew, the British colonial administration laid out the main administrative and commercial centre in the neighbourhood of the **Sule Pagoda**, with broad streets running east to west parallel to the river and north to south ending at the river. The main streets have names (Burmese now replacing the original English names) and the side-streets have numbers, beginning with the north-south streets in the west, and then progressing to the east of the city and finishing with the less carefully laid-out streets north of the railway line. The **Shwedagon pagoda**, a more than 2,500-year-old, richly gilded Buddhist stupa, rises almost 100 m from the top of Singuttara Hill, the last of the Pegu range, about 6.5 km north of the city centre. The Shwedagon Pagoda Road runs north from the riverside, past the city's main shopping centre to the base of the pagoda hill. Buses and taxis ply the route and a 15-minute bus ride will take you to the pagoda. Admission costs US$5.

At the base you can either take the lift up to the pagoda platform or walk up the stone steps which are flanked by stalls selling gilded Buddhist images and shrines of all shapes and sizes, flowers and incense to be offered at the pagoda, wooden and papier mache toys for children, etc. It is necessary to remove your

---

The following are some of the names which have been changed by the present government from their previous colonial spelling, in line with changing the name of the country from Burma to Myanmar.

TOWNS

Rangoon	to	Yangon
Pegu	to	Bago
Moulmein	to	Mawlamyine
Akyab	to	Sittwe
Bassein	to	Pathein
Prome	to	Pyi (or Pyay)
Maymyo	to	Pyin Oo Lwin
Syriam	to	Tanyin

RIVERS

Irrawaddy	to	Ayeyarwady
Salween	to	Thanlwin
Sittang	to	Sittoung
Chindwin	to	Chindwinn

ETHNIC GROUPS

Karen	to	Kayin
Burman	to	Bamar
Arakanese	to	Rakhine

---

footwear once you reach the pagoda precincts, which start from the base of the hill right up to the pagoda platform.

The treasure vault of the pagoda is believed to contain the sacred relics of the Buddha. Legend has it that, apart form the relics, it contains a fabulous collection of gold, jewellery and precious stones which successive kings and nobles of Burma donated to the pagoda for more than 2,500 years. (The original, a much smaller one, was believed to have been built in 524 BC.)

Once on the pagoda platform, you will experience the serene tranquillity of a Buddhist place of worship. The soft tinkling of the bells from the diamond bud at the pinnacle of the pagoda sooths away worldly worries. Described by Sir Edwin Arnold, a British scholar on Buddhism, as the great pyramid of fire and by the poet Kipling as the "waking, winking, tinkling wonder," the pagoda has 68 smaller pagodas and numerous shrines and prayer halls on its 432-m base platform. The stupa has a plantain-bud-shaped pinnacle which since 1900 has been sheathed in gold plates, each one foot square. The latest layer of gold plates, numbering 2,562, was affixed in a picturesque 13-day ceremony in March 1986. The pagoda now has a total of 20,912 plates weighing about 1.9 tonnes. At the top of the bud is the crown called *hti* (meaning umbrella) fitted with a vane studded with 5,448 diamonds and more than 2,000 other precious and semi-precious stones. In the pagoda precincts packets of gold leaf (25 to 100 leaves per packet) are sold for the convenience of pilgrims wishing to have them pasted on to the pagoda or to many of the Buddhist images in the surrounding shrines.

On the northwest corner of the platform is a giant bronze bell with an interesting history. Just over 2 m high and weighing about 16 tonnes, it was donated to the pagoda by a Burmese king in 1778. After the second Anglo-Burmese war in 1824, which ended in British annexation of lower Burma, the victorious British troops tried to carry the bell away to Calcutta as a war trophy. But the great bell fell into the Rangoon river and defied all attempts by British military engineers to salvage it. Subsequently, the Burmese rescued it from the bottom of the river by the simple device of diving and tying bamboo poles to the bell until it floated. The bell was thus restored to the pagoda. Describing this incident, an English civil servant named H. Fielding Hall remarked: "The river gave back to them [the Burmese] what it had refused to us."

Another notable stupa is the *Sule pagoda*, a

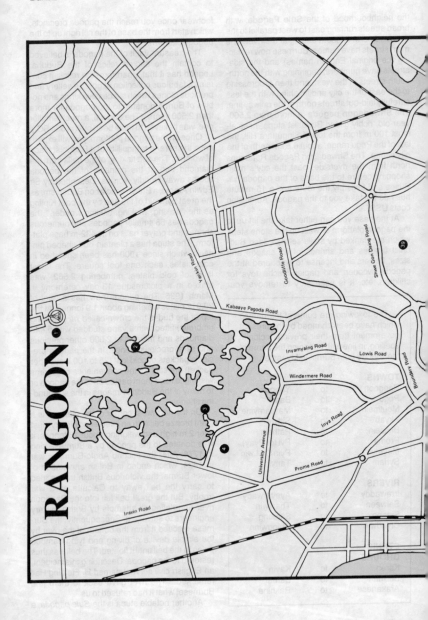

RANGOON

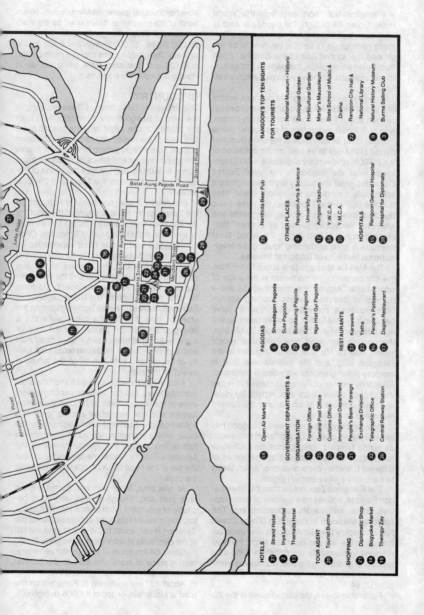

HOTELS
- 27 Strand Hotel
- 2 Irya Lake Hotel
- 13 Thamada Hotel

TOUR AGENT
- 20 Tourist Burma

SHOPPING
- 21 Diplomatic Shop
- 14 Bogyoke Market
- 19 Theingyi Zay

GOVERNMENT DEPARTMENTS & ORGANISATION
- 10 Foreign Office
- 25 General Post Office
- 26 Customs Office
- 33 Immigration Department
- 31 People's Bank - Foreign Exchange Division
- 32 Telegraphic Office
- 36 Central Railway Station

PAGODAS
- 6 Shwedagon Pagoda
- 24 Sule Pagoda
- 1 Botataung Pagoda
- 30 Kaba Aye Pagoda
- 39 Nga Htat Gyi Pagoda
- 18 Open Air Market

RESTAURANTS
- 37 Karawek
- 23 Yatha
- 16 People's Pattisserie
- 17 Dagon Restaurant

OTHER PLACES
- 28 Nanthida Beer Pub
- 4 Rangoon Arts & Science University
- 12 Aungsan Stadium
- 34 Y.W.C.A.
- 35 Y.M.C.A.

RANGOON'S TOP TEN SIGHTS FOR TOURISTS
- 10 National Museum - Historic
- 7 Zoological Garden
- 8 Horticultural Garden
- 11 State School of Music & Drama
- 22 Rangoon City Hall & National Library
- 9 Natural History Museum
- 3 Burma Sailing Club

HOSPITALS
- 15 Rangoon General Hospital
- 38 Hospital for Diplomats

few minutes' walk northwest from the Strand Hotel. Some 48 m high, the pagoda is said to have been built about 2,250 years ago by a Burmese minister. In its vault is believed to be enshrined the sacred hair of the Buddha. Apart from being a holy place, the pagoda and its surrounding structures now form a picturesque traffic island.

The city has other important pagodas worthy of a visit. The **Kaba Aye** (meaning world peace) pagoda about 11 km north from the city centre, was built under the orders of the former prime minister U Nu as the venue of the Sixth Buddhist Synod (1954-56) to be held on the occasion of the 2,500th anniversary of Buddha's enlightenment. Near the pagoda is the great Sacred Cave, designed and built by Burmese engineers specifically for holding the synod. It was here that the text of the Tripitakas (the three basic Buddhist canons) was recited, interpreted and wherever necessary revised by eminent Burmese Buddhist abbots during the synod. Near the cave is another building housing the **International Institute of Buddhist Studies**.

The **Mae La Mu** pagoda is about 13 km from the city centre to the northeast at the edge of open fields. Around the main pagoda are a number of beautiful images showing scenes from Buddha's previous lives. Said to have been built by Mae La Mu, so-called because she was believed to have been born of a La Mu tree, the pagoda remained neglected until recent years. Mae La Mu later became queen to the Rangoon king, and the pagoda was built in memory of her grandson who died in childhood. An elderly woman of Rangoon started to repair the pagoda a few years ago, reportedly in response to a dream in which the long-dead queen requested her to do so.

Besides pagodas and shrines, Rangoon has several places of worship of different faiths such as Hindu temples, Islamic mosques, Chinese temples, Jewish synagogues and churches of different Christian denominations, which testify to the country's freedom of religion.

The **Rangoon Zoo**, not far from the Shwedagon Pagoda, houses rare species of birds, reptiles, apes, wild beasts, crocodiles etc. **The National Museum** in Pansodan (Phyre Street) has on display the Mandalay regalia, once belonging to the last two Burmese kings, that was returned to Burma by the British in 1964 as a gesture of goodwill to the new Burmese government headed by Gen. Ne Win. Price of admission: US$4.

For orchid lovers, the place to visit is the 20-acre horticultural garden at Mingaladon, 16 km north of the city centre. Maintained by the state Agricultural Corp., the garden has more than 88,000 native, 23,000 foreign and 5,500 hybrid orchids. The garden forms part of a more ambitious 120-acre **National Park** being set up in Rangoon's northern environs.

UPCOUNTRY

The Irrawaddy Delta town of **Bassein**, lying to the west of Rangoon is a 30-minute flight from the capital, or one might take the boat to get a fine view of the region and its people. The town is most noted for its artistic umbrellas. It is also of historic interest and 6th-century writers mentioned it. Subsequently, it was the scene of frequent battles between the Mons and the Burmese.

Moulmein, a town southeast of Rangoon on the Tennasserim coast and lying at the mouth of the Salween river, can be reached by rail, road or air — the flight taking only 40 minutes. Once an important port, it has been superseded by Rangoon and Bassein owing to the difficulties of navigation on entry. The scenery in the surrounding country is pleasant, and the view from the pagoda-topped hills overlooking the town from the east is superb. The **Uzina** pagoda has beautifully carved life-size figures depicting the story of how the Buddha-to-be, while still a young unenlightened prince, saw the four visions — an aged man, a sick man, a dead man and a monk — which made him realise the futility of his life and sent him off to the jungle in search of the truth.

Also of interest are the caves a short distance from the town. You can have an exciting experience at the bigger caves by tackling the narrow tunnels with the help of an electric torch or a lighted candle. Starting from the entrance of the cave, where you will notice some weird figures nature has formed through the centuries, the tunnels will take you to some opening at or near the top of the huge block of rock which contains the cave.

At one time, Moulmein was Burma's great teak port and, though now downgraded because of insurgent interference with timber extraction in the forests in the upper reaches of the Salween River, a visit to the timber yard will still show elephants at work moving the great logs.

Some 64 km south is a large war cemetery, resting place of many who died on the Burma-Thailand railway built during World War II.

About 177 km northeast of Rangoon on the road to Moulmein, on top of a 1,066-m-high cliff, lies one of Burma's most famous pagodas, the **Kyaiktiyo** or **Golden Rock** pagoda. The 5.4-m-high pagoda stands on a big, gilded boulder, which rests precariously on a downward-sloping, narrow ledge, separated from the main cliff by a 6-m gap. When pushed by pilgrims, the heavy boulder gives a mild shake, but hundreds of years of pushing by generations of pilgrims have not yet toppled the boulder. Burmese Buddhists regard this phenomenon as a miracle induced by the supernatural power of a lock of Buddha's hair believed to be enshrined in the pagoda. Foreign visitors may not subscribe to the "miracle" theory but nevertheless cannot help marvelling at the ingenious way the original builder of the pagoda used the force of gravitation to secure a fine balance of the huge boulder on a sloping slab of rock.

To visit the pagoda, you have to take a 160-km busride from Rangoon to the town of Kyaikto, and from there another bus to a base-camp called Kinpun Skhan. From this camp, you have to trek up some 11 km of low, densely wooded hills, past dozens of wayside eating stalls, rest-houses and souvenir and curio shops. You can hire porters at reasonable rates at the base camp to carry your personal effects. The climb should take from three to five hours.

Pegu, 83 km to the north of Rangoon, can be reached by road or rail and makes a good day-trip since the journey by car takes only two hours. It is said to have been founded in AD 573 and was at one time the capital of the Talaing (Mon) kingdom. It used to be Burma's greatest seaport, and many 16th and 17th-century travellers commented on its size and magnificence. The town was destroyed by one Burmese king (Alaungpaya) in 1757 and rebuilt by another (Bodawpaya) between 1782 and 1819. However, with the changing of the course of the river, Pegu has never regained its greatness.

En route from Rangoon to Pegu is the **Kyaikpun pagoda**, a favourite picnic spot for residents of Rangoon. The pagoda was erected by King Dhamazedi in AD 1476 and is distinguished by a sitting image of Buddha. The images are built of brick and stucco, are 30 m high and lean back against a square pillar. One of the images facing west was destroyed in the 1930 earthquake.

Shwemawdaw (Great Golden God) pagoda lies to the east of the railway station in Pegu. It, too, is believed to contain relics of the Buddha (two of his hairs) and so is among the most venerated shrines in the country. It ap-

pears to be almost as large and as high as the Shwedagon but it rises only 88 m above the platform. The pagoda was almost destroyed by an earthquake in 1930, but was rebuilt in the early 1950s. Murals along the main entrance steps depic the destruction and the stages of reconstruction of the pagoda. The word Shwemawdaw is derived from the Khmer language meaning at the tip of the peninsula — a reference to Pegu's former position as a thriving seaport.

Tradition has it that Lord Buddha, in his lifetime, bestowed on two devout Buddhist brothers two of his hairs. The brothers took them back to Pegu and enshrined them on a hill. There they built a pagoda 21 m high. In AD 825 and AD 840 the two kings of Pegu raised the height of the pagoda to 24 m and 27 m respectively. Throughout history it continued to be an important place of religious veneration, drawing large crowds and the most powerful of Burmese kings. Successive kings repaired, heightened or regilded it. King Tabinshwehti (1573-1650) decided to have his ears pierced at the pagoda, while Kign Bayinnaung (1651-81) broke up his crown and used its jewels to adorn the pagoda's spire. King Bodawpaya (1791-1819) constructed many edifices on the pagoda platform and raised the height to 90 m. He elevated the *hti* (umbrella) on the full moon day of Tagu (April) in the year AD 1796. Since then Tagu Full Moon Day has been the festival day of the pagoda. Although destroyed several times by earthquakes, the pagoda has always been rebuilt by devotees.

The **Hinthagone hill** behind the Shwemawdaw has a high-roofed platform over the remains of a pagoda and offers a good view. It is an ideal spot for a picnic lunch but remember to take off any footwear since it is considered to be the grounds of a pagoda named after the mythical Hintha bird. According to mythology, male and female Hintha birds flying over the sea could not find land to rest. Soon, they espied a little mound, later known as Hinthagone, which had just enough room for one bird to land. The male alighted on that speck of land and the female bird, having no place to rest, had to alight on the male's back. And thus you will find the statue of two birds, one on top of the other, in front of the pagoda. Some of the local people joke that they do not dare to marry girls from Pegu since they would suffer the same fate as the male Hintha bird of the story — the life of a hen-pecked husband.

As Pegu was once a seaport before the silt of

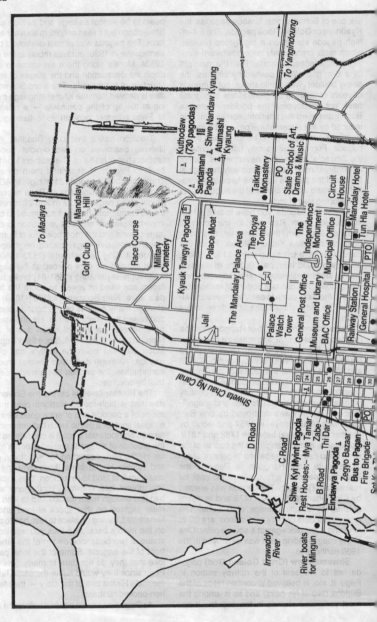

The map shows: To Yangindoung, To Yangindaung, Kuthodaw (730 pagodas), Shwe Nandaw Kyaung, Sandamani Pagoda, Atumashi Kyaung, Mandalay Hill, Taiktaw Monastery, State School of Art, Drama & Music, PO, Circuit House, Mandalay Hotel, Race Course, Palace Moat, The Royal Tombs, The Independence Monument, Tun Hla Hotel, Kyauk Tawgyi Pagoda, Golf Club, Military Cemetery, The Mandalay Palace Area, Municipal Office, PTO, Railway Station, General Hospital, To Madaya, Museum and Library, General Post Office, BAC Office, Jail, Palace Watch Tower, Shweta Chau Ng Canal, D Road, C Road, Shwe Kyi Myint Pagoda, Rest Houses:- Mya Tamar, Zabe, Thi Dar, Zegyo Bazaar, Bus to Pagan, Fire Brigade, B Road, PO, Eindawya Pagoda, Irrawaddy River, River boats for Mingun, To Pagan

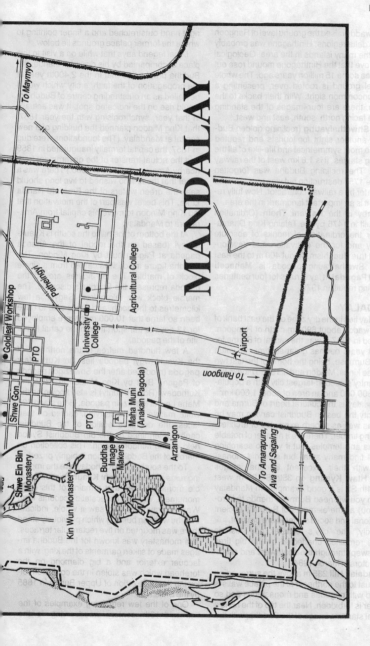

the Irrawaddy raised the ground level of Rangoon and the delta regions, Hinthagone was probably one of the many islands in the area. Geological tests prove that the Hinthagone mound rose out of the sea some 15 million years ago. The whole top-level ground is roofed over, presenting a rather uncommon sight. With their backs to the pagoda, there are four images of the standing Buddha facing north, south, east and west.

The **Shwethalyaung** (reclining golden Buddha) is another sight for tourists and reputed to be the most symmetrical and life-like of all the reclining statues. It is 1.6 km west of the railway station. The reclining Buddha was forgotten after the 1757 destruction but was rediscovered much later by a railway contractor. Now fully restored, it is an important landmark in the area.

Nearby is the **Kalyani Thein** (Ordination Hall) built in 1476 by the Talaing King Dhamazedi for the ordination of monks of absolute integrity and for the cultivation and development of true Buddhism. About 400 m to the east of the Swethalyaung pagoda is **Mahaceti (Grand Pagoda)**. It lay in ruins for four centuries until being rebuilt in 1979.

MANDALAY

Mandalay lies in the dry zone on the east bank of the Irrawaddy about 690 km north of Rangoon. Founded in 1857, it was the capital of Burma for only 28 years but has great sentimental value for the Burmese, being the home of the last two Burmese kings, Mindon and his son Thibaw. It is the country's second-largest city with a population of 600,000 and an area of about 1,600 km^2.

Mandalay is the cultural heart of Burma and in the city the best in Buddhist carving can be found as well as superb examples of architecture using timber. There are a number of notable pagodas and temples, but if you go searching you will find many small but splendid monasteries with their excellent Buddha images (**Tahat Htaw Kyaung** on 35th St, 90 m west from 84th St, is a good example). In Mandalay (though you will need Burmese friends to introduce you) all the elements of Burma's ancient educational and social systems are present.

Luckily, the city's cultural and historic edifices remained unaffected by the big fires which swept through the southwest and northeast sectors in March 1984.

Mandalay Hill 235 m above the surrounding plains just to the northeast of the palace walls is covered with pagodas and monasteries and so footwear is forbidden. Near the top of the hill is a colossal standing image of the Buddha, with the right hand outstretched and a finger pointing to where the former palace grounds lie below.

Local legend says that while on a visit to this place accompanied by his disciple Ananda, the Buddha prophesied that in the 2,400th year of the propagation of the faith, a city which would be hailed as an outstanding centre of Buddhism would rise on the indicated spot. It was actually in that year, synchronising with the year 1857, that King Mindon planned the building of a new capital at Mandalay. (The foundations were dug in 1857, the capital formally inaugurated in 1859 and the actual transfer of the government from nearby Amarapura made in 1860.) There was a belief that those who wished to live long should seek the green waters of the **Emerald Nanda Lake**. This belief was part of the motivation that led King Mindon to move his capital from Amarapura to Mandalay.

At the bottom of the hill to the south is Kyauktawgyi (based on the model of the Ananda pagoda at Pagan) built by King Mindon. The Buddha figure inside was carved from a single block of marble. The 90 figures around the pagoda represent the Buddha's disciples. The marble block was taken from Sagyin, a few kilometres to the north, and it was said to have been so large that 10,000 men were employed for 13 days to transport it from the canal to the site of the pagoda.

A few hundred metres to the northeast of the Kyauktawgyi pagoda lies the **Kuthodaw pagoda** (modelled after the Shwezigon pagoda of Pagan). Built by King Mindon in 1857, the Kuthodaw (Royal Bounty) is also known as the Maha Lawka Marazein pagoda. Here stand 728 white marble tablets carrying, carved on their faces, the definitive edition of the Buddhist canon determined by the 5th Buddhist Synod held during Mindon's reign. This collection on marble of the Buddhist canon is highly prized.

To the south of the Kuthodaw are the imposing ruins of the **Atumashi Kyaung** (incomparable monastery). All that remains of this great monument, which drew ecstatic accounts from Western travellers who saw it whole, indicate that the wooden building which previously stood there was mounted on five rectangular terraces. The monastery was known for the Buddha images made of silken garments of the king, with a lacquer exterior and a big diamond on the forehead which was stolen in the confusion following the annexation of Upper Burma in 1885 by the British.

One of the few remaining examples of the fine mid–19th century woodcarving is the

Shwenandaw monastery a few hundred metres further to the south from the Kuthodaw. Much of the material used in the construction of the monastery was moved by King Thibaw from the palace occupied by his father (Mindon) and his chief queen, Satyadevi. The monastery contains a replica of the royal throne, a couch used by King Thibaw when he visited, some glass mosaics and magnificent wood-carvings. The Royal Palace was once a royal city within the city of Mandalay. Now, because of British bombing (of which the Burmese have long been resentful) during World War II, the palace grounds offer little more than a walk in the hot sun. The walls form a square with each side wall 1.6 km long, punctuated by fine watchtowers and gates. A 77-m-wide moat surrounds the whole.

In the palace grounds is a small museum exhibiting models of the original palace buildings.

The ruined clocktower and the relic tower lie to the east of the museum. A little to the north of the clocktower are the mausoleums, of which the most important historically is King Mindon's tomb. It was gilded and covered with glass mosaic. The work now seen is of recent origin and nothing of the old craftsmanship remains.

Close to the clock tower are inscription sheds housing more than 600 inscribed stone slabs, being original lithic documents collected by King Bodawpaya. They were removed from Amarapura to the present site just before World War II.

Mandalay's famed **Zegyo bazaar**, designed in 1903 by an Italian named Count Caldrari, the first secretary of the Mandalay municipality, colourfully displays all sorts of wares. This is where you can buy Burmese silk and other locally made handicrafts. The Diamond Jubilee Clocktower stands at the northern end of the bazaar.

In the heart of Mandalay stands the **Shwe Kyi Myint** pagoda built by King Monshinsaw (1114-67) of Pagan. This shrine on 24th St between 82nd and 83rd streets, predates Mandalay by many centuries. It is noted for two things: the image is the original one consecrated by the builder himself and it has now become the repository of many images made of gold and silver, salvaged from the palace and adorned with invaluable precious stones representing the collection of successive monarchs. There is also a small golden palanquin used by a lesser queen. Many Buddha images can also be seen in the quadrangle of the pagoda.

The **Mahamuni** or **Arakan pagoda** is the town's best-known and lies about 3 km south of the market just off to the east from 84th St. The main Buddha figure is believed to be of great antiquity and was brought from Mrohaung — once the capital of Arakan — by King Bodawpaya (1782-1819) in 1784. The road the king built from his capital (nearby at Amarapura) to the pagoda can still be seen.

The Buddha image is enshrined in the pagoda and became the object of fervent devotion for his people and is still paid homage to by Buddhists throughout the world. It was originally cast out of metal but the body of it has for long been so lavishly gilded that it has assumed an irregular outline. The image, which is in the usual sitting posture of Buddha, is 3.8 m high. The original pagoda was damaged by fire in 1884. The present pagoda, which has a terraced roof of gilded stucco, is therefore of late construction. In the inner courtyard are hundreds of stone slabs bearing inscriptions recording religious endowments. Not far from the western entrance is a group of six bronze figures — two of men, three of lions and one of a three-headed elephant. They were part of the spoils which King Bayinnaung brought back from Ayudhia (Ayutthaya) in Thailand in 1663 and later taken by the Arakanese King Razagyi from Pegu.

Local legend has it that, by rubbing the appropriate anatomical part of the two bronze figures of men, one can be cured of similarly located diseases. On the way to the pagoda can be seen the workshops of local stonemasons who carve Buddha figures.

The **Eindawya** pagoda was built by the Pagan Min (Pagan Prince) in 1847 on the site of the palace he lived in before ascending the throne. It lies in the centre of the city. Heavily gilded, this beautifully proportioned shrine houses an image of the Buddha made of chalcedony (a type of quartz mineral with an admixture of opal) said to have been brought back from Buddha Gaya (India) in 1839.

In east Mandalay lies the **Sandamuni** pagoda built on the ground on which the temporary palace of King Mindon stood while the new palace was being erected. This pagoda is also known to have been raised over the graves of the Crown prince and some members of the royal family who lost their lives in the palace rebellion of 1866 when an attempt was made on the life of King Mindon.

The manufacturing of gold leaf flourishes in the southeastern part of the city. It is a hereditary occupation carried on as a cottage industry. Small bits of gold are laboriously beaten for days to get the required film-like thinness. The beating is done by men while the piecing together of the film is done by women. The pieces are sold in packets which the devotees buy for gilding pagodas and images.

Buses run to the outskirts of the town where many of the previously mentioned sites are located.

Surrounding Mandalay are three towns (or ruins of such) which were in their time capitals of Burma. These are the towns of **Amarapura**, **Ava** and **Sagaing**. The town of **Mingun**, though never a capital, is also of note.

A few kilometres south of Mandalay is the **Ava Bridge**, the only one spanning the Irrawaddy. About a 1.6-km long, the 16-span bridge was built in 1938 to link Mandalay with Sagaing, a beautiful town with pagoda-and-temple-studded green hills in the Irrawaddy's west bank. The bridge was destroyed in 1942 by withdrawing British troops but was rebuilt after the war and completed in 1954.

Some people find Mandalay disappointing: if you are one of these, **Maymyo** is an alternative place to visit. A remote hill station, once a favourite refuge for the British during the wet season and hunting ground for expatriate spinsters, this incredible anachronism can be reached by a taxi service which leaves from near Mandalay bazaar. The trip takes about two hours, but the views are breathtaking and a night at the former **Canda Craig** hotel, now renamed the **Maymyo Inn**, will not be forgotten.

The altitude — as in Taunggyi — makes Maymyo very cold and warm clothing should be taken. Transport in the town is by primitive horse-carriage and the town itself is a curious mixture of Burma and the English Home Counties. The **Government Botanical Garden** is worth a visit. Established in 1914 by the then British Government, the garden has 170 acres of land and 70 acres of well-maintained lakes.

Amarapura (Immortal City) lies a few kilometres to the south of Mandalay and can be reached cheaply by bus or by multiload taxi. Founded by King Bodawpaya in 1781, it was the capital from 1782 to 1882. Ava became the capital for some years until Amarapura was restored to favour from 1837 to the founding of Mandalay in 1857.

Today the villages in the vicinity are centres for silk weaving and practically every house has its loom. The Kathe villages are famous for weaving of chequered long-yi — the intricately patterned open skirt worn by Burmese women on ceremonial occasions. The industry is strictly

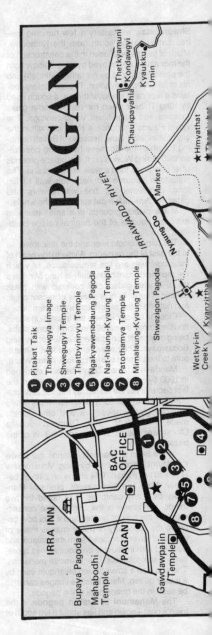

PAGAN

1 Pitakat Taik
2 Thandawgya Image
3 Shweguyi Temple
4 Thatbyinnyu Temple
5 Ngakyawenadaung Pagoda
6 Nat-hlaung-Kyaung Temple
7 Patothamya Temple
8 Mimalaung-Kyaung Temple

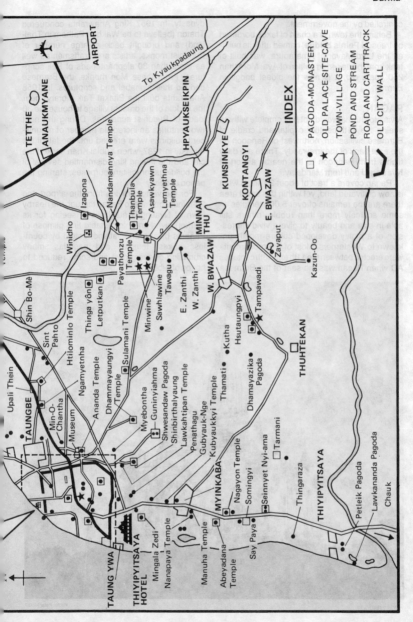

INDEX

- ● PAGODA-MONASTERY
- ★ OLD PALACE SITE-CAVE
- ⬠ TOWN-VILLAGE
- ⬭ POND AND STREAM
- ═══ ROAD AND CARTTRACK
- ⌐ OLD CITY WALL

AIRPORT

To Kyaukpadaung

TETTHE

ANAUKMYANE

Izagona

Winidho

Shin Bo-Mè

Sint Pahto

Upali Thein

TAUNGBE

Min-O-Chantha

Museum

Ananda Temple

Ngamyetna

Dhammayaungyi Temple

Htilominlo Temple

Thinga yón

Letputkan

Nandamannya Temple

Thanbula Temple

Asawkyawn

Lemyethna Temple

Payathonzu Temple

HPYAUKSEIKPIN

KUNSINKYE

KONTANGYI

MINNAN THU

E. BWAZAW

W. BWAZAW

Tawagu

Sawhlawine

Minwine

E. Zanthi

W. Zanthi

Zayaput

Kazun-Oo

Sulamani Temple

Myebontha

Guninyiahma

Shwesandaw Pagoda

Shinbirthalyaung

Lawkahtipan Temple

Penathagu

Gubyauk-Nge

Kubyaukkyi Temple

Thamati

Kutha

Dhamayazika Pagoda

Hsutaungpyi

Tampawadi

THUHTEKAN

Tarmani

THIYIPYITSAYA

Nagayon Temple

Somingyi

Seinnyet Nyi-ama

Thingaraza

MYINKABA

Manuha Temple

Say Paya

Abeyadana Temple

Mingala Zedi

Nanapaya Temple

THIYIPYITSAYA HOTEL

TAUNG YWA

Petleik Pagoda

Lawkananda Pagoda

Chauk

73

controlled by the government.

Behind the town is a chain of lakes bordered by trees. **U Pein's bridge**, named after its builder, the Lord Mayor of Amarapura, was built of teak from the deserted palace of Ava. More than 250 years old, it is now the oldest bridge in Burma.

PAGAN

A visit to Burma would not be complete without seeing the 11th-century capital and cradle of Burmese civilisation, northwest of Rangoon on the east bank of the Irrawaddy. There are daily flights from Rangoon to the nearby airport at **Nyaung-U** and from Mandalay.

Pagan covers a tract of about 25 km of what is now cultivated land, yet within this small area there are the remains of over 5,000 temples — some scarcely more than rubble, others still able in size and beauty to give a vivid impression of a highly developed culture mostly unknown to Westerners. Most of the monuments were erected between the 11th and 13th centuries AD when Pagan was the seat of the Burmese dynasty. In 1057 King Anawrahta conquered Thaton (believe to be Wakhon Pathom in Thailand) and brought back a large number of Buddhist monks, artists and craftsmen as well as more than 30 elephant-loads of Pali scriptures. From these Mon monks, the Burmese derived their alphabet and scriptures. In 1058 Anawrahta built the Pitakat Taik (library) near the middle of the present village to house the 30 loads of Buddhist scriptures. During the next two centuries an incredible number of magnificent buildings were erected until the fall of the dynasty in 1287, when Kublai Khan sacked the city and the fleeing king dismantled several of the buildings for military purposes, starting the period of decay.

For the visitor arriving from the airport, the 20-minute bus ride to Pagan through the nearby town of Nyaung-U (itself worth seeing for its market) gives an unforgettable first glimpse of Pagan's bizarre arid flatland, dotted by countless spires, temples and pagodas, many crumbling or overgrown and some reduced to heaps of rubble.

Pagan pagoda.

Photo: Peter McGill

Pagan village is little more than a collection of wooden houses lined along the main road linking it to Nyaung U. The **Sarabha Gateway** still serves as the market for the present village perimeter. It is the only structure remaining of the old city built in the ninth century AD, and was originally the main gate of the east wall. The entrance is guarded by two *nat* or spirit sculptures, representing a brother and sister.

The best way to see Pagan is to hire a local guide and one of the many horse buggies. Next to the gateway is the huge white **Ananda** temple. Built in 1091, it is highly venerated for the relics of the Buddha it supposedly contains. The plan of the building is that of a perfect Greek cross. Inside is a maze of corridors studded with inset statues of the Buddha and plaques inscribed in Mon script. The overall effect is not unlike that of some catacombs. In the centre lies a stone block with each side facing either directly north, south, east and west, and housing four colossal standing Buddhas. The centre corridor contains 80 statues in the lower niches showing the stages from birth to Nirvana of the Boddisatva. In the west-facing porch are two Buddha footprints on pedestals. The local museum is nearby.

Just south of the main street is **Thatbyinnyu temple**. Surrounded by the remains of red-brick stupas, the temple is easily recognised by its soaring white exterior, resembling a multi-storey wedding cake. Thatbyinnyu (omniscience) contains two main storeys connected by dark, perilously steep stairs on the inside to the passage on the first floor, and an external flight of stone stairs to the Buddha image on the upper storey. Further climbing on the outside to the narrow ledges on the top reveals magnificent panoramas.

The **Manuha** temple is named after the captured king of Thaton and its cramped style, including uncomfortably seated Buddhas, reflects the claustrophobia and stress suffered by the king.

Mingalazedi pagoda was constructed a few years before the Mongol invasion and in many ways is the most developed in style of the Burmese buildings in Pagan. The terraces have beautiful inscribed terracotta tiles.

This is by no means an exhaustive itinerary. **Htilominlo** should not be missed, nor **Mahabodhi** on the track to the **Irra Guest House**, a pagoda of Indian Bihar influence, or indeed many of the thousands of other relics of this period of Burmese renaissance.

When sightseeing becomes too tiring, visitors are usually welcome to a free bowl of tea at any of the eating houses along the main street. Accommodation is a problem only if one is incurably addicted to Western-style comfort; then the **Thiripyitsaya** is the only place available. Built at great expense by the government, some way out of the village on the banks of the Irrawaddy for a captive market, it is an ugly imitation of a modern resort hotel and, by Burmese standards, extremely expensive. Other privately-run rest-houses offering lodging facilities at moderate rates are for spartan living, but much better value.

Pagan still has good-quality lacquerware for sale: but be sure to bargain over the price, and beware of buying gemstones; the stones are most likely fakes.

LAKE INLE

The people of the Shan state are fiercely independent of the central government, which sends troops to the area to combat local insurgency forces and attempts to curb widespread smuggling operations with bordering Thailand. The Shan area is the only place in Burma where Coca Cola is available, and the powerful motors for the fishermen's boats are mostly smuggled in from across the border.

The chief attraction to visitors in this often-troubled region is the beautiful lake; an enormous, tranquil expanse of water surrounded by mountains, and home of the famous Shan legrowers who paddle and steer their long boats with one leg wrapped round the oar, releasing their arms to cast their fishing nets. Fast boats can be hired in the lakeside village of **Yaunghwe**; at least four hours are required to make a round trip.

At Kyats 350, hiring is expensive; but since each boat accommodates at least five people, the cost can be shared. From the boat you will be able to see the rowers and stops can be made at lake villages and pagodas resting on stilts. A normal part of the trip should be a visit to a hand-weaving industry managed by the government, but most of the materials, as well as the hand-woven Shan shoulder-bags, can be purchased much cheaper elsewhere.

Open trucks (Burmese term them buses) and Toyota vans run the 32 km from Yaunghwe up precipitous mountain roads to **Taunggyi**, the old British hill station and Shan capital, whose museum deserves a visit for its interesting relics and a good natural history section. Get there by daily flight from Rangoon or Mandalay to **He Ho**, then by bus to Yaunghwe/Taunggyi.

INDIA

India captivates the spirit and justifies every superlative ever written about it. At the same time, it can easily give the visitor a culture shock from an overdose of experience. For the traveller with sufficient time to explore properly, it is so large that there is somewhere and something in India to suit every taste.

Tradition is of the utmost importance and there is a strong resistance to change. Cows — sacred to Hindus — still wander down the congested roads of many major cities. Holy men, palmists and astrologers sit on the pavement outside modern scientific laboratories.

Immigration and customs officials receiving foreign visitors can still be maddeningly thorough when they wish to be, working laboriously through lists of ritual questions and form-filling.

A surprising aspect for any visitor is the number of reminders of days of the British Raj — memorials and buildings in large numbers, but more particularly the political and educational systems, which in many respects reflect the system of the British administrators who once ruled the country.

But India in many other respects does things in its own way — in many cases slowly, when officialdom is involved, as most businessmen will point out. India is run by a massive bureaucracy, which requires an Indian-style tolerance to cope with. India also contains extreme contrasts between the staggeringly rich and the appallingly poor, which visitors often find difficult to accept. Despite this, there seems to be little bitterness towards obviously more affluent visitors.

India is a country which should be visited partly for pleasure but also as an educational experience — not always pleasant.

The British were just the last of a long string of invaders of India. Around 1500 BC, Aryan tribes swept down into India from the northwest to conquer and merge with earlier Dravidian inhabitants of the land. The Greeks under Alexander the Great came in 327 BC, but their supply lines were stretched too thin and they were soon driven out. The first Indian empire to extend its authority across the whole of North India rose under Chandragupta Maurya, with its capital at the site of present-day Patna, capital of Bihar state. The Maurya empire reached the peak of its glory under the rule of Changdragupta's grandson, Ashoka, who ruled from 273 to 232 BC. Ashoka, a convert to Buddhism, was instrumental in the spread of that belief throughout and beyond India. A great traveller, Ashoka left

evidence of his wise rule in columns bearing his edicts, many of which still stand today.

But by the 1st century BC, the Mauryas had lost their power. Other empires rose and fell. One of them, the Gupta empire, held sway in northern India during the 4th and 5th AD. The period, during which the arts and sciences flourished, became known as the Golden Age of India; the greatest of India's Sanskrit poets, Kalidasa, lived in this age.

By the end of the 5th century, marauding Asiatic tribes had established their rule in northern India, which was divided into various kingdoms held together by Hinduism, which expanded in scope and influence.

The development in Dravidian southern India had been markedly different from those in the increasingly Aryanised north. Seldom did the rulers of the north venture into the south. The south had its own dynasties and its own maritime trade relations with countries as far east as Indonesia and even perhaps the Philippines. This helps to explain the essential difference between northern India and the south which continues to this day.

By the 11th century, a new influence appeared in India — Islam. The Muslim kingdoms to the west of India had been growing in power and India was soon to fall under their sway, despite the resistance of such fabled fighters as the Rajputs, who were unfortunately too concerned with internal squabbles to be able to mount any real resistance. The Delhi Sultanate was established in 1206, and from then on Muslim rule was to spread over most of India with the exception of the far south.

Although ancient trade contact between India and Europe existed intermittently in the Greek and Roman eras, the European Age of Discovery brought Portuguese explorer Vasco da Gama to Calicut (Kozhikode) in the present-day state of Kerala, in 1498.

By 1510 the Portuguese had taken possession of Goa on the west coast of the subcontinent. The British East India Company arrived in 1613, establishing itself on the eastern coast. For some time British power remained localised there as the Moghuls continued their powerful rule in the north. After Akbar there was Emperor Shah Jahan (the builder of the Taj Mahal) and then Emperor Aurangzeb, a religious zealot.

Eventually, the British began moving north. In the Battle of Plassey in 1757, Robert Clive defeated the Nawab of Bengal and established control over that extensive region. Calcutta became the centre of British power, which now began to expand until it extended over almost the whole country. The East India Company handed over control to the British crown following the Indian Mutiny of 1857. In 1876, Queen Victoria was crowned Empress of an empire comprising British India and a patchwork of smaller states. For the first time, a single authority ruled over all India which, at that time, included the present Pakistan and Bangladesh.

As early as 1885 there were already significant signs of growing nationalist opposition to British rule. The movement which crystallised under the leadership of Mahatma Gandi and the Indian National Congress brought independence to India on August 15, 1947. But India was divided for the purpose and the Muslim-

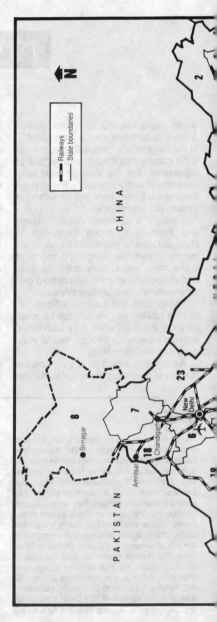

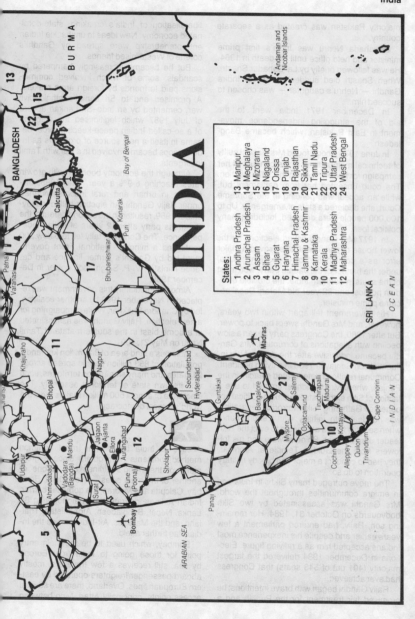

INDIA

States:

1. Andhra Pradesh
2. Arunachal Pradesh
3. Assam
4. Bihar
5. Gujarat
6. Haryana
7. Himachal Pradesh
8. Jammu & Kashmir
9. Karnataka
10. Kerala
11. Madhya Pradesh
12. Maharashtra
13. Manipur
14. Meghalaya
15. Mizoram
16. Nagaland
17. Orissa
18. Punjab
19. Rajasthan
20. Sikkim
21. Tamil Nadu
22. Tripura
23. Uttar Pradesh
24. West Bengal

BURMA

BANGLADESH

Bay of Bengal

SRI LANKA

INDIAN OCEAN

ARABIAN SEA

Andaman and Nicobar Islands

Calcutta
Patna
Varanasi
Konarak
Puri
Bhubaneshwar
Khajuraho
Bhopal
Nagpur
Udaipur
Ahmedabad
Vadodara (Baroda)
Surat
Mandu
Jalgaon
Ajanta
Ellora
Aurangabad
Pune (Poona)
Sholapur
Bombay
Panaji
Secunderabad
Hyderabad
Guntakal
Bangalore
Mysore
Ootacamund
Salem
Tiruchirapalli
Madurai
Madras
Cochin
Kottayam
Alleppey
Quilon
Trivandrum
Cape Comorin

majority Pakistan was created as a separate country.

Jawaharla Nehru was India's first prime minister and held office until his death in 1964. He was followed briefly by Lal Bahadur Shastri. When Shastri died suddenly in 1966, Indira Gandhi — Nehru's daughter — was chosen to succeed him.

In December 1971 India went to the aid of the struggling independence movement in East Pakistan, which became Bangladesh.

In June 1975 a court found Mrs Gandhi guilty of technical malpractices in the conduct of her campaign for her own seat in the 1971 election. The court unseated her from parliament but, while an appeal was pending in the Supreme Court, she declared a state of emergency. Up to 100,000 people were detained, including many political foes.

In 1977 Mrs Gandhi risked elections for the lower house of parliament: this proved a major error as a combination of opposition groups, under the banner of the Janata party, won most of the seats in northern India, the crucible of Indian politics, and 82-year-old Morarji Desai became prime minister.

His government fell apart within two years, however, and Mrs Gandhi swept back to power. But after 1980, the Congress party began a slow decline with allegations of corruption. Mrs Gandhi became indecisive after the death of her influential son Sanjay in 1980 in a flying accident. Communal relations deteriorated steadily in the Punjab, where Mrs Gandhi attempted to use a faction of Sikh extremists to weaken political opponents. Gathering Sikh terrorist separatism was not dealt with, initially, with a strong hand; when security forces attempted to evict the Sikh leader Jarnail Singh Bhindranwale and his followers from the Golden Temple at Amritsar, they had to conduct a major and bloody military operation to do so.

The move outraged many Sikhs in India and in emigre communities throughout the world. Mrs Gandhi was assassinated by two Sikh bodyguards on October 31, 1984. Her remaining son, Rajiv, had entered parliament a few years earlier and despite his inexperience most Indians accepted him as a rallying figure. Elections in December 1984 delivered the largest majority (401 out of 543 seats) that Congress had ever achieved.

Rajiv Gandhi began with brave intentions: he promised fair treatment for the Punjab and a liberalisation of India's creaking, state-dominated economy. New ideas to unshackle Indian entrepreneurship were spread by Gandhi's coterie of Westernised friends.

But he became increasingly hampered by scandals, some of which involved commissions paid to friends by foreign arms makers. A promised end to Sri Lanka's ethnic civil war, cemented by an Indo–Sri Lankan accord of July 1987 which legitimised the dispatch of a so-called Indian peace-keeping force, became in itself a new source of problems as Indian troops became involved in a war with Tamil insurgents.

Although the economy boomed, with growth rates reaching 6-9% a year, after 1985, disparities in urban and rural income widened under Rajiv Gandhi. An election called in November 1989, resulted in the second defeat of the Congress party after 42 years of Indian independence. The Congress tally fell to below 200 seats and a minority, National Front government led by Gandhi's former finance and defence minister, V. P. Singh, took power in December 1989.

Almost immediately this government was replaced in November 1990 by another coalition, led by Chandra Shekhar. While campaigning for a new election, Rajiv Gandhi was assassinated in a bomb blast in the southern state of Tamil Nadu on May 21, 1991.

India has a land area of 3.2 million km^2 and a population of 853 million people spread across 24 states and many small union territories, each with its own state or territorial assembly. The electorate of almost 500 million makes India the world's largest democracy.

Access to India by air (the most common method) presents no problem since a great many of the world's airlines call at one or another of the main cities — New Delhi, Bombay, Calcutta and Madras; the domestic carrier, Indian Airlines, operates into neighbouring Sri Lanka, Nepal, Bangladesh. Afghanistan, Thailand, and the Maldives. Air-India carries the Indian flag further afield.

Bombay, which used to be the main entry point for those going to India from Europe by sea, still receives a few travellers, mostly aboard passenger/freighters operated by eastern European lines. Overland, there are several access points, principally Attari, lying between

Taj Mahal, Agra. ▷

India

Pakistan's city of Lahore and India's Amritsar. To the east, on India's border with Bangladesh, the crossing is at Haridaspur.

Up-to-date information on the state of border crossing-points into India can be obtained from Indian overseas missions or government tourist information officers.

There is a tax of 10% of the basic fare for all passengers on internal Indian air routes, except those tourists who pay their fare in foreign currency.

All foreigners wishing to visit India need a valid passport and a visa before arrival.

Normally, Indian missions abroad grant a multi-entry visa valid for 120 days to tourists. The visa is valid for entering India within six months of the date of issue.

A "collective" visa, for group tours of no fewer than four and sponsored by a government-recognised travel agency, is also available, usually for 30 days, upon presentation of a travel itinerary. Although the tour parties may split into smaller groups they must reassemble and depart the country as the original group.

Business travellers should apply for a multi-

EMBASSIES, HIGH COMMISSIONS AND CONSULATES

AFGHANISTAN — Bombay (8128577), New Delhi (606625, 603331); **ALGERIA** — New Delhi (6441805); **ARGENTINA** — New Delhi (671345, 671348); **AUSTRALIA** — Bombay (217366), New Delhi (601336, 672637); **AUSTRIA** — Bombay (2042044), Madras (476038, 812131), New Delhi (601238, 601112); **BAHRAIN** — Bombay (217023, 217428); **BANGLADESH** — New Delhi (6834065, 615668); **BELGIUM** — Bombay (4939261), Calcutta (443886), New Delhi (608295, 608067); **BHUTAN** — New Delhi (609217, 609218); **BRAZIL** — New Delhi (3015086, 3017286); **BULGARIA** — New Delhi (607411, 607413, 607716); **BURMA** — New Delhi (600251, 600252); **CAMBODIA** — New Delhi (693414, 623157); **CANADA** — Bombay (2024343), New Delhi (608161); **CANARY ISLAND** — New Delhi (3015892); **CHILE** — New Delhi (671718); **CHINA** — New Delhi (600328, 600872); **COLOMBIA** — New Delhi (3012771); **COSTA RICA** — Bombay (250351); **CUBA** — New Delhi (6445775, 6442897); **CYPRUS** — Bombay (244294), New Delhi (697503, 697508); **CZECHOSLOVAKIA** — Calcutta (733316), New Delhi (609318, 608382); **DENMARK** — Bombay (264462), Calcutta (287476, 287477, 287478), Madras (473333), New Delhi (616273); **DOMINICAN REPUBLIC** — Bombay (241416); **EGYPT** — Bombay (212425), New Delhi (602074, 608904); **ETHIOPIA** — New Delhi (604411, 604407); **GERMANY** — Bombay (232422, 232517), Calcutta (45-9141, 45-9142, 45-9143, 45-4886), Madras (471747, 473542), New Delhi (604861); **FINLAND** — Bombay (4150271), Calcutta (444757), Madras (87724, 83817), New Delhi (605409/205, 616006); **FRANCE** — Bombay (4949808), Calcutta (290978), Madras (811469), New Delhi (604004, 604300); **GHANA** — New Delhi (670788); **GREECE** — Bombay (8112539), Calcutta (298194), New Delhi (617800); **GUYANA** — New Delhi (674195/4); **HOLY SEE VATICAN** — New Delhi (606921, 606520); **HUNGARY** — New Delhi (608414 608415, 608152); **ICELAND** — Bombay (251931), New Delhi (3321122, 3321172); **INDONESIA** — Bombay (368678), Calcutta (460297), New Delhi (602352, 602353, 602354); **IRAN (ISLAMIC REPBLIC)** — Bombay (293925), New Delhi (3329600, 3329601, 3329602, 3329603); **IRAQ** — Bombay (8123887), New Delhi (618011/3/2); **IRELAND** — Bombay (2872045), New Delhi (615485, 617435); **ISRAEL** — Bombay (362793, 362794, 362795); **ITALY** — Bombay (2874794/95-7), Calcutta (45-1411, 45-1412), New Delhi (618311, 618312); **JAPAN** — Bombay (262583), Calcutta (611811), Madras (475792), New Delhi (604071); **JORDAN** — New Delhi (650977, 661954); **KENYA** — New Delhi (672303, 672312, 672003); **KAMPUCHEA** — New Delhi (693417); **KOREA, DPR (NORTH)** — New Delhi (617140); **KOREA REPUBLIC OF (SOUTH)** — New Delhi (601601/603); **KUWAIT** — Bombay (2871897, 221941), New Delhi (600791, 600821/944); **LAOS** — New Delhi (6873125, 6873124); **LEBANON** — New Delhi (3013174, 3015406); **LIBERIA** — Calcutta (461164), New Delhi (600569); **LIBYA** — New Delhi (697717, 697926); **LUXEMBOURG** — New Delhi (3015855, 3011569); **MALAYSIA** — Madras

entry business visa, which are normally given readily with a validity of one year but with a maximum stay in India of not more than 120 days.

Conference participants can receive a visa to cover the conference as well as for tourism. Special visas also exist for trekking, botanical expeditions, sports and journalistic purposes. Foreign nationals of Indian origin can obtain a two-year, multi-entry visa which is also available to dependent members of their families.

Visa extensions may be obtained but nor-

mally there are no extensions beyond a maximum of six months.

Visitors may move about freely throughout the country, except to restricted and/or protected areas or prohibited places. These include the entire northeast region (comprising the states of Assam, Arunachal Pradesh, Nagaland, Manipur, Meghalya, Mizoram and Tripura, plus the Mikir and North Cachar Hills districts).

Immigration officials at Bagdogra airport will grant entry to visitors provided they leave after 15 days, that they arrive and depart

---

(473534, 478397), New Delhi (601291, 601292); **MAURITIUS** — New Delhi (3011112, 3011113); **MEXICO** — New Delhi (697992/1, 698193); **MONACO** — New Delhi (623193, 617067); **MONGOLIA** — New Delhi (618921, 617989); **MOROCCO** — New Delhi (611588, 611038, 619349, 617067); **NAURU** — New Delhi (667977, 651274); **NEPAL** — Calcutta (452024), New Delhi (3327594); **NETHERLANDS** — Bombay (296840), Calcutta (26-2160/64), Madras (811566), New Delhi (609571); **NEW ZEALAND** — New Delhi (697296, 618281); **NICARAGUA** — New Delhi (6442022); **NIGERIA** — New Delhi (679150, 670545, 670405); **NORWAY** — Bombay (242042), Calcutta (444757), Madras (517950), New Delhi (605003, 605982, 606517); **OMAN** — Bombay (244821, 244830), New Delhi (671704); **PAKISTAN** — New Delhi (600603/01); **PALESTINE** — New Delhi (676605); **PANAMA** — Bombay (217866), New Delhi (6438620); **PERU** — Bombay (244664, 244743), New Delhi (674085, 673937); **YEMEN** — Bombay (213956, 2172570), New Delhi (6414623, 6414731); **PHILIPPINES** — Bombay (2024792, 2026340), Calcutta (200514), Madras (608492, 433241), New Delhi (601120, 608842); **POLAND** — Bombay (8123863, 8123864), Calcutta (44-2811, 44-7030), New Delhi (608321, 608762); **PORTUGAL** — Bombay (221868), Calcutta (455586), New Delhi (6441263); **QATAR** — Bombay (2027192), New Delhi (673745); **ROMANIA** — New Delhi (670700); **SAN MARINO** — New Delhi (3016675); **SAUDI ARABIA** — Bombay (217768), New Delhi (645419); **SENEGAL** — New Delhi (6872720); **SINGAPORE** — Bombay

(2043205/ 209), Madras (473795, 476637, 476393), New Delhi (608149); **SOMALIA** — New Delhi (619559, 619277); **SPAIN** — Bombay (244664), Calcutta (45-1388, 45-5771), Madras (72008), New Delhi (3015892); **SRI LANKA** — Bombay (2048303), Madras (470831), New Delhi (3010201-2-3); **SUDAN** — New Delhi (6440434/36-38); **SWEDEN** — Bombay (262583), Calcutta (213621), Madras (475792), New Delhi (604961/051); **SWITZERLAND** — Bombay (2043550, 2042591), New Delhi (604225-26); **SYRIA** — Bombay (221999), New Delhi (670285); **TANZANIA** — New Delhi (694351); **THAILAND** — Bombay (8226404-17), Calcutta (460836), New Delhi (605985, 605679); **TRINIDAD & TOBAGO** — New Delhi (618186, 618187); **TUNISIA** — New Delhi (676204, 676174); **TURKEY** — Bombay (240992), Calcutta (445605, 447748), Madras (51853), New Delhi (601921/667); **UAE** — Bombay (213021, 215527), New Delhi (670830, 670945); **UGANDA** — New Delhi (693514, 693585); **UK** — Bombay (274874), Calcutta (445171), Madras (473136), New Delhi (601371); **US** — Bombay (8223611), Calcutta (44-3611), Madras (473040), New Delhi (600651); **USSR** — Bombay (8223628), Calcutta (442006, 444982), Madras (71112), New Delhi (606026, 606558, 600022); **VENEZUELA** — New Delhi (6436535); **VIETNAM (SOCIALIST REPUBLIC)** — New Delhi (3017714, 3018059); **YEMEN ARAB REPUBLIC** — Bombay (213956), New Delhi (674064, 674472); **YUGOSLAVIA** — New Delhi (606022, 605251); **ZAIRE** — New Delhi (619455/6); **ZAMBIA** — New Delhi (619328); **ZIMBABWE** — New Delhi (677460, 677436)

India

by air and that they remain in the Darjeeling environs.

All foreigners wishing to visit India need a visa from the Indian mission in the country from which they are arriving. They must have a valid passport to enter India, unless they are Bhutanese or Nepalese nationals.

Normally, Indian missions grant a multi-entry visa valid for 120 days to tourists. The visa is valid for entering India within six months of the date of issue.

A collective visa, for group tours of no fewer than four people and sponsored by a travel agency recognised by the Indian Government is also available, usually for 30 days, upon presentation of a travel itinerary. Although the tour parties may split into smaller groups they must reassemble and depart the country as the original group.

Business travellers should apply for multi-entry business visas, which are normally given readily with a validity of one year but with a cumulative maximum stay in India of not more than 120 days.

Special visas also exist for trekking, botanical expeditions, sports and journalism. Foreign nationals of Indian origin can obtain a two-year, multi-entry visa which is also available to dependent members of their families.

Foreigners coming to India for 120 days or less do not need to register at the Foreigners' Regional Registration Offices (FRRO) maintained by the Home Affairs Ministry in all major cities. Visa extensions may be obtained but registration at an FRRO then becomes necessary. Normally there are no extensions beyond a maximum time of six months. Usually tourists and other foreigners are required to give passport and personal particulars checking into hotels or guesthouses.

Visitors may move about freely throughout the country, except to restricted and/or protected areas or prohibited places. These included, in 1990, the entire northeast region (comprising the states of Assam, Arunachal Pradesh, Nagaland, Manipur, Meghalya, Mizoram and Tripura plus the Mikir and North Cachar Hills districts). Those wishing to visit Sikkim must apply for a permit from the Home Affairs Ministry at least eight weeks in advance.

Special permits are also needed for Maziranga and Jaldapara, in West Bengal; these can be obtained from the FRRO.

Apart from yellow fever vaccinations for people coming from infected areas, there are no vaccination requirements for visitors to India. Those coming from yellow fever infected areas without a vaccination certificate are liable to be detained in quarantine for up to six days. Visitors should remember that they may arrive in countries which impose health restrictions on arrivals from India; the requirements can be checked with the resident missions of those countries while you are in India.

Visitors to India should consider basic protection and care against contacting various diseases, notably cholera. Protection is best gained by strict attention to drinking water and sanitation. Vaccination against cholera is now regarded by many health authorities in Europe and North America as ineffective.

A more reliable step is a multiple vaccination against typhoid, paratyphoid A and B, and against tentanus. The first two diseases result from poor sanitation while the last normally results form a skin puncture. Visitors to India should also ensure that they have had a recent anti-polio booster which lasts for five years. The risk of contacting infectious hepatitis can only be reduced by not eating uncooked food. Injections of gamma globulin, which is thought to give protection against hepatitis by some for up to six months is considered ineffective by many medical authorities.

Protection against malaria is strongly advised, by taking a daily or weekly tablet as advised by a doctor.

The most important health precaution is to treat all drinking water with suspicion. It is sensible to carry water purification tablets or to use the "Steriliq" brand of liquid water purifier. Adding iodine solution to water is the best way to sterilise it.

If you do not have water purification tablets, confine yourself to tea made from boiled water or to bottled drinks. Rabies is widespread and not only dogs but monkeys, squirrels and other mammals should avoided.

Visitors possessing more than US$1,000 or the equivalent in traveller's cheques or bank notes must fill in a currency declaration form. Customs clearance has improved at some airports, where Green (for passengers with nothing to declare) and Red (for dutiable articles) clearance chan-

Kerala fishermen.

Photo: Gavin Greenwood

nels now speed up the arrival procedure.

Duty-free import of items for personal use by those over 17 years include: personal jewellery; one camera; one cine camera; one pair of binoculars; one portable music cassette recorder; one portable radio; one portable typewriter; one perambulator; one tent and camping equipment, and sports equipment such as a canoe, bicycle and a sporting firearm or pair of skis. Those weapons permitted to be brought into the country must have a licence granted by an Indian mission abroad.

Items subject to duty include: motorcycles, fire-arms, more than 200 cigarettes or 50 cigars; more than one litre of alcoholic liquor; a video camera or VCR or a colour TV. Non-sporting firearms, which include 303 or 7.62 mm calibre rifles as well as weapons using 410, 380 or 455 rimmed cartridges, are not allowed. The importation of gold bullion or coins or dangerous drugs is strickly prohibited and penalties are heavy.

There are restrictions on the export of antiquities. To ascertain whether purchases made by tourists are considered antiquities or not, the following authorities may be consulted:

Superintending Archaeologist, Antiquities, Archaeological Survey of India, Sion Fort, Bombay; Eastern Circle, Archaeological Survey of India, Narayani Bldg, Brabourne Rd, Calcutta 700 013.

Skins of all animals, snakes, etc. and articles made from them used or unused, as personal baggage, are banned. For details contact the nearest Government of India Tourist Office.

The unit of currency is the Indian rupee, which is divided into 100 paise. Coins of 5, 10, 20, 25, 50 paise, 1 and 2 rupees, and notes of Rs 1, 2, 5, 10, 20, 50 and 100 are in use. The most recent conversion rate is Rs 18:US$1.

Visitors are not allowed to bring in or take out any Indian currency except in the form of travellers' cheques. There is no limit to the amount of foreign currency a tourist can bring in, but receipts of currency exchanges are needed in order to convert rupees when leaving the country. Foreigners are often required to pay hotel bills in foreign currency.

Exchanging foreign currency other than through banks or authorised money changers is an offence. One also risks receiving forged rupees. Facilities for the exchange of foreign-currency notes exist at airports and docks and

85

authorised money changers generally display the rates of exchange.

American Express and Diners Club credit cards are now widely accepted in India. The American Express offices in India's major cities have the usual facility to provide cash. The major hotel chains (Taj, Oberoi, Sheraton) accept all major international credit cards, as do most higher class restaurants and shops catering to tourists, as in Jaipur and other well visited cities where the gem trade is important.

English continues to be widely used throughout India, often serving as a *lingua franca* between Indians of different regions. Indian-English is often heavily overlaid with the phonetic habits of the speaker's native tongue. But a great many Indians speak good English and one can easily get about. Railway station ticket-clerks, for example, can always speak English.

Hindi, the official language, is the most universally known of the Indian languages, especially in the north. But a working knowledge of the language may prove of little help in the south where the Dravidian languages (Telugu, Malayalam, Tamil and Kannada) prevail.

Written English appears commonly enough (on sign-posts on major roads, for example) so that the visitor can usually find his way around, and there are many English-language newspapers.

A variety of locally written English-Hindi phrase books exist and can be bought in most book shops or hotels. In New Delhi the best bookshops include the **Oxford Bookshop** in Connaught Circle and **Faqir Chand's** in Khan market.

India has three major seasons: winter, summer and the monsoon. The winter months (November to March) are pleasant in most of India with bright sunny days. In the northern plains, the minimum temperature at times drops steeply and there is snowfall in the hills. In Maharashtra and the south and in eastern India, however, December and January are pleasantly cool, never really cold, though New Delhi's homes — built to keep cool in summer months — can become clammily cold during December and January. It can become bitterly cold in the Himalayan regions and Himalayan foothill states such as Himachal Pradesh and Kashmir,

in winter months. Snow can still fall in the foothills of the Himalyas as late as March or early April.

The summer months are hot in most parts of India and it is during this season that hill resorts are popular retreats. In New Delhi the temperature can reach over 38°C (100°F) in summer.

The southwest monsoon usually breaks about the beginning of June on the west coast and reaches elsewhere later. With the exception of the southeast, India receives the major share of its rainfall between June and September. The southeastern areas receive most of the rainfall from the northeast monsoon between mid-October and the end of December.

Light, easily laundered clothing is best for the south and the northern plains from April to September. Warmer clothes, including woollens, will be needed for the north during winter. Even an overcoat may be required in New Delhi during December and January. Warm clothing is also needed for the hill stations throughout the year, especially in the northern hills and mountains in winter, where clothing for snow conditions is required.

Formal dress is not insisted on except in dining rooms of a few hotels. It is advisable to wear a jacket and tie whem meeting senior officials or ministers as a mark of respect.

Business hours for government and commercial offices, post offices and shops vary from one part of India to another, but 10 am to 5 pm is fairly standard. Half or all of Saturdays and Sundays are observed as a holiday by just about all offices. Restaurant and nightlife hours may vary considerably.

Central government offices in New Delhi and their branches in the states normally work 9 am to 6 pm, with a lunch break from 1 pm to 2 pm, Monday to Friday. Staggered hours have now been introduced for some offices, and these may begin work any time from 9 am to 10:30 am and finish between 4 pm and 5:30 pm.

State government hours may be different from those of central government. In Calcutta, for example, state government offices work 10:30 am to 5:30 pm, Monday to Friday, and 10:30 am to 2 pm on Saturday. Sunday is a holiday. Some other state government offices work only a five-day week.

At the major airports tourist offices are open 24 hours a day. Commercial firms work from 10 am to 5 pm weekdays and often a half-day on Saturday.

Banks are open to the public from 10 am until 2 pm weekdays, and from 10 am to 12 mid-day on Saturdays. In New Delhi, there is a bank branch at the **Ashoka Hotel** open 24 hours a day, including holidays, for purposes of money exchange.

The larger shops in New Delhi are open from 9:30 am to 1:30 pm and from 3:30 pm to 7:30 pm. Smaller stores stay open longer. Except for a few up-market hotels with 24-hour restaurant service, most restaurants close around 11 pm.

MAIN CITIES

FROM THE AIRPORT: International airports have, in addition to taxis, coach services. New Delhi, Madras and Bombay have two terminals. There are coaches from both to the city centre. Coaches operate from the airports in Calcutta, Madras and New Delhi to the city centres. The fare ranges between Rs 150 to Rs 350 from Bombay International. The prices in Madras, New Delhi and Calcutta are lower, ranging between Rs 75-150 (depending on the hotel destination) in New Delhi, and Rs 130 in Madras and Calcutta to the city centres.

TAXIS: Taxis are fairly easy to come by in the streets of India's main cities. Their fares keep changing as the price of fuel rises periodically, but they are still fairly cheap.

While in the larger cities all taxis have meters, they may not show the current fare because of delays in calibration. In such cases the driver usually carries a printed card showing old fares and new fares issued by the transport authority. But there have been many complaints that strangers arriving at main ports of entry are subjected to fleecing by taxi drivers who show the card even when the meter registers the current correct fare or will refuse to use their meters. A word at the airport information counter on the approximate fare for your destination is well advised, though even then tourists must be prepared to either fight hard or give in. Taxis are usually available at the main tourist hotels. Most drivers speak passable English.

A pre-paid taxi service now operates at most airports and, while it involves a bit of bureaucracy (paying at one counter, receiving a chit, going to another pick-up point to collect the taxi) the set price is agreeably hassle-free.

BUSES: Buses operate over many suburban routes in the main cities, but are usually crowded. Fares are very cheap, at less than Rs 1.50-2 for the vast majority of journeys within the city area. Prices depend on distance travelled. English may or may not be spoken and often destination boards are in Indian script only. In some cities, such as Bombay and a few states such as Tamil Nadu and Kerala, the bus service is reasonably efficient and comfortable.

TRAINS: Bombay has the best suburban railway system in India though Madras has steadily expanded its own, much smaller system. Calcutta now has a limited but surprisingly efficient and clean underground railway line which opened in 1984 while its above-ground trains, much grubbier, make a number of suburban stops. Fares fluctuate according to the whims of central and state government finance ministers but are cheap, even for first class, by comparison to Western standards.

SCOOTERS (MOTORISED TRISHAWS): Scooter taxis (also known as "three-wheelers") are a convenient, fast (sometimes excessively) and cheap means of getting around the city. They are metered and the drivers can speak some English. They can carry up to four passengers at a pinch.

HIRECARS: Chauffeur-driven cars carrying a licence plate beginning with the letters "DLY" may carry four passengers. Rates depend on petrol prices. It is normal and preferable to hire a car with a driver, given the erratic driving skills of many local drivers. In 1989, the government gave approval to three foreign car-hire firms to begin Indian operations with a majority equity partner but start-up has been slow. Bombay no longer offers self-drive hire cars.

OTHER MEANS: Various other means of transport are available: rickshaws in Calcutta and tongas and Victoria carriages (horse-drawn vehicles) in several other cities. Pedal trishaws still operate in many cities and smaller towns.

UPCOUNTRY

AIR: Domestic air services are operated by **Indian Airlines**, a government corporation. A network of services connects more than 57 cities including many centres of tourist attraction as well as 10 cities outside India. Aircraft used are Airbus A300s, Boeing 737s, Fokker Friendships and HS 748s. Indian Airlines also operates regular flights to the neighbouring countries of Bangladesh, Nepal, Pakistan, Sri Lanka, Thailand, Afghanistan and the Maldives. India Airlines' domestic fares quoted in US dollars out-

Cochin fishing nets.

Photo: Gavin Greenwood

side India are considerably lower than the fares on domestic sectors in many developed and developing countries of the world.

Dollar fares are used for India Airlines' domestic sector tickets sold outside India. Fares for domestic sectors in Indian rupees, available for sale in India are approximately 30% cheaper. India Airlines offers a US$400 fare to be paid in foreign currency for 21 days known as the **Discover India** ticket. It can be bought at Air-India offices abroad or at India Airlines' offices in India.

In addition, there are **India Wonder** fares, consisting of four fares, each priced at US$200, each of which permits unlimited, economy class travel for one week anywhere in India, provided the passenger does not touch the same point more than once except for the purpose of transfers and connections. Payment for both packages can be paid in foreign currency at either Air India offices abroad or at India Airlines offices within India.

Cancellation of confirmed India Airlines tickets on the domestic sector less than one hour before a flight means the fare is forfeited. Children up to 12 years pay 50% of the fare and infants below two years 10%. One travel operator can travel free with a group of 15 or more passengers.

With its **Youth Fare India** India Airlines offers a savings of 25% on US dollar air fares on domestic and Indo-Nepal sectors to people between 12 and 30 years. Travel is permitted year-round to all those permanently residing outside India including foreign nationals of Indian origin. Foreign residents in India are also eligible if payment is made in convertible currency.

Its 21-day South India excursion trip offers a 30% discount on normal US dollar fares applicable for travel between Madras-Tiruchirapalli-Madurai-Trivandrum and Cochin-Coimbatore and Bangalore when combined with India–Sri Lanka or India-Maldives fares.

The free baggage allowance per adult passenger is 20 kg. International passengers holding first-class tickets are allowed 30 kg provided they change from the international service to the internal service or vice versa within 30 days of arrival at the point of trans-shipment.

No firearms, ammunition or other weapons will be allowed to be carried by passengers without specific authorisation from the Director-General, Civil Aviation. Firearms should be declared. Unloaded firearms and ammunition may be handed over to India Airlines before embarkation for delivery at the destination. Carriage of explosives is prohibited. In addition to Indian Airlines, there is **Vayudoot**, a feeder airline, which serves remote destinations.

RAILWAYS: The great legacy left to India by the British Raj is its railway system, which opened up the country to commerce and travel. The 61,810 km of railway criss-cross nearly 3.2 million km^2 of Indian territory, knitting together the far-flung parts of the vast country. **Indian Railways** has several classes: first air-conditioned, first, second air-conditioned sleeper, air-conditioned armchair car and second. Obviously, travelling in the air-conditioned coaches is most comfortable and relaxing.

Indian Railways' fares are among the lowest in the world. Air-conditioned first class costs Rs 241 for 200 km and Rs 877 for 1,000 km. Air-conditioned armchair car costs Rs 80 for 200 km and Rs 290 for 1,000 km. First-class fare is roughly half of the air-conditioned first-class fare and ordinary second class is roughly half of air-conditioned chair fare.

New Delhi is linked with Bombay and Calcutta by air-conditioned super-fast Rajdhani Express trains running five to six times a week. Tickets for these trains include meal charges. There are other super-fast trains on several routes in addition to ordinary express and mail trains.

Tourists are advised to make reservations for which a nominal fee is charged. While there is no extra charge for sleeper accommodation in the air-conditioned and ordinary first class, a surcharge for the first two nights (subsequent nights being free) is charges for second-class travel. Since the Rajdhani Express and other super-fast trains provide a higher degree of comfort and are faster, there is a surcharge.

Bed-rolls are provided in the air-conditioned class free of charge and on certain routes in first class on payment of Rs 5. Prior arrangements of bed-rolls in the first class can be made either through the railway authorities or through a travel agent.

Indian Railways have introduced **Indrail** passes for unlimited travel by any train within

the period of validity. These tickets are sold only to foreign nationals and non-resident Indians on payment in convertible currencies. No separate charge is payable for meals provided on Rajdhani Express trains, sleepers for night journeys, travel by super-fast trains or reservation fee for reserved berths/seats.

The ticket is non-transferable and hence the tourist must show his passport whenever asked. Normal free allowance of luggage is permitted: 50 kg for air-conditioned, first class or air-conditioned chair car and 35 kg for second class. Children between five and 12 years are entitled to child Indrail passes at half rates and are allowed half the free allowance. Children below five years travel free. The ticket can be used within one year of issue, but the period of validity is computed from the date when the first rail journey starts and ends on the midnight of the last day of validity. If tourists are held up en route owing to reasons beyond their control, such as a train accident or hospital treatment, they may ask for an extension of the validity date to the extent of days lost.

The Indrail pass is neither refundable nor replaceable when lost, stolen or mutilated, nor is it refundable if submitted after one year of issue or for travel in a lower class. However, full refund is given if it is surrendered at the office of issue before commencement of the first rail journey provided no advance reservation has been made. If advance reservation has been made, a full refund will be given if the journey is cancelled and the ticket surrendered more than two days in advance, excluding the date of journey. If it is cancelled less than two days in advance the refund will be subject to deduction of a cancellation fee of 10% of the value of the ticket.

Indrail pass tickets are sold at:

Railway Tourist Guide, Northern Railway, Baroda House, New Delhi. **Central Reservation Office**, Northern Railway, Churchgate, Bombay. **Railway Tourist Guide**, Central Railway, Bombay, Victoria Terminus. **Central Reservation Office**, South Eastern Railway, Esplanade mansions, Calcutta. **Central Reservation Office**, Southern Railway, Madras Central, Madras.

Some travel agents also sell Indrail pass tickets. Tourists can obtain reservations up to one year in advance. The booking railway/travel agency will arrange reservations for the entire itinerary given in advance.

In view of the popularity of the Indrail passes, there are plans to make them available through agents abroad who, besides booking reserva-

INTERNATIONAL CARRIERS

Air India
Bombay: Tel: 2024142, (*Airport*) 6329090, 6326767; Calcutta: 442356, 286012, (*Airport*) 572611 Ext. 346; New Delhi: 3311225, (*Airport*) 5482621; Madras: 474477, 476507, 479523, (*Airport*) 474488.

Aeroflot Soviet Airlines
Bombay: 221743, (*Airport*) 6320178; New Delhi: 3310411, 3310426, (*Airport*) 5452294; Calcutta: 449831.

Air Canada
Bombay: 2021111, 2029730, (*Airport*) 643-5653; Madras: 8250884; Calcutta: 298363; New Delhi: 604755.

Air France
New Delhi: 604775, (*Ticketing and Reservations*) 3310407, (*Airport*) 5452294; Madras: 868377, 862569; Bombay: 2025021, 2024818, (*Airport*) 6328070; Calcutta: 296161.

Air Lanka
Calcutta: 431730; Bombay: 223288, (*Airport*) 63322829, 6327050; New Delhi: 3327909.

Air Mauritius
Bombay: 20288474, 2026740, (*Airport*) 636-6767; Calcutta: 442356; New Delhi: 3311225.

Alitalia
Calcutta: 432140; New Delhi: 3311019, 3310785, (*Airport*) 5483174; Bombay: 222112, 222144, (*Airport*) 6329082.

Alyemda
Bombay: 2024229, (*Airport*) 6320700, Ext. 522.

American Airlines
Calcutta: 442394; New Delhi: 3329349.

Ariana Afghan Airlines
New Delhi: 3311432, (*Airport*) 5452173.

Bangladesh Biman
New Delhi: 3313331; Calcutta: 2922832; Bombay: 224580, (*Airport*) 6366700, Ext. 524.

British Airways
Madras: 477388; New Delhi: 3327735, 3327428, (*Airport*) 5452078; Bombay: 2020888, (*Airport*) 6329061/3/4; Calcutta: 293436.

Burma Airways
Calcutta: 231624.

Canadian Pacific Airlines
Bombay: 215207, (*Airport*) 6329666.

Cathay Pacific
Bombay: 2029112/3, (*Airport*) 6321965/66; Calcutta: 293211; Madras: 833372; New Delhi: 3323919.

Continental
Bombay: 211431; Madras: 471195, 477905; New Delhi: 3325559.

Czechoslovak Airlines
Bombay: 220736, (*Airport*) 6366767; GSA Air India, 442354; New Delhi: 3311833.

Druk Air
Calcutta: 441301; New Delhi: 3322859.

Egypt Air
Bombay: 221415, 221562, 224088, (*Airport*) 6320700, Ext. 512, 6326089; Madras: 849913, 840323; New Delhi: 697232.

Emirates
Bombay: 2871648, 2871645/7, (*Airport*) 636-5730, 6365731; New Delhi: 3324824/03, (*Airport*) 394154/4021.

Ethiopian Airlines
Bombay: 2028787, 2029378, 2024525, (*Airport*) 6328068, 636700, Ext. 514; New Delhi: 3329235; Madras: 471195, 477905.

Finnair
New Delhi: 3315454.

Garuda Indonesian Airways
Madras: 867957, 869832; Bombay: 243825.

Gulf Air
Madras: 867872; Bombay: 2024067, (*Airport*) 6327588; New Delhi: 3324293.

Iberia Airlines
Madras: 471195, 477905; Calcutta: 442697; Bombay: 211431; New Delhi: 3327582.

Indian Airlines
New Delhi: 3310071, 3310085, (*Airport*) 548-3535; Bombay: 2023031, (*Airport*) 6144433; Calcutta: 200731, 263135, (*Airport*) 569611, 569846; Madras: 4788339, 477098, (*Airport*) 433954.

Iraqi Airways
Madras: 811740; New Delhi: 3318742, (*Airport*) 5452011; Bombay: 221399, (*Airport*) 632-7538.

Iran Air
Bombay: 2047070, (*Airport*) 632997; New Delhi: 600412, 600121.

Japan Airlines
Madras: 867957, 869832; Calcutta: 297920; New Delhi: 3327104, 3324858, (*Airport*) 545-2083, 5452058, 5452059; Bombay: 233136.

Kenya Airways
Bombay: 224580, 220064, (*Airport*) 6322577; New Delhi: 3318502; Calcutta: 445576; Madras: 869832, 867957.

KLM Royal Dutch Airlines
Madras: 860123; Calcutta: 292451, 297462; New Delhi: 3313319, 3317474, (*Airport*) 545-2297; Bombay: 221372.

Korean Airlines
New Delhi: 3329561, 3323676.

Kuwait Airways
Calcutta: 444697; Madras: 811810; New Delhi: 3314221; Bombay: 2045351, (*Airport*) 632-769, 6300329; Telex: 011-2487 KAC IN.

LOT Polish Airlines
Bombay: 211440; New Delhi: 3324308, 324-454.

Lufthansa
Calcutta: 299365; Madras: 869095; New Delhi: 3327268, (*Airport*) 5452063; Bombay: 202-0887, 2023430, (*Airport*) 6321485.

Malaysian Airlines Systems
New Delhi: 3325786; Madras: 868970, 868985.

Middle East Airline Co.
Bombay: 224580.

North West Airlines
Calcutta: 299218.

Pakistan International Airlines
Madras: 810619; New Delhi: 3313161, 331-3162, (*Airport*) 5452011.

Philippine Airlines
New Delhi: 3325888, 3325890; Bombay: 224-580.

Qantas
Calcutta: 442394, Ext. 2965, 440718; Bombay: 2029297, 2029299, (*Airport*) 6127219; Madras: 478649, 478680; New Delhi: 3329732, 3320070.

Royal Jordanian Airlines
Calcutta: 484262; Bombay: 224580, 223025; New Delhi: 3323710, 3327667.

Royal Nepal Airlines
New Delhi: 3325222, (*Airport*) 5452093; Madras: 471195, 477905; Calcutta: 298534.

Sabena (Belgian) World Airlines
Bombay: 2022724, 2023817, (*Airport*) 634-8847; Madras: 451598; New Delhi: 3312928.

Saudia Airlines
Bombay: 2020457, 2020049, 2020199, (*Airport*) 6323126, 6327633; New Delhi: 3310464, (*Airport*) 5482179.

Scandinavian Airways System (SAS)
Calcutta: 292655; New Delhi: 3327503; Madras: 450400; Bombay: 215207, 219191, 214224, 214180.

Singapore Airlines
Bombay: 2023365, 2023835, (*Airport*) 632-7861; Calcutta: 299293, 291525; Madras: 862871, 861872; New Delhi: 3320145, 3326373, (*Airport*) 5452011, Ext. 2389.

Swissair
Madras: 862692, 861583; New Delhi: 3325511; Calcutta: 2998467/8/9; Bombay: 222402, 222559, (*Airport*) 6326084.

Syrian Arab Airlines
Bombay: 2232996, (*Airport*) 6366700, Ext. 564; New Delhi: 343218.

Thai Airways International
Madras: 450400; New Delhi: 3323608, 332-3638, 3327761, 3327668, 3327346, (*Airport*) 5482672, 5482526, 5483898; Calcutta: 299-846-9; Bombay: 215207, 213647, 214180.

Trans-World Airlines (TWA)
Bombay: 224580; New Delhi: 3325890, 332-3710; Madras: 812775.

Turkish Airlines
Bombay: 2043605, (*Airport*) 6322220; New Delhi: 3326602, (*Airport*) 394296, 5452021, Ext. 2439.

United Airlines
New Delhi: 3315013; Bombay: 6146583.

Yemen Air
Madras: 849913, 840323.

Yugoslav Airlines
Calcutta: 441561.

Zambian Airways
New Delhi: 3328129; Bombay: 241251.

tions on trains, will provide information on accommodation and places of interest.

A new experience in holiday travel, introduced early in 1982, is the **Palace on Wheels**, running through Rajasthan. The Palace-on-Wheels comprises 16 non–air-conditioned vintage saloon wagons including 13 residential saloon cars, two dining cars and a lounge car. the train takes visitors through Rajasthan in the fashion of 19th-century travel done by British Viceroys or Indian Maharajas. The original style and decor has been preserved and refurbished. The oldest coach was built in 1898 for the maharajah of Bikaner. It is a journey into the past, through desert landscapes, with stops for camel and elephant rides, tours of fortresses and palaces — all accompanied by fabulous cuisine. The train leaves New Delhi every Wednesday evening and travels to Jaipur, Chittaurgarh, Udaipur, Jaisalmer, Jodhpur, Bharatpur, Fatehpur Sikri and Agra, returning to New Delhi the next Wednesday morning.

The train operates between October and March each year, the cooler months of the year on the central plain.

A twin bedded cabin (in 1991) cost Rs 1,980 per person on a sharing basis, or Rs 3,360 for single occupancy. Four bedded cabins are cheaper depending on the numbers using the cabin. Children travel half fare. There is full catering on board and on the ground during the tour including morning and evening tea, plus three full meals a day. Entrance fees for palaces and monuments are also included. For reservations in India contact the Rajasthan Tourism Development Corp., Central Reservation Office, Chanderlok Bldg, 36 Janpath, New Delhi. Tel: 332-1820 or 3322332. Bombay (Tel: 267162) or 2 Ganesh Chandra Ave, Calcutta (Tel: 234261).

"Retiring rooms" at railway stations are available in all principal centres to bona fide railway passengers. Tourists can reserve these in advance for a period not exceeding 72 hours. Apply to the station master. The railways have tourist guides at important stations to help foreign tourists to plan their tours and secure rail accommodation.

For large parties, tourist cars equipped with crockery, cutlery, linen, refrigerators and other amenities are available on some sections of the railways.

Important train times are given in the tourist railway timetable published annually by the railways on behalf of the Department of Tourism and available at all government tourist offices. Round-the-clock reservation facilities are available in New Delhi, Calcutta, Bombay, Madras and Ahmedabad.

PRIVATE VEHICLES: India has a network of metalled roads which connect all the important cities. Tourists who wish to travel by car can obtain full information on road conditions, driving regulations and licences from the recognised automobile associations: **The Automobile Association of Upper India**, Lilaram Bldg, 14F, Connaught Place, New Delhi 110 001; **Western India Automobile Association**, Lalji Narainji Memorial Bldg, 76, Veer Nariman Rd, Bombay 400 020; **Automobile Association of Southern India**, 187, Anna Salai, Madras 600 006; **Automobile Association of Eastern India**, 13, Promothesh Barua Sarani, Calcutta 700 019; **UP Automobile Association**, 32A Mahatma Gandhi Marg, Allahabad.

Third-party insurance is compulsory for all motor vehicles less than 5.5 m long and must be paid to a company registered in India or to a foreign insurer who has a guarantor in India.

BUSES: In many parts of India there are now increasing numbers of long-distance bus services, some offering excellent air-conditioned expresses. Usually the bus routes complement the railway system, fanning out into the countryside from the railway station. But the relatively new popular routes run parallel to the railways. These include Bombay to Goa; Madras to Bangalore; New Delhi to Jaipur; Bangalore to Hyderabad; Pathankot to Srinagar, and New Delhi to the Himalayan Hill stations.

Sometimes it is convenient to combine train and bus travel — for example going overland to Kashmir from New Delhi, one takes the train as far as Jammu and from there goes by bus on to the capital, Srinagar. The security situation in Jammu and Kashmir since late 1989 means that this route is subject to interruption and should be checked.

HIRE CARS: Chauffeur-driven cars may be hired in all the main cities for trips upcountry.

SHIPS: Ships operate on a number of coastal runs. Of special interest is the daily sailing between Bombay and Goa (and return), stopping only during the bad weather in the monsoon season, June to September.

Many of the tours, both city and upcountry, offered in India are arranged either by national or state government tourism corporations. Their city tours in particular are very cheap and on the whole of a good standard. A limited number of

Chinese shops in Ootacamund.
Photo: Gavin Greenwood

private operators offer tours though tending to serve groups rather than the individual traveller.

Half-day city tours of the sights of New Delhi are offered by the government's **India Tourism Development Corp.** (ITDC). Non–air-conditioned buses cost less but air-conditioning is especially welcome for the afternoon tourist in the New Delhi summer.

Half-day tours of Bombay by government and private company tours are available.

Daily tours out to the **Elephanta caves** are available. A similar tour is offered by the state government twice a week at a cheaper rate. A full-day tour of Calcutta is offered by the state government. Such tours cover the major temples, monuments, museums and gardens in the cities and provide an idea of the city which then makes it easier to get around by yourself.

Upcountry tours out of New Delhi include one to Agra, site of the **Taj Mahal**. Taking the train out at 7:15 am arriving in Agra at 10:15 am then transferring to a sightseeing bus to see the Taj Mahal and **Agra Fort** among other places, taking a train from Agra at 7 pm and arriving back in New Delhi at 10 pm.

There is also a wide variety of hill trains such as the trains to **Darjeeling** (the famous "minature train"), to **Ooti** in the Nilgiri hills starting at Mettupalayam (the blue-and-cream train with wooden coaches that was featured in the film *Passage to India*) and to Matheran near Bombay.

The Ooti train has a central toothed rail in the centre of the track that engages a grooved wheel when the train makes steep climbs.

English-speaking guides are available at fixed charges at all important tourist centres through the government tourist offices. French, Italian, Spanish, German, Russian and Japanese-speaking guides are available in some major cities. Unregistered guides are not permitted to enter protected monuments and tourists are, therefore, advised to use guides who carry a certificate issued by the Department of Tourism.

Travellers may arrange for their own car for sightseeing under a scheme offered by the ITDC. A car able to take four passengers is available for a two-day excursion from New Delhi to Agra and back. Details of this and similar trips available to other places can be obtained from government and tourist offices.

Government tourist offices also make available trained guides for excursions in the city area and upcountry.

WILDLIFE: Almost one-fifth of India's land area is covered with forests harbouring a wide variety of wildlife. Rare species like the Asian lion, the white tiger, the one-horned rhinoceros, the blackbuck and the Kashmir stag are protected animals. Twenty national parks, 191 wildlife sanctuaries and nine bird sanctuaries all over the country constitute a year-long tourist attraction. They include: those at **Dudhwa** (famous for tiger), **Corbett National Park** (for tiger, sambhar and chital); **Kaziranga National Park** (one-horned rhinoceros and bison); **Kanha National Park** (tiger and barasingha antelope); **Palamau National Park** (tiger and panther); **Periyar Wildlife Sanctuary** (elephant and wide boar); **Bandipur Wildlife Sanctuary** (elephants, bison, spotted deer, tiger and panther); **Gir Lion Sanctuary** (Asian lion); **Jaldapara Wildlife Sanctuary** (rhinoceros, kakar and peafowl); **Sariska Wildlife Sanctuary** (tiger, elephant, sloth, and wild dog); **Bharatpur Bird Sanctuary** (indigenous and migratory waterbirds); the **Vedanthangal Bird Sanctuary** (waterbirds) and **Chilka Bird Sanctuary** (waterbirds). Two lion safari parks have also been developed, one at Hyderabad and the other at Borivili near Bombay.

Some of the sanctuaries are closed for parts of the year, and it is advisable to check on this with the tourist office or travel agents.

TREKKING: India offers a wide variety of opportunities for trekking vacations, from the towering grandeur of the Himalayas to the more sedate woodlands and fragrant orchards of the Western Ghats or Aravalli hills to the south. The best seasons for trekking are April to June and September to November. Trekking in India is organised by the following agencies: Western Himalayan Institute of Mountaineering, Skiing and Allied Sports, Manali, Himachal Pradesh; Nehru Institute of Mountaineering, Uttarkashi, Uttar Pradesh; Director of Tourism, Jammu and Kashmir government, Srinagar, Kashmir; Tourist Bureau, Government of West Bengal, 1 Nehru Rd, Darjeeling, West Bengal; Guajarat Mountaineering Institute, Mt Abu, Rajasthan; Trek and Mountain tours, Air India, 15 Barakhamba Rd, New Delhi; Youth Hostels Association of India, 5 Nyaya Marg, Chanakyapuri, New Delhi. Many travel agencies also organise treks.

GOVERNMENT OF INDIA TOURIST OFFICES

Agra, 191 The Mall. Tel: 72377/67959.

Aurangabad, Krishna Vilas, Station Rd. Tel: 4817.

Bangalore, KFC Bldg, 48 Church St. Tel: 579517.

Bhubaneswar, B-21 Kalpana Area. Tel: 54203.

Bombay, 123 M Karve Rd, Opp. Churchgate. Tel: 291585, 293144.

Calcutta, Embassy, 4 Shakespeare Sarani. Tel: 441475, 443521, 441402.

Cochin, Willingdon Island. Tel: 6045.

Guwahati, B K Kakati Rd, Ulubari. Tel: 31381.

Hyderabad, 3-6-369/A/25 & 26, Sandozi Bldg, 2nd Fl., 26 Himayat Nagar. Tel: 66877.

Imphal, Old Lambulane, Jail Rd. Tel: 21131.

Jaipur, State Hotel. Tel: 72280.

Khajuraho, Near Western, Group of Temples. Tel: 47.

Madras, 154 Anna Salai. Tel: 88685, 88686.

Naharlagun, Sector 'C'. Tel: 328.

New Delhi, 88 Janpath. Tel: 3320342, 332-0005, 3320008, 3320109, 3320266.

Panaji, Communidade Bldg, Church Square. Tel: 3412.

Patna, Paryatan Bhawan, Birchand Patel Path. Tel: 26721.

Port Blair, VIP Rd, Junglighat (Andaman & Nicobar Islands). Tel: 21006.

Shillong, G. S. Rd, Police Bazar. Tel: 25632.

Trivandrum, Trivandrum Airport.

Varanasi, 15-B The Mall. Tel: 43744.

GOVERNMENT OF INDIA TOURIST OFFICES ABROAD

Australia, Level 5, 65 Elizabeth St, Sydney, New South Wales 2000. Tel: 232-1600/1796, 233-7579; Fax: (02)2233003.

Bahrain, P. O. Box 26106, Manama, Bahrain.

Canada, 60 Bloor St, West Suite 1003, Toronto, Ontario, Canada M4 W3 B8. Tel: 962-3787; 962-3788; Fax: 962-6279.

France, 8 Blvd de la, Madeleine, 75009 Paris. Tel: 65-83-86; Fax: 65-77-06, 65-0116.

Germany, 77-(111) Kaiserstrasse, D-6000 Frankfurt. Tel: 235423, 235424; Fax: 234724.

Italy, Via-Albricci 9, Milan 20122. Tel: 804952, 8053506; Fax: 72021681.

Japan, Pearl Bldg 9-18, 7-Chome Ginza, Chuo-Ku, Tokyo 104. Tel: 571-5062/63; Fax: 571-5235.

Malaysia, Wisma Hla, Jalan Raja Chulan, 50200 Kuala Lumpur. Tel: 2425285; Fax: 2425301.

Netherlands, Rokin 9-15, 1012 KK Amsterdam. Tel: 208991.

Singapore, 5th Fl., 05-01 Podium Block, Ming Court Hotel, Tanglin Rd, Singapore 1024. Tel: 2355737, 2353804; Fax: 7328820.

Spain, c/o Embassy of India, Avenida PIO XII 30-32, Madrid 28016. Tel: 4570209, 4570265.

Sweden, Sveavagen 9-11, 1st Fl., Stockholm-11157. Tel: 215081, 101187; Fax: 210186.

Switzerland, 1-3 Rue de Chantepoulet, 1201 Geneva. Tel: 321813, 315680; Fax: 27315660.

Thailand, Singapore Airlines Bldg, 3rd Fl., 62/5 Thaniya Rd, Bangkok. Tel: 2352585.

UAE, Post Box 12856, Nasa Bldg, Al Makhtoum Rd, Deira, Dubai. Tel: 274848, 274199; Fax: 274013.

UK, 7 Cork St, London WIX 2AB. Tel: 437-3677/8, (Gen.), 434-6613 (Direct line); Fax: 494-1048.

US, 3550 Wilshire Blvd, Rm 204, Los Angeles, California, 90010. Tel: 380-8855; Fax: 380-6111.

230 North Michigan Ave, Chicago, Illinois, 60601. Tel: 236-6899, 236-7869; Fax: 236-7870.

30 Rockefeller Plaza, Suite 15, North Mezzanine, New York, NY, 10112. Tel: 586-4901, 586-4902, 586-4903; Fax: 582-3274.

Maharashtra, A-8 State Emporia Complex, Baba Kharak Singh Marg. Tel: 343773/4.

Manipur, C-7 Baba Kharak Singh Marg. Tel: 344026.

Meghalaya, Meghalaya House, 9 Aurangzeb Rd. Tel: 3015605, 3015139.

Mizoram, Mizoram Bhawan, Circular Rd, Chanakyapuri. Tel: 3015951.

Nagaland, 29 Aurangzeb Rd. Tel: 3014289, 3012245.

Orissa, B4 Baba Kharak Singh Marg. Tel: 345515.

Pondicherry, F-407 Kasturba Gandhi Marg. Tel: 387486.

Punjab, Punjab Bhawan, Copernicus Marg. Tel: 387532, 385431-4.

Rajasthan, 2 Baba Kharak Singh Marg. Tel: 351746.

Sikkim, Sikkim House, 12 Panchsheel Marg, Chanakyapuri. Tel: 3013026; 10, Hotel Janpath. Tel: 3324589.

Tamil Nadu, Tamil Nadu House, 6 Kautilya Marg, Chanakyapuri. Tel: 3015297, 301-4652-7.

Tripura, Tripura Bhawan, Kautilya Marg, Chanakyapuri. Tel: 3015157.

Uttar Pradesh, Chandralok Bldg, 36 Janpath. Tel: 3326640, 3321068.

West Bengal, A-2 State Emporia Bldg, Baba Kharak Singh Marg. Tel: 343775.

STATE INFORMATION OFFICES IN NEW DELHI

Andaman & Nicobar, F 104/105, Carzon Rd Hostel, Kasturba Gandhi Marg. Tel: 387015.

Andhra Pradesh, Andhra Pradesh Bhavan, 1 Ashoka Rd. Tel: 389182.

Arunachal Pradesh, Arunachal Bhawan, Kautilya Marg. Tel: 3013915, 3013786.

Assam, B-1 State Emporia Complex, Baba Kharak Singh Marg. Tel: 343961.

Bthar, Baba Kharak Singh Marg. Tel: 311087.

Gujarat, A-6 State Emporium Bldg, Baba Kharak Singh Marg. Tel: 343173, 316305.

Haryana, Haryana Bhawan, Copernicus Marg. Tel: 386131, 386141.

Himachal Pradesh, Himachal Bhawan, 27 Sikandra Rd. Tel: 383521, 386124-7.

Jammu & Kashmir, Kashmir House, 5 Prithviraj Rd. Tel: 611217.

Karnataka, C-4 State Emporia Bldg, Baba Kharak Singh Marg. Tel: 343862.

Kerala, Kerala House, 3 Jantar Mantar Rd. Tel: 3323424.

Madhya Pradesh, B-8 State Emporia Complex, Baba Kharak Singh Marg. Tel: 344026.

STATE TOURIST OFFICES IN NEW DELHI

Assam Tourist Office, B-1 State Emporia Complex, Baba Kharak Singh Marg. Tel: 325897.

Tourism Corp. of Gujarat Ltd. Tel: 352107.

Haryana Tourist Bureau, Chandralok Bldg, 36 Janpath, Tel: 3324910/11; Haryana Tourism, Faridabad, Tel: 8122204; Motel (Badkhal), Tel: 8122202; Grey Falcon (Badkhal), Tel: 8122203; Magpic (Faridabad), Tel: 8123473.

Himachal Pradesh Tourist Information Office, Chandralok Bldg, 36 Janpath. Tel: 3324764, 3325320.

Himachal Bhawan, 27 Sikandra Rd. Tel: 387473.

Jammu & Kashmir Tourist Bureau, 202 Kanishka Shopping Plaza, Ashoka Rd. Tel: 3325373, 3327400.

Kerala Tourist Information Office, Kanishka Shopping Plaza, Ashoka Rd. Tel: 3316541.

Madhya Pradesh Tourism Development Corp., Kanishka Shopping Plaza, Ashoka Rd. Tel: 3321187, 3324422, 23, 53.

Meghalaya Tourist Information Centre, 9 Aurangzeb Rd. Tel: 3014477.

Maharashtra Tourist Information Centre, State Emporia Complex, Baba Kharak Singh Marg. Tel: 343774.

Orissa Tourist Information Centre, B/4 Baba Kharak Singh Marg. Tel: 344580.

Punjab Tourism, Kanishka Shopping Plaza, Ashoka Rd. Tel: 343054.

Rajasthan Tourism Development Corp., Chandralok Bldg, 36 Janpath; Tourist Office, Tel: 33222332; Place on Wheels Reservation, Tel: 3321820.

Sikkim Tourism Development, 10, Hotel Janpath. Tel: 3324589.

Tamil Nadu Tourist Information Centre, State Emporia Complex, Baba Kharak Singh Marg. Tel: 344651.

Uttar Pradesh Tourist Bureau, Chandralok Bldg, 36 Janpath. Tel: 3322251.

West Bengal Tourist Bureau, State Emporia Complex, Baba Kharak Singh Marg. Tel: 353840.

For other states please consult the list of State Government offices in New Delhi.

India is now recognised as a leading tourist destination and efforts are being made to project India as the destination of the 1990s. The Department of Tourism Government of India has produced a great number of colourful pamphlets which cover most areas of tourist interest in India.

These include:

Adventure Sports, India by Rail, Tourist Information Booklet, Ajanta and Ellora Caves, The Bundelkhand-Orchha Circuit, Shekhavati, the Painted Havelis of Rajasthan, Discover India — East India, West India, North India, South India. They also include Andhra Pradesh Circuit, Orissa, Trekking in the Himalayas, Golf in India.

Also available are map guides to the west, the north, the south and the east. In addition to the above-mentioned pamphlets, individual pamphlets on well-known tourist areas (e.g. New Delhi, Agra, Jaipur) have also been produced and are available through the various information offices.

TRAVEL AND TOUR OPERATORS
Bombay

Ambassador Travels Pvt Ltd, 14 Embassy Centre, Nariman Point. Tel: 231046, 234748.

American Express International Travel Division, Majithia Chamber, DN Rd. Tel: 2048291, 2046361.

Asiatic Travel Service, 12 Murzban Rd. Tel: 2048151.

BAP Travels, Mittal Towers 'A', Nariman Point. Tel: 244068.

Cox & Kings (Agents) Ltd, Grindlays Bank Bldg, DN Rd. Tel: 2043065.

Diners World Travel, Raheja Chambers, 213 Nariman Point. Tel: 224949.

Eastman Travel & Tours Pvt Ltd, 21 Dalmai Chambers, New Marine Lines. Tel: 317343.

Mercury Travels (I) Ltd, Oberoi Towers. Tel: 2024785.

Sanghi International Travels, 39 A Patkar Rd. Tel: 8225061.

Sita World Travel (I) Pvt Ltd, 8 Atlanta, 1st Fl., Nariman Point. Tel: 240666, 233155.

Thomas Cook Overseas Ltd, Cooks Bldg, DN Rd, Post Box 46. Tel: 2048556.

Travel Corp. (I) Pvt Ltd, Chandermukh, 1st Fl., Nariman Point. Tel: 2021881, 2027120.

Uni Pacific Travel & Tours, 205 Tulsiani Chambers, Nariman Point. Tel: 242644, 243821.

Universal Express Travels & Tours Ltd, 14 K Dubash Rd. Tel: 2047982, 233411.

Calcutta

American Express Co. Inc., 21 Old Court Houe St. Tel: 288896, 280266.

Balmer Lawrie & Co., 21 N. S. Rd. Tel: 201759.

Mercury Travels (India) Ltd, 46C J. L. Nehru Rd. Tel: 443555.

Trade Wings (Calcutta) Pvt Ltd, 32 J. L. Nehru Rd. Tel: 299531.

Sita World Travel (India) Pvt Ltd, 3B, Camac St. Tel: 293003.

Indian Air Travels, 28 Chittaranjan Ave. Tel: 272040.

Travel Corp. of India, 46C J. L. Nehru Rd. Tel: 445469.

Chetak Travels, 12/1A Lindsay St, 1st Fl. (opp. New Market), — for railway tickets. Tel: 248627.

Madras

Jetwings Travels, 111 Anna Salai. Tel: 840457, 848499, 848899, 842786; Cable: JET INDIA; Telex: 041-6332 JET IN.

Ganesh Overseas Travel & Tours, First Fl., 1-C Ram Mansion, Pantheon Rd, Egmore. Tel: 860256.

The Orient Express Co. Ltd, 150 Anna Salai. Tel: 861823, 869616.

Indtravels, 4445 Thiru Complex, Pantheon Rd. Tel: 584119, 584122.

Mercury Travels (India) Ltd, 191 Mount Rd. Tel: 869498.

Sita World Travel, 26 Commander-in-Chief Rd. Tel: 478861.

Travel House, 826 Anna Salai. Tel: 833485, 833488-89.

Balmer Lawrie & Co. Ltd, 10 Spur Tank Rd. Tel: 864454, 863214.

STIC Travels, Continental Chambers, 142 Nungambakkam High Rd. Tel: 471195.

Thomas Cook (India) Ltd (Freight Office), 20 North Beach Rd. Tel: 584976, 589994.

Travel Corp. of India, 734 Anna Salai. Tel: 868813.

Cox & Kings (India) Ltd, A-15 Kodambakkam High Rd. Tel: 470162.

New Delhi

STIC Travels, G-55 Connaught Circus. Tel: 3324789.

American Express Co. Ltd, Wenger House, Connaught Place. Tel: 3327617; Cable: AMEXCO; Telex: 031-2587.

Ashok Travels & Tours, Kanishka Shopping Plaza, 19 Ashok Rd. Tel: 3324422; Telex: 031-61858.

Bird Travels (P) Ltd, E-9 Connaught Place. Tel: 3320466; Telex: 031-3045.

Balmer Lawrie & Co. Ltd, Bldg No. 32/33, Flat No. 1 & 2, Nehru Place. Tel: 6419222; Cable: BAIMBERTRAV; Telex: 031-3806.

Combines Travels (I) Pvt Ltd, N-2 Market, Greater Kailash Part I. Tel: 6418387, 6418369; Cable: COMFLY.

Cox & Kings (I) Ltd, Indra Palace, Connaught Place. Tel: 3321028; Cable: COXSHIP; Telex: 031-3309.

Holiday Maker (I), 4 Yashwant Place, Chanakyapuri. Tel: 673227, 605848; Cable: RECREATION.

Indebo Travels (I) Pvt Ltd, 117 Aurobindo Place. Tel: 665155.

Mercury Travels (I) Ltd, Jeevan Tara Bldg, Parliament St. Tel: 312008; Cable: MERC-TRAVEL; Telex: 031-3207.

Holiday Nepal, Hotel Ambassador, Sujan Singh Park. Tel: 615227, 690391; Telex: 031-61116.

IN-Air, E-69 South Extension Part I. Tel: 697987/89; Telex: 031-65999.

Sita World Travel (I) Pvt Ltd, F-12, Connaught Place. Tel: 3313103; Cable: SITATRAVEL; Telex: 031-2343.

Student Travel Information Centre, Rm 6, Hotel Imperial, Janpath. Tel: 3328512; Cable: STICKAIN; Telex: 031-2170.

Travel India Bureau Pvt Ltd, S-13, Green Park. Tel: 667434; Cable: VISITOR; Telex: 031-3258.

Thomas Cook (I) Pvt Ltd, Hotel Imperial, Janpath. Tel: 3328468; Cable: THOMASCOOK; Telex: 031-3725.

Travel Corp. (I) Pvt Ltd, Hotel Metro, Janpath. Tel: 3327468; Cable: TRAVELAIDS; Telex: 031-3569.

There are modern Western-style hotels in all large cities as well as at tourist centres. These have been classified as top-class hotels, fully air-conditioned with all luxury features, hotels which are functional and have air-conditioned rooms, and hotels which offer basic amenities. Most offer a choice of first-class Western as well as Indian cuisine.

At many tourist centres there are travellers' lodges or tourist bungalows which offer comfortable lodging and meals and are run by the ITDC, which is an Indian Government undertaking, or by the state governments.

Houseboats fully furnished and staffed are moored to the banks of the river Jhelum and Dal and Nagin lakes in Srinagar in Kashmir and are known for their comfort and convenience. For reservations, contact Director (Tourism), Jammu and Kashmir government, Srinagar.

The Government of India Tourist Offices in Delhi, Bombay, Calcutta and Madras arrange for tourists to stay with an Indian family as a paying guest. This facility is also available at certain other tourist centres through respective government tourist offices.

Many centres of tourist interest in India are situated in out-of-the-way places. At most of these there are government-owned rest houses (semi-hotel establishments) where tourists can stay. These establishments, in certain places, are also called circuit houses or dak bungalows. There are hundreds of such rest houses all over India, and while they are meant primarily for government officials on tour, foreign tourists may stay in them under certain conditions. The dak bungalows, rest houses and circuit houses are all situated near national highways and are convenient for tourists travelling by road. It is advisable to make reservations in these rest houses in advance through district or local authorities.

There are YWCAs and YMCAs in important towns. A large number of youth hostels exist all over the country. Details can be obtained from the National Council of YWCA or YMCA, New Delhi, and the Youth Hostels Association of India. The National Council of YMCAs of India is

Doorway in Cochin spice centre. ▷
Photo: Gavin Greenwood

located at Massey Hall, Jainsingh Rd, New Delhi (Tel: 310-769).

Voltage in most places is 220 AC, 50 cycles, though a few areas have DC supply as well. The tourist is advised to check the voltage before using his electric shaver or any other electric appliance in a hotel.

Discovering the immense variety of Indian food and learning the more sophisticated and delicate dishes is one of the supreme pleasures of a visit to India. The Indians, above all others in Asia, are masters of the art of spicing food. Doubtless the hot climate of the country has led them to devise ways of preserving their food, but from that bare necessity the ways of flavouring food have developed as prolifically as the Hindu gods until there is one for absolutely every occasion. Much of the excellence of Indian spicing technique is due to the preparation (i.e. grinding or rolling) of the individual ingredients immediately prior to use.

Not every dish in India is in the form of a curry. A great deal of Indian food — especially in the north — is not hot, only richly garnished to provide exciting flavours complementary to the meat or vegetable of the dish.

Each region has its own cuisine, some enriched by the influence of foreign cuisines. Bombay's Parsee food, for instance, is the contribution fo the Zoroastrians who fled religious persecution in Persia 1,300 years ago. What is known as Goanese food is Indo-Portuguese cooking, a result of Goa's five centuries of rule by Portugal. Outside Goa, the best Goanese food is to be found in Bombay, though the major restaurants in other Indian cities have Goanese dishes on their menus.

Chinese food has been growing in popularity and the bigger hotels almost all have Chinese dishes, while Chinese food is to be found in abundance in Calcutta — the only Indian city with a Chinatown. Tibetan restaurants cater mainly to the Tibetan settlers in hill towns (Dalhousie, Mussorie, Kalimpong and Darjeeling) where they live in large numbers . Although ridiculously inexpensive, they are far from clean and therefore not popular with tourists.

Of necessity, eating in India is something of an adventure. Even if you are familiar with most ingredients of a particular dish, you probably still would not recognise it by the name on the menu. *Rogan josh*, for example, is to north India what hamburgers are to America and fish-and-chips

to Britain, but until you learn that under that piece of Oriental terminology hides tasty, only mildly hot, curried lamb, you are likely to remain hungry.

It takes a bold eater just to sit down at a restaurant on his or her first day in India and take pot luck on something as mysterious as *rogan josh*, not to mention **saag meat**, **lassi** (after a childhood spent at the cinema!), *brain masala*, **kali mash dal** or *aloo mattar*. You just have to ask what things are and then proceed by trial and error to an understanding of what is good in your interpretation of the word. But good it will be, and once you are familiar with the vigorous flavourings of Indian dishes you have added a whole new world of gastronomic experience. As a result, you would not be the first person to head home planning to liven up your domestic eating with the aid of more than a little asafeotida, cardamom, coriander, cumin, fenugreek, mace, saffron and turmeric.

Sorting out the many types of curry is something best done at the table over a number of sessions. Even though there are relatively standard forms like *masala*, *do piaza* and *rogan josh*, it is obvious that with at least 25 common spices available for mixing there can be any number of curries depending largely on the region and, of course, the cook's special skills. And about the only precaution necessary when taking Indian curry for the first time is to have a large glass of (boiled or bottled) water ready at hand; water is far more cooling than beer with hot food. Very weak tea is a good way to take boiled, and therefore safe, water.

Tandoori-style dishes are becoming increasingly popular throughout India. Visitors usually enjoy them immediately as there is no problem of hot spices. Brought by the Moghuls from the northwestern areas beyond India, tandoori dishes are cooked in the tandoor — a special clay oven, kept at a very high temperature with charcoal on the oven floor to lend the food a slightly smoked taste — after being marinated for up to 48 hours in yoghurt together with a special blend of Himalayan herbs and spices. Chicken is the most popular dish to be prepared in this manner, but lamb, mutton and seafood are also available, either in tasty chunks on a shaslik or as a seekh (i.e. minced and moulded into long thin patties). Tandoori dishes are usually eaten with the bread known as naan.

Chappati — basically a wheat flour and water mixture cooked as a pancake — and *paratha* — flour and water mixed with butter or other fat and rolled and tossed very thin before being folded on itself and cooked — are the other main types of bread more usually taken with curry. *Poori* is another type that comes small and light and is common with vegetarian dishes. It is made the same way as *chappati*, but fried.

Another Muslim contribution to Indian eating pleasure are the dishes known as *biryani* — chicken, lamb and fish cooked in chunks after being liberally spiced and usually added in a casserole to rice which is spiced and laced with dried fruits and nuts; the whole dish being lightly sprinkled with scented rose-water before being served.

PROHIBITION: Laws on alcohol vary from state to state, and even in those where there is official prohibition for Indians, the law is largely ignored. Alcohol is obtainable in most hotels, in bars and in better restaurants.

Nevertheless, visitors should not risk infringing laws, and liquor permits can be required for inspection on rare occasions. Details of prohibitions should be obtained from Indian missions and tourist offices abroad where, along with their visas, visitors will be issued liquor permits on request. Those who do not require visas for entry into India, or those who have not been able to obtain a liquor permit before departure, can get one from any Government of India Tourist Office in Bombay, Calcutta, New Delhi or Madras on arrival.

In many states, such as Haryana and the other northern Indian states, have at least two "dry" days a month, sometimes as many as six, timed to coincide with the animal slaughtering days plus the first and last day of the month.

In New Delhi, the 20-year-old restrictions making the second and seventh day of each month "dry," were abolished in 1990, but only for hotels, clubs and restaurants with bar licences. They may now serve liquor on all days of the month. But the relaxation does not apply to liquor shops, which must stay closed on these two days of each month. In addition, draft beer is now available in hotels, where it was previously not allowed.

The Indian entertainment scene — in the Western sense of the term — is not at all comparable to what goes on in places like Tokyo or Manila. As a nation, India neither has the money nor the liberal morals that allow a freewheeling nightlife. True, the middle classes of Bombay, New Delhi and Calcutta are straining at the leash in such matters and there are now increasing numbers of hotels featuring dinner-dancing and floor shows, and discotheques with both live and recorded music, but that is about as far as it goes.

In New Delhi, popular discos include **Ghungroo** at the Maurya Sheraton; the **Number One** at the Taj Mahal; **Annabelle's** at the Holiday Inn; **My Kind of Place** at the Taj Palace and **CJ's** at the Meridien. The best guide to what's going on in Delhi can be found in the pages of the *Indian Express* or the *Delhi Diary* found in all bookshops and hotels and costing Rs 3.

In Calcutta, there is the **Pink Elephant** for guests and members. Elsewhere there are the **Peter Cat** and **Capaccino**, catering mostly to younger local couples of some means. Calcutta offers a rich choice of the performing arts, centred on traditional dance and music and vibrant Bengali theatre. Daily newspapers list venues and also *Calcutta* produced once a fortnight by the West Bengal Tourist Office.

The traditional entertainments of India, its marvellous music and dance, can be enjoyed at the special evenings put on for the visitors at some of the hotels or at the occasional concert. There are many professional drama, dance and music troupes, but few professional theatres or concert halls.

Indian and foreign films are shown at a great many theatres in the main centres. The Indian film industry (using Hindi, Bengali, Tamil, Telugu, Marathi) produces more feature films than Hollywood every year.

India is still what is described as a developing country. Add to this the fabulous wealth of regional cultures and the result is a wide variety of beautiful as well as utilitarian objects made by hand or simple machines.

There are many regional specialities to look for during your travels: Kashmir's handloomed rugs, furs, papier-mache utensils and paisley shawls; the jewels and brassware of Jaipur; silks from Varanasi (Benares) and Bangalore; the ivory work of Delhi — but do not forget that many countries now forbid the import of ivory because of the endangered status of elephants. New Delhi brings together in Connaught Place handicrafts from distant regions, each sold in regional craft shops.

At the **Central Cottage Industries Emporium** on Janpath Rd and, nearby, along Baba Kharak Singh Marg, are found various state emporia each run by state governments. In addition, an old but still very serviceable guide to

Delhi shopping is the book *Explore and shop in the Delhi markets*, published in 1985 by Collette Galas.

Other premier cities also have government-run emporia for cottage industries.

Miniature paintings are sold in the north of India. Generally of Rajput style, these are usually later, unimpressive copies of earlier fine works. It is best to consider all you see as of recent origin unless you are really in the hands of a recommended dealer, and then of course the prices will be high. In the south, bronze copies of the gods are widely offered — especially those of the god Siva dancing — and they make fine ornaments if not art.

Getting lost among the bazaars is one of the pleasures of a visit to India. If you have an Indian friend who can accompany you, then all the better. As for tourist guides as shopping companions, you should know that a great many of them — as elsewhere in Asia — are on a commission arrangement with certain retailers. Bargaining is in order in most places. Some salesmen have the ability to make it seem that their mother's evening meal depends on your buying a certain thing; if not, tomorrow she will be dead and by inference you are to blame.

Antiques are widely offered throughout India. Genuine antiques (i.e. objects more than 100 years of age) are often restricted for export.

Bombay remains the centre of India's jewellery trade which, together with illicitly imported gold, is one of the country's biggest businesses. The country's biggest gems trade turnover comes from the cutting and re-export of diamonds imported largely, though not entirely from South Africa through London merchants.

Throughout India a visitor can find literally hundreds of thousands of establishments dealing, in large or small way, in the gold, silver or precious stone business. In the larger centres, however, one may choose particular settings, or even have designs from photographs copied. This practice is especially advanced in Bombay and New Delhi.

The gems available are numerous: diamonds, emeralds, amethysts, blue sapphires, topaz, star rubies, moonstone, cat's-eye, cinnamon stone, aquamarine, garnet and touramaline are among the most popular. Of these, only rubies, sapphires and cat's-eyes are still mined within India.

Even the famed "pearls of Golconda," said to come from the oysters of the Hyderabad lakes, most often originate now in China and Japan. The processing of the pearls remains the work of Hyderabad artisans, however.

Similarly, the "diamonds of Surat," equally famous around the world, no longer originate from there, while the once famous Kashmir sapphire mines have now been closed for over 85 years.

Indian women have a reputation for being gem-addicted and may if not most have a long tradition of doing business with a "family jeweller." Visitors do not have this benefit and must either rely on introductions via Indian friends or rely, riskily, on the blandishments of the jewellers themselves.

In this situation it is wise to consult the Gem Testing Laboratories at the **Indian Gemology Institute** before making a purchase, especially if it is a large one. Buyers in New Delhi have the advantage as the Institute, which is connected to the government's Ministry of Commerce, and is located at F-32, Flatted Factories Complex, Rani, Jhansi Rd, New Delhi 110 055. Tel: 779-732. Its hours of business are between 11 am and 3 pm but visitors should telephone ahead for an appointment prior to arriving at the Institute.

Gold in India fetches a premium and is constantly being smuggled in. Visitors to India are inspected by metal detector with far more vigour on their arrival than on departure: the customs authorities are searching for incoming gold. Yet, a large part of the gold circulating in India is still the metal brought to India 2,000 years ago during the last centuries of the Roman era, in exchange for South and Southeast Asian products sold at Indian emporia.

India is no longer the land of big game hunting. Shikar (safari-style hunting) is now forbidden and the only hunting is for small game such as wild duck. One may of course fish. Hunting is normally managed by one of the registered agencies in India, a list of which is to be obtained by writing to the Government of India Tourist Office in New Delhi.

Fishermen may go after the masheer that inhabit the upper reaches of some of India's larger rivers, which reputedly gives better sport than even salmon, and there is also the fresh-water goonch which can reach a weight of 150 kg. In Kashmir you may fish for trout (the season is from April 1 to September 30 and you will need a licence). Trout are also found in the streams of the Nilgiri Hills in Tamil Nadu state. Deep-sea fishing is also possible off Kerala's coast. Most

Brass and Bell metal shop.

Photo: John R. Thompson

fishing gear is available locally for both inland and deep-sea fishing.

There are many golf courses scattered around the country, especially in the hill stations. Those in Kashmir are excellent: there are 18-hole courses in both Srinagar and Gulmarg. Visitors should contact club secretaries directly to request permission to play. In New Delhi, one can play at the Delhi Golf Club: green fees are Rs 25 on weekdays and Rs 30 on weekends and holidays.

Hockey, cricket, polo, football, volley-ball and basketball are all enjoyed by Indians and in many hill stations ponies may be hired for excursions. Skiing is the up-and-coming sport in north India. One may ski at either the new resort at **Gulmarg** in Kashmir or at some of the other Himalayan snow fields to the northeast. The season usually runs from December until February. The mountains in the north and the Western Ghats attracted many trekkers.

There is a wide offering of adventure sports, including white water canoeing in the tributaries of the Ganges. The most popular rivers are the **Zanskar, Indus, Chenab** and **Lidder** (all in Kashmir); the **Sutlej** in Himachal Pradesh; the **Bhagirathi** and **Alaknanda** in Uttar Pradesh

and the Rangit in Sikkim.

Motor rallyists find climatic and topographical diversity in India: deserts, forests, mountain passes, swamps and wasteland. Ballooning has also become popular, with the national club located at **Safdarjung** airport, New Delhi. Other adventure sports include camel safaris, heli-skiing and hang-gliding in the Himalayas.

Thanks to its several religions and its regional distinctions, India offers a brilliant confusion of celebrations to the curious visitor. The Hindu festivals often derive from agricultural events even though they might appear superficially to be purely religious festivals; the gods are either asked to bless the crops or are thanked for the harvest.

Modern events commemorated in the festive calendar usually have fixed dates, while the majority of traditional occasions are linked to the lunar calendar and so celebrated on a different date from one year to the next. The Muslim calendar is especially variable and holidays may fall at any time. In the following listing of important occasions, those having variable dates show only the months during which they fall. Most of the events are celebrated nationally and the public holidays shown are national public holidays. However, some of the more important regional festivals are included. There are a great number of other regional festivals and many of them result in local public holidays not shown on the listing.

Mid-January: Pongal/Sankranti is celebrated by the Tamils and Andhras of the south as well as Bengalis and others in the north, marking a successful harvest and venerating cattle.

January 26: Republic Day commemorates the day in 1929 when the Indian National Congress took a pledge to work unceasingly for the establishment of a sovereign democratic republic in India — a goal which was reached on January 26, 1950 when the new constitution came into force. Celebrations take place in all state capitals, but are most grand in Delhi. One needs to book ahead to view the Delhi parade (public holiday).

January (variable): Muharram is a Muslim festival commemorating the martyrdom of Imam Hussain, the grandson of the holy prophet Muhammad (public holiday).

February-March: Holi is celebrated boisterously by the throwing of water and coloured powder over all and sundry. Do not be caught out in your best clothes (public holiday).

March-April: Ramanavami is the birthday of the Hindu god, Lord Rama, and is celebrated in temples throughout India (public holiday).

Mahavir Jayanti is a Jain commemoration of the birthday of the 24th Vardhamana Mahavira (599 BC: public holiday).

Good Friday is observed by the Christian community (public holiday).

May-June: Buddha Purnima celebrates the birth, enlightenment and reaching of Nirvana of the Lord Buddha. Each of these events took place on the same date in different years of the Buddha's life (public holiday).

June-July: Car festival of Lord Jagannath takes place in Puri in Orissa state and several other places. There is a grand procession when the gods are taken out on huge vehicles.

August 15: Independence Day celebrates the achieving of Indian Independence on August 15, 1947. The prime minister speaks from the ramparts of Delhi's Red Fort (public holiday).

August-September: Janmastami is the birth anniversary of Lord Krishna (one of the incarnations of the god Vishnu). Mathura, Bombay and Agra are the main centres of celebration though the occasion is observed nationally (public holiday).

Onam harvest festival is celebrated in Kerala state and is the occasion of snake-boat races in Aranmulal and other towns.

Ganesh Chaturhi is a popular festival dedicated to the elephant-headed god Ganesa (God of Wisdom). Bombay, Pune and Madras are the main centres of observance.

September-October: Dussehra is the most popular of all Indian festivals. The occasion celebrates the killing by Rama (hero of the epic Ramayana story) of the evil demon king Ravana. The festival runs for 10 days and is observed in Delhi (where it is known as Ram Lila) by enactments of the Ramayana and fireworks; in Mysore by a splendid procession; in West Bengal (known as Durga Puja) by music, dance and drama, and also in the south; Kulu, in the north, celebrates later with colourful processions (public holiday, two days).

September (variable): Idu'l Fitr is a Muslim occasion marking the end of the month-long Ramadan Fast (public holiday).

October 2: Mahatma Gandhi's birthday is solemnly observed and there are prayer meetings at the Raj Ghat in Delhi where Gandhi's body was cremated (public holiday).

October-November: Diwali is the gayest of all the country's festivals when a multitude of lights mark what was originally Rama's return from exile; now they venerate the goddess of Wealth — Lakshmi — in Bombay and elsewhere except Calcutta where the goddess Kali is supreme (public holiday).

November: Govardhana Puja is a Hindu festival celebrated by the public veneration of cattle (public holiday).

Pushkar Fair, which takes place in the town of Pushkar not far from Ajmer in Rajasthan, where the celebrations include colourful camel races.

Nanak Jayanti commemorates the birthday of the founder of the Sikh religion, Guru Nanak (1469-1539). There are prayer readings followed by processions, especially in the towns of Amritsar, Taran Taran, Patna and Anandpur (public holiday).

Early December: Feast of St Francis Xavier (December 3) and feast of Our Lady of Immaculate Conception (on December 8) are two highlights of the rich festival calendar in Goa.

December (variable): Id-Uz-Zuha is a Muslim festival celebrating the sacrifice of Abraham. Prayers are offered at the mosques and there is feasting (public holiday).

December 25: Christmas Day (public holiday).

Bombay

American Express Bank, Dalamal Towers, 1st Fl., 211 Nariman Point, Bombay.

Citibank, Sakhar Bhavan, Nariman Point, Bombay. Tel: 2870871.

Standard Chartered Bank, Dr Dadabhai Rd, Bombay. Tel: 2045056.

Bank of Borroda, Colaba Causeway, Bombay. Tel: 2020723, 232827.

ANZ Grindlays Bank, 90 Mahatma Gandhi Rd, Bombay. Tel: 270162.

State Bank of India, New Administrative Bldg, Madam Cama Rd, Bombay. Tel: 2022426, 2045338; Telex: 011-3813/3814.

Central Bank of India, Chandramukhi, Nariman Point, Bombay. Tel: 2026428; Telex: 011-4428.

Bank of India, Express Towers, Nariman Point, Bombay. Tel: 2023020; Telex: 011-2281.

Bank of Credit and Commerce International (Overseas) Ltd, Maker Chambers III, Nariman Point, Bombay. Tel: 241091; Telex: 011-5839.

Canara Bank, Mahatma Gandhi Rd, Cochin 16. Telex: 0885 306.

Bank of Baroda, Mandvi Rd, Baroda. Telex: 0175 344.

Calcutta

Reserve Bank of India, 15 Netaji Subhas Rd. Tel: 286019.

State Bank of India, 1, Strand Rd. Tel: 289331, 201653.

Central Bank of India, 13 Netaji Subhas Rd. Tel: 208921.

United Bank of India, 16 Old Court House St. Tel: 287471.

American Express International Banking Corp., 21 Old Court House St. Tel: 286281.

Bank of America, 8 India Exchange Place. Tel: 272824/25.

Bank of Tokyo, 2 Brabourne Rd. Tel: 261125.

Citibank, 43 J. L. Nehru Rd. Tel: 299220.

Grindlays Bank Ltd, 19 Netaji Subhas Rd. Tel: 205264.

Standard Chartered Bank, 4 Netaji Subhas Rd. Tel: 206907.

Algemene Bank of Nederlands N. V., 18A Brabourne Rd. Tel: 262100.

UCO Bank, Brabourne Rd, Calcutta 700 001. Tel: 260120; Telex: 021 5019.

Banque Nationale de Paris, 4A B. B. D. Bagh East. Tel: 202318.

Hongkong & Shanghai Banking Corp., 8 Netaji Subhas Rd. Tel: 201833.

Madras

Bank of India, 827 Mount Rd. Tel: 370041.

Canara Bank, 787 Mount Rd. Tel: 832071.

Central Bank of India, 803 Mount Rd. Tel: 566817.

Punjab National Bank, Bharat Insurance Bldg, 92 Mount Rd. Tel: 849861.

Bank of America, 748, Mount Rd. Tel: 863856.

Citibank, 768 Mount Rd. Tel: 860750.

Standard Chartered Bank, 70 Wallajah Rd, Anna Salai. Tel: 841649, 841667.

Hongkong and Shanghai Banking Corp., 30 Rajaji Salai. Tel: 512708.

Grindlays Bank, 164 Mount Rd. Tel: 861-168.

New Delhi

Central Bank of India, Hotel Ashok. Tel: 601848.

State Bank of India, Palam Airport. Tel: 392807.

Bank of Tokyo Ltd, Jeevan Vihar, Sansad Marg. Tel: 310033.

Banque Nationale de Paris, 2nd Fl., Barakhamba Rd. Tel: 3313883.

Mercantile Bank Ltd, ECE House, 28 Kasturba Gandhi Marg. Tel: 3314356/57/58/59.

Sanwa Bank, The World Trade Centre, 1 Barakhamba Rd Extension, New Delhi 110 001. Tel: 331-4100.

Bank of Baroda, 16 Parliament St. Tel: 3321901, 3321537.

Bank of India, Jeevan Bharati Bldg, Tower Level 15, 24 Connaught Place. Tel: 3317302, 3311647.

Canara Bank, F-19, Connaught Circus. Tel: 3313916, 3310855.

Bank of America, Hansalya, 15 Barakhamba Rd, New Delhi 220 001. Tel: 311 5101; Telex: 031-65205-65294-62104.

American Express Bank Ltd, (Travel Related Services), Wenger House, A Block, Connaught Place, New Delhi.

Grindlays Bank, 10 Sandad Marg, New Delhi 110 001. Tel: 312004, 310761.

Citibank, Jeevan Bharati Bldg, 124 Connaught Circus, New Delhi 110 001. Tel: 3326685.

Hongkong & Shanghai Bank, 28 Kasturba Gandhi Marg, New Delhi 100 001. Tel: 3314355/9.

Standard Chartered Bank, 17 Parliament St, New Delhi 100 002. Tel: 273157; Fax: 011 34598; Telex: 031-65328, 031-63154.

Punjab National Bank, 28 Kasturba Gandhi Marg. Tel: 3316183.

State Bank of India, SBI Bldg, Sansad Marg. Tel: 310635.

Hindu sculpture. ▷

Punjab National Bank, Sansad Marg, New Delhi 110 001. Tel: 387387; Telex: 031-2694.

Addresses

CHAMBERS OF COMMERCE

The Associated Chambers of Commerce and Industry of India, The Allahbad Bank Bldg, 17 Parliament St, New Delhi 110 001. Tel: 310704, 310749, 310779, 344031, 344252; Telex: 031-61754 ASSO IN; Fax: 11-312193; Cable: ASSOCHAM.

Indo-American Chambers of Commerce, PHD House, 4/2 Siri Institutional Area, Opposite Asian Games Village, New Delhi 110 016. Tel: 6863801, 668201, 665425; Telex: 031-73058 PHD IN; Cable: IYACHAM.

Indo-French Chambers of Commerce and Industry, PHD House, 4/2 Siri Institutional Area, Opposite Asian Games Village, New Delhi 110 016. Tel: 657259, 604300, 665425; Telex: 31-73058 PHDL IN.

Indo-German Chamber of Commerce, 85 FG Himalaya House, New Delhi. Tel: 3314151, 3316491, 3310645; Telex: 031-61229 IGCC IN; Cable: INDKAMMER.

Hungarian Chamber of Commerce, 1-A Janpath, New Delhi. Tel: 3012798.

Indo-Polish Chambers of Commerce, PHD House, opp. Asian Games Village, New Delhi. Tel: 3327421, 6863801/4; Telex: 31-73058 PHDC IN; Cable: CHAMBER.

Indo-American Chamber of Commerce, 1-C Vulcan Insurance Bldg, Veer Nariman Rd, Bombay 400 020. Tel: 221413, 221485; Telex: 011-3891 IACC IN; Cable: INDAM CHAM.

Indo-French Chamber of Commerce and Industry, Bakhtawar, Nariman Point, Bombay 400 021. Tel: 2023540, 2027950; Telex: 3599 MUBY IN; Cable: INDIAFRA.

Indo-German Chamber of Commerce, Maker Towers 'E,' Cuffe Parade, Bombay 400 005. Tel: 216131, 216118; Telex: 001-4254 IGCC IN; Fax: INDKAMMER.

Bombay Chamber of Commerce and Industry, Mackinnon Mackenzie Bldg, Ballard Estate, Bombay 400 038. Tel: 264681, 262051; Telex: 011-73571; Cable: CHAMBER.

Bengal Chamber of Commerce & Industry, Royal Exchange, 6 Netaji Subhas Rd, Calcutta 700 001. Tel: 20-8393 (14 lines); Telex: 021-7369; Cable: BENCHAM.

Madras Chamber of Commerce and Industry, 41 Kasturi Ranga Rd, Alwarpet, Madras 600 018. Tel: 451451, 451871; Telex: 41-7306; Cable: MASCHAM.

Publications

Among other publications available in India, and found in most bookshops in the major hotels as well as in bookshops in the larger cities are:

INDIA: a travel survival kit
India in Luxury: A Practical Guide for the Discerning Traveller by Louise Nicholson
The APA Guide to India

STOCK EXCHANGES

New Delhi Stock Exchange, 34/4B Asaf Ali Rd, New Delhi. Tel: 3271302, 3279000, 3272493; Telex: 031-65317.

Bombay Stock Exchange, Dalal St, Bombay. Tel: 275626; Telex: 011-5925.

Madras Stock Exchange, Second Line Beach, Madras. Tel: 510845.

DISCOVERING INDIA

NEW DELHI

India's capital, New Delhi (really a kind of twin city with New and Old sections), lies in the plains of northern India, on the main invasion route to India. With the obvious exception of the Europeans, who came by sea, India received most of its new blood from the northeast — Aryans, Greeks, Kushans, Huns and finally the Muslims.

Some believe that the city of Indraprastha was located on the site of present-day Delhi. But verified history only goes back to the 11th century. A little after this time the Hindu king reigning in Delhi, Pritvi Raj, was killed in 1192, battling to save the city from the armies of Muhammad of Ghor. From then on Delhi became the capital of the Muslim empire in India. In 1324, the new dynasty of Tughluq Shah founded a new capital 6 km to the east called Tughluqabad. A later ruler of the same dynasty founded yet another at Ferozabad, some 12 km to the north. The Afghan dynasty of Lodhi, which seized power in 1451, was swept away in 1526 by Bahur, founder of the Moghul empire. The early Moghuls preferred to rule from Agra or Lahore, but eventually the capital was brought back to the region of Delhi by Shah Jahan (1627-58), where it remained until the final extinction of the moghul empire in 1857.

British power was originally centred on Calcutta, but the capital yet again returned to Delhi with the foundation of New Delhi in 1911; the new capital was not formally inaugurated until 1931. The British set out to build a spacious capital, succeeding most obviously with the central vista of the **Rajpath** and its surrounding majestic buildings (the **Rashtrapati Bhavan** — once the Viceroy's residence and now the President's home — and the Central Secretariat), parklands, and fountains. One cannot but be impressed with such trappings of authority.

Rajpath cuts through the centre of the city, from Rashtrapati Bhavan in the west to the memorial arch dedicated to India's war dead, known as the **India Gate**, 3 km to the east. Parliament House lies to the north of the Secretariat buildings. The commercial centre of New Delhi lies approximately 2 km to the north of Rajpath and around its nucleus — **Connaught Place** — can be found shops, airline booking offices, restaurants and the **Government of India Tourist Information Office**.

South and southwest of Rajpath, the upper-class suburbs spread spaciously with ambassadorial mansions set in fine gardens. It is here that several of the city's best hotels (the Akbar and Ashoka, both named after great Indian emperors) offer their interpretations of Indian hospitality.

Old Delhi adjoins the New in the north of the city, and across **Asaf Ali** and **Desh Bandhu Gupta Roads** one is at once out of the modern capital and back in India with its milling masses.

The **River Yamuna** runs along the eastern boundary of the city proper, bearing on its right bank the cremation sites of Mahatma Gandhi and prime ministers Jawaharlal Nehru, Lal Bahadur Shastril and Indira Gandhi, Nehru's daughter. Both the Mahatma, father of the Indian independence movement, and Mrs Gandhi (who were not related) were victims of assassination.

Much of historic interest in the present city of Delhi lies within the scattered remains of the walls to be found in the old section. Built by Shah Jahan to surround his city of Shahjahanabad, their total circumference was nearly 9 km. **The Ajmeri** and **Delhi** gates are parts of this old wall. The most splendid inclusion within the ancient city was the **Red Fort** of Shah Jahan (which was in fact the palace) begun in 1638 and completed nine years later. The Red Fort lies on the bank of the Yamuna River, though the actual watercourse has shifted some way to the east since the fort was constructed, leaving the eastern approach relatively poorly fortified.

It is entered by the **Lahore Gate** at the eastern end of Chandni Chowk St. You come first to a magnificently vaulted hall, 114 m, which once contained the Moghul emperor's private bazaar and now houses small shops selling postcards and souvenirs. Next to the bazaar is the **Naubat Khana**, the music chamber where the emperor's musicians performed five times a day, which is now an open courtyard. On the far side of the central courtyard is the **Dewan-i-Am** (the Hall of Public Audience), a splendid building in the Hindu style with 60 pillars of red sandstone supporting a flat roof. The building is of white marble and in the interior the art of the Moghuls reached the perfection of its jewel-like decoration. Unfortunately the pavilion has been vandalised over the years, but one can still imagine the past splendours of life on its cool, polished marble floors centuries ago. The emperor's throne was once located in the richly decorated recess to be seen in the rear wall.

Through a gate to the north side of the Dewan-i-Am, one passes yet another pleasantly grassed courtyard where there are several graceful buildings (including the residences of the harem girls). *Son et lumiere* (sound and light) displays, relating the Red Fort's history, are held between the months of September and July. You can check the times and dates with the tourist office.

Nearby is the marble **Moti Masjid** (Pearl Mosque) where one leaves one's shoes in the care of a guard before entering.

Chandni Chowk (Silver St), once supposed to have been the richest street in the world, is now chiefly a market for silver and cloth. It was made wide enough to accommodate Shah Jahan's great processions. Many of the old city mansions in this quarter still exist — balconied inside and out and approachable only through narrow alleys. Visitors fortunate enough to be invited inside are astonished by the grace and coolness of these old buildings, surrounded by crowded and rather unclean bazaars. Off Chandni Chowk is a lane, **Dariba Kalan**, with shops offering a wide range of jewellery, antique and modern.

Just to the south of Chandni Chowk is the **Jama Masjid**, another monumental creation of Shah Jahan built between 1650 and 1656.

Between the walled city and new New Delhi proper, near the river bank, stands the

Yamauna River

To Calcutta

Grand Trunk Road

Vijay Ghat

Shanti Vana

Raj Ghat

Power House Rd.

Ashoka Pillar

Blea Road

Red Fort

Netaj Subhash Marg

Sikandra Rd.

Upper Bela Road

Hamilton Road

Shyama Prasad Mukerjee Marg

Chandni Chowk

Nai Sorak

Chilli Kabar

Asaf Ali Road

Jawahar Lal Nehru Marg

Rouse Avenue

Connaught Place

Barakhamba Rd.

Kasturba Gandhi

Lal Kuan

Garstin Bastion Road

Qutb Road

Desh Bandhu Gupta Rd.

Panel Ganj Rd.

Street

Baba Kharak Singh Marg

Jai Singh Rd.

Court Road

Rajpur Road

Sadar Thana Rd.

Panchkuin Road

Tilak Marg

Sahib

Market Rd.

Ridge Road

Roshanara Road

Roshanara Road

Sarai Rohila Rly. Stn.

Bahadurgarh Road

Rani Jhansi Road

Link Road

Mandir Marg

Kali Bari Marg

Subzi Mardi Rly. Stn.

Rash Bihari Marg

To Jaipur

Sir Ganga Ram Hosp Rd.

Sadhu Waswani Marg

Arya Sanaj Road

Original Road

East Park Road

Faiz Road

Upper Ridge Road

Shankar Road

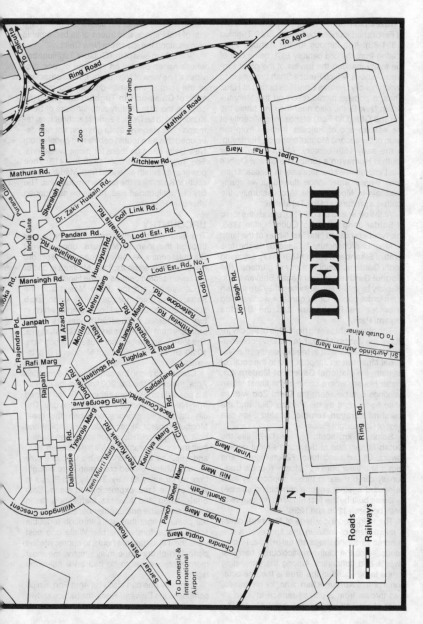

DELHI

Roads
Railways

To Calcutta
To Agra
Ring Road
Mathura Road
Humayun's Tomb
Zoo
Purana Qila
Kitchlew Rd.
Lajpat Rai Marg
Mathura Rd.
Shershah Rd.
Purana Qila Rd.
Dr. Zakir Hussain Rd.
Golf Link Rd.
Cornwallis Rd.
Pandara Rd.
Lodi Est. Rd.
India Gate
Shahjahan Rd.
Humayun Rd.
Lodi Est. Rd. No. 1
Lodi Rd.
Ashoka Rd.
Mansingh Rd.
Nehru Marg
Lodi Est. Rd.
Rajendra Pd.
M Azad Rd.
Motilal Rd.
Akbar Rd.
Prithviraj Rd.
Rajendra Pd.
Rafi Marg
Tees January Marg
Aurangzeb Rd.
Jor Bagh Rd.
Rajpath
Dr. Rajendra Pd.
Hastings Rd.
Tughlak Road
Sri Aurbindo Ashram Marg
To Qutab Minar
Janpath
Dupley Rd.
Safdarjang Rd.
King George Ave.
Race Course Rd.
Ring Rd.
Dalhousie Rd.
Tyagraja Marg
Teen Kushak Rd.
Kautilya Marg
Club Marg
Vinay Marg
Willingdon Crescent
Teen Murti Marg
Niti Marg
Shanti Path
Chandra Gupta Marg
Nyaya Marg
Panch Sheel Marg
Patel Road
Sardar Road
To Domestic & International Airport

N

Ferozeshah Kotla — all that remains of the city of Ferozabad founded by Feroze Shah Tughluq (1351-88). It is famous for the **Ashoka Pilar** (dating from the 3rd century BC), being one of the many marking the travels of the great Emperor Ashoka, which Feroze Shah brought in to enrich his city. Feroze Shah lies buried at Hauz Khas, a popular picnic resort off the Mehrauli Rd. In New Delhi, also near the river bank, the **Purana Qila** (Old Fort) stands magnificently at the eastern end of Rajpath. It dates from the reign of the second Moghul emperor, Humayun, in the early 16th century. About 2 km to the south is **Humayun's tomb**, one of New Delhi's most impressive structures set in pleasant gardens where water once flowed down many channels in Moghul style. Architecturally, the tomb is a precursor of the Taj Mahal.

At the other end of Lodhi Rd, stands the tomb of **Safdar Jang**, a ruler of Oudh: built in 1753, this has been called "the last flicker of the lamp of Moghul architecture." Close by is the fine tomb of **Sikander Lodhi** (1489-1517), adjoining Lodhi Gardens. Delhi is a city of gardens. The **Moghul Gardens** in Rashtrapati Bhavan are in full glory by mid-February when they are thrown open to the public. Other gardens worth seeing in winter are **Roshanara** and the **Buddha Jayanti Park**.

The other sightseeing highlights of the city include: the **Jantar Mantar** (a massive observatory) in Parliament St in the city centre; the **National Museum** on Janpath, just to the south of Rajpath; the **National Gallery of Modern Art**, Jaipur House, where some of the finest Indian paintings can be seen; the **Delhi Zoo** with its white tigers right by the Purana Qila; and the **Lakshmi Narayan Temple**, located 2 km due west of Connaught Place.

Some 11 km south of New Delhi lies the **Qutab Minar**, one of the world's most perfect towers. Of red sandstone, 72 km high — and with a fine view from its balcony (people traditionally climb there in threes supposedly as a safeguard against anyone committing suicide) — it was built by the first Muslim conquerors of Delhi between 1206 and 1236.

The neighbouring village of **Mehrauli** offers a microcosm of India in the space of a few hundred yards. Its shops are full of typical Indian goods — cotton cloth, multicoloured bangles, sweets and softdrinks. Among the interesting tombs to be found in the area is the fine octagonal one of **Adham Khan**, who, for his crimes, was thrown from a palace terrace at Agra by order of his half-brother, the great Akbar. The

Qutab actually marks the centre of Prithvi Raj's city of Rai Pithora, and traces of its battlements remain along the road from New Delhi.

Some 8 km east of the Qutab is Tughluqabad whose ruined citadel, on its ledge of rock, provides a fine view of New Delhi. On the other side of the road is the white-domed and massive tomb of **Ghias-ud-Din Tughluq** and just to the south is the 11th century amphitheatre of Suraj Kund, said to be Delhi's earliest architectural remains. The Haryana state government has developed this as a tourist centre and people from New Delhi often go there for picnic weekends. The Tughluqs ruled from 1320 to 1413. Their power at its zenith extended from Madurai in the south to Kashmir in the northern mountains. The city of Tughluqabad was, however, abandoned after only 15 years.

UPCOUNTRY

The main road south from New Delhi passes through the town of **Mathura**, once a great Buddhist centre. As the legendary scene of Lord Krishna's frolicsome exploits, Mathura is one of the seven sacred centres for the Hindus.

Of interest are the Jame Masjid and the Katra; here a great mosque built by Aurangazab stands on the ruins of a Hindu temple, which in turn supplanted a Buddhist monastery dating probably from the first years of the Christian era. The town's archaeological museum (open from 10:30 am to 4:30 pm except Mondays) is of interest.

Continuing along the same road one reaches Agra, the city of the Taj, 200 km from the capital. It is possible to visit Agra either by air, rail or road from New Delhi and be back the same day. The city came into prominence when the great Moghul emperor Akbar made it his capital and built a huge fort. His grandson, Shah Jahan, built the incomparable Taj Mahal between 1630 and 1652 as a memorial to his favourite wife Mumtaz Mahal. Skilled craftsmen were brought from as far away as Italy, Turkey and Persia to work on the finer expressions in stone. Both Shah Jahan and Mumtaz Mahal now lie in tombs alongside one another beneath the central dome in light that filters through a double screen of perforated marble. While one best visits the Taj in daylight hours to appreciate the perfection of the stone inlay artistry, the most memorable view is to be had on a full-moon night.

In the city one can also visit Agra Fort, which comprises the Dewan-i-Khas, the palace known as the Jahangiri and the Moti Masjid built by

Shah Jahan. Also worth seeing are the tomb of Itmadud-Daulah across the River Yamuna and the impressively simple tomb of Akbar at Sikandra, about 8 km away along the road back to New Delhi. The city possesses a golf course. Just 50 km away is the famous Bharatpur Bird Sanctuary, best visited between October and March.

Forty kilometres west of Agra is Fatehpur Sikri, built as a new capital by Akbar, but soon abandoned for lack of adequate water supply. Its circuit of about 11 km comprises a splendid mosque, palace buildings and tombs, many of them perfectly preserved.

About 160 km to the south of Agra is the ancient city of Gwalior, famous for its magnificent fort and the palaces within it — notably Man Mandir built by the Tomber dynasty king, Man Singh (1486-1516), and the Karan Palace of about the same date. The palaces are unequalled in central India for picturesque beauty. Some fine Jain sculptures are carved from the solid rock under the fort. The old town that lies beyond the fort has a beautiful mosque and the fine early Moghul tomb of Mohammed Ghaus.

From Gwalior it is a day's drive via the town of Jhansi to the village of Khajuraho, once the capital of the Chandela kings, and now famous for the splendid temple ruins with some of the masterpieces of India's erotic sculpture.

The temples fall into three main groups of which the western is the best. The oldest temple in Khajuraho, Chausat Yogini, and the only one built of granite, dates from about 900 AD and is dedicated to the goddess Kali. Of the original 65 cells arranged around the courtyard, 35 still remain. North of it is the Kandariya Mahadev temple dedicated to Siva — the largest of them all and boasting magnificent sculptures. Almost the entire outer and inner surface presents examples of Hindu art at its most brilliant.

At the entrance is an exquisitely carved archway. Three bands of sculpture surround the temple with a luxury of embellishment — lovers deep in fond embraces, flying nymphs, musicians and crocodiles. To the north again, the Chitragupta (Bharatji) Temple enshrines a lovely image of the Sun God, Surya, who is driving a seven-horse chariot. The carvings on the outside depict hunting scenes, elephant fights, royal processions and dancers. Other fine temples in this western group are the Viswanath-nandi and lakshman Temple, all with first-class carvings. A colossal statue of the monkey god, Hanuman, which has been installed in a modern temple halfway to the village, is dated 922 AD,

thus making it one of the oldest pieces to be found in Khajuraho.

The eastern group of temples lies close to the village and comprises six shrines, three Hindu and three Jain. Of these, the Javari Temple, dedicated to Vishnu, and the remains of the Ghantia Temple(Jain) are outstanding. The latter includes a number of pillars richly decorated with girdles, strings of pearls and bells. Parsvanath, the largest of the Jain shrines, is a compact structure without balconied openings. The ambulatory passage receives light from small perforated windows, and excellent sculptures of women depicted engaged in various activities adorn the outer walls of the sanctum.

The southern group consists of the Duladeo and Chaturbhuj temples lying about 3 km from Khajuraho village. The tower of Duladeo differs from all the others in being formed of successively diminishing circles of overlapping stones, and the sculptures show some decline in the artistic sensibilities of the carvers. The Chaturbhuj Temple enshrines a splendid statue of the four-armed Vishnu, 9 ft high. A striking sculpture is that of a lion-headed figure who may be the female counterpart of Narasimha, an incarnation of Vishnu.

There are daily return flights linking Khajuraho, Delhi, Agra and Varanasi.

From Khajuraho the road runs east through Panna and Satna until it reaches the main road running north to Allahabad. The most conspicuous feature of this old city is the fort at the confluence of the Yamuna, the Ganga (Ganges) and the mythical river Saraswati which is believed to have gone underground; the spot is called Triveni, or the confluence of three rivers, sacred to all devout Hindus. The fort contains an Ashoka Pillar, the remains of a palace erected by Akbar and once a favourite residence of his, and an important arsenal. Outside the fort the places of most historical interest are the tomb and gardens of Khusrau, son of the Emperor Jahangir (1605-27), and the Jama Masjid, scene of a bathing festival known as the Magh (January-February). Every 12th year this becomes the Kumbh Mela when as many as 2 million devotees arrive from all over India.

Northwest of Allahavad the vast industrial city of Kanpur offers little to the tourist except its memories of what was formerly called the Indian Mutiny.

Across the Ganga, two hours away from Kanpur by train, lies the city of Lucknow on the Gomti River. Famous alike as the capital of the former

Jaisalmer, Rajasthan.

Kingdom of Oudh, whose annexation in 1856 did much to provoke the Mutiny, and for the defence of its residency in the following year, Lucknow is now the thriving capital of the state of Uttar Pradesh.

The monuments of Oudh were somewhat jerry-built and consequently have not worn well. Of prime interest is the Great Imambara (mausoleum) built by the Nawab Asaf-ud-Daula in 1784. This is one of the world's largest halls with an arched roof which has no direct support. Behind the hall is a warren of passages through which you may mount to emerge near the roof of tiny balconies originally designed for musicians. Going west from this building along the Husainabad Road you pass through the Rumi Darwaza (Turkish Gate), and then reach the Husainabad Imambara, bulit by Mohammed Ali Shah in 1837. A small building in the grounds of this Imambara contains a series of Portraits of the Nawabs and Kings of Oudh, which provide an interesting study in degeneration. In the other direction, the large but unattractive Kaiser Bagh was the palace of Wajid Ali Shah, last ruler of Oudh, whose absurd existence is described by an eye-witness in a well-known work *Private Life of an Eastern King.*

East of Allahabad, on the Ganga, lies Baranasi (previously called Benares), a centre of worship and the most holy Hindu city in the country. The Ganga is considered especially sacred at this point.

Varanasi is very old: Hsuan Tsang, the celebrated Chinese pilgrim, visited it in the seventh century and described it as containing 30 Buddhist monasteries and about 100 Hindu temples. However, by the 12th century, it was occupied by the Muslim Sultan of Delhi who destroyed all the temples. Consequently, none of the buildings are now of any great antiquity. On the dismemberment of the Moghul empire, Varanasi was seized by Safdar Jung, Nawab Vizir of Oudh, whose grandson ceded it to the East India Company in 1975.

The sacred area of Varamaso is bounded by a road 80 km in circuit which every Hindu hopes to tread once in his life. Many thousands make the pilgrimage every year for bathing in the sacred river; thousands of elderly people come to Varanasi to die, believing it to be a way to ensure the soul's immediate salvation.

Most of the temples are small, placed in the angles of the extremely narrow and winding streets. These are mostly below the ground floors of the houses, which are often embellished with carved balconies and paintings of gods and animals. The most important temple — the holiest spot in the holy city — is the Viswanath (Golden Temple), dedicated to Siva, Lord of the Universe. It dates from about 1750. The most famous building perhaps is the Durga monkey Temple, a 17th-century building (constructed during the time of the Maratha empire which had replaced the Moghuls) in the southern suburbs, where monkeys scramble about the temple. There are also two conspicuous mosques: the Alamgir mosque in the northern quarter and the Aurangazeb mosque in the middle of the Hindu town. The observatory of Raja Jai Singh is a notable building of the year 1693.

It is impossible to take in the details of Varanasi in a short visit. Since non-Hindus may not enter the temples, perhaps the best plan is to stroll about and observe the multitudinous scenes of religious devotion, all the time taking glimpses of whatever temple interiors are visible from the streets. Many of the locally available guides will be able to lead you to windows offering a revealing view of some temples. Be ready to sense something eerie about the city, especially if you take a boat trip on the river around dawn. The river is lined by a stone embankment on and behind which the temples and other buildings rise in dense tiers; some of the temples are more or less submerged when the river is high. As you travel down the river you pass the bathing ghats (stepped landings on the river bank) where pilgrims take their ceremonial dips. Then you see the burning ghats where on every side burn the funeral pyres on which the bodies of the dead are rotated to ensure their complete consumption by the flames.

Also worth seeing are the small shops where the city's Muslim weavers turn out brilliant fabrics woven on handlooms with borders of gold and silver thread. One of the best universities in India, the Benares Hindu University, is also located here. Benares silk is well-known all over the world.

About 8 km north of Varanasi is the town of Sarnath, where in the Deer Park, Gautama delivered his first sermon after becoming the Enlightened One or the Buddha. Here lie the foundations of monasteries built over 2,000 years ago and several shrines and stupas which attract Buddhists from all over the world. The Mahabodhi Society of India has built a new shrine in which the frescoes have been completed by a Japanese artist. Sarnath also possesses the famous Ashoka Pillar whose lion crest has been adopted as the national emblem of the Repulic of India. A fine museum close by houses finds from the excavation of Saranath, which was started with Viceroy Lord Curzon's encouragement in 1904.

Some 350 km to the southwest of Allahabad is the modern cantonment town of Jabalpur. Just 18 km from the town the Narbada River, after a fall of 30 ft, forces its way through the famous Marble Rocks Gorge, while closer to the town is an ancient fortress built by the Gond Kings on a huge outcrop of rock.

In the northwest corner of the country is the large state of Rajasthan, home of the martial Rajputs. The former princely city of Alwar, 165 km almost due south of New Delhi, stands in a valley overhung by a fortress 1,000 ft above, and is surrounded by a rampart and a moat with five gates, containing fine palaces, temples and tombs. Just 35 km from Alwar is the Sariska Wildlife Sanctuary where accommodation is available at the Tourist Bungalow. Forest Rest House and Sariska Palace Hotel.

Also in Rajasthan is the pink city of Jaipur, 300 km by rail southwest of New Delhi. It was founded in 1728 by the warrior-astronomer Maharaja Jai Singh. Well laid out and lighted, with wide and regular main streets which divide it into six rectangular blocks, the city is home for a people noted for their colourful clothing; the women wear enormous swing skirts. Houses with latticed windows line the streets. At sunset the rose-pink of the buildings is best appreciated. The city is surounded by crenellated walls overhung by ragged hills crowned with forts. Most famous of the buildings are the Hawa Mahal (Palace of the Winds) and the observatory with huge stone instruments constructed by Jai Singh the Second — even more fascinating than the ones at New Delhi and Varanasi, also built by him. Eleven kilometres from Jaipur lies Ambet, with its 17th-century palace.

Further, to the southwest are Ajmer, which has ruins of a very fine ancient Jain temple, partly converted into a mosque, and Udaipur which is called the city of sunrise and stands in a valley on the bank of the Pichola Lake with palaces built of granite and marble. The maharaja's palace, which crowns the ridge on which the city stands, dates originally from about 1570, though later conditions have made the present structure a conglomerate of architectural styles. It is noted for its walls inlaid with mosaic peacocks, tiled floors and roof gardens. In the lake are two islands with palaces (one a hotel) of the 17th and 18th centuries. At the ancient village of Ahar, 2 km away, are the cenotaphs of the maharajahs and suttee (the old custom of Indian wives immolating themselves on the funeral pyre of their husbands) stones in memorial to self-sacrificing Rajput women of the past.

West of Jaipur is Jodhpur (founded in 1459), another walled town endowed with a fort and a number of excellent palaces. About 8 km north of Jodhpur are the ruins of Mandor, capital of the Parihar princes of Marwar (Jodhpur) before its conquest by the Jajput Rathors in the 13th century. Rosita Forbes' *India of the Princes* provides a fascinating background account of Jodhpur, Jaipur and other former princely states.

Jaisalmer, in the far west, famous for its buildings of yellow stone, rises from the desert sands as if it was built entirely of gold. Dating from 1156, the town has recently become largely deserted owing to both its proximity to the Pakistan border and the shortage of regular water. When there is water it is usually taken from the rain-fed lake in the town; the women — noted for their exceptional beauty — visit the lake throughout the day carrying shining brass vessels on their heads. Dominating the town is a great fort, the second oldest in Rajasthan, encircled by a base of stone blocks each 15 ft high. Inside the formidable entrance are many beautifully carved temples with exquisite stone figures and the old palace. Many of the Jain temples house ancient manuscripts and paintings on palm leaf and paper, some of which date back to the 12th century. The Maharawal's palace, crowned by a large metal umbrella (Chatri) still preserves the stone cannon balls which were once stored for its defence. The town itself is a picturesque jumble of narrow bazaars, intricately carved balconies, archways and lattices all cut from locally quarried stone. Jaisalmer is also the home of India's finest breed of camel — the Jaisalmer Risala. The camels are raced in a thrilling annual event.

The annual three-day Desert Festival held at Jaisalmer at full moon over January and February features music and dancing from the region.

Bikaner, northwest of Jaipur, can be reached by a branch line of the railway from Jaipur to Jodhpur. The city is enclosed by a wall with a circuit of 5.5 km, and there are the usual forts and palaces. The relative economic well-being of the towns in the region has been attributed to their being the ancestral homes of the astute Marware merchants.

Amritsar, the centre of the Sikh religion, lies some 500 km by rail northwest of New Delhi in the state of Punjab near the Pakistan border. The border crossing point (the only one at present between the two countries) at Attari lies between Amritsar and Pakistan's city of Lahore. Amritsar is noted for its Golden Temple, its dome covered with gold leaf, which stands in the middle of a vast square tank populated by large and voracious sacred fish. Visitors may attend the readings of the Sikh scriptures which are held every day in the temple.

The bazaar in the town is rather attractive with many houses possessing carved overhanging balconies. Halfway between New Delhi and Amritsar (take the road to the north at the cantonment town of Ambala) is Chandigarh, the new town designed by the famous French architect Le Corbusier, which is the capital of Punjab.

North of Chandigarh is the hill station of Simla where the former British Goverment of India migrated every summer. North of Simla again lie the twin valleys of Kulu and Kangra which rival the Vale of Kashmir in beauty. Green with apple orchards and dotted with ancient Rajput forts on the summit of immense crags, these valleys provide an endless scenic spectacle. In the Kulu Valley one should see the fine temple at Bajaura 14 km south of Sultanput. Further up the valley is Manali, a beautiful village in full view of snow-covered mountains and set in pine woods where there is a rest-house. Accommodation can also be had at tourist bungalows and loghuts. It possesses the remarkable wooden Dhoongri Temple to the Goddess Hadimba Deve. Other beauty spots such as Katrain (famous for its trout fishing) and Naggar dot this region.

From Kangta you can reach the hill station of Dharamsala where the Dalai Lama has his residence. To the northwest, via Pathankot, is the hill station of Dalhousie where there is a golf course. From there it is a short and spectacular drive to the former princely state of Chamba. The town — said to have been founded in the sixth century — is picturesquely set above the Ravi Gorge. In the region northeast of New Delhi are the well-known summer resorts of Mussoorie, Nainital and Ranikhet, the latter two possessing golf courses.

The predominantly Muslim state of Jammu

and Kashmir (often known simply as Kashmir) with its fast-running mountain streams, limpid lakes fed by Himalayan snows, flowers and garden and forests ringed by snow-clad peaks is the scenic showplace of India. Srinagar, the capital, which dates from the sixth century, straddles the River Jhelum. Its eastern side is bounded by the Dal Lake, along whose shores are moored the famous houseboats which may be rented by visitors and on whose waters ply the shikara gondolas, also for hire. Further out is the Nagin Lake, whose houseboats are less suburban and preferable for a longer stay. The river is traversed by nine bridges; fragments of masonry from demolished Hindu temples can be seen on the embankment.

The city runs above a network of canals and consists chiefly of wooden houses attractively carved and balconied to make a renowned spectacle.

The city's most conspicuous sight is the Sankaracharya Temple which stands on a hill rising 300 m above the Kashmir plain. It is probable that a temple was first built here by Jaluka, son of Ashoka, in about 200 BC. It was later rebuilt between 253 AD and 326 AD. The superstructure is of the eighth century and displays a fine early example of the horseshoe arch. The abandoned fort outside the city is also well worth the climb (a permit to visit can be obtained from the local tourist office).

Kashmiris used to be known throughout India as Sastra-Silpine (architects). Characteristic of Kashmiri architecture are high, pyramidal roofs, pediments and lofty trefoil pillars. Lalitaditya, ruler of Kashmir in the years 724-760 AD, is generally credited with being the patron of the sophisticated Aryan style of Kashmiri architecture. Later came the Islamic influences and the construction of wooden buildings. A superb example of this Muslim style is the Jama Masjid at Srinagar, built originally between 1389 and 1413. The building has been razed by fire three times: the present structure was restored on the original plan by the Moghul Emperor Aurangazeb in 1674.

The carpets, woollen goods. wood carvings, leather work and other handicrafts of Kashmir have a high reputation.

A few kilometres out of Srinagar are the Moghul Gardens of Shalimar (Abode of Love), Nishat (Garden of Pleasure) and Chashma Shahi (Royal Spring); gardens the likes of which exist nowhere else in the world. *Son et lumiere* displays are held most evenings at Shalimar.

The Moghuls — like their present-day successors — developed Kashmir as a resort to escape from the heat and the dust of the lowland plains.

Some 40 km from Srinagar is Gulmarg (Meadow of Flowers) at an altitude of 8,500 ft. Gulmarg is an excellent resort for the golfer with the upper course (one of the highest in the world) reputed to be the best in Asia. Further on and 600 m higher is Khilanmarg, where one can ski. The Indian Government has recently completed the construction of a top-class resort complex in the area.

About 100 km from Srinagar at 7,000 ft, lies Pahalgam, meeting point of two snow-fed rivers and famed for its scenic beauty. Blue forests of pine and fir crowd up the mountains. About 50 km from Pahalgam in a hinterland of rock and ice is the sacred cave of Amarnath, a centre for pilgrimage. Sonamarg (Path of Gold) lies 80 km from Srinagar, 8,750 ft up at the end of the road which offers fabulous views. Nearby is Thajiwas, an excellent camping site consisting of miniature plateaux naturally separated into compartments, and providing a view of the glaciers on the Thajiwas Range.

Ladakh, closed to foreigners until a few years ago, is a desolate, wind-swept plateau, separated from the lush Kashmir Valley by the Zoji-La pass, 11,578 ft above sea level on the Himalayan range. Leh, its picturesque capital, provides a glimpse into what is essentially Tibetan culture and architecture. It is also a base for visits to the mahayana Buddhist monasteries of hemis Gumpa, Spituk and others. Srinagar and Leh are linked by air. From mid-May to mid-November there is also a daily bus service, with an overnight stop at Kargil. Cars can also be hired at Srinagar for the journey.

Although facilities at Leh have vastly improved in recent years, it is advisable to carry a sleeping bag and a light mountain tent, as well as basic provisions, in view of the limited accommodation facilities at Leh. A trip to Ladakh is still something of an adventure and should not be undertaken by those unable to take collapse of arrangements and other uncertainties in their stride.

THE WESTERN REGION
BOMBAY

Bombay, which the king of Portugal gave as dowry to Charles II of England in 1661, has grown in 300 years from a marshy fishing village to one of the world's greatest seaports, one of Asia's largest industrial centres and India's most cosmopolitan city. While New Delhi, with

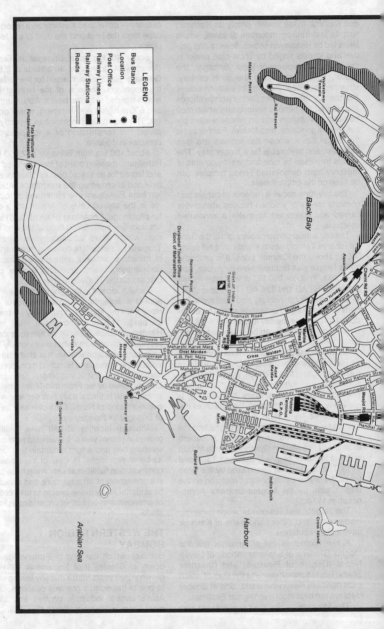

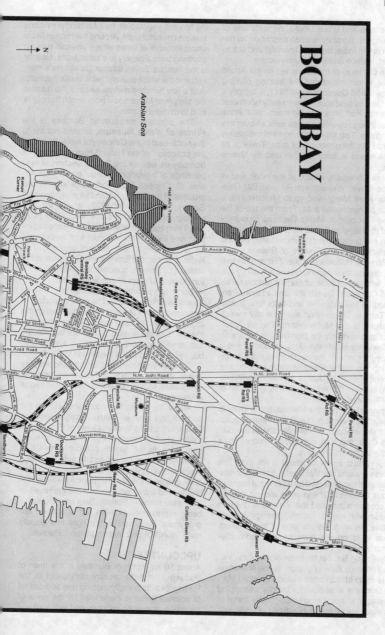

its avenues and office blocks, reminds one of Washington. Bombay is often described as the New York of India, being its financial and stock-market, fashion and film industry centre.

The Gateway of India, erected on the Apollo Bunder to commemorate the landing of King George V and Queen Mary in 1911, is the city's most famous landmark. Immediately northwest of it is the Fort area and the main commercial centre, though business areas exist all over this thriving city. Two kilometres north of the gate is Ballard Pier, the general dock area. Towards its southern end is Back Bay, skirted by Marine Drive.

From Chowpatty Beach at the north end of Marine Drive, Walkeshwar Rd and Bal Gangadhar Kher Marg wind up to Malabar Hill, a well-to-do residential area. From the top of the hill the Ferozeshah Mehta Gardens (popularly called the Hanging Gardens) afford a view of the ocean and parts of the city. Immediately beyond the gardens are the Towers of Silence where the Parsees (followers of the Zoroastrian religion) expose their dead to be consumed by vultures; entry is not allowed. Back down the hill towards Chowpatty Beach is Kamala Nehru Park (named for Nehru's wife) and at its foot, Bahulnath Temple. To the north along the city's western shore is the Mahalakshmi Temple, dedicated, appropriately for Bombay, to Lakshmir, the Goddess of Wealth. And as Bombay is a money-minded city, the best horses in the country also run at the Mahalakshmir race-course (November-March). Just to the north again and jutting out into the Arabian Sea is the Tomb of Haji Ali, a Muslim saint.

Going inland from the Mahalakshmir Temple one reaches a number of sporting venues; apart from the race-course, there are the Willingdon Sport Club, the National Sports Club of India and the Vallabhai Stadium.

Going east again for about 2 km from this sporting area, is the Veermata Jijabai Bhonsle Udyan (still better known by its original name of Victoria Gardens). These were laid out in 1861 and contain a zoo and the Victoria and Albert Museum with natural history, geology and agriculture sections. To the east of the museum stands a stone elephant brought from Elephanta Island.

On Palton Rd, not far to the north of the Victoria Terminus railway station, is the **Mahatma Phule market** (still often called Crawford Market). Once the focal point for the city's shopping activities, it is now being upstaged by some of the newer areas, but its hundreds of stalls selling flowers, vegetables, fruit, fish and provisions make a colourful sight. Around the market lies a whole network of lanes where you can pick up anything from a canary to a cabin trunk. Nearby is the famous Zaveri Bazaar (Jewellers's market) and the wholesale and retail textile markets. Just a few hundred metres away to the north is the temple of Mumbadevi from which the city is said to derive its name.

The principal museum in Bombay is the **Prince of Wales Museum**, located not far to the north-east of the Gateway of India. It houses the collection of the Natural History Society of Bombay as well as the Tata collection of rare paintings of the Moghul school and fine examples of Chinese jade and porcelain. In the grounds of the museum stands the Jehangir Art Gallery, completed in 1952, where art and photographic exhibitions are frequently held. The Town Hall's Asiatic Society collection of Indian and Eastern manuscripts and records will be of interest to the serious student. The Rajabai Tower, the Elphinstone College and the Institute of Science opposite the museum mark the Bombay University academic area.

Bombay's picturesque lake district is only an hour's drive from the city. The more important of these are Vihar, Tulsi and Tansa from which the city also draws its water supply. Transport within the city is cheap and fast; there are two electric suburban train services, besides a municipal bus system considered the best in India.

The city has many fine churches and temples and is also the location of the Cancer hospital, the Bhabha Atomic Research Centre and two oil refineries.

About 10 km to the southeast across the harbour, on a small island locally known as Gharapuri, are the famous **caves of Elephanta**. Seven in all, these caves, hewn from the rock, date back to the eighth century. The Great Cave, which once served as a temple, has huge sculptures and panels in relief. The most striking of the images is the Maheshmurti, a 19-ft-high triple-headed figure with each of the members of the Hindu trinity — Rahma, Siva and Vishnu — being represented. To the left is a huge androgynous Siva, and to the right two equally huge figures of Siva and his consort, Parvati.

UPCOUNTRY

About 50 km north of Bombay is the town of **Bassein**, the 16th century stronghold of the Portuguese. Its once flourishing role as a citadel of colonial times is evidenced by the ruins of churches, convents, manors and fortifications.

Gujarat.

Photo: Lincoln Kaye

An ideal picnic spot, it is a worthwhile side trip from Bombay.

Karla, 8 km from Lonavala Station on the Bombay-Poona line, is famous for its rock caves. **The Great Cave of Karla** (second century) is the finest and largest *chaitya* (i.e. a place of worship) cave in India. The large hall is 38 m long, 14 m wide and 14 m high. A row of ornamental columns rises on either side to the ribbed teak roof. In the same district, the caves of Bhaja and Bedsa display other fine *chaitya* halls.

Pune (or **Poona**), 190 km from Bombay and three hours away by the Deccan Queen railway express, was the capital of the Maratha empire under the Peshwa (1750-1817). It is pleasantly situated amid extensive gardens, with many modern buildings besides temples and palaces dating from the 16th to the 19th centuries. It is an important industrial centre. The city's fair climate caused it to be used during the British Raj as the residence of the governor of Bombay during the monsoon season, and as a military base.

Aurangabad is an hour from Bombay by air to the northeast; it is a dry and dusty region, and can be uncomfortable in the dry season. The **Bibi-da-Maqbara**, the mausoleum of the wife of the Moghul emperor Aurangazeb (1685-1707), which is modelled on the Taj Mahal, is of interest. Nearby are some Buddhist rock *chaitya*.

The most famous of all the complexes of rock temples are to be found at **Ellora and Ajanta** 30 km and 100 km respectively north of Aurangabad. The nearest railhead for those visiting Ajanta is the town of Jalgaon, though Aurangabad is almost as close. Limited accommodation is available in the vicinity of both temples.

At Ellora the caves extend along the face of the hill for 2 km and are divided into three distinct series — Buddhist, Brahmanical (Hindu) and Jian — and are arranged almost chronologically. The most splendid is the **Kailasa**, which is a copy of a complete Dravidian Temple, the rock having been cut away both internally and externally. First the great sunken court was hewn out of the solid rock of the hillside, leaving the mass of the temple wholly detached. A rock bridge once connected the upper storey of the temple with the upper row of galleried chambers surrounding three sides of the court. The temple was constructed under Krishnadeva Rashtrakuta, king of Malkhed from 760-783 AD.

At Ajanta, the caves — 30 in number, and all Buddhist — are excavated in the south side of the precipitous bank of a ravine and, like Ellora, are made up of both places of worship and monastic living quarters.

Daulatabad Fort, on the way from Aurangabad to Ellora, is a magnificent 13th century citadel, with a moat, scarp and spiral passage hewn out of the solid rock. You may take tea close by at the tea shop.

The picturesque **ruined city of Mandu** lies in the state of Madhya Pradesh off the main Bombay–New Delhi Rd some distance to the southwest of the towns of Indore and Mhow. Lying 600 m up, it extends for 13 km along the crest of the Vindhya mountains. It reached its greatest splendour in the 15th century under Hoshang Shah (1405-34). The circuit of the battlemented wall is nearly 37 km, enclosing many palaces and mosques. The oldest mosque dates from 1405; the finest is the **Jama Masjid**, a notable example of Pathan architecture. Hoshang Shah's marble-domed tomb is also magnificent.

Sanchi, the site of what are almost certainly the oldest buildings in India still standing, lies near Bhopal, also in Madhya Pradesh — site of one of the world's worst environmental disasters when poison gas escaped from a local factory. Buddhist buildings were first erected in the area not long after the time of the Buddha himself. Following the visit of the Buddhist emperor, Ashoka, Sanchi was to become an important centre for the religion. The structures consist of stupas (memorial mounds) standing on the level top of a small sandstone hill about 90 m high on the left bank of the River Betwa.

On the Sanchi hill itself there are 10 stupas, of which the Great Stupa is by far the most important. It is a solid dome of stone, about 160 m in diameter and now about 13 m high. It must have formerly been much higher, the top having originally formed a terrace 10 m in diameter on which stood lofty columns. Round the base is a flagged pathway surrounded by a stone railing and entered at the four points of the compass by gateways some 6 m high. Both the gateways and railings are elaborately covered with bas-reliefs and inscriptions.

In Gujarat state is the city of **Ahmedabad**, founded in 1411 by King Ahmed Shah. The city was built on the site used for earlier Hindu towns. Besides its cotton mills, the city is famous for such handicrafts as brocades and other fancy fabrics, copper, brass, woodwork and jewellery.

Owing to its many changes of fortune, Ahmedabad became a meeting place of Hindu, Muslim and Jain architecture; Ahmed Shah pulled down Hindu temples in order to build mosques with the materials. The beautiful Jama Masjid (completed in 1424) with its 300 fantastically carved pillars is one building which has undergone a similar metamorphosis. There are many other fine mosques and tombs along with other examples of Indian Muslim architecture. Two of the windows in Sidi Said's mosque, of filigree marble work, are marvels of artistic delicacy and grace — better than anything of the kind to be found in Agra or Delhi.

Further up the railway north from Ahmedabad (alight at Abu Rd Station) is **Mount Abu** which emerges from the surrounding plains of Marwar like a precipitous granite island, rising to a height of 1,200 m above sea-level.

The elevations and platforms of the mountain are covered with elaborately sculptured shrines, temples and tombs. On the very top is a small round platform containing a cavern with a block of granite bearing the impression of the feet of Data Bhrigu (an incarnation of Vishnu).

The two principal temples at **Dilwara**, at about the middle of the mountain, are of white marble. The more modern of them was built by two rich merchant brothers between 1197 and 1247 and is almost unrivalled for the delicacy of its carving. The other was built by a local governor, apparently about 1032. Simpler and bolder in style, it is one of the oldest and most complete examples of Jain architecture.

The **Gir Forest Sanctuary** located in Gujarat on the Kathiawar Peninsula is one of the best of the Indian wildlife sanctuaries and is renowned as the home of the Indian lion. There is a small guesthouse in the area. The sanctuary is closed during the monsoon period, and is accessible only from mid-October to mid-June.

GOA

Goa was captured by the Portuguese Alfonso de Albuquerque in 1510 and the capital of Portuguese India was transferred there from Cochin. In the 18th century the Portuguese added to their possessions around Goa and the whole was to remain in Portuguese hands until forcibly retaken by Indian forces in 1961. As a result of this long Portuguese presence, some 40% of the population is Christian and the territory shows a remarkable mingling of Eastern and Western cultures. Panaji or New Goa (previously called Panjim), can be reached daily by air, road or sea transport, though sea passage is suspended during the monsoon months (June to October usually).

Old Goa reached the height of its prosperity between 1575 and 1625; it is now for the most part a city of ruins, but there are some splendid buildings which have survived. Among the most notable is the fine **Basilica of the Bom Jesus** (built between 1594 and 1603). This contains the tomb of St Francis Xavier who lies in a silver coffin atop an elaborate monument in a side chapel. Next to the Bom Jesus is the **Convent of the Jesuits** (1590) from which many missionaries went forth in their attempts to convert the East. Across the square is the **Cathedral of St Catherine**; founded by Albuquerque in 1511 and rebuilt in 1623, it is still used for public services. West is a converted mosque, rebuilt in 1661 except the portal of carved black stone which is the earliest relic of Portuguese architecture in India. The **Church of St Cajetan** (1665), some way north of Bom Jesus, is one of the best preserved buildings of old Goa.

THE EASTERN REGION
CALCUTTA

Calcutta is incredible: often apparently inhuman, though at the same time permeated with a vitality and spirit that forces one to an admiration of man's staying power under the most difficult of conditions. Long after you have gone from the city, it continues to tug at your consciousness like the persistent hand of a begging child.

Only a fishing village three centuries ago, Greater Calcutta is now the second-biggest city on the Asian mainland (after Shanghai). It is the home of local and foreign firms which export jute goods and tea, the mainstays of India's economy; the port of Calcutta handles nearly half of India's sea-borne trade.

Calcutta is also the metropolis of the sociable and intellectually curious Bengalis, who reputedly find something like intoxication from prolonged, impassioned talk over a cup of coffee. Calcutta was not the earliest centre of British power in India, though it soon became the principal one. From the time of Clive's victory over Suraj-ud-Dowlah at the Battle of Plassey (1757) until the foundation of New Delhi, Calcutta was the centre of Britain's Indian Empire and most of the city's monuments are relics of the British Raj.

Dalhousie Square (named after the governor-general between 1848 and 1856), located centrally in the sprawling mass of the city and not far from the Hooghly River — one of the delta tributaries of the Great River Ganga — is a small stretch of parkland, flanked on the north by the splendid red brick **Writers' Building** which now houses most of the ministries of the state of West Bengal. Next to it is the **Scotch Kirk of St Andrew** (opened in 1818), and adjacent to the west side of the square the General Post Office with its massive white columns and golden dome. Inside the Post Office is a brass plaque marking the boundary of the old Fort

William that was captured by Suraj-ud-Dowlah in 1756. A similar plaque marking the infamous Black Hole — where many of the imprisoned British perished at that time — has been removed.

Just off Council House St, nearby Dalhousie Square, is **St John's Church**, built in 1784. In the church graveyard can be found the octagonal monument to Job Charnock (who died in 1692), the founder of Calcutta. Charnock is also remembered for having married a lovely Brahmin widow whom he saved from committing ceremonial suicide at the funeral pyre of her husband.

Further to the south, between Council House St and Old Court House St, is the **Raj Bhawan**, the residence of the Governor of West Bengal. Built in 1804, it is modelled on Kedleston Hall in Derbyshire, birthplace of Lord Curzon who was viceroy of India from 1898 to 1905.

North of Dalhousie Square, Netaji Subhas Rd leads past banks and offices of shipping and commercial firms — among which is the vast, cathedral-like Chartered Bank building on the right-hand side — to the huge **Howrah Bridge** which here crosses the Hooghly River and leads to Howrah Railway Station. (Calcutta's other railway station is Sealdah, located on the Calcutta side of the river.)

Mahatma Gandhi Rd, off the north end of Netaji Subhas Rd, brings you to the **Nakhoda Mosque**, the largest mosque in the city. It is modelled on Akbar's tomb at Sikandra, though the vicinity is too crowded to permit a full appreciation. From here it is about 3 km via Acharya Profulla Chandra Rd to the famous **Swetamber Jain Temple**, built in 1967.

Just over 1 km south of Dalhousie Square brings you to the beginning of the great expanse of parkland known as the **Maiden** where rises the tail column of the **Ochterlony Monument** built in 1828. Nearby is the city's tram terminus from where, via a seeming maze of random tracks, trams fan out through the suburbs. From this point one of Calcutta's main thorough-fares, Nehru Rd (perhaps better known by its old name of Chowringhee) runs south in the direction of the **Victoria Memorial** down the east side of the Maidan. The Grand and the Ritz hotels can be found on the eastern side of Nehru Rd, while behind them and stretching for several blocks is the interesting bazaar area known as the New (or Hogg) Market. Close to where Park St (the location of several of the city's best restaurants) runs off Jawaharlal Nehru Rd lies the large India Museum with a collection which includes some

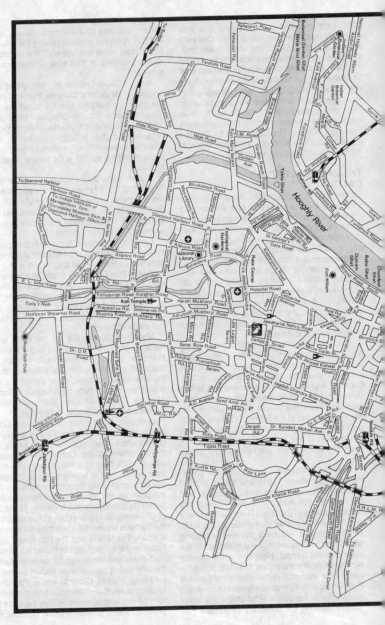

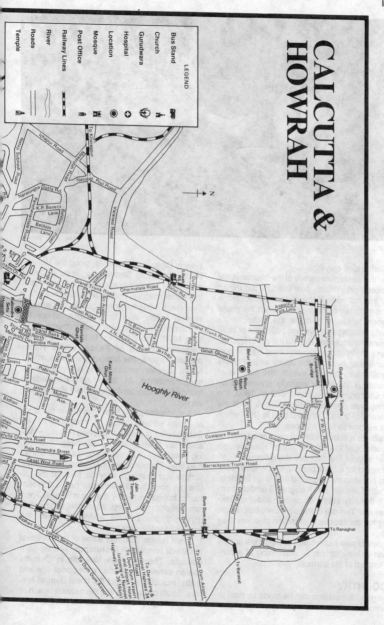

CALCUTTA & HOWRAH

LEGEND

Bus Stand	
Church	
Gurudwara	
Hospital	
Location	
Mosque	
Post Office	
Railway Lines	
River	
Roads	
Temple	

Hooghly River

To Ranaghat

To Khargpur

To Dum Dum Airport

To Darjeeling & National Highway 34

To Barasat

125

Photo: John R. Thompson

College St market, Calcutta.

excellent stone carvings.

On the western extremity of the maidan is the enclosed Fort William, now used by the Indian Army and not open to the general public. In the southern corner of the maidan stands the grand memorial to Queen Victoria, the white marble building housing a fascinating collection of India memorablia under the Raj. All the great figures, Indian and British, are remembered in print, portrait or stone; even for the visitor almost totally unfamiliar with colonial events, the place is of tremendous interest. Originally conceived by Lord Curzon, viceroy from 1899 to 1905, the building was opened in 1992. Close by is the Anglican St Paul's Cathedral built in 1847 which has a window by Burne-Jones.

Calcutta's suburbs are of greater interest to the sociologist than to the tourist. However, on the far side of the river are the Botanical Gardens noted for a huge banyan tree whose many stems cover as much ground as a large building. In south Calcutta the **Kalighat Temple**, from which the city takes its name, and the **Dakshineswar Temple** to the north, are both worth a visit for the spectacle of Indian customs they offer.

Calcutta now has a clean and efficient underground railway ststem — something of a contrast to most of the surface.

UPCOUNTRY

Some good excursions can be made by train or bus into Calcutta's neighbouring villages for a view of Bengali peasant life, or up the Hooghly River, notably to **Serampore**, once a Danish settlement where there is a church built in 1805; to Chandernagore, French until 1951 but where the French influence only lingers in the names of several hotels; and to Chinsura, where the Dutch once lived and which has a church dating from 1678. About 160 km to the north is **Santiniketan (Abode of Peace)** where Rabindranath Tagore, the famous Bengali poet and Nobel laureate, whose songs became the national anthems of India and Bangladesh, founded the non-conformist Visva Bharati University.

It is now one of the finest centres for the study of Indian art and culture. A good time to visit Santiniketan is during the spring festival — Vasantotsav — which usually falls in March, or during Paus Mela, a winter fair held around Christmas time. Tagore's personal belongings, manuscripts and paintings may be seen at the Uttarayan complex. Santiniketan has a 20-room tourist bungalow run by the West Bengal Tourism Development Corp. as well as a couple of university guesthouses where, however, the food and facilities are poor.

West Bengal also has some of India's finest terracotta temples at **Bishnupur**, 146 km from Calcutta. The Ashutosh Museum in Calcutta has an excellent collection of regional arts and crafts, including some of the finest Bengali textiles. South of Calcutta lies the nearest beach at Digha, though at 250 km distance (six hours by bus), it is not too accessible.

Calcutta is also one of the take-off points for Kathmandu (capital of Nepal), Gangtok (capital of Sikkim), and in India itself, Darjeeling and Kalimpong in the northern mountains of West Bengal (with a view of the Himalayas).

Patna, 480 km by rail from Calcutta, stands on the site of the ancient city of Pataliputra, which, under Emperor Ashoka, was the capital of an empire extending from the Bay of Bengal to the Hindu Kush (in present-day Afghanistan). After some centuries of fame as a great Buddhist centre, it fell into decline, but recovered in the mid–16th century when it became the capital of the state of Bihar. It has several noteworthy mosques and a Sikh temple which marks the birthplace of the great Govind Singh, 10th and last Guru of the Sikhs, who was assassinated in 1708; in the temples are preserved his cradle and shoes. The city's Khudabuksh Oriental Library, famous for its rare collection of Arabic and Persian manuscripts, possesses the only volumes saved from the sacking of the Moorish University of Cordoba. The curious beehive-shaped structure next to the university was built in 1786 for rice storage.

Some 80 km to the south, the district of **Gaya** has many archaeological remains associated with the early history of Buddhism. Bodh Gaya, 10 km south again from the town of Gaya, is one of the holiest places in the Buddhist world, for it was here under the Bodhi tree that the Prince Gautama finally reached the absolute enlightenment of Buddhahood. In the third century BC Ashoka erected a temple here; part of the stone railing enclosing this temple and the *vajrasan* (diamond throne) marking the spot where the Buddha sat, are preserved.

Ashoka's temple having fallen into ruin, it was replaced by another identified with that now standing and which was restored in the 11th century and again in 1882. The main tower rises to 50 m, and in the courtyard are ranged many stone stupas which Buddhist pilgrims have left as memorials of their visit. A pipul tree outside the temple is held to be a lineal descendant of the sacred Bodhi tree; the tree is perpetuated from time to time by dropping seeds into the fork or hollow of the parent tree.

The **Barabar Hills**, 25 km north of Gaya, houses cave shrines of the time of Ashoka — the most ancient excavated in India.

Some 100 km southeast of Patna by road lie the ruins of the great Buddhist monastery of **Nalanda** where the Chinese pilgrim Hsuan Tsang studied for five years. At that time — the

seventh century — the monastery housed about 10,000 monks.

Lying on the coast in the state of Orissa, almost 500 km southwest of Calcutta by rail (an overnight run) is **Puri**. The bungalows on the wide and almost deserted beach, which here stretches for miles, is an alternative accommodation to the town's hotels. At daybreak people stand to worship in the water, facing east with heads bowed and hands folded.

Puri is above all the town of the great temple of **Jagannath**, the god identified with Krishna and consequently ranked as an incarnation of Vishnu. Only Hindus are admitted to the temple but locally available guides may take non-Hindus on to the surrounding house balconies or roofs which offer a good view of the temple. The temple was built in the 12th century. The tower, which is lightly carved and has been covered with white plaster, rises 58 m. On top are the symbolic flag and wheel of Vishnu and the principal entrance (the Lion Gate) is a fine monolithic grey stone pillar, 10 m high, surmounted by the image of a garuda bird which formerly stood before the Sun Temple at Konarak. Inside the sanctum are three images: Jagannath with his brother Balbhadra and his sister Subhadra. They are in the form of grotesque wooden busts with very large faces. Small reproductions of these can be bought in Puri's colourful bazaar.

The famous **Rathyatra Car Festival** takes place in June or July (depending on the lunar calendar). On this occasion the images are brought out through the Lion Gate and placed on enormous wooden chariots. The largest, that of Jagannath, is 14 m high while those for the other images are not much smaller. Thousands of pilgrims drag the cars along Baradand Rd to the Gundicha Bari (Garden House). Non-Hindus are barred at the time of the festival.

Bhubaneswar, capital of Orissa, is 100 km from Puri, and contains splendid temples dating from between the eighth and the 13th centuries. The town is dominated by the 40-m-high tower of the great **Lingaraj Temple** (built in about 1050). Visitors may not enter the temple, which is in use, but quite good views of the exterior can be obtained from surrounding vantage points. The outer surface is intricately carved.

Near the Lingaraj Temple is the **Vaital Temple**, striking for its small size and minuteness of its carvings; the reliefs have the delicacy of jewellers' work. The characteristic ribbed tower of the region is notable for its oblong plan and

Photo: Gavin Greenwood

Madras traffic.

semi-cylindrical roof, which seems to show southern influence. The **Mukteshwar** and **Rajrani** temples are also outstanding and can be entered by non-Hindus. The museum at Bhubaneswar is well worth a visit.

Eight km south of Bhubaneswar, at **Dhauli**, a set of edicts by Ashoka is engraved on a rock facing a bridge over the River Daya. The rock is crowned by a carved elephant. Going in a different direction from Bhubaneswar, 8 km to the west, the twin Udayagiri and Khandagiri hills are honeycombed with decorated caves, both natural and artificial. Notable in the Udayagiri Hills are the Chota-hathi cave which has some fine sculptures of plant life; the Rani Nahar (Queen's Palace), a two-storeyed structure supposed to have been built by King Kharavela (a ruler who achieved independence on the breakup of Ashoka's kingdom) for his queen; and the Ganesh Gumpha, which has eight very fine tableaux which seem to depict a stormy wooing. On the Khandagiri hill the Ananta cave is Buddhist but the others are mostly Jain, though these contain several Buddhas in meditation.

On the coast to the north of Puri and some 65 km by road (there is a bus) from Bhubaneswar, is the stupendous **Sun Temple of Konarak** (also known as the Black Pagoda), which stands within a vast compound in a desolate stretch of sand about 5 km from the sea. This structure, built about 1250, marks the peak of Orissan architectural art. It was conceived as a mythical chariot of the Sun God, Surya, borne on 24 brilliantly carved wheels. What now remains is only a fragment of the original since the tower — which is thought to have been over 60 m high — has collapsed, and some exceptionally erotic carvings.

South of Puri is **Chilka Lake**, India's largest fresh-water lake, which is famous for its migrating duck in winter. There are bungalows on the lake at Balugaon and Brakul. Those who are interested in the modern as well as the ancient world may care to visit the **Hirakud Dam** and the giant Hindustan steel plant at Rourkela in the extreme north of the state.

Darjeeling, in the northernmost part of West Bengal, derives its name from the Tibetan Dorje Ling (Place of Thunderbolts). It stands at 2,133 m and commands one of the most beautiful views in the world. The eyes sweep up from the valleys to a succession of ranges culminating — when not hidden in cloud — with Kanchenjunga (8,570 m) and, a little further off, the world's highest mountain, Mount Everest. Other peaks white with perpetual snow fill the horizon. From May to October, however, Darjeeling and the surrounding high country is veiled in mist.

Visitors going by air to Darjeeling no longer need a special pass (the town and surroundings are considered a restricted area by the Indian Government) as long as their stay does not exceed 15 days. The issuing of such passes for visitors going by land transport is merely a formality. Contact the Ministry of Home Affairs.

The town of Darjeeling is located on a series of terraces on the hillside and offers a good number of resort hotels. For those who are fit, there are many interesting hikes in the beautifully forested hills, but for the less energetic, the local network of roads provide access by car to sites such as **Tiger Hill** (where there is a Tourist Lodge), 11 km from Darjeeling, and from where the sunrise over the Himalayas is breathtaking.

Some 50 km east of Darjeeling, and accessible either from there or from Siliguri, is Kalimpong, once a frontier market to which wool and mules were brought from Tibet. Permission (over and above that to visit Darjeeling) to go to Kalimpong can be obtained from the Deputy Commissioner at Darjeeling, but for a stay no longer than 48 hours.

Travellers heading to **Gangtok** (the Sikkim capital) can go either by road via Darjeeling or directly from Siliguri.

To the east lies Assam, a land of rice fields, bamboo and tea estates and the mighty Brahmaputra River. The other states in this almost detached portion of India include Tripura, Manipur and Nagaland, Meghalaya and the protected areas of the North East Frontier Agency. From Siliguri a railway runs east to a number of places deep in Assam. **Shillong**, in the Khasi-Jaintia Hills, is a popular hill station featuring an excellent golf course. It is an easy bus ride from Shillong to Cherapunji, 1,370 m up on a small plateau offering a view to the south.

THE SOUTHERN REGION
MADRAS

The tropical and crowded south of India with its towering temples and distinctive languages has some claim to be more authentically Indian than other regions in the land. The people, culture and language of the south are Dravidian and indigenous to India in contrast to the north's Aryan culture. In some respects the south has been more influenced by things foreign, for example, the English language and Christianity. But this may only reflect a special gift for assimilation. The south has undeniably kept its special traditions intact and the Western visitor will find the south a rather different sort of experience from the north.

The foundations of the city of Madras, capital of Tamil Nadu state, were laid in 1639 when Francis Day, chief of the East India Co.'s settlement at Armagon, obtained a grant of the city's present site from the representative of the local Raj. A fort was constructed which later became known as **Fort St George** and a gradually increasing population settled around its walls. During the 18th century the town had to resist attack from the Marathas and the French; the latter actually took it from 1746 to 1748. The neighbouring fort of San Thome, which had been founded by the Portuguese in 1504, was subsequently held by the French and the Dutch until occupied by the British in 1749.

Today, Fort St George in the north of the city close by the harbour area, retains many of its original features; the moated enclosure surrounded with battlements and ramparts standing much as it did 300 years ago. Within the fort are the old barracks, the original officers' quarters and two houses of interest in Charles and James Sts: one where Robert Clive, founder of the East India Co., lived and, a little further on, Wellesley House where Col Wellesley — the future Duke of Wellington — lived in 1798.

The most important monument in the fort is the **Church of St Mary**, consecrated in 1680 and the oldest Anglican church in India. Within the church are preserved many monuments of the early days of the fort. **The Fort Museum**, overlooking the sea, was at one time an exchange for merchants of the East India Co. It has been a museum since 1948 and among its holdings are the registers of baptisms, marriages and burials since 1680. The marriages of Elihu Yale (founder of Yale University) and Robert Clive are noteworthy.

The pride of Madras is its wonderful beach — the marina. About 200 m wide, it stretches south from the harbour, well past the southern reaches of the city beyond the Adayar River. One comes upon the beach from the city with something like surprise. At dawn, with the sun rising over the Bay of Bengal, the fishermen return from the sea, dragging their longboats — unchanged for centuries — through the breakers while yoga devotees practise their exercises on the beach. At dusk the monumental expanse of sand attracts promenading locals, rich and poor, ice-cream vendors and even an ad hoc brass band.

At the northern end of the marina, just outside the fort, is an imposing war memorial. Going south across the bridge over the River Cooum, the buildings of Madras University are seen on the right with the clock tower of the library dominating the scene. Conspicuous is the **Senate House**, built in the Indo-Saracenic style with its brilliantly painted towers. A short distance further along is the **Chepauk Palace**, built in the Moorish style, where once the Nawabs of the Carnatic held court.

Some 3 km further south along the beach is **San Thome** (also called Mylapore), a residential area containing the homes of the leaders of

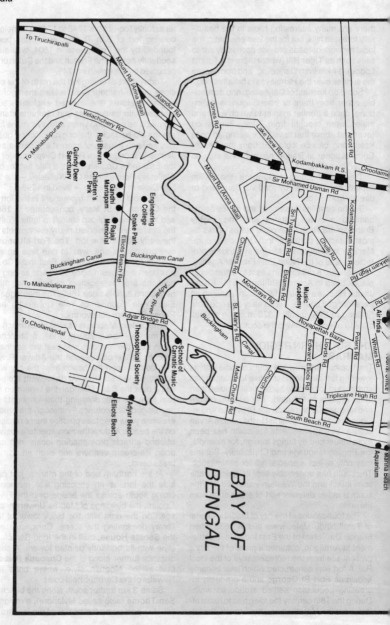

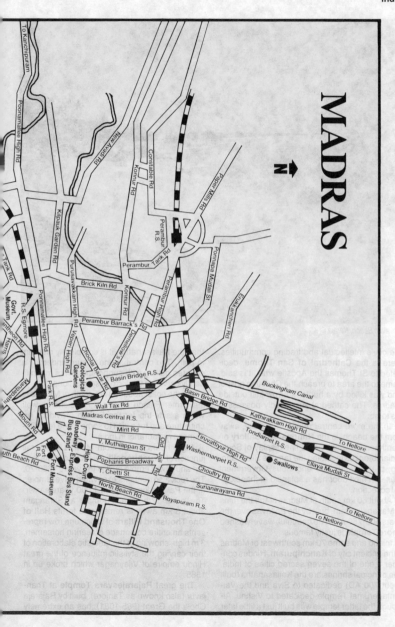

MADRAS

N

To Kanchipuram

Poonamallee High Rd

Tank Rd

Govt. Museum

R.S. Egmore

Pantheon Rd

Harris

Mount Rd

Mambalam

South Beach Rd

Kilpauk Garden Rd

Ponnamallee High Rd

Purusawakkam High Rd

Choolai Bazar Rd

Park R.S.

Fort R.S.

Zoological Gardens

Wall Tax Rd

Madras Central R.S.

Broadway Bus Stand - Express Bus Stand

High Court

V. Muthiappan St

Pophanis Broadway

T. Chetti St

North Beach Rd

Fort Museum

Kilpauk Garden Rd

Brick Kiln Rd

Konnur Rd

Perambur Barrack's Rd

Demellows Rd

Vepery High Rd

Perambur High Rd

Perambur Tank Rd

Konnur Rd

Constable Rd

New Avadi Rd

Paper Mills Rd

Perambur R.S.

Perambur Tank Rd

Pornapa Mudali St

Erukkancheri Rd

Buckingham Canal

Basin Bridge R.S.

Basin Bridge Rd

Kathirakkam High Rd

Mint Rd

Old Jail Rd

Tiruvattiyur High Rd

Washermanpet R.S.

Choultry Rd

Surinarayana Rd

Royapuram R.S.

Tondiarpet R.S.

Ellaya Mudali St

• Swallows

To Nellore

To Nellore

To Nellore

Kovalam Beach. Kerala.

the city's intellectual and trading communities. Here is the **Cathedral of San Thome**, dedicated to St Thomas the Apostle who, it is said, came to the area to preach the Christian gospel and was killed by a hunter's arrow just outside Madras. The cathedral supposedly possesses his tomb.

In the more central region of the city, away from the beach, is the **National Art Gallery** on Pantheon Rd which has a fine display of South Indian bronzes including the famous Siva dancing, the Nataraj. The enormous Government Museum next door has a splendid archaeological collection.

About 60 km south of Madras stand the ruins of Mahabalipuram, built by the Pallavas over the years 500-750 AD. The beautiful, wave-washed **Shore Temple** is justly famous.

Inland and some 70 km southwest of Madras is the ancient city of **Kanchipuram**. Hindus consider it one of the seven sacred cities of India. The principal shrines are the Kailasanatha (built about 700 AD) dedicated to Siva and the Vaikuntaperumal Temple dedicated to Vishnu. Although the latter temple was built just a little later

than the Kailasanatha, it is completely different in plan. The central shrine is surrounded by a covered gallery with supporting pillars magnificently carved in the form of seated lions.

On the coast about 50 km south of Madras is the former French colony of Pondicherry, well worth a side-trip for the French provincial architecture and for a visit to some of the few Vietnamese restaurants in India.

Eight hours by rail from Madras is the rail junction of **Tiruchirapalli**, celebrated for its rock fort and Siva Temple built in the years 1660-70. The rock also contains excavated cave temples of the Pallava kings, about 1,000 years earlier. The great 17th-century temple at Srirangam about 3 km away is remarkable for its **Hall of One Thousand Pillars** of which one row represents an entire colonnade of rearing horsemen, 3 m high, showing in the fantastic elaboration of their carving the stylistic influence of the great Hindu empire of Vijaynagar which broke up in 1565.

The great **Rajarajesvara Temple** at Thanjavur (also known as Tanjore), built by Rajaraja Chola the Great (985-1081), has an extremely beautiful tower 60 m high capped by a single stone weighing 80 tonnes. A ramp 6 km long was necessary for its installation. Other noteworthy temples in the vicinity of Thanjavur are those of Tiruvarur (17th century) and Kumbakonam.

At the southernmost tip of India is **Kanya Kumari** (Cape Comorin) there is a Gandhi memorial shrine, already visited by so many pilgrims that the steps are deeply worn.

Kerala (Land of Coconut Palms) is the green lush state that runs as a narrow strip along the western coast of southern India, the hills known as the Western Ghats forming a natural inland border. The state has always maintained a certain independence from the rest of India and was manifesting this in 1957 when it became the first state in the world to elect a communist government (against non-communist alternatives).

Trivandrum, the capital, lies in the very south of the state by the sea. Only Hindus are admitted to the local Padmanabhaswami Temple. Also of interest in the city is the Kaudiyar Palace, the residence of the last reigning Maharaja of Travancore, and the ancient palaces of previous rulers which may be found in the fort area.

The pride of this region is **Kovalam**, about 8 km south of Trivandrum, where the government has built a comfortable beach resort complex. Kovalam is famous for what is said to be one of the clearest blue seas in the world. A memorable dip and sunbathing on the expanse of white sand are only a taxi ride away from Trivandrum. A scuba-diving centre has recently been established at Kovalam — check with the Tourist Office for details.

If you are heading south of **Kanya Kumari** from Trivandrum you can stop in at the interesting old fort of Padmanabhapurtam which was once the capital town of the now non-existent Travancore state. (Along with Cochin and Malabar, Travancore now forms the state of Kerala whose people speak Malayalam.)

Heading north from Trivandrum along the coast, one reaches **Quilon** some 75 km away. In the past Roman, Arab, Portuguese, and Dutch ships all used Quilon as a port of call. From Quilon you can travel all the way to Alleppey and beyond by motorboat along the backwaters, a continuous palm-fringed chain of lagoons and canals, past quiet village backyards and sometimes over wide blue expanses of water. The coconut palms of the region ensure a ready supply of the mildly alcoholic (and a little raw to the taste buds of the uninitiated) "toddy" which is the fresh sap tapped from the toddy palm. The milk of tender coconuts is also a delight.

Some 80 km north of Quilon (pronounced Koylou) is the town of **Kottayam**, centre of India's rubber industry. From there it is a further 120 km to the **Periyar Wild Life Sanctuary** on a lake formed by the damming of the Periyar River. Across the lake lies a vast forest where wild animals roam at will. While cruising on the lake you can often see herds of elephant, bison, deer and sambhar drinking at the water's edge. There is a state-run hotel and one can also obtain a fishing permit during the season.

From Kottayam the port of **Cochin** is three hours away by road. It is a complex of three towns and several picturesque islands — one of them man-made — set in the Arabian Sea and merging with the backwaters. There are many ancient churches while the **Santa Cathedral**, consecrated in 1557, has been rebuilt in modern form.

The tomb of Portuguese explorer Vasco da Gama, the first man to reach India from Europe round The Cape of Good Hope and who died in Cochin in 1524, is in St Francis' Church. The local community of Jews has a synagogue, built in 1568, in which is preserved a land grant inscribed on a copper plate made by a ruler in (it is thought) the seventh century. It also has a floor of beautiful Canton blue, willow-pattern tiles, located on a street whose houses resemble those of an old Dutch village.

Adjacent to Cochin is **Ernakulam**, and further north **Cheruthuruthy**, the centre of the revival of the Kathakali dime drama featuring elaborately masked actors. Some distance north is **Trichur**, famous for its ancient temple and Puram Festival in either April or May of each year — a great spectacle of fireworks, drums and gold-caparisoned elephants in procession. Up the coast again is Calicut (now called Kozhikode) where Vasco da Gama first made land after his great voyage in 1498.

Accessible by road, rail and air from many corners of the country, the centrally located and modern city of **Bangalore** is capital of Mysore state. Perched 1,000 m above sea-level, the city was once famous as a hill station, cantonment town and home for British pensioners, though it is now better known for its rapidly expanding industries. **Nandi Hills**, 70 km from Bangalore at an altitude of 1,4980 m, is a popular resort.

It is 130 km by road to the garden city of **Mysore**, amid wide roads and beautiful fountains. One of the best times to visit the city is during the **Dusserah festivities** (October or November) which are observed with pomp and pageantry. Headed by elephants, richly decorated and painted horses, silver coaches and standard bearers, the procession is one of the most spectacular in the world. The Maharaja once rode in a golden howdah on his elephant.

Around 290 km to the south of Mysore city are the hill resorts of the Nilgiri mountains; Ootacamund (2,130 m), Coonoor (1,850 m) and Kotag Kotagiri (2,000 m). Of these, Ootacamund is the principal one. There are fishing, shooting, hiking and other recreational activities. The nearest airport is almost 90 km away at Coimbatore, though both road and rail transport is available from both the east and west coasts of South India.

East of Mysore, some 35 km, by the village of Somnathpur, is a small but famous temple erected in 1268 under the Hoysala Dynasty which ruled in Mysore from the 11th to 14th centuries. It has three star-shaped sanctuaries preceded by a single hall. North of Mysore lies the temple of Halebid, which is the site of Dwarasamudra, capital of the Hoysala dynasty.

The great Hoysalesvara Temple in this place and other Hoysala shrines are extraordinarily photogenic because of the intricate sculpture that covers them from top to bottom. Other Hoysala temples may be found at Belur to the north.

In the northern part of the state, on the railway between Gadag and Bellary, lies **Hampi**, site of the capital of the Vijaynagar empire which rose in the early 14th century to embody Hindu resistance to Muslim raiders. It was eventually destroyed by an alliance of three Muslim sultans at the Battle of Talikota in 1565. The outstanding edifice here is the Pattabhirama Temple.

Between Hampi and Bijapur lie the ancient caves of Badami and the temples at Pattadakal and Aihole. The latter are the oldest Hindu temples in India (fifth century AD) and all are well maintained in gardens tended by the Archaeological Survey of India.

Hyderabad, once the capital of the Nizams, is now capital of the state of Andhra Pradesh which faces the Bay of Bengal immediately to the north of Tamil Nadu state. The city is well served by road and rail from the neighbouring states and there are frequent air connections with the main Indian cities.

The city proper, founded in 1589, is surrounded by a stone wall with 13 gates, completed in the time of the first Nizam (1724-48). In the centre of the city, where four of the main roads meet, is the **Char Minar Gate** (Four

Minarets) which was built in 1591. It rises from arches facing the cardinal points. The Ashur Khana (built in 1594) which is a ceremonial building, the hospital, the Gostha Mahal Palace and Mecca Mosque are other buildings of the early period.

The **Salar Jung Museum** contains fine jewellery and precious stones, paintings, statues, wood and ivory carvings. Chinese porcelain and remarkable pieces of furniture from Japan, China, Italy and Britain.

About 3 km away is Golconda, once capital of the powerful kingdom of the Kutb Shahi Dynasty until captured by Aurangazeb in 1687. The fortress of Golconda, on a granite ridge, is commanded by the massive mausolea of the ancient kings who ruled the area in the 16th and 17th centuries.

ANDAMAN AND NICOBAR ISLANDS

Tourism has yet to make an impact on the Andaman and Nicobar Islands, partly because of their remoteness from the mainland (1,255 km from Calcutta and 1,190 km from Madras) and the paucity of inter-island boat services. There are 204 islets, and the limited services between them are subject to disruption by sea and weather conditions. However, the lack of guided tours and strict schedules allows a restful holiday to those who have the time to allow for delays in shipping between islands to see the variety of lifestyles.

SIKKIM

The small, once independent, Himalayan state of Sikkim has been described as the land of mountains and orchids. It has the third-highest mountain in the world, the 8,585-m Kanchenjunga. The 22nd state of the Indian union, it is bounded by Tibet in the north and Bhutan in the east, Nepal in the west and West Bengal in the south.

Sikkim offers the tourist an eyeful of nature's grandeur. The magnificent vistas of ice-clad peaks framed by dense tropical vegetation, forested slopes and ridges, fast-flowing rivers plus its natural tranquillity, makes Sikkim a truly unique experience.

Hotel accommodation has increased in quantity and quality in recent years. A number of private and government hotels have been developed in various parts of the state. Apart from the **Norkhill**, the other hotel in Gangtok which offers a high standard of service is the newer **Tashi Delek**. Both offer a variety of Chinese, Western and Indian dishes.

HOTEL GUIDE

Hotel address	Phone	Fax	Telex	Cable	〜	🍴	🍷

A (US$100 or above) **B** (US$70-100) **C** (US$40-70) **D** (Under US$40)

AGRA
B

Hotel address	Phone	Fax	Telex	Cable	〜	🍴	🍷
Welcomgroup Mughal Sheraton Fatehabad Rd, Taj Ganj	64701-30		0565-375	WELCOTEL	▲	▲	▲
Taj View Fatehabad Rd, Taj Ganj	64171-75		0565-202 TAJVIN.	TAJVIEW	▲	▲	▲

C

Hotel address	Phone	Fax	Telex	Cable	〜	🍴	🍷
Agra Ashok The Mall	76223-27		0565-313	ASHOKOTEL	▲	▲	
Clarks Shiraz Taj Rd	72421		0565-211	SHIRAZ AGRA	▲	▲	▲

D

Hotel address	Phone	Fax	Telex	Cable	〜	🍴	🍷
Mumtaz Fatehabad Rd	64771-5		0565-222	MUMTAZTEL		▲	
Amar Fatehabad Rd	65696-98		0565-341 AMAR IN.			▲	▲
Grand Station Rd	74014			GRANDHOTEL		▲	
Shahanshah Inn Fatehabad Rd	6500		0565-212			▲	▲

AHMEDABAD
C

Hotel address	Phone	Fax	Telex	Cable	〜	🍴	🍷
Cama Khanpur Rd	25281		0121-6377 CAMA IN.	HOTELCAMA	▲	▲	

D

Hotel address	Phone	Fax	Telex	Cable	〜	🍴	🍷
Karnavati Ashram Rd	402161		0121-6519 CSCO IN.	SHREE HOTEL		▲	▲
Natraj Ashram Rd	448747		021-6685 SHIV IN.	ATITHI		▲	
Riviera Khanpur	24201		021-6598 STAY IN.	RIVERHOTEL		▲	▲

Hotel address	Phone	Fax	Telex	Cable	〜	🍴	🍽
AHMEDABAD – *Cont'd* **D**							
Siddharta Palace Shahibag Dafnala	66505, 67736			CHARMING		▲	▲
Ambassador Khanpur Rd	353244, 342245			HOTAMBASS			
Capri Tilak Rd (Relief Rd)	354643-46			CAPRI		▲	
KINGSWAY Relief Rd	26221-5			KINGSWAY			
Capital Chandanwadi, Mirazpur Khanpur	24633-7			HOTCAP		▲	
Balwas Relief Rd	351135					▲	
Prithvi International L. G. Corner, Maninagar	366634					▲	
ALLAHABAD **D**							
Presidency Sarojini Naidu Marg	60097, 60460				▲	▲	▲
Allahabad Regency Tashkant Marg.	56043, 56735				▲	▲	▲
Yatrik Sardar Patel Marg	56920, 56020				▲	▲	
Samrat M. G. Marg, Civil Lines	60888, 60081					▲	▲
Taoosi Stanley Rd	56377			TAOOSI		▲	
Milan Leader Rd	56021, 36721					▲	
AMRITSAR **D**							
Airlines Cooper Rd	44545			PANKAJ		▲	

Hotel address	Phone	Fax	Telex	Cable	〰	🍴	🍽
AMRITSAR – *Cont'd*							
D							
Mohan International Albert Rd	34146		384-291		▲	▲	
Ritz The Mall	44199		384-242	RITZHOTEL	▲	▲	
Amritsar International Amritsar	31991					▲	▲
AURANGABAD							
C							
Welcomgroup Rama International R-3 Chikalthana	82340-44		0745-212 RAMA IN	WELCOTEL	▲	▲	
Ajanta Ambassador Chikalthana	82211, 82215		0745-211 AMBA IN	AMBASSADOR	▲	▲	▲
D							
Aurangabad Ashok Dr Rajendra Prasad Marg	24520-29		0745-229	TOURISM	▲	▲	
BANGALORE							
B							
Welcomgroup Windsor Manor Sankey Rd	79431		0845-8209 WIND IN	WELCOTEL	▲	▲	▲
C							
Holiday Inn Sankey Rd	79451		0845-354 MARCHIN		▲	▲	▲
Bangalore Ashok Kumara Krupa High Grounds	79411		0845-2433	ASHOKOTEL	▲	▲	▲
West End Race Course Rd	29281		0845-337 WEND IN	WESTEND	▲	▲	▲
Taj Residency MG Rd	568888		0845-8367 TBLR IN	RESIDENT	▲	▲	▲
D							
Gateway Hotel Residency Rd	573265-9		0845-2567 LUX IN	GETAWAY, BANGALORE	▲	▲	
Harsha Venkataswamy Naidu Rd, Shivajinagar	565566		0845-561	HOTHARSHA	▲	▲	

Hotel address	Phone	Fax	Telex	Cable	〰	🍴	🍷
BANGALORE – *Cont'd* **D**							
Bangalore Int'l Crescent Rd	25801-7		0845-2340	SWEETOME		▲	
BARODA **C**							
Express R. C. Dutt Rd	67051		0175-311	EXPRESSHOTEL		▲	▲
D							
Utsav Prof. Manekrao Rd	51415		0175-274	UTSAV		▲	
Surya Sayajiganj	66592		0175-482	SURYA		▲	▲
BHOPAL **D**							
Hotel Panchanan New Market	551647						
Lake View Ashok Shamla Hills	540452						
Jehan Numa Palace Shamla Hills	540100-109			JEHANUMA		▲	▲
Ramsons Int'l Hamidia Rd	72298-99			SETHIBROS		▲	▲
Rajdoot Hamidia Rd	72691-92			RAJDOOT		▲	▲
Hotel Surya Sheraton Hamidia Rd	76925-26						
Hotel Siddhartha Hamidia Rd	75680						
Hotel Mayur Berasia Rd	76418-19						
Hotel Taj Hamidia Rd	73161-68						

Hotel address	Phone	Fax	Telex	Cable	〰	🍴	🍷
BHUBANESWAR							
C							
Oberoi Bhubaneswar Nayapalli	56116				▲	▲	
D							
Kalinga Ashok Gautam Nagar	53318		0675-282	TOURISM	▲	▲	▲
Swosti Janpath	54179			SWOSTI		▲	
Prachi Janpath, Unit III	52689		0675-278	DESTINY			
The Kennilworth Gautam Nagar	53330		0675-343	SWAGATAM	▲	▲	
Safari Int'l Rasulgarh	54240		0675-345	SAFARI		▲	▲
Nagpur Janpath	54254					▲	
Hotel Meghdoot	55802						
BIKANER							
D							
Hotel Lallgarh Palace	3263, 5963			PALACE	▲	▲	
Hotel Karni Bhawan Palace	3308						
Hotel Gajner Palace Gajner	3915						
Hotel Joshi Station Rd	6162					▲	
Hotel Thar Ambedkar Circle	6480					▲	▲
BODHGAYA							
D							
Hotel Bodhgaya Ashok nr Archaeological Museum	22708-9 (Gaya exchange)			TOURISM		▲	▲

139

Hotel address	Phone	Fax	Telex	Cable	〰	🍽	🍸
BOMBAY							
A							
The Leela Kempinski Sahar	6363636		011-79236, 011-79241 KEMP IN			▲	▲
Oberoi Bombay Adjacent to Oberoi Towers	2025757				▲	▲	▲
Taj Mahal Hotel & Taj Mahal Inter-Continental Apollo Bunder	2023366		011-24411 TAJB IN	INHOTELS, BOMBAY	▲	▲	▲
Welcomgroup SeaRock Sheraton Land's End, Bandra	6425421		011-71230		▲	▲	▲
B							
Centaur Bombay Airport	6126660		011-71171		▲	▲	▲
Centaur Juhu Beach Tara Rd	6143040		011-78181 THJB			▲	
Holiday Inn Balraj Sahani Rd, Juhu Beach	6204444		011-71266, 011-71432		▲	▲	
Oberoi Towers Nariman Point	2024343		011-4153, 011-4154	OBHOTEL	▲	▲	▲
President Cuffe Parade, Colaba	4950808		011-4135		▲	▲	
C							
Ambassador Veer Nariman Rd, Churchgate Extn.	2041131		011-2918	EMBASSY		▲	▲
Fariyas Off Arthur Bunder Rd	2042911		011-3272	FARIYAS	▲	▲	
Horizon Juhu Beach	6148100		011-71218	BEACHREST	▲	▲	▲
Natraj Marine Drive	2044161		011-2302			▲	▲
Ramada Inn Palm Grove Juhu Beach	6149395		011-71419		▲	▲	
Ritz J. Tata Rd	220141		011-2520	RITZ		▲	▲
Sea Princess Juhu Tara Rd	6129865						
Sun-n-Sand Juhu Beach	6204945		011-71282	SUNANDSAND	▲	▲	▲

Hotel address	Phone	Fax	Telex	Cable	〰	🍴	🍷
BOMBAY – *Cont'd*							
C							
West End New Marine Lines	299121		011-2892	BESTIN		▲	
D							
Airport Plaza Nehru Rd, Santa Cruz Airport	6123390		011-71365		▲	▲	▲
Ajanta Juhu Rd	6124890			BEACHSIDE		▲	▲
Apollo Lansdowne Rd	2020223			APOLLOTEL		▲	▲
Ascot Garden Rd	240020		011-6261	ASCOHOTEL			
Diplomat Mereweather Rd	2021661					▲	
Garden Garden Rd	241476						
Godwin Garden Rd	241226			HOSHEE		▲	▲
Grand Sprott Rd, Ballard Estate	2613558, 2618212			GRANDHOTEL		▲	▲
Hilltop Worli Sea Face	4930860		011-71361	ONDEROCKS		▲	▲
Jal Nehru Rd	6123820		011-71037				
Kings Juhu Tara Rd	579141						
Kumaria Presidency Andheri Kurla Rd	6343882					▲	
Mayura Linking Rd, Khar	545561					▲	
Metropole Paltan Rd	266338						
Regency Nepean Sea Rd	8120002					▲	
Riviera Juhu Rd	628122			HOTRIVER	▲	▲	▲
Royal Inn Opp Khar Telephone Exchange	539888					▲	
Rosewood Tulsiwadi, Tardeo	4940322					▲	

Hotel address	Phone	Fax	Telex	Cable	〜〜	ᵢᵢ	▽
BOMBAY – *Cont'd*							
D							
Sahil J. B. Behram Marg	391423						
Samrat 3rd Rd, Khar	535441		011-71063			▲	
Sea Green Marine Drive	222386			SEZHOTEL		▲	▲
Sea King Juhu Tara Rd	6128225		011-71429			▲	▲
Sea Side Juhu Beach	621972						
Shalimar August Kranti Marg	8221311					▲	
Transit Off Nehru Rd	6121087					▲	▲
Host-Inn Int'l Marol Naka, Andheri Kurla Rd	6360105					▲	
CALCUTTA							
A							
Oberoi Grand J. L. Nehru Rd	292323		021-7248, 021-7854	OBHOTEL	▲	▲	▲
B							
Taj Bengal Belvedere Rd	283939	033281766	021-5718			▲	▲
Park Hotel Park St	297336		021-5912	PARKOTEL	▲	▲	▲
C							
Hotel Airport Ashok Calcutta Dum Dum Airport	575111		021-2271	AIRPORTEL	▲	▲	▲
Hindusthan Int'l AJC Bose Rd	442394		021-7167	MODERN	▲	▲	▲
D							
Great Eastern Hotel Old Court House St	282331		021-7571	GREATERN		▲	▲

Hotel address	Phone	Fax	Telex	Cable	≋	🍴	🍷
CALCUTTA – *Cont'd*							
D							
The Astor Hotel Shakespeare Sarani	449957		021-2020	KINGCOLE		▲	▲
New Kenilworth Int'l Little Russell St	448394-99		021-3395	NEWKEN		▲	▲
Hotel Rutt-Deen Loudon St	431691		021-8163	RUTT-DEEN		▲	▲
Lytton Hotel Sudder St	291872		021-3562	LYTTOTEL		▲	▲
Fair Lawn Hotel Sudder St	244460			FAIROTEL		▲	▲
Hotel Minerva Ganesh Chandra Ave	263365, 264505						
Hotel Shalimar Banerjee Rd	285030					▲	▲
CHANDIGARH							
D							
Hotel Chandigarh Mountview Sector 10	21257, 21583		0395-337	MOUNTVIEW		▲	▲
Hotel Piccadily Sector 22-B	32223-7		PICC IN 0395-256	PICCOTEL		▲	▲
Hotel Sunbean Sector 22	32057, 41335		0395-444	SUNBEAM		▲	▲
Hotel President Sector 26	40840-44		0395-490 HYG IN	COMFORTS		▲	▲
Hotel Maya Palace Sector 35-B	32118					▲	▲
Hotel Kapil Sector 35-B	33366						
COCHIN							
C							
Malabar Hotel Willingdon Island	6811		0885-661 MLBR IN	COMFORT	▲	▲	▲

Hotel address	Phone	Fax	Telex	Cable	〰	🍴	🍽
COCHIN – *Cont'd* **D**							
Casino Hotel Willingdon Island	6821		0885-6314 SAFE IN	CASINO	▲	▲	▲
Bolgathy Palace Hotel	355003			RELAX			
Hotel Presidency Paramara Rd	363100		0885-6201 TOUR IN	ASHOKOTEL		▲	
Abad Plaza M. G. Rd	361636		0885-6587 ABAD IN			▲	
COONOOR **D**							
Ritz Hotel Orange Grove Rd	6242, 6465			RITZ		▲	▲
Hampton Manor	6244, 6961-64			HAMPTON		▲	
DALHOUSIE **D**							
Aroma-n-Clair Court Rd	99			AROMAHOTEL		▲	
Grand View Bus Stand	20, 94			GRANDVIEW		▲	▲
DARJEELING **D**							
Hotel Sinclairs Gandhi Rd	3431-2			SINCLAIRS		▲	▲
Hotel New Elgin H. D. Lama Rd	3314, 2882			NEW ELGIN		▲	▲
Hotel Windamere Observatory Hill	2841, 2397		201 WNDH IN	WINDAMERE		▲	▲
Hotel Central Robertson Rd	2033, 2746			NADAM		▲	
Hotel Valentino Rockville Rd	2228					▲	▲

Hotel address	Phone	Fax	Telex	Cable	〰	🍴	🍽
DEHRA DUN **C**							
Madhuban Rajpur Rd	24094			MADHUBAN		▲	▲
President Astley Hall	27082			PRESTRAVEL		▲	
Hotel Nidhi Rajpur Rd **D**	24611						
Kwality Rajpur Rd	27001			KWALITY			
GANGTOK **D**							
Tashi Delek M. G. Rd	2038, 2991			TASHIDELEK		▲	▲
Nor Khill Paljor Namgyal Stadium Rd	3186, 3187			NOR KHILL		▲	▲
Mayur Stadium Rd	2752, 2825			SIKKIM TOURISM		▲	▲
Tibet Stadium Rd	2523, 2568					▲	▲
GOA **C**							
The Aguada Hermitage and Fort Aguada Beach Resort Singuerim	87501-9		0194-291 TAJ IN	FORT AQUADA, GOA	▲	▲	▲
Taj Holiday Village Singuerim	87514-17		01946206 TAJ IN	FORTAGUADA, GOA	▲	▲	▲
Hotel Oberoi Bogmalo Beach Bogmalo	2191-92		0191-297 OBGA IN	OBHOTEL	▲	▲	▲

Hotel address	Phone	Fax	Telex	Cable	〰	🍴	🥤
GOA – *Cont'd*							
C							
Majorda Beach Resort Majorda, Salcete	20025		0196-234 MBR	MBR		▲	
Cidade De Goa Vainguinim Beach, Dona Paula	3301-7		0194-257 DONA IN	WELCOTEL	▲	▲	▲
Ronil Beach Resort Baga	Calangute 68		0194-252 ALCON IN	ALCON			
D							
Fidalgo 18th June Rd, Panaji	6291-99		0194-213 REST IN	MABEREST	▲	▲	▲
Mandovi D. B. Bandodkar Marg	6270-9		0194-226 SHOME IN	MANDOVI		▲	▲
Keni's Hotel 18th June Rd, Panaji	4581-3			KENIHOTEL		▲	▲
Hotel Nova Goa Dr Atmaram Borkar Rd, Panaji	6231-39						
Hotel Metropole Avenida Concessao Margo	21169						
La Paz Gardens Vasco da Gama	21216		0194-291			▲	▲
Hotel Golden Goa Dr Atmaram Borkar Rd, Panaji	6231-39						
Dona Paula Beach Resort Dona Paula	4255-6			OPESCADOR			
Hotel Airport Airport Rd, Chicalim	3192		0191-318 SHON IN				
Hotel Summit Menezes Braganza Rd	5309		0194-212 KMSF IN	SUMMIT			
GULMARG							
D							
Hotel Hilltop	245, 277			HILLTOP		▲	▲
Hotel Highlands Park	207, 230			HIGHLANDS		▲	▲
Hotel Asia Green Heights	204			ASIAOTEL		▲	▲
Hotel Pine Palace	266			GLACIER		▲	

Hotel address	Phone	Fax	Telex	Cable	〰	🍴	🍸
GULMARG – *Cont'd*							
D							
Hotel Nedou's	223			NEDOU'S		▲	
Hotel Welcome	212			SAFETY		▲	
Hotel Affarwat	202					▲	▲
GUWAHATI							
D							
Brahamaputra Ashok M. G. Rd	32632-33		0235-2422	BRAHMASHOK		▲	▲
Hotel Coronet Dynasty S. S. Rd	24353		0235-2362			▲	
Hotel Belle Vue M. G. Rd	28639-41			BELLEVIEW		▲	▲
Hotel Urvashi nr Guwahati Airport	28893					▲	▲
Hotel Kuber Int'l Hem Barua Rd	32601		0235-2251	HOTELKUMBER		▲	
Hotel Chilarai Regency H. P. Brahmachari Rd, Paltan Bazar	26877		0235-2401	REGENCY		▲	▲
Hotel Prag Continental Motilal Nehru Rd, Pan Bazar	33785-87		0235-2403	ATITHI		▲	▲
Hotel Siddharth Hem Barua Rd, Fancy Bazar	33746-49			SIDDHARTH		▲	▲
Hotel Pragjyotish Paltan Bazar	27882					▲	▲
Hotel Empire Hem Barua Rd	31670		0235-2377	EMPIRE		▲	▲
GWALIOR							
C							
Welcomgroup Usha Kiran Palace Jayendraganj	23453			USHA KIRAN		▲	▲
D							
Hotel Tansen Gandhi Rd	21568					▲	

Hotel address	Phone	Fax	Telex	Cable	〰	🍴	🍽
GWALIOR – *Cont'd* **D**							
President Station Rd	24673						
Fort View M. L. B. Rd	23409						
HYDERABAD **B**							
Krishna Oberoi Banjara Hills **C**	222121		0425-6931 OBH IN	OBH-IN	▲	▲	
Gateway Hotel Banjara Hills	222222	0842-222218	0425-6947 GATE IN	BANJARA	▲	▲	▲
Bhaskar Palace Ashok Banjara Hills **D**	226141		0425-6182 BPA IN		▲	▲	▲
Basera Sarojini Devi Rd, Secunderabad	843200		0425-6152				
Ritz Hillfort Palace	233571		0425-6215		▲	▲	▲
Sampurna Int'l M. I. Rd	40165					▲	
Ashoka Lakdi-ka-pul	230077			PROHOTEL			
Asrani Int'l M. G. Rd	842267			ASRANIS			▲
Deccan Continental Minister Rd	840981		0425-665	HOTDECON			
Emerald Chirag Ali Lane Abids	237835			STAYFINE	▲	▲	▲
Karan Sarojini Devi Rd	840191-3			MALWALA		▲	▲
Nagarjuna Basheerbagh	237201		0425-6260	MAGNIFIQUE		▲	▲
Parklane Parklane Rd, Secunderabad	70148		0425-6679	HIARCHES		▲	▲

Hotel address	Phone	Fax	Telex	Cable	〰	🍴	🍽
HYDERABAD – *Cont'd*							
D							
President Mozzamshahi Market	44444						▲
Sarovar Secretariat Rd	237642		0425-66425	SAROVAR			▲
INDORE							
C							
Indotels Manor House A. B. Rd	33121-9		0735-273				▲
D							
Kanchan	33394-97						▲
Ambassador	33216						▲
Shreemaya RNT Marg	34151						▲
JAIPUR							
B							
Rambagh Palace Bhawani Singh Rd	75141	(0141) 73798	03652254 RBAG IN	RAMBAGH, JAIPUR	▲	▲	▲
C							
Rajmahal Palace Sardar Patel Marg	61257	(0141) 73798	0365-313	RESIDENCY	▲	▲	
Jai Mahal Palace Jacob Rd	68381	(0141) 68337	03652250 JMPH IN	JAIMAHAL, JAIPUR		▲	▲
Ramgarh Lodge Jamuva	75141	(0141) 73798	03652254 RBAG IN			▲	
Clarks Amer Jawaharlal Nehru Marg	822616		0365-276	CLARKSAMER	▲	▲	
Hotel Mansingh Sansar Chandra Rd	78771		0365-2344 WICO IN	WELCOMTEL		▲	▲
D							
Jaipur Ashok Collectorate Circle	75171		0365-2262	ASHOKOTEL	▲	▲	▲

Hotel address	Phone	Fax	Telex	Cable	≈	⑪	⬛
JAIPUR – *Cont'd* **D**							
Meru Palace Sawai Ram Singh Rd	61212-5		0365-2259	HOTELMERU		▲	
Narain Niwas Narain Singh Rd	65448		0365-2482	NARAINNIWAS	▲	▲	▲
Lakshmi Vilas Sawai Ram Singh Rd	61368-9			LAKSHMI		▲	
Khasa Kothi M. I. Rd	75151-5		0365-431	KHASA KOTHI	▲	▲	▲
Gangaur Tourist Hotel M. I. Rd	60231-7					▲	▲
L. M. B. Johari Bazar	48844			ALAMBE		▲	
Jaipur Emerald M. I. Rd	70476			LUXURY		▲	▲
Aditya Bhawani Singh Rd	75726		0365-2428	ARTAGE		▲	▲
JAISALMER **C**							
Himmatgarh Palace Ramgarh Rd	2213					▲	
Jawahar Niwas Palace	2208			JAWAHAR		▲	
Narayan Niwas Palace Malka Rd	2408			JAISAL		▲	▲
JAMMU **D**							
Ashok Jammu Tawi Opp. Amar Mahal	43127		0377-227 ASOK IN	TOURISM	▲	▲	▲
Asia Jammu-Tawi Nehru Market	49430		0377-224 ASIA IN	ASIAOTEL	▲	▲	▲
COSMO Veer Marg	47561			COSMOHOTEL		▲	

Hotel address	Phone	Fax	Telex	Cable	~~~	▮▮	�ображ
JAMMU – *Cont'd* **D**							
Premier Veer Marg	43234					▲	
Mansar Denis Gate	46161					▲	▲
Moti Mahal Gurdwara Sunder Singh Rd	43307					▲	
JODHPUR **C**							
Welcomgroup Umaid Bhawan Palace **D**	22366		0552-202	WELCOTEL	▲	▲	
Ratanada Int'l Residency Rd	31910-14		0552-233	POLO	▲	▲	▲
Ajit Bhawan nr Circuit House	20409					▲	
Karni Bhawan Defence Laboratory Rd	20157			KARNIMA		▲	▲
Ghoomar Tourist Hotel High Court Rd						▲	
KHAJURAHO **C**							
Chandela	54	TACH IN	01501-201	CHANDELA	▲	▲	▲
Jass Oberoi **D**	66, 85-89				▲	▲	
Hotel Payal	76						
Khajuraho Ashok	24					▲	

151

Hotel address	Phone	Fax	Telex	Cable	〰	🍴	🍷
KANPUR **D**							
Meghdoot The Mall	211999		0325-282 A/B MGDT IN	MEGHOTEL	▲	▲	▲
Grand Trunk G. T. Rd	245435			PIGMENTS	▲	▲	
Geet The Mall	211042-46			GEETINN		▲	
Saurabh Birhana Rd	67971			TEWARIBROS		▲	
KOVALAM (*TRIVANDRUM* **)** **C**							
Kovalam Ashok Beach Resort Trivandrum **D**	68010		0435-216 KBR IN	TOURISM VIZHINJAM	▲	▲	▲
Hotel Samudra	62089			SAMUDRA		▲	▲
Hotel Palmanova Vizhinjam	494					▲	▲
Hotel Neptune Light House Beach	548 (Vizhinjam)						
Raja Hotel Vizhinjam	355 (Vizhinjam)			RAJDOOT		▲	
LUCKNOW **C**							
Clarks Avadh Mahatma Gandhi Marg **D**	24031-33		0535-243	AVADH		▲	▲
Hotel Carlton Shahnajaf Rd	244021-24		0535-217	CARLTON		▲	▲
Hotel Kohinoor Station Rd	35421			SAPNA		▲	▲
Charans International Vidhan Sabha Marg	2472-21					▲	
Hotel Deep Avadh Naka Hindola	36521-25					▲	

Hotel address	Phone	Fax	Telex	Cable	〰	🍴	🍽
LUCKNOW – *Cont'd* **D**							
Taj Lucknow Vipin Khand (expected opening late 1990)							
MADRAS **A**							
Welcomgroup Park Sheraton Mowbrays Rd **C**	452525		041 6868		▲	▲	▲
Taj Coromandel Nungambakkam High Rd	474849	(044) 470070	041 7194 TAJM IN	HOTELORENT, MADRAS	▲	▲	▲
Connemara Hotel Binny Rd	860123	(044) 860193	041 8197 CH IN	CONNEMARA, MADRAS	▲	▲	
Fisherman's Cove Chingleput Dist	6268	(044) 470070	041 7194 TAJM IN	FISHCOVE, MADRAS	▲	▲	▲
Welcomgroup Chola Sheraton Cathedral Rd	473347		041 7200		▲	▲	▲
Trident G. S. T. Rd	434747	(044) 434343	041 26055	TRIDENT HOT	▲	▲	▲
Ambassador Pallava Montieth Rd **D**	868584		041-7453 AMB PIN	PALAMBAS	▲	▲	▲
Savera Dr Radhakrishnan Rd	474700		041-6896	SAVERA	▲	▲	▲
Madras Int'l Anna Salai	861811		041-7373	HOTELINTER		▲	▲
Sindoori Greames Lane	477197		041-8859 SIND IN			▲	▲
New Victoria Hotel Kennet Lane, Egmore	8253638		041-7897	HOTEL VICKY		▲	▲
Shrilekha Inter-Continental Anna Salai	453132		041-6873	LEKHA		▲	▲
President Dr Radhakrishnan Rd	832211		041-6699	GAYTIME	▲	▲	▲

Hotel address	Phone	Fax	Telex	Cable	〰	🍴	🍵
MADRAS – *Cont'd* **D**							
Palmgrove Kodambakkam High Rd	471441		041-7115	HOTELPALM		▲	▲
MAMALLAPURAM (*MAHABALIPURAM*) **D**							
Temple Bay Ashok Beach Resort	251, 252, 253			TOURISM	▲	▲	▲
Shore Temple Beach Resort	235, 268				▲	▲	
Silver Sands Beach Village	228, 283			VEECUMSEES		▲	▲
Golden Sun Hotel & Beach Resort	245, 246			GOLDENSUN	▲	▲	▲
Ideal Beach Resort Kovalam Rd	240, 243				▲	▲	▲
MANALI **D**							
Hotel Piccadily The Mall	113,114		03904-205	PICCOTEL		▲	▲
Hotel Preet NH 21	129		03904-206			▲	▲
Hotel Panchratan Resorts nr Log Huts	164-172					▲	▲
Hotel Holiday Home Int'l Zarim Resorts nr Circuit House	101			NEERMAL		▲	▲
Zarim Resorts	252					▲	▲
MADURAI **D**							
Pandyan Race Course	42471		0445-214	TEMPLECITY		▲	▲
Madurai Ashok Alagarkoil Rd	42531		0445-297	TOURISM	▲	▲	▲
Supreme West Perumal Maistry St	36331		0445-232	SUPREME		▲	▲

Hotel address	Phone	Fax	Telex	Cable	≋	🍴	🥣
MANGALORE **D**							
Welcomgroup Manjarun Old Port Rd	31791		0832-316 WELH IN	WELCOTEL	▲	▲	
Moti Mahal Falnir Rd	21222		0832-314	MOTI MAHAL	▲	▲	▲
Summer Sands Ullal	6400			SUMMERSAND	▲	▲	▲
Vimlesh Int'l G. H. S. Rd	31575			CHEKKIN		▲	
MUSSOORIE **C**							
Savoy Hotel Library Area	2510, 2601			SAVOY		▲	▲
Hotel Classic Library Area **D**	2297						
Shilton Hotel Library Area	2842			SHILTON			
Padmini Niwas Bet Library & Ropeway	2793						
Hotel Holiday Inn Bet Library & Ropeway	2693						
Hotel Hill Queen Ropeway Area	2868						
Hotel Mid Town Ropeway Area	2558						
Brentwood Hotel Ropeway Area	2702, 2536						
Hotel Samrat Ropeway Area	2707						
Shiva Continental Ropeway Area	2980			SHIVA			

India

Hotel address	Phone	Fax	Telex	Cable	〰	🍴	🍲
MYSORE C							
Lalitha Mahal Palace Hotel T. Narasipur Rd D	26316		0846-217	TOURISM	▲	▲	▲
Quality Inn Southern Star Vinobha Rd	27217-9		0846-256 OSSM IN		▲	▲	▲
Hotel Metropole Jhansi Lakshmi Bai Rd	10681, 20871		0846-214 RITZ IN	METROPOLE		▲	▲
Rajendra Vilas Palace Chamundi Hills	22050		0846-231 HRVI-IN	PALASCHAIN		▲	▲
Dasprakash Paradise Vivekananda Rd, Yadavgiri	26666		0846-266 DASA-IN	PARADISE		▲	▲
Kings Court Hotel Jhansi Lakshmi Bai Rd	25250		0846-263 KING-IN	KINGSCOURT		▲	▲
Ritz Hotel Krishnarajasagar			0846-214 RITZ IN			▲	▲
NAINITAL C							
The Naini Retreat Ayarpatta Slopes D	2108, New Delhi 656147			RETREAT		▲	▲
Vikram Vintage Inn Mallital	2877			VINTAGE INN	▲	▲	▲
Hotel Arif Castles Mallital	2801-3		05703-201	CASTLES	▲	▲	▲
Shervani Hilltop Inn Mallital	2504			HILLTOPINN		▲	▲
Hotel Swiss Mallital	2603					▲	▲
Hotel Royal Mallital	2007			ROYAL		▲	▲
Hotel Armadale Mallital	2855			ARMADALE		▲	

Hotel address	Phone	Fax	Telex	Cable	〰	🍴	🥣
NEW DELHI							
A							
Taj Mahal Mansingh Rd	3016162	(011) 301-7299	031-4758 TAJD IN	TAJDEL	▲	▲	▲
Holiday Inn Crowne Palace Barakhambha Ave	3320101	3325353	031-61186 HIND IN		▲	▲	▲
Le Meridien Windsor Place	383960		031-63076/ 4397	MERID HOTEL	▲	▲	▲
The Oberoi Dr Zakir Hussain Marg	363030	(011) 238347	031-63222		▲	▲	▲
Welcomgroup Maurya Sheraton Diplomatic Enclave	3010101	(011) 3010908	031-61447	WELCOTEL	▲	▲	▲
B							
Taj Palace Inter-Continental Sardar Patel Marg	3010404	(011) 301-1252	031-62756 TAJS IN		▲	▲	▲
Ashok Chanakyapuri	600412		031-6527 ASHOK IN	ASHOKAHOTEL	▲	▲	▲
Hyatt Regency Delhi Ring Rd	609911	678833	031-61512 HYT IN		▲	▲	▲
Park Parliament St	352477		031-66598	PARKOTEL	▲	▲	
Samrat Chanakyapuri	603030		031-73122	HOTEL SMRAT	▲	▲	▲
Vasant Continental Vasant Vihar	678800		031-72263	CONTIHOTEL	▲	▲	▲
C							
Ambassador Sujan Singh Park	690391		031-74177 MISR IN			▲	
Centaur Delhi Airport	5481411		031-62744, 5477	CENTAUR	▲	▲	▲
Claridges Aurangzed Rd	3010211		031-71266	CLARIDGES	▲	▲	▲
Janpath Janpath	3320070		031-61546	RESTWELL		▲	▲
Kanishka Ashok Rd	3324422		031-62788	KANISHOTEL	▲	▲	▲
Imperial Janpath	3325332	91-11- 3324542	031-62603		▲	▲	▲

Hotel address	Phone	Fax	Telex	Cable	≋	🍴	🍽
NEW DELHI – *Cont'd*							
C							
Oberoi Maidens Sham Nath Marg	2525464	(011) 238347	031-66303	OBMAIDENS	▲	▲	
Qutab off Sri Aurobindo Marg	660060		031-62537	QUTABOTEL	▲	▲	
Siddharth Rajendra Place	5712511		031-61293	IRONHOTEL	▲	▲	
Sofitel Surya New Friends Colony	6835070		031-66700	SUROTEL	▲	▲	▲
Ranjit Maharaja Ranjit Sing Marg	3311256		031-66001	STAYWELL	▲	▲	▲
D							
Diplomat Sardar Patel Marg	3010205		031-61042	DIPLOMATIC		▲	▲
Lodhi Lala Lajpat Rai Marg	362422		031-74068	LIVEWELL	▲	▲	▲
Marina Connaught Place	3322698		031-62969	MARINA			
Nirula's Connaught Place	3322419		031-66224	NIRLABROS		▲	▲
York's Connaught Place	3323769			YORKHOTEL		▲	▲
OOTACAMUND							
C							
Savoy Hotel Club Rd	4142-49		0853240 SAHO IN	SAVOY, OOTACAMUND		▲	▲
D							
Southern Star Havelock Rd	3601-09		0853-249	QUALITY INN	▲	▲	
Nilgiris	3556-7					▲	
Fernhill Palace	3910		0853-246	PALASCHAIN		▲	▲
PAHALGAM							
C							
Hotel Senator Pine-N-Peek	11, 75					▲	▲

Hotel address	Phone	Fax	Telex	Cable	〰	🍴	🥣
PAHALGAM – *Cont'd*							
C							
Hotel Pahalgam	26, 52, 78				▲	▲	▲
Hotel Woodstock	27			WOODSTOCK		▲	▲
D							
Hotel Pine View	42, 70			PINEVIEW		▲	
Hotel Heevan	17			HEEVAN		▲	▲
Hotel Mountview	21			MOUNTVIEW		▲	▲
PATNA							
C							
Welcomgroup Maurya Patna Fraser Rd	222067-69		022-352	MAURYA	▲	▲	▲
D							
Pataliputra Ashok Birchand Patel Path	226270-79		022-311	ASHOKOTEL		▲	▲
Chanakya Birchand Patel Path	223141-42			SWAGAT		▲	▲
Samrat Int'l Fraser Rd	31841-43		022-405	SAMRAT		▲	▲
Republic Lawlys Bldg	55021-24		022-261	LYSWAL		▲	▲
Marwari Awas Griha Fraser Rd	31866-67		022-241	AWASGRIHA		▲	
Satkar Int'l Fraser Rd	31886-88			SATKAR		▲	▲
PONDICHERRY							
D							
Pondicherry Ashok Chinnakalapet	460-468 (Kalapet)		0469-239	PONDYASHOK		▲	
Mass Marai Malai Adigal Salai	27221			MASS		▲	▲

Hotel address	Phone	Fax	Telex	Cable	〰	🍴	🥣
PORT BLAIR (*ANDAMAN & NICOBAR ISLANDS*) **D**							
Andaman Beach Resort Corbyn's Cove	3381, 2599			TRAVELAIDS		▲	▲
Welcomgroup Bay Island Marine Hill	2881-88			WELCOTEL	▲	▲	▲
PUNE **D**							
Ajit Deccan Gymkhana	59076					▲	▲
Amir Connaught Rd	661840		0145-292	HOTEL AMIR		▲	▲
Blue Diamond Koregaon Rd	663775		0145-369		▲	▲	▲
Executive Ashok University Rd	57391		0145-565 HEAP IN	EXECOTEL	▲	▲	▲
Sagar Plaza Bund Garden Rd	661880				▲	▲	
PURI **D**							
Nilachal Ashok adj. Raj Bhawan Complex	2973				▲	▲	▲
Toshali Sands	2888				▲	▲	
S. E. Railway Hotel	2063			SURF		▲	
RISHIKESH **D**							
Ganga Kinare Virbhadra Rd	566			GANGA KINARE		▲	▲
Natraj Dehra Dun Rd	728			NATRAJ	▲	▲	▲
Baseraa Ghatt Rd	720, 767			BASERAA		▲	▲

Hotel address	Phone	Fax	Telex	Cable	〰	🍴	🍶
SHILLONG **D**							
Pinewood Ashok Shillong	23116		237-222 PINE IN	PINEWOOD		▲	▲
Alpine Continental Quinton Rd	25361			ALPOTEL		▲	▲
SHIMLA **C**							
Oberoi Clarkes The Mall **D**	6091-95			OBHOTEL		▲	▲
Woodville Palace The Mall	2722					▲	▲
Hotel Asia The Dawn Tara Devi	5858		0391-205		▲	▲	▲
Maharaja Fingask Estate	77788					▲	
Lords Grey Circular Rd	5146					▲	▲
SRINAGAR **C**							
Oberoi Palace Gupkar Rd	71241-42		0375-201 LXSR IN	OBHOTEL		▲	▲
Centaur Lake View Cheshma Shahi **D**	75631-33		0375-205 CLVH IN	CENTAUR	▲	▲	▲
Broadway Maulana Azad Rd	75621-3		0375-212	BROADWAY	▲	▲	▲
Shahenshah Palace Blvd	71345-46		0375-335 SPEC IN	SHAHENSHAH	▲	▲	▲
Welcome Blvd	74104			SAFETY		▲	▲
Asia Brown Palace Blvd	73903			ASIAOTEL		▲	▲

Hotel address	Phone	Fax	Telex	Cable	〰	🍴	🍽
SRINAGAR – *Cont'd* **D**							
Shah Abbas Blvd	79334		0375-273 YALI IN	RESTWELL		▲	▲
Zabarvan Blvd	71441-42		0375-269	FEELHOME		▲	▲
Zamrud Blvd	73123-24					▲	▲
Duke Blvd	79427			CARNES		▲	▲
Pari Mahal Blvd	71235			PARISTAN		▲	▲
Tramboo Continental Blvd	73914			HOST		▲	▲
Ahdoo's Residency Rd	72593			AHDOO'S		▲	▲
Green World Blvd	75050		0375-220	GREENWORLD		▲	
TIRUPATI **D**							
Vishnu Priya opp Central bus stand	20300		0403-246 HSVP IN	SRIVISH		▲	▲
Hotel Mayura T. P. Area	20901			KAMATH		▲	
Sree Oorvasi Int'l Renigunta Rd	20202			OORVASI		▲	
TRIVANDRUM (*KOVALAM*) **D**							
Mascot Palayam	68990		0435-229 KTDC		▲	▲	
Horizon Aristo Rd	66888		0435-546 HRZN IN			▲	
Pankaj M. G. Rd	76667		0435-323 PANKAJ-IN	PANKAJ		▲	
Geeth nr G. P. O.	71987		0435-318 GEET IN	GEETH HOTEL		▲	

Hotel address	Phone	Fax	Telex	Cable	〰	🍴	🍵
TRIVANDRUM (*KOVALAM*) – *Cont'd* **D**							
Luciya Continental East Fort	73443		0435-330 LUCY-IN			▲	▲
UDAIPUR **A**							
Shiv Niwas Palace City Palace **B**	28238-41		033-226	PALACE	▲	▲	▲
The Lake Palace Pichola Lake **C**	23241-5		033-203 LPAL IN	LAKEPALACE, UDAIPUR	▲	▲	▲
Laxmi Vilas Palace Fateh Sagar Rd **D**	24411-13			TOURISM	▲	▲	▲
Anand Bhawan Fateh Sagar Rd	23256-7			ANANDBHAWAN		▲	
Lake Pichola Chandpole	29197		033-257	PICHOLA		▲	
Hilltop Ambavgarh, Fateh Sagar	28708-9			HILLTOP		▲	▲
Lakend Fateh Sagar	23841			LAKEND	▲	▲	▲
Raj Darshan Pannabai Marg	23271-3			DARSHAN		▲	
Shikarbadi Goverdhanvilas	83201-5		033-227	IMPERIAL/ SIKARBADI	▲	▲	▲
Fountain Kumbha Marg	26646			FOUNTAIN		▲	▲
Meera Meera Marg	27554					▲	

Hotel address	Phone	Fax	Telex	Cable	≋	⫴	◪
VADODARA							
C							
Welcomgroup Vadodara R. C. Dutt Rd	323232		0175-525		▲	▲	▲
D							
Express R. C. Dutt Rd	323131	0265-325980	0175-488	EXPRESS HOTEL		▲	▲
Surya Palace opp. Parsi Agyari, Sayajigunj	329999		0175-500	JINDAL	▲	▲	▲
Surya Sayajigunj	328213-17		0175-482	SURYA		▲	▲
Express Alkapuri Alkapuri	325744	0265-325980	0175-488	EXPRESS ALKAPURI		▲	▲
Rama Inn Sayajigunj	329567		0175-668	RAMA INN	▲	▲	▲
VARANASI							
C							
Taj Ganges Nadesar Palace Grounds	42485		0545-219	TAJBEN	▲	▲	
Clarks Varanasi The Mall, Cantt	42401-06		0545-204	CLARKOTEL	▲	▲	▲
D							
Varanasi Ashok The Mall, Cantt	42551-59		0545-205	TOURISM	▲	▲	▲
Hindustan Int'l Maldahia	57075		0545-247			▲	
Pallavi Int'l Hathwa Market	54894			PALLAVI		▲	▲
Diamond Bhelupur	56561-66			DIAMOTEL		▲	▲
Hotel De Paris The Mall, Cantt	43582-85		0545-323	HOTELPARIS		▲	▲
Malti Vidyapith Rd	64703					▲	▲

Hotel address	Phone	Fax	Telex	Cable	〰	🍴	🥂
VIJAYAWADA **D**							
Kandhari Int'l Bandar Rd	471311		0475-271	HOT KAN		▲	▲
Manorama Bandar Rd	77221			BLISS		▲	▲
Mamata Eluru Rd	65251					▲	▲
VISAKHAPATNAM **D**							
Hotel Park Beach Rd	63081		0495-230	PARKOTEL	▲	▲	▲
Dolphin	64811		0495-316 HOST IN	DOLPHIN	▲	▲	
Aspara Waltair Main Rd	64861		0495-404	ASPARA		▲	▲
Palm Beach Beach Rd	54026-27		0495-436	PALMBEACH	▲	▲	▲

MALDIVES

The Republic of Maldives is one of the world's last remaining unspoilt, yet easily accessible, tropical-island paradises.

Its natural attractions include year-round sunshine, white sandy beaches and crystal-clear waters, offering a spectacular underworld of multi-coloured coral reefs teeming with an abundance of marine life. It is also a haven for seabirds.

An archipelago in the Indian Ocean, some 600 km southwest of India and Sri Lanka, the Maldives comprises 26 atolls and close to 1,200 islands, of which only 202 are inhabited. They form an 820-km-long chain, straddling the equator.

With a population of only 216,000, the Maldives is the smallest nation in South Asia. About 60,000 of its inhabitants live on Male, the capital, an island of only 1.5 km². And most of the tourist resorts are located on Male atoll, within a couple of hours' ferry ride from Male and the international Hulule airport.

Islam is the strength of Maldivian society and no other religion exists, or is permitted, among Maldivian citizens.

But while the Muslim faith is taken very seriously, Islam in the Maldives has its own unique character, a delicate blend of tradition and modernity. Women are much freer than in other Muslim countries.

The origins of the Maldivian people are shrouded in mystery but it is thought there was a Dravidian population from south India as early as the fourth century BC. Perhaps two millennia ago, a second wave of settlers, Aryans from India and Ceylon, came to dominate the islands. Archaeological findings and legends tell that the Maldivian people practised Buddhism before the sultan, converted by a Moroccan saint, embraced the Islamic faith in 1153 AD and then ordered that his country become Muslim.

Throughout history the Maldivians have depended for their livelihood on the sea, and most of the people have been involved in one way or another with fishing. Only Male, the capital the sultan has always lived, has urban traits acquired from the town's role as government and commercial centre of the country.

Although the Maldivians have never been conquered or ruled for long by any foreign power, they had to fight off Portuguese invaders several times in the 16th century and time and again they had to battle marauding pirates from southern India. The Maldivians, though never

very wealthy or major traders, always participated in the ancient Indian Ocean trading system borne annually by the monsoons. They were known in the trade for their cowrie shells, dried fish, ambergris and tortoise-shell.

In 1887, the Maldives became a protectorate of the British and in 1965 the country gained independence. Under the former president, Ibrahim Nasir, who was then prime minister under the last titular sultan, the Maldives became a republic in 1968 with an elected president and national assembly. The current president, elected on November 11, 1978, is Maumoon Abdul Gayoom, now in his third term of office. The country has no major industry — its main economic activities are fishing, shipping, tourism and coconut farming.

In November, 1988, there was a coup attempt launched by a disgruntled Maldivian businessman using Tamil mercenaries from Sri Lanka. The government survived, thanks to the intervention of Indian commandos. Tourism, which is now the Maldives' major foreign-exchange earner, was developed only relatively recently. In 1975, a mere 9,000 visitors were recorded. In 1988, there were 155,000.

◁ *Indian Ocean paradise.*
Photo: E. Colton

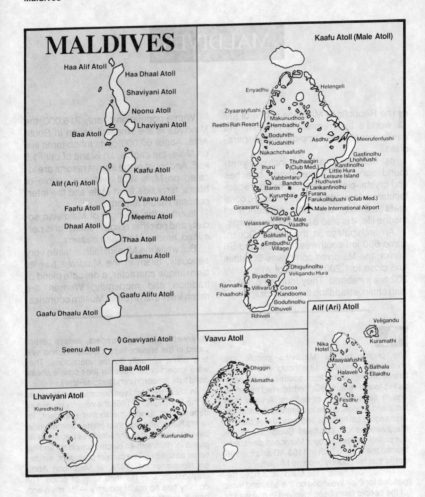

MALDIVES

Haa Alif Atoll
Haa Dhaal Atoll
Shaviyani Atoll
Noonu Atoll
Lhaviyani Atoll
Baa Atoll
Kaafu Atoll
Alif (Ari) Atoll
Vaavu Atoll
Faafu Atoll
Meemu Atoll
Dhaal Atoll
Thaa Atoll
Laamu Atoll
Gaafu Alifu Atoll
Gaafu Dhaalu Atoll
Gnaviyani Atoll
Seenu Atoll

Kaafu Atoll (Male Atoll)

Eriyadhu
Helengeli
Ziyaaraiyfushi
Makunudhoo
Reethi Rah Resort
Hembadhu
Boduhithi
Asdhu
Meerufenfushi
Kudahithi
Nakachchaafushi
Gasfinolhu
Lhohifushi
Thulhaagiri (Club Med.)
Kanifinolhu
Ihuru
Little Hura
Vabbinfaru
Leisure Island
Bandos
Hudhuveli
Baros
Lankanfinolhu
Kurumba
Furana
Farukolhufushi (Club Med.)
Giraavaru
Male International Airport
Villingili
Male
Velassaru
Vaadhu
Bolifushi
Embudhu Village
Dhigufinolhu
Biyadhoo
Veligandu Hura
Rannalhi
Villivaru
Cocoa
Fihaalhohi
Kandooma
Bodufinolhu
Olhuveli
Rihiveli

Baa Atoll
Kunfunadhu

Lhaviyani Atoll
Kuredhdhu

Vaavu Atoll
Dhiggiri
Alimatha

Alif (Ari) Atoll
Veligandu
Kuramathi
Nika Hotel
Maayaafushi
Bathala
Halaveli
Ellaidhu
Fesdhu

The Republic of Maldives is an archipelago in the central Indian Ocean. Today, a few visitors still come by sea, either on private yachts or freighters (about two full days from Colombo, Sri Lanka, for around US$40). But the primary means of visiting the Maldives now is by air to Hulule International Airport, adjacent to the capital island of Male.

Since the modernisation of Hulule Airport in 1981, it has been able to handle wide-body aircraft and direct charter flights operate from various points in Europe, the Maldives' major tourism market. Singapore Airlines also has three weekly scheduled Boeing 747 services into Male — an intermediate stop on its Singapore-Europe routes — and is due to start a fourth. The full economy round trip fare from Singapore is about US$976, though a range of discounted fares and all-inclusive package rates is available.

Direct scheduled flights to the Maldives are also operated daily from Colombo by Air Lanka (about US$177 for the round trip), twice weekly from Trivandrum in south India by Indian Airlines (US$129) and, on an irregular basis, from Colombo and Madras by Maldives Airways.

The Air Maldives agency in Male (Tel: 322 4368) handles bookings for all airlines. Bookings are usually quite heavy, especially during the tourist season from December to March. There is a passenger service charge of US$7 for each outgoing passenger. It is advisable to book your return flight when making an inward booking.

Until 1978, Maldives was one of the few countries in the world that did not require a passport from visitors, but today a valid passport is needed. No visa is required for landing at Male, where a 30-day visa is granted automatically. On expiry of this period, extension is granted for a further 60 days.

Any visitor coming from areas infected with cholera and/or yellow fever must have certificates of inoculation. This also applies to those transiting affected areas. Persons coming from malaria-infected areas are requested to give a blood sample. The Maldives has mosquitoes but reportedly no malaria, though visitors venturing beyond Male or the resort islands would be wise to take anti-malaria pills as a precaution.

The Maldives has the barest of customs formalities. A strict ban, however, is imposed on the import (but not export) of nude pictures, firearms, ammunition, saltpeter, explosives, narcotics, intoxicants including all types of alcoholic beverages, poisons, dangerous animals, dogs, pigs and statues of idolatry. Tortoise shell and black coral can now only be exported as ornaments.

The currency used in all tourist resorts, in Male's government guesthouses, at the central tele-

graph office, for airline tickets, at Hulule airport and souvenir shops, used to be US dollars, but since February 1983, it has been decreed that all transactions should be made in rufiya. The US dollar is still widely accepted, though. All other major currencies can be exchanged at the resorts or at one of the five banks in Male. Travellers cheques are also accepted.

The Maldivian rufiya, which is divided into 100 larees, is the unit of currency. It is pegged to the US dollar at around Rufiya 9.15=US$1. Maldivian money is divided into notes in denominations of 1, 2, 5, 10, 50 and 100 rufiyas and coins of 1, 2, 5, 10, 25 and 50 larees and 1 rufiya. American Express/Visa/MasterCard are acceptable at main hotels on Male' and at most resorts.

Dhivehi is the national language. Found only in the Maldives, it is one of the Indo-European family of languages and very similar to Sinhala spoken in Sri Lanka. Since the Maldives' conversion to Islam in the 12th century, many Arabic words have been brought into the language. English is widely spoken in Male and on all the resort islands, as well as in the country's southernmost Addu Atoll, where a British airbase was formerly located. No phrase books in Dhivehi, the Maldivian language, are available. Guidebooks are also scarce, and should be bought beforehand, though some may be had at **LEMON** at Chandhani Magu, Male. A common and appreciated form of greeting is the Arabic "Salaam Alekum."

The Maldives has a tropical climate which is warm throughout the year but because the coral islands are so small, there is always a cooling breeze. The islands are only a few feet above sea level and the highest elevation in the country is about 2 m. Like other Indian Ocean islands, the Maldives has the two seasons of southwest and northeast monsoons. The climate remains much the same, however, throughout the year with daily temperature variations between 78.8°F and 87.8°F (26-31°C). Even during the rougher, stormy southwest monsoon months (any time between May and November), there are seldom more than a few days of rain at a time and usually there are periods of sunshine during the day.

Only light, informal clothing is necessary in the Maldives.

In the early years of tourism, many tourists showed little regard for local customs by wearing hardly any clothing in the capital, Male.

Now there are regulations requiring that visitors there wear appropriate clothes so as not to offend the locals.

A man doing business in Male, especially if dealing with senior government officials, is expected to wear a jacket and a tie.

Some of the resorts do not permit nudity around staff quarters, in the bars, restaurants and places of business. But most resort islands do not enforce any clothing regulations.

Most Maldivian workers have only a one-day weekend on Friday, the Muslim day of rest. Schools are closed on Thursdays as well, while banks are the only institutions that are also closed on Saturdays.

Government offices are open most of the year from 7:30 am until 1:30 pm. But during the Islamic fasting month of Ramadan which is determined according to the lunar calendar, offices seldom get going before 9 am.

Persons wishing to meet government officials can usually obtain appointments from 9 am onwards.

It is recommended that any foreigner wishing to meet government officials should write in advance or at least go first through the Protocol Officer in the Ministry of External Affairs.

The General Post Office is open six days a week from 8:15 until 11:45 am in the mornings and in the afternoons from 1:30 until 3:30 pm. Banking hours are from 9 am until 1 pm. Sunday through Thursday.

Unlike the telex service, which is reasonably efficient, the postal service is unreliable. Sometimes it takes weeks for mail to reach its destination from the resort islands.

Most shops in Male are open from 8 am until 1:30 pm, then again from about 2:30 pm or 3 pm until 5:30 pm and again in the evenings from 7 pm until 10:30 pm. Even on Fridays many shops are open some time during the day, except from 11:30 am until 2 pm — the time for Friday prayers.

FROM THE AIRPORT: Most visitors to the Maldives go directly from Hulule airport to one of the resort islands. Each resort provides ferry services at charges varying from US$10-40 depending on distance and type of craft. A locally built vessel called a Dhoni can be hired at Hulule airport to Male for about Rufiya 40 — though occasionally the traveller may find a ferry for Rufiya 10.

The island of Gan, 467 km south of Male on Addu Atoll (Seenu) has an international standard runway and can be reached by an infrequent Indian Airlines' service from Hulule airport (a continuation of some of its Trivandrum-Male flights) or by an equally irregular Air Maldives 18-seater Shorts 330 charter operation. Services are basically geared to traffic demand for Gan Holiday Village and fares are expensive (around US$150 for the round trip).

A 20-seat amphibious Twin Otter aircraft flying the colours of Inter Atoll Air is used for airport-to-resort transfers, reducing a two-and-a-half-hour ferry journey down to about 10 minutes and adding an average US$10-15 only to ferry transfer fares.

In addition, helicopters, hydrofoils and a hovercraft are in operation.

Between Hulule airport and Male there are regular ferry services operating almost hourly, except during meal times (12-3 pm and 5-7 pm), costing about US$1 one way. Arrangements can also be made to hire diesel launches or speedboats (fares negotiable but expensive).

IN MALE: The capital is only 1.5 km^2 in area and hence the most practical way of covering distances is to walk. Some cars, motorcycles and bicycles are available for hire. Taxis are also available. Some of them have radio service, and can be telephoned for, while most can be hired by walking to the Male Government Hospital where they have a stand. Taxis do not cruise around the town in search of fares. Their rates average around US$1-2, depending on the number of passengers and the amount of baggage. They usually travel very slowly, since Male is such a small place that anything above first gear would be liable to land you straight in the sea.

INTER-ISLAND: Visitors to the Maldives can make their own arrangements with local boatmen in Male about travelling to other islands and atolls. There are passenger boats plying from Male to distant atolls. These are very cheap and uncomfortable. Tourists can also hire the local fishing boats, called dhonis, but there are no set rates and sometimes the price may remain in dispute throughout the voyage.

Most resorts can make more expensive arrangements for their clients to charter yachts and other boats for sailing around the islands.

INTERNAL AIR TRANSPORT: The irregular Air Maldives 18-seater Shorts 330 charter operation to Gan has been joined by a 20 seater amphibious Twin Otter of Inter Atoll Air for airport to resort transfers. Helicopter, hydrofoil and hovercraft services supplement these limited air services.

The Maldivian Government also has a number of small aircraft, such as two-seater Cessnas and six-seater Senekas, which it makes available for hire for sightseeing. Arrangements can be made through the Airport office on Marine Drive in Male.

Each resort offers several basically similar kinds of excursion tours. There are half-day excursions to Male and day-trips to nearby uninhabited and inhabited fishing-village islands for about US$25 per person including a barbecue picnic. Resorts also offer night fishing trips and moonlight cruises, as well as diving safaris lasting some three to four days.

Most visitors to the Maldives go for the sun and sea and would not enjoy staying long in Male, which has no beaches and only limited accommodation. Even people going to the Maldives primarily to do business in Male frequently stay at one of the nearby resorts and arrange to go into the capital by boat every day. **Villingili** is the most convenient resort for making daily trips to Male.

All resorts and guesthouses in the capital offer rates that include full board with three meals a day. In Male, besides two modern guesthouses and two hotels, there are usually rooms with minimum facilities available for rent. Some tourists have even hired islands by the month.

There is basically very little to choose between the resort islands, though some have larger lagoons, others are situated closer to the outer reef and some are more affected than others by mosquitoes or non-flying insects. All resorts now have to have fresh water and most either have installed, or are installing, air conditioning.

Water is the Maldives' main problem and visitors to Male are advised to be extremely careful. But all the tourist resorts offer rainwater for drinking, which is safe.

Despite strict local laws against the consumption of alcohol, liquor is freely available for visitors to the resort islands. A Singapore beer costs about US$2 and prices are similar for most spirits. Wine is more expensive, from around US$15 for the cheapest bottle. Since the opening of a large-scale bottling factory in Male in 1983, soft drinks have halved in price to around 50 US cents. The factory was opened primarily to lessen the Maldives' dependence on Sri Lanka for imported soft drinks, but has also helped solve the problem of empty cans being dumped in the sea by resort staff.

Food is not one of the Maldives' major attractions as virtually everything has to be imported except fish, coconuts and some fruits. Set meals at the resorts usually consist of bland Western food, sometimes mixed with a Maldivian curry. But à-la-carte meals of a much higher standard are available and some of the more expensive resorts, or those catering to specialised markets, like the French or Italians, have imported European chefs to improve their catering services.

Maldivian cuisine is monotonous, basically fish, usually tuna. Such fruits as water melon and bananas are seasonally available. Despite the large quantities of tuna, there is no sushi or shashimi, but devilled fish is recommended. The **Rendezvous** (near the Alia Hotel) on Haveeree Higun, Male, Tel: 32795 is a good new French restaurant run by M. Philippe Maurella, a fine source of island lore. **The Newport** on Marine Drive, and the **Downtown**, on Majeedi Magu, are also popular. All three are unlicensed. **Nasandura Palace Hotel** and **Hotel Alia** have their own licensed restaurants.

Although the Maldives has one TV station which transmits in colour for a few hours each evening, the resorts do not provide TV sets in guests' rooms. Some of them place a TV in the common lounge, but they are not too popular since transmission ends as early as 9 pm. But video-films are becoming more widespread for guests' entertainment. Various resorts, including Kurumba, Bandos and Velassaru, offer weekly dances with live music by various local rock bands. Tourists staying at the other resorts are encouraged to hire boats to attend the dances on other islands. Often, too, the traditional Maldivian dance **bodu beru** — said to have been brought long ago from East Africa — is performed for the tourists.

In Male there are three cinemas which usually show Indian and English films and sometimes video-taped TV shows.

Historically the Maldives exported tortoiseshell, shark's fin, ambergris, cowrie shells and lacquerware in the ancient Indian Ocean dhow trade. Tortoise shell from the Hawksbill turtle and the shells and stuffed carcasses of that and other sea turtles are being sold by the Maldives in limited quantities to tourists and markets in Singapore and Hongkong. Exports of turtle products have waned dramatically, however, since a government regulation was passed prohibiting the killing or catching of sea turtles of less than 60 cm in length and tortoises of less than 75 cm. The export of whole turtle shells is banned and only smaller items made of them can now be bought.

The best buys are seashells, some specially woven sarongs called felis, in wide black-and-white stripes, and woven grass mats in black, brown and orange designs. Chinese ceramics are also considered good buys by collectors. The Palm Store has duty-free goods, and the Japanese-run Lemon Souvenir Shop has local souvenirs, books and magazines. Both are on Chandhani Magu, the main shopping street.

Aquatic sports and especially the spectacular diving opportunities are the chief attractions for tourists coming to the Maldives.

All the resorts have equipment (snorkelling and scuba) for hire, and most also have full-time professional diving instructors. The better-known diving groups are **Barakuda Club** and **Eurodivers**.

Besides diving, resorts offer wind-surfing, sailing and water-skiing. Indoor games, such as table-tennis, snooker, and chess are also available.

The Maldivians enjoy various sports and hold tournaments throughout the year in Male. The annual sports·calendar for these tournaments follows roughly this schedule: bicycle races, January; tennis, February; cricket, March; soccer, June; table tennis, August; dhoni racing, September; volleyball, October; swimming, November; and hockey, December. Basketball is also played. Soccer is currently the most popular spectator sport in the capital.

There is very little public celebration of Maldivian holidays. Except for the observances of Independence Day, and Republic Day on November 11, when there are usually parades, programmes in the national stadium and fireworks, the other festivals for special Muslim days are celebrated more by private feasting and visiting. Following the lunar calendar, the observance of these Islamic events varies annually. Maldivian holidays:

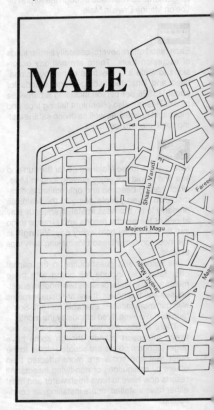

January 1: New Year's Day.
July 26: Independence Day.
November 11: Republic Day.
November 24: National Day.
Variable: Prophet Muhammad's birthday; first of the fasting month of Ramadan; the day marking the end of the fasting month; the 10th day of the last month of the Muslim calendar; the first day of the first month of the Muslim calendar (New Year).

Addresses

The Maldives Department of Tourism, which runs the guesthouses in the capital, is under the office of the president. Some 47 private agencies operate the 56 resorts outside the capital. The largest of them, Universal (Marine Drive,

Male), runs Kurumba, Velassaru, Bandos, Villingili, Baros and Fesdu. It also has an office at 15, Chandanee Rd, Male.

Publications

A small map of the Republic of Maldives, showing all the atolls with their new administrative names plus a detailed map of Male Atoll, can sometimes be purchased in Male and the resorts. It can be ordered from Adam Maniku, Maizandosuge, Male. However since Male can be comfortably walked round in a morning, a map is not really necessary. Large, detailed, but often out-of-date maps of the Maldives produced by the British Admiralty can be purchased at ship's chandlers in Colombo, Sri Lanka. *The West Indian Pilot* giving details of

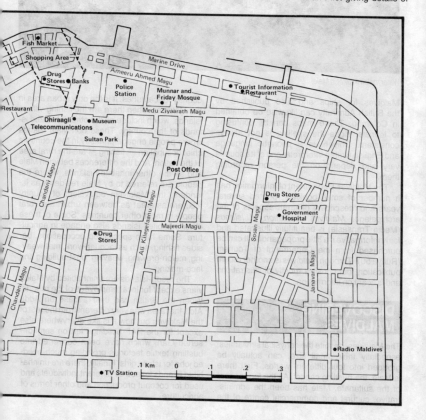

Water melon market in Male.

Photo: Jim Pringle

Maldives for ships and also published by the British Admiralty can likewise be obtained in Colombo. These maps can be confusing to tourists, since the spelling is not always consistent. Dhivehi is a phonetic language and English written interpretations of its sounds vary and depend on the person recording them.

The Maldives Department of Information has a number of small booklets, printed several years ago, describing different aspects of the archipelago. *Maldives, a Nation of Islands* (Media Transasia) is beautifully illustrated and fairly informative if a little propagandist. It can be purchased from the Department of Tourism (Rufiya 50). *Through Maldives* is another recent publication, but consists mostly of illustrations and is scant on information.

DISCOVERING MALDIVES

The Maldives, despite their physical similarities, especially their small size, can actually be grouped into four different worlds. First there is Male, the bustling capital. As the former seat of the sultanate, Male has been the administrative, cultural and commercial centre of the country for centuries. It is the only urban area in the Maldives. Then there are the fishing-village islands, which include all the other inhabited islands of the country. These non-Male islands where people engage primarily in the country's chief occupation — fishing — are the rural area of the nation. And the differences between Male and all the other inhabited islands, where the people are referred to by Male residents as islanders, the Maldivian equivalent of country folk, are as great as between urban and rural people in most other countries. Some of these other inhabited islands also engage in agriculture. Some have specialised occupations, besides fishing, such as lacquer-work, mat-weaving, melon-growing, weaving, boat-building and lace-making.

The resort-islands are uninhabited by Maldivians except for local employees of the resorts. When the British had their airbase on Addu Atoll, that area was very different from the rest of the Maldives but now it is like everywhere else except for the RAF buildings left on semi-deserted Gan, which have been converted into bustling textile factories providing much-needed jobs for island girls. Finally, there are uninhabited islands leased by different individuals and used for coconut production and other forms of agriculture.

HOTEL GUIDE

Hotel address	Phone	Fax	Telex	Cable	〰	🍴	🍜
Resort hotel rates (double, full board) **Summer Rates (1 May–31 Oct. '91)** **A** (US$180-380) **B** (US$100-180) **C** (US$70-100) **D** (US$55-70) **Winter Rates (1 Nov.–30 Apr. '91)** **A** (US$150-180) **B** (US$90-140) **C** (US$60-90) **D** (US$45-60)							
MALE ATOLL							
These are not resort hotels, but business hotels in the capital, and rates do not include board. **C**				Rates include full board — three meals a day. None of the resorts has or needs to have a swimming pool since all are by the sea. There is no TV in guests' rooms. All feature communal dining-rooms, with set meals, though some do have separate à-la-carte restaurants. Address is always Name of Resort, Republic of Maldives.			
Nasandhura Palace Hotel Marine Drive, Male	323380, 322360, 323525	324300	66091 POLYCOM MF				
Hotel Alia Haveeree Higun Male **D**	323445, 322080, 322935, 322197		77032 HOTALIA MF				
Sosunge Sosun Magu, Male	323025		66019 TOURISM MF				
RESORTS **A**							
Biyadhoo Tourist Resort 29 km from airport	343516, 343742, 343978	343742	77003 TAJ MF				
Cocoa Island 29 km	343713		77037 COCOA MF				
Farukolhufushi Tourist Resort (Club Med) 1.5 km	344552, 343749, 343021	342415	66057 MEDMALD MF				
Kurumba Village 3 km	342324, 343081, 343084	343885	77083 KURUMBA MF				

Hotel address	Phone	Fax	Telex	Cable	≈	⫙	◺
RESORTS – *Cont'd*							
A							
Kudahithi Tourist Resort 29 km	344613	344613	66030 SAFARI MF				
Rihiveli Beach Resort 40 km	343731	344775	66072 PITTMAT MF				
B							
Bandos Island Resort 8 km	342527, 342674, 343310, 343876	343877	66050 BANDOS MF				
Baros Tourist Resort 16 km	342672	343497	66024 UNIENT MF				
Fun Island Resort (Bodufinolhu) 39 km	344558, 343958, 343597	343958	77099 FUNISLE MF				
Boduhithi Coral Isle 29 km	343198, 343981, 345905	342634	77044 BODHITI MF				
Bolifushi Island Resort 13 km	343517	345924	66043 IOB MF				
Gasfinolhu Tourist Resort 18 km	342078	342078	66027 DHIRHAM MF				
Hudhuveli Beach Resort 10 km	343982, 343396, 343983	343849	77035 HUDVELI MF				
Kanifinolhu Resort 16 km	343152, 344859	344859	77096 EUROKAN MF				
Lankanfinolhu Tourist Resort 10 km	344546, 344623, 344582, 343597	344576	66088 LANFIN MF				
Little Hura Club 16 km	345934, 344231	344231	77032 HOTALIA MF				
Nakatchafushi Tourist Resort 22 km	342665, 343846, 343847	343848	66024 UNIENT MF				
Reethi Rah Resort (Medhufinolhu) 35 km	342077	342077	77046 RERARE MF				
Thulhagiri Island Resort 11 km	342816	342876	66053 THULA MF				

Hotel address	Phone	Fax	Telex	Cable	≋	⊞	◢
RESORTS – *Cont'd*							
B							
Vaadhu Diving Paradise 8 km	343977, 343976	343397	77016 VADOO MF				
Vabbinfaru Paradise Island 16 km	343845, 343147	343843	77026 VABBIN MF				
Velassaru Tourist Resort 10 km	343041, 343042	343041	66071 SEASAND MF				
Veligandu Huraa 20 km	343882	343882	77006 PALMTRI MF				
Villivaru Island Resort 28 km	345716, 343598	343742	77003 TAJ MF				
C							
Asdhu Sun Island 43 km	345051	345051	66091 POLYCOM MF				
Dhigufinolhu Tourist Resort 20 km	343599, 343611	343886	77006 PALMTRI MF				
Embudhu Finolhu Island Resort 8 km	344451	345925	66081 DOLPHIN MF				
Embudhu Village 8 km	344776, 342673	342673	66035 KAIMOO MF				
Eriyadhu Island Resort 38 km	344487	344487	66031 ERIYADU MF				
Fihaalhohi Tourist Resort 41 km	342903	343803	66065 LHOHI MF				
Giraavaru Tourist Resort 11 km	344203, 343880, 343881	344818	66059 GIRAVAR MF				
Helengeli Tourist Village 50 km	344615	344615	66022 ENGELI MF				
Hembadhu Island Resort 39 km	343884	343884	66084 JEWORLD MF				
Ihuru Tourist Resort 16 km	343502		66099 IHURU MF				

Hotel address	Phone	Fax	Telex	Cable	〰	🍴	🥂
RESORTS – *Cont'd*							
C							
Lohifushi Tourist Resort 17 km	343651	343451	66047 ALTAF MF				
Makunudhu Club 35 km	343064, 345092, 345093	345089	77059 MAKU MF				
Meerufenfushi 40 km	343157	343157	77002 CHAMPA MF				
B							
Olhuveli Club 35 km	342788	342788	66064 LAABA MF				
Rannalhi Tourist Village 43 km	345931, 342688	342688	66086 JETAN MF				
Sunset Club Kadooma 20 km	344452	344452	77073 KANDOO MF				
Ziyaaraiyfushi Tourist Resort 34 km	343088	343088	66107 HORIZON MF				
ARI ATOLL AND OTHERS							
A							
Nika Hotel 70 km	350516	350577	66124 NIKA MF				
B							
Bathala Tourist Resort 58 km	350504	350504	77017 TIEL HQ MF				
Fesdu Fun Island 64 km	350541	350541	66024 UNIENT MF				
Gangehi Resort 70 km	350505, 350506	350506	66021 VCZ MALE MF				
Halaveli Tourist Resort 55 km	350561	350561	77017 TIEL HQ MF				
Kuramathi Tourist Resort 58 km	350556, 350527	355327	66024 UNIENT MF				

Hotel address	Phone	Fax	Telex	Cable	〰	🍽	🍵
ARI ATOLL AND OTHERS – *Cont'd*							
B							
Maayaafushi Tourist Resort 60 km	350529	350529	77017 TIEL HQ MF				
Madoogali Resort 49 km	350581		66126 MADUGAL MF				
Mirihi Island Resort 116 km	350500	350500	66131 MOBINA MF				
Veligandu Island 60 km	350549, 350519, 350594	350519	66095 CROWN MF				
C							
Angala Island Resort 113 km	350510	350510	66155 ANGALA MF				
Dhiggiri Resort 60 km	350592	350592	66030 SAFARI MF				
Ellaidoo Resort 59 km	350614	354614	66030 SAFARI MF				
Kuredu Island Resort 130 km	330337	330337	66095 CROWN MF				

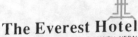

NEPAL

After 40 years of being open to the rest of the world, Nepal still offers a rare combination of old and new in terms of art, culture and civilisation. Crossing a street in Nepal may also mean travelling back 200 or 300 hundred years. The pagoda-style architecture scattered all over the independent kingdom, the fascinating array of temples honouring various deities and the old-style way of life practised by most of the population make the country a living museum. Add to this the almost mystic appearance of the Himalayan mountain range in the north of the country and even the most hardened traveller will find a trip to Nepal a spur to imagination and meditation.

The kingdom still bears signs of its long isolation. The capital, Kathmandu, seemingly floating between the world's tallest mountains and lowland tropical jungle, is very much rural in character. The Nepalese are proud, both as Buddhists and as Hindus, because their country was the birthplace of Gautama Buddha (at Lumbini in the lowlands) and of Sita, heroine of the epic Hindu Ramayana (at Janakpur, also in the lowlands).

Another reason for their pride is their boast that in more recent years they did not give way to either Muslim or British encroachments as did the peoples on the Indian plain.

Nepal is still a country of small villages where men and women work hard and long and where the gods are felt to be as close and as real as the huge mountains which form a dazzling white, jagged barrier to the north.

The country is trying to strike a balance between traditional values and the realities of the modern world. This be-comes obvious when one travels or walks around the towns of the Kathmandu valley where buildings using contemporary materials are replacing the old-style structures noted for their wood-carved windows and other features created by Nepalese craftsmen.

Above all, the Nepalese are a friendly people, perhaps a little shy on first contact with a newcomer but nonetheless willing to go to any lengths to help outsiders feel welcome in their country. For instance, if your taxi-driver is unable to find the place you want to visit (usually because of the language barrier rather than lack of knowledge), and you stop to ask someone to interpret for you, it is odds-on that your new-found interpreter will get into the taxi to show the driver the way — all with a great show of smiles and goodwill.

Nepal is a beautiful, gentle country with none of the tensions of Western civilisation. Small wonder that many young people flock to its towns and villages, either by air or overland, looking for a tranquillity they cannot find elsewhere.

Until the early 1950s the country was relatively unknown to the travel industry and this, too, is one of its great attractions. The age of the organised, hyper-efficient group tour has not yet reached Kathmandu on any scale and so there is, as yet, little or no sense of the visitor being an intruder merely collecting another country's stamp in a passport. Instead, the visitor is welcomed as a friend or a guest.

With the passage of time, and the introduction of jet services to and from Kathmandu, the inflow of foreign tourists is creeping higher every year. In 1989 a total of 240,000 foreign tourists visited Nepal.

Nepal

The early history of Nepal is veiled in mythology. Its recorded history stretches back to the Lichavi dynasty, which ruled from the fifth to 12th centuries AD. when it was replaced by the Malla dynasty. Before the fall of the Mallas in 1768, Nepal split into 46 independent principalities that were constantly at war with each other. Even three principalities in the Kathmandu valley were at war with each other.

The modern history of the country began with the followers of a Rajput ruling family self-exiled from north India for political and religious reasons, pushing eastwards at Riddi in 1494 AD. In the second half of the 16th century they based themselves in the town of Gurkha in central Nepal, from which they now take their name. The Gurkha king, Prithvinarayan (The Unifier), conquered the whole of Nepal in 1768, founding the Shah Dynasty that reigns to this day.

From 1846-1950, Nepal was, in effect, ruled by a family of hereditary prime ministers, the Ranas, who pursued a policy of close cooperation with the British powers in India. However, the movement against British rule by the Indian Congress had its repercussions among Nepalese intellectuals and politicians, who agitated through the Nepali Congress Party for a more democratic government. This led to a revolution by which the royal line, represented by King Tribhuvan — ninth of the dynasty — returned to power.

A general election in 1959 resulted in an overwhelming victory for the Congress, but at the end of 1960 King Mahendra, who had succeeded Tribhuvan, dismissed the ministry and imprisoned Congress prime minister B. P. Koirala. A system of Panchayat (village democracy) government was installed and political parties were not allowed. The party-less Panchayat system was abolished by his son and successor, King Birendra, who succeeded him on his death on January 31, 1972. It was done by royal proclamation on April 8, 1990 after eight weeks of violent unrest during which the king's forces killed 500 and wounded 1,000 others in addition to rounding up and arresting more than 10,000 political activists, including boys, girls and college students.

Under pressure from further agitation and political demands from the pro-democratic Nepali Congress and an alliance of seven communist groups under the banner of the United Left Front, King Birendra finally gave way to calls for a more democratic system of government. In November 1990 he appointed the acting president of the Nepali Congress, Krishna Prasad Bhattarai, as prime minister of an interim coalition government and introduced a constitutional monarchy, with elections scheduled for a multi-party bicameral parliament in April 1991.

Nepal covers 151 600 km^2 (after the signing of the Sino-Nepalese joint boundary protocol on November 20, 1979) and has a population of 18.5 million (1990). To the north, in the highest mountains and valleys, dwell the Bhotes (Tibetan-Nepalese in origin), to the west the Gurungs and Magars. The Brahmins, Chettris, Tamangs, Gurungs and Newars occupy the central parts and the Kirats Limbus and Rais the eastern. A majority of the country's population is Hindu, the country being the Hindu dominated kingdom in the world. Buddhism, the other important religion, is followed by the Bhotes, Gurungs, Rais and a section of the Newars. But there is a high degree of intermingling between the two faiths. The installation of a multi-party democracy made religious freedom universal, including the practice of Islam and Christianity, but proselytising continues to be banned by law.

The country is traversed from north to south by four great rivers and split into four main areas: the plains, the foothill jungle (terai), the great central trough of hills and valleys and the Inner Himalayas whose peaks range from 6,000 m to the 8,848 m of the world's highest peak, Mt Everest.

Along the southern border there are the beginnings of industrial development — textiles, sugar and cement — and this area also has the best network of roads. Some 25% of the country's trade is with India, with most exports consisting of food-grains by mid-July 1990. The famous Gurkha soldiers were for a long time Nepal's largest foreign-currency earners, remitting much of their earnings home, but now tourism, woollen carpets and garment exports earn more — US$208 million in 1989.

Kathmandu's Tribhuvan International Airport is served by nine Asian airlines with links to Hongkong, Bangkok, Lhasa, Karachi, Rangoon, Dhaka, Colombo, Calcutta, Delhi, Varanasi and Patna. Thai International flies four times a week from Bangkok and the Union of Burma Airways twice a week from Rangoon. There are four flights a week by Bangladesh Biman from Dhaka and two a week by Pakistan International Airlines from Karachi via Dhaka. Indian Airlines

Trekking in the Himalayas. ▷
Photo: K. M. Singh

flies daily from Delhi, Calcutta and Varanasi. Nepal's own national carrier Royal Nepal Airlines has three flights a week from Hongkong, four from Bangkok and two from Calcutta. It also has daily flights from Delhi, but service from Colombo has been suspended. Twice weekly connections to Dubai via Karachi, and to Singapore via Bangkok were introduced in 1985. The airline also operates flights to Frankfurt (US$450) via Dubai and to London via Dubai (US$500).

The following are samples of one-way fares: from Hongkong US$275, Bangkok US$190, Colombo US$180, Delhi US$142, Calcutta US$96, Varanasi US$80, Dhaka US$80, Rangoon US$170, Dubai US$250, Karachi US$150 and Singapore US$275. Airport tax of Rs 450 must be paid on departure from Tribhuvan; the charge is Rs 30 for internal flights.

By land there are 15 points of entry: Kakar Bhitta (Mechi), Rani Sikhiya (Kosi), Jaleswor (Janakpur), Birgunj (Narayani), Kodari (Bagmati — on the Tibet-Nepal border), Sunauli (Lumbini), Nepalgunj (Bheri), Koilabas (Rapti), Dhangadi (Seti), Mahendranagar (Mahakali). The most common and recommended entry points are Birgunj (near Raxaul in India), Kakar Bhitta (approached from Siliguri, Darjeeling and Assam) and Sunauli (near Gorakhpur and best approached from Delhi). There are regular bus services to Kathmandu from these points in the evenings and mornings. The 13-hour journey from Kakar Bhitta (no morning service) costs Rs 170, the eight-hour journey from Birgunj approximately Rs 75 and that from Bhairahwa (close to Sunauli) takes 10 hours and costs about Rs 78. Buses are tolerable but not air-conditioned. Regular deluxe bus services are in operation between Kathmandu-Pokara (Rs 140) and Bhairahawa (Rs 168).

Passports and visas are required for all except Indian nationals. Visas for one month can be obtained from Nepalese diplomatic missions or consulates abroad for a fee of US$10. A seven-day visa may also be obtained upon arrival at Tribhuvan airport or other entry points by land for the same fee, which may be extended at Central Immigration at Pridevi Marg (418573) for another three weeks at no extra cost. Extensions for a second month cost Rs 75 a week and for a third month Rs 150 a week. Travellers who want their visas extended must present a currency declaration form or receipts from the Nepal Rastra Bank showing they have converted foreign currency to the equivalent of US$5 per day for the intended period of stay. Extensions beyond three months are granted on the recommendation of the Home Ministry.

Note that the visa is valid only for Kathmandu, Pokhara, Chitwan and areas linked by highways. For trekking, a special permit is required, also obtainable from Central Immigration. Indian nationals are exempt from visa requirements provided they carry an identity card issued by a city or district magistrate in India.

Yellow fever vaccination is required for those arriving within six days of leaving or transiting an infected area. Inoculations against typhoid, paratyphoid and gamma globulin shots against hepatitis are recommended. Travellers are advised only to drink boiled water, served at major hotels. Filtered but unboiled water, served at smaller establishments and restaurants, is unsafe.

Baggage is spot-checked on arrival. The following personal effects are allowed duty-free entry (provided they are taken out on departure): one pair of binoculars, one perambulator, one camera, 12 rolls of film (officials are fairly flexible on this), one portable gramophone, 10 records, one tape-recorder and five tapes, one radio, one musical instrument and one fishing rod and accessories. Photographers can generally bring additional equipment provided it is taken out of Nepal on departure.

Duty-free facilities are available both on arrival and departure from Tribhuvan airport. Items permitted: one carton of cigarettes, 20 cigars, one bottle (limit, 1.15 litres) of alcoholic liquor and two bottles or 12 cans of beer.

Firearms and ammunition, explosives, transmitter-radios, walkie talkies and narcotic drugs cannot be imported. Firearms may be brought in with prior permission of the Foreign Ministry. Permission is needed from the Ministry of Forests to export animal and bird trophies. The export of antiques requires the approval of National Archives, Ram Shah Path; objects more than 100 years old cannot be taken out.

Cars entering the country require a carnet de passage with which no customs duty is levied for three months. On arrival in Kathmandu, car registration with the police is necessary to obtain a temporary licence and number plate.

EMBASSIES AND CONSULATE OFFICE IN KATHMANDU

Address	Tel
Australian Embassy Bhat Bhateni	4-11578
American Embassy Panipokhari	4-11179
Bangladesh Embassy Naxal, Bhagawati Bahal, Bangladesh House	4-14943
British Embassy Lainchaur	4-10583
Myanmar Embassy Chakupat, Patan Dhoka	5-21788
Chinese Embassy Baluwatar	4-11740
Egyptian Embassy Pulchowk, Lalitpur	5-21844
French Embassy Lazimpat	4-12332
Germany Kantipath	2-21763
Indian Embassy Lainchaur	4-10900, 4-11940
Israeli Embassy Lazimpat	4-11811
Italian Embassy Baluwater	4-12743
Japanese Embassy Panipokhari	4-14083
Embassy of the Democratic People's Republic of Korea Lalitpur	5-21084
Embassy of the Republic of Korea Tahachal	2-70812, 2-70584
Pakistan Embassy Panipokhari	4-11421

Address	Tel
Russian Embassy Baluwatar	4-11063
Thai Embassy Thapathali	2-13910
UNDP Pulchowk, UN Bldg	5-23200
SAARC Secretariat	2-16350, 2-21794
Belgium Consulate Lazimpat	4-14760
Austrian Consulate Kupondol, Lalitpur, G. P. O. Box 1457	5-21144
Netherlands Consulate Kumari Pati, Lalitpur G. P. O. Box 1966	5-22915
Belgium Consulate Lazimpat Kathmandu G. P. O. Box 1426	4-14760
Sri Lankan Consulate Kamal Pokhari, Kathmandu, G. P. O. Box 2669	4-14192
Finnish Consulate Khichhapokhari, Kathmandu	2-20939
Danish Consulate Khichhapokhari, Kathmandu	2-20939
Norwegian Consulate Jawalakhal, Kathmandu	5-21646
Swedish Consulate Khichhapokhari, Kathmandu	2-20939
Swiss Consulate Jawalakhal, Kathmandu	5-23468

Nepalese rupees come in banknotes of 1,000, 500, 100, 50, 10, 5, 2 and 1. A rupee is made up of 100 paisa which come in coins of 50, 25, 10, 5 and 2. The value of foreign currencies against the rupee fluctuates from day to day as the exchange is based on a floating system. The official exchange rate in July 1990 was Rs 29.3:US$1. The exchange rate for Indian currency is fixed at Indian Rs 100 to Nepalese Rs 168.

Foreign currency must be exchanged through official banks or authorised hotels. Foreign currency can be imported in reasonable amounts except for Indian rupees which may be brought in by Indian and Nepali nationals only. Nepalese rupees may not be imported. The US dollar fetches 20% more at the black market. International credit cards are accepted by most major shops and hotels.

On entry, visitors are given a currency-exchange declaration form on which all exchange transactions must be entered and stamped by the authorised dealer or bank.

According to a recent regulation, all payments to hotels and travel agencies (those authorised to deal in foreign currency) and Royal Nepal Airlines must be made in foreign currency.

On leaving Nepal, up to 10% of converted Nepalese rupees can be re-converted to hard currency at the airport exchange counter against presence of currency exchange bank or hotel receipts.

Nepali is the national language and is written in its own distinctive Devanagari script. English is widely spoken and understood in Kathmandu, particularly by those who regularly come into contact with tourists.

The popular tourist season is from October (13-26°C) to mid-June (19-30°C). Kathmandu is, however, cooler than most cities in Asia during summer and can still be pleasant to visit then; short treks from Kathmandu, sightseeing in the Kathmandu valley and raft trips are all still feasible. The only real disadvantage of summer is the monsoon rains, which cloud views of the mountains and make trek trails slushy.

November (6.6-22.5°C) to February (2.6-8.6°C) is winter, when mornings and evenings are especially cold, with night temperatures often dropping to zero. During the day when the sun is out it is warm and pleasant. Late September (18.4-27°C) to October (18-23°C) is autumn, with warm days and mildly cold nights. March (10.9°C) to mid-May (14.6°C) is spring, with weather similar to that of autumn. Late May to mid-September is the warm season, with rains from mid-June (19°C) to mid-September. Between mid-December to the end of January the weather is extremely cold (−1-1.7°C) in the mornings and reaches an average 18°C in the afternoons.

It is severely cold in the mountains between November and February, but otherwise pleasant the rest of the year.

The terai lowland is hot for most of the year and pleasant in winter.

In Kathmandu, light clothing with perhaps a jacket for the evenings, is all that is required for the warm months of April (11°C) to September (18°C). For the rest of the year warm clothing is needed, particulary from November to February when a down jacket would serve well. An umbrella might help during the monsoon (mid-June to mid-September).

Those going on treks in winter should be prepared for severely cold conditions (−6-−15°C) when good-quality warm, windproof jackets and trousers and thermal underwear are necessary. Medium-weight boots with gripping rubber soles that give ankle support are best for walking in the mountains.

Government offices are open from 10 am to 5 pm Sunday through Friday, Saturday being the day of rest in Nepal. Offices close at 4 pm in winter. Embassies and international organisations take a two-day weekend; their office hours are from 9 am to 5:30 pm. Commercial offices keep the same hours but open on Sunday, and travel agencies are open seven days a week.

Banks keep government office hours, but exchange facilities in some branches are open from 8 am to 8 pm; main banks close exchange facilities at 2 pm and at 12 noon on Fridays. Shops generally open around 10 am and close at 8 pm, some remaining open seven days a week.

Overland transport is difficult in Nepal, though an increasing number of motor roads are being built. At present the main road links are the Tribhuvan Raj Path, a 200 km road and Gorkha Narayanghat via Naubise that links Kathmandu to Raxaul at the Indian border, the Arniko Highway (110 km) which links Kathmandu to the Tibetan border at Kodari, the Prithvia Raj Marg (225 km) between Kathmandu and Pokhara (this road also has extensions from Durche to Gorkha and Mugling to Narayanghat), the 188-km road between Pokhara and Sunauli on the Indian border, and the 1,040 km east-west thoroughfare in the terai called the Mahendra Raj Marg, and the extension from Dharan to Dhankuta in the east. A 400-km road linking Pokhara and Baglung in the west is under construction.

Travel by air, remains the best means of covering long distances, and aircraft are the only means of access — apart from walking — to most areas in the northern highlands.

KATHMANDU

FROM THE AIRPORT: Metered taxis are available from the airport and a ride into the city costs Rs 45-60. Taxis often choose not to use the meter, particularly in the evenings when fares go up to Rs 75-100. Royal Nepal Airlines has a Blue Bus Service to its city office on New Rd, which costs Rs 25. Some hotels provide their own transport, but charges are almost double those of metered taxis.

TAXIS: Metered taxis are usually easily available, except when it rains and also after 9 pm. Best places to find them are in front of larger hotels and in Thamel Durbarmarg and New Rds. Fare is Rs 2.50 for flag-fall and rarely exceeds Rs 40 for a ride within city limits. A 50% surcharge on the meter-reading is demanded at night.

RICKSHAWS: Pedal rickshaws (three-wheelers) are plentiful and are good for distances of a mile or so. Expect to pay about Rs 20-30, subject to bargaining before getting in. Rickshaws are often available late at night at hotel entrances.

MAJOR AIRLINES
(all addresses in Kathmandu)

Aeroflot: Kantipath	212397
Air Canada: Durbar Marg	215271, 213871, 412138, 222838
Air France: Durbar Marg	223339
Air-India: Kantipath	212335
Dragon Air: Durbar Marg	223162
Alitalia: Durbar Marg	222339
Bangladesh Biman: Durbar Mar	222544
British Airways: Durbar Marg	222266
Cathay Pacific: Kamaladi	214705
Indian Airlines: Durbar Marg	223053
Japan Airlines: Durbar Marg	222838, 224854
KLM: Durbar Marg	224896, 224845
Korean Air: Kantipath	212080, 216080
Lufthansa: Durbar Marg	223052, 224341
Northwest Orient Airlines: Kantipath	226139, 225552
Pakistan International Airlines: Durbar Marg	223102

Singapore Airlines: Durbar Marg	220759, 223284
Royal Nepal Airlines (Domestic booking office): New Rd	220757, 214491
SAS: Durbar Marg	224917
Swissair: Durbar Marg	212455
Thai International Airways: Durbar Marg	223565, 224387
Trans World Airlines: Kantipath	226704, 411725
Union of Burma Airways: Durbar Marg	224839
Vayudoot: Durbar Marg	411419, 414067
CAAC: Kamaladi	411302, 416541
Kuwait Airways: Kantipath	222884
Panam Airways: Durbar Marg	411824
Druk Air Corp. (G. S. A.): Durbar Marg	227229, 225166
Saudi Arabian Airlines: Kantipath	222452, 222787

BUSES: Buses and mini-buses are available to most places within the city and to outlying areas. They are cheap — most fares are Rs 2 or less — but crowded and very slow. Buses for Boudhnath, Patan and the airport leave from Ratna Park. A regular trolley-bus service operates between Kathmandu (from Tripureswor) and Bhaktapur, a conch shell shaped city of Hindu and Buddhists devotes.

SCOOTERS AND TEMPOS: The former are three-wheel taxis painted black with yellow tops, have meters and cost about two-thirds the fare of a regular taxi. Flagfall is Rs 1.50; plus a 10% surcharge. Tempos are the same vehicles, generally painted grey or blue, which operate like buses, packing up to six passengers in the back; cost Rs 3 or so per person. They go to most places and are found at Rani Pokhari, Ratna park and near the Post Office at Sudhara.

HIRE CARS: These can be arranged through travel agencies and at Avis (represented by Yeti Travels at Hotel Mayalu Annex, Durbar Marg, tel: 223596) and Hertz (represented by Gorkha Travels, Durbar Marg, Tel: 224895). Toyota Corollas are available for half-day or extended trips, prices depending on mileage and the quality of the road. All cars are chauffeur-driven.

MOTORCYCLES: These can be hired for Rs 100 an hour or Rs 700 per day from 8 am to 6 pm.

BICYCLE HIRE: The valley is ideal for cycling, which is cheap at Rs 2-3 per hour and Rs 20 per day. No deposit is required.

UPCOUNTRY

BUSES: From Kathmandu buses are available to the following destinations: Pokhara (approximate fare Rs 140 — but the Swiss Mini Express leaving from Sundhara is available at Rs 150); Kakar Bhitta (Rs 169 — night service only); Sunauli (Rs 78); Birgunj (Rs 75); Narayanghat (Rs 60); Trisuli (Rs 20); Nepalganj (Rs 168); Gorkha (Rs 60); Janakpur (Rs 104), and Kodari (Rs 70). Mini-buses and Land-Rovers can also be hired for most trips from Pako and Dharmapath.

AIR: RNAC is the only domestic carrier. It has an extensive network using a fleet of three HS748s, 10 DHC6s (Twin Otters) and one Pilatus Porter. Some of the tourist destinations served by RNAC are: Pokhara (US$61), Meghauly (US$60), Jomsom (US$83), Manang (US$80), Nepalgunj (US$99), Phaplu (US$70), Simra (US$44), Tumlingtar (US$80), Jumla (US$127), Lukla (US$83) and Jiri (US$75). There are flights to Jomsom from Pokhara and

to Jumla from Nepalgunj. Most flights to the remote mountainous areas do not operate from June to late September. Tourists have to pay Rs 30 airport tax at each point. In addition to flying and driving, walking is the other major means of travel in Nepal.

Travel agencies operate half-day or day sight-seeing tours to the cities of Kathmandu, Patan and Bhaktapur, and other sights in the valley and outside such as Dakshinkali, Pashupatinath, Boudhnath, Swayambhu, Dhulikhel, Changu Narayan and Nagarkot. The cost varies according to the type of vehicle, number of passengers, distance and time involved. A charge of about US$20-30 for a four-hour tour for a car for three, plus guide, would be reasonable. Coach tours would cost US$48 per person, depending on the number of passengers, for a four-hour trip. Some agencies — Everest and Kathmandu Travels, for example — operate daily scheduled tours. Some of the better known agencies (all in Kathmandu) are:

Adventure Travel Nepal, Durbar Marg (Tel: 223328); **Annapurna Travel & Tours**, Durbar Marg (223530); **Everest Express Travel & Tours**, Durbar Marg (223284); **Gorkha Travel & Tours**, Durbar Marg (224895); **Himalayan Travels & Tours**, Durbar Marg (228485); **Kathmandu Travels & Tours**, Gangapath (224536); **Malla Travels & Tours**, Lekhnath Marg (410635); **Natraj Travel & Tours**, Durbar Marg (222532); **Pokhara Travels & Tours**, New Rd (22038); **Shangrila Tours**, Kantipath (226138); **Shanker Travels & Tours**, Lazimpat (411465); **Yeti Travels**, Durbar Marg (221234); **Alpine Travel and Tours**, Durbar Marg (410115); **Panorama Tours and Travels**, Nagasthan Sundhasa (214290); **Marco Polo Travels**, Kamalpokhari (414192); **Nepal Travel Agency**, Ranshahpath; **Nirvana Journey Travel Trekking and Rafting**, Lazimpat G. P. O. Box 2116, Tlx: 2543, Fax: 977-1-271607; **Peace Travel and Tours**, Kantipath (225368); **Tibet Travel and Tours**, Thamel (410303) Tlx: 2672 (Tibtvl NP); **President Travel and Tours**, Durbar Marg (220245); **Students' Travel and Tours**, Pri Devi Marg (220334).

TREKKING: Nepal offers arguably the best trekking holidays in the world and every year it attracts more than 30,000 visitors — mainly from the Western world — who set out on treks which last from one week to a month. The trekking season extends from late September to

White water rafting. Photo: K. M. Singh

May. Travellers need a trek permit and should apply two days in advance at Central Immigration Office at Tridevi, enclosing two passport photographs and a fee of Rs 60 per week, which rises to Rs 75 per week for a second month.

Trekking agents will make all arrangements and provide camping gear, food, guides, porters and other services for a fee of US$25-45 per day per trekker, depending on the size of the group, the length and difficulty of the trek and the quality of the service. Trekkers who want to go on their own must allot several days for preparation, which is generally too troublesome for the first-time visitor. If you want to live in village huts and eat at tea-houses along the trail (possible only on a few treks) you can expect to spend about US$6 a day. If you want to organise your own crew, the cost is Rs 100 a day for a sherpa guide, plus meals and Rs 75 per porter, who should also be supplied with food. Read one of the many books available on trekking or write to a trekking agency for further information.

Some trekking agencies in Kathmandu: **Asian Trekking Travel**, Keshar Mahal (Tel: 412821); **Annapurna Mountaineering and Trekking**, Durbar Marg (222999); **Glacier Safari Treks — Thamal Himalayan Journeys**, Kantipath (226139); **Himalayan River Trek**, Langimpat (412667); **International Trekkers**, Durbar Marg (220594); **Lama Excursions**,

Durbar Marg (220186); **Mountain Travel Nepal** (414508); **Natraj Trekking**, Kantipath (226644); **Nepal Treks and Natural History Expeditions**, Gangapath (222511); **Sherpa Cooperative Trekking**, Durbar Marg (224068); **Sagarmatha Trekking**, Kantipath (226639); **Trans Himalayan Trekking**, Durbar Marg (224854); **Snow Leopard Trek**, Naxal (414719); **Summit Nepal Trek**, Kupondol (521810).

RAFTING: This has become very popular with visitors, being a novel way to see the countryside as well as an exciting sport. Rafting agencies offer one to nine days of rafting and camping trips on rivers with scenic stretches and some rousing whitewater rapids. The most popular are the two-to-three-day trips that begin at points on the Kathmandu-Pokhara road and end in the Terai lowlands, often with a two-night stay at one of the wildlife lodges in the Chitwan National Park. Raft trips cost from US$60-80 per person per day, inclusive of all gear, food and guides but not transport to the starting point and back from the finishing point. High-quality inflatable rafts — operated by an oarsman or by everyone on board handling paddles — life-jackets and water-proof protection for cameras and personal items are all provided.

Some rafting agencies: **Great Himalayan Rivers**, Kantipath (Tel: 226798); **Himalayan**

189

River Exploration, Naxal (418491); Nepal Himal Treks, Keshar Mahal (411494); Last Frontier Trekking, Lainchour (416146); Lama Excursions, Durbar Marg (410786); Gorkha Treks, Lainchour (413806); Himalayan Adventures, Lazimpat (413806); Rover Trek and Expedition, Naxal (414373); International Trekkers, Hitty Durbar 224157); Treks and Expeditions Services, Kamal Pokhari (412231); Wilderness Experience, Kantipath (227152).

WILDLIFE VIEWING: The Chitwan National Park, 120 km south of Kathmandu, has become a permanent attraction for visitors. Several jungle lodges operate in and around the 960 km² national park, offering comfortable accommodation and high quality service, with wildlife viewing from elephant back, excursions by Land-Rover and on foot, bird-watching, canoeing in dugouts, and cultural tours to nearby Tharu villages.

At the top of the list is the famous Tiger Tops Junel Lodge, with its Tented Camp and Tharu Village at US$250 per person per night, plus US$140 air transport. Others offering similar activities at more moderate prices include Gaida Wildlife, Elephant Camp and its Chitwan Jungle Lodge and the Jungle Safari Camp. Rates range upwards from US$150 for two nights at Jungle Safari.

Besides flying, trekking offers the only means of seeing Nepal's central hills and valleys and all the northern highlands. The main trekking areas are the Everest region, approached via Lukla airstrip (more than 3,000 m), for visits to Sherpa villages, the monasteries of Thyangboche and Pangboche, the peaks of Kala Pathar (5,045 m) and Gokyo (5,483 m) for the best views and the Everest Base Camp; the region north of Pokhara, including Jomsom and the Annapurna Sanctuary and the villages of Ghandrung and Landrung, the Helambu-Langtang and Gosaiklund Lake area, approached via Sundarijal or Trisuli, and the Jumla and Rara area, approached via Jumla airstrip. Royal Nepal Airlines operate scheduled flights to all the trek regions; aircraft can also be chartered if a booking is made six months in advance.

TREK PERMIT FEES: Kanchengjunga — US$10 per person per week for the first four weeks; US$15 per person per week for the following weeks. Other areas — US$2.50 per person per week for the first four weeks; US$3 per person per week for the following weeks. A trek permit includes visa extension during the trek.

Newly permitted trek areas in the Kanchan-

junga region are: Taplejung, Sekhathum, Gyabla, Ghunsa, Mirgin la, Seram, Ramze up to Yalung Glacier, Serman, Torontan, Chitre, Yamphudin, Mamankhe, Khesewa, Bhanjang, Tambawa and Taplejung. Restricted areas in the district of Taplejung are Olangchung, Gola, Lelep and Pabung.

The newly permitted trek areas in the district of Dolpo are Rimi, Kaigaon, Sharmi, Naku, Kalika, Laha, Lekhu, Pahada, Tripurakot, Suhu, Gufal, Mazfal, Dunai, Raha, Laban and Sahar Tara.

MOUNTAIN FLIGHTS: Royal Nepal Airlines operates a one-hour mountain flight to the Everest region daily from October to March, weather permitting. Aircraft used are the pressurised 44-seater HS748s, or sometimes a Boeing 727, which flies within 20 km of the world's highest mountains, including Everest at 8,848 m. The cost is US$94, plus Rs 30 airport tax. Helicopters and light aircraft may be chartered. The costs are: Puma helicopter (load 1,070 kg) US$1,070 per hour; Allouette helicopter (load 362 kg) US$436 per hour; Skyvan — fixed wing — (load 800 kg) US$312 per hour; Pilatus (PC-6) — fixed wing — (load 350 kg) US$550 per hour; Twin Otter — fixed wing — (load 1,300 kg) US$855 per hour.

KATHMANDU

Kathmandu has a wide range of hotels from first-class establishments that are about the lowest-priced in the region to budget-class lodges of excellent value. First-class and tourist-class hotels include the Soaltee Oberoi, Yak and Yeti, Annapurna, Everest, Sherpa, Malla, Shanker, Hunalaya, Shangri-La, Summit, Narayani, Yellow Pagoda, Dwarika'd Village Hotel, Blue Star, Hotel Kathmandu, Woodlands and Tara Gaon Village. Good low-cost hotels are the Evergreen Nook, Vajira, Kohinoor, Blue Star, Blue Diamond, Kathmandu Guest House, International Guest House, MM International Central, Manaslu, and Sayapatri Hotel, Mansyangdi Hotel Thanel, Ambassador, Tridevi, Puja, Gautam and Janak.

UPCOUNTRY

Two excellent and unusual hotels upcountry are Tiger Tops and the Everest View at 4,330 m in the Everest region. West Nepal Adventures, an affiliate of Tiger Tops runs the Karnali Tented Camp in West Nepal. Other tourist-class hotels

Discover Your Shangri-la
Aboard Royal Nepal

orld travellers have long supposed
pal Himalayas to nestle a heaven-
earth, a hidden Shangri-la. Many
d their own personal paradise at
gh points among the sacred
ountains of Nepal..... near Thorang-
a 5,400 metre pass in the
nnapurna; accross Ganja-la in
ngtang Himal; atop Rupi-la in
orkha Himal; or near Khumbi-la,
med for the guardian god of
numbu.

But before you even land in the
magical Kingdom of Nepal, you will
experience another sort of Shangri-la
at 11,000 metre high in the sky. Royal
Nepal's Shangri-la Executive class is
that heaven above the cloud.

Sail in true bliss on our quiet Boeing
757s, pampered under the tender
loving care of our charming hostesses.

Royal Nepal's exclusive Shangri-la
executive class can prove to be your
personal paradise in the sky.

Royal Nepal
Airlines

A taste of Shangri-la in the sky

| gkok | Calcutta | Delhi | Dubai | Kathmandu | Hong Kong | Singapore | London | Frankfurt |

include **Gaida Wildlife, Elephant Camp** and **Chitwan Jungle Lodge** in the Chitwan National Park, and the **Narayani Safari Hotel**, with swimming pool and tennis court, in Bharatpur.

In Pokhara there is the charming **Fish Tail Lodge**, plus the **New Crystal, Hotel Dragon** and **Mount Annapurna**. An ambitious project, the **Begnas Lake Resort**, with houseboats and water sports, is also under way. Two recently added properties are the **Dulikhel Mountain Resort**, 35 km from Kathmandu (ideal for bird-watching, seeing the sun rise and set over Mt Everest and for white water rafting, and **Tara Gaon Resort** in Nagarkot, also 35 km from the capital. Apart from these, smaller hotels with basic facilities are to be found in all places patronised by tourists.

Nepali food is basically rice, curry and lentils prepared in hot spices, though it is not as rich as Indian cuisine. Newari cuisine, indigenous to the Kathmandu valley, is more exotic with rice-and-meat pancakes and offal and blood fried with spices. Mountain-goat curry and wild fowl are everyone's favourites. Beef, though officially banned, is available in most hotels and restaurants. Fresh fish, shell-fish and canned food are imported from Calcutta, the EC and Scandinavia.

Hotel Annapurna has two excellent outlets — the **Arniko Room** for Chinese and **Ghare-Kabab** for Indian meals. At the Soaltee, **Al Fresco** serves the best Italian food in town and **Himalchuli** is good for Indian and Nepali fare. The **Chimney Room** at the Yak and Yeti serves fine Russian and Continental cuisine and exotic local cocktails. Good Indian food can be had at **Kabab Corner** on Kantipath and at **Amber** (owned by the well-known Amber Restaurant in Calcutta). Good Chinese food is served at Hotel Malla's **Mountain City restaurant**, which has two cooks from Sichuan, and **Top in Town Restaurant & Bar**, New Rd, which specialises in Peking cuisine. The best Japanese food is offered at **Kushifuji** on Durbar Marg, **Fuji** on Kantipath, and the **Sakura-Ya Restaurant and Garden** and **Molisyu** in Lazimpat. **Sun Kosi** on Durbar Marg is good for Nepali dishes, while the **Dhulikhel Mountain Resort**, 35 km from Kathmandu, serving Indian and Continental meals, makes for a pleasant evening out and overnight stop.

In the medium and lower-priced category (less than US$7 a head) **K. C.'s** in Thamel serves excellent Continental meals. **Rum Doodle** and the **Red Square**, also in Thamel, are also good. Chinese and Tibetan food is best at **Meihua** on Kantipath, **Kaushung** in Thamel, **Nanglo Chinese Room** on Durbar marg, **Kowloon** Lazimpat and **Astha Mangal** in Thamel. **The Nest** at Hotel Ambassador in Lazimpat and **Ras Rang** have good Nepali, Chinese and Indian food. Decent and even cheaper meals can be had at **Tripti** and **Top in Town** on New Rd, and **Mt Fuji Kanti Patyh** for good Japanese food. The **Nnanglo Cafe** on Durbar Marg offers light Western meals and a popular fixed Nepali lunch. The **Paradise** in Jochhe does good Western vegetarian dishes and crepes. Nepali and Newari food is available at the **Gallery Room** at the Kathmandu Guest House and **Kumari** in Jochhe. The **Annapurna Coffee Shop** and **Nanglo Cake Shop**, both on Durbar Marg, have good pastries, chicken, mutton and vegetable patties, and white and brown bread. For ice cream and pizzas, try **Nirula's** on Durbar Marg. The **Airang Korean Restaurant**, the **Old Vienna Restaurant** and **New Kabab Corner** have reasonably priced meals.

Only the larger hotels have bars stocked with a wide range of imported drinks. Most restaurants serve only local drinks — Nepali rum, vodka, gin, whisky and two brands of beer, Star and Eagle Gorkha Brewery's Tuborg. These are moderately expensive, a large bottle of beer costing Rs 32 and a rum-and-Coke about Rs 38. Imported soft drinks are available. Home-brewed alcohol such as chhang — fermented wheat, millet or corn — and rakshi, a rice alcohol, can be purchased everywhere.

There is no night life to speak of in Kathmandu. Nepali folk-dance and music performances are held every evening at 6 pm at the **Everest Cultural Society** at Lal Durbar, New Hinalchuli, which charges US$7 for an elaborate meal and cultural show. Hotels like the **Soaltee** and **Yak and Yeti** feature cultural programmes. The **Sheraton** features dancing. **Ghare-Kabab** on Durbar Marg has excellent Indian classical music to go with an Indian dinner. The Soaltee has a casino, open from 12 noon to 4 am, with roulette, keno, blackjack, pontoon, flush, poker, jackpot machines and a video room for non-gamblers. Transport is provided free after 8 pm. Most bars in hotels and restaurants close at 10 pm. See *The Rising Nepal* for news of concerts, plays, dances and other happenings in town.

Craftsmanship is high and relatively inexpensive. Thus Kathmandu offers a wide range of souvenirs or items for use that will interest the visitor. Wood-carving of pagodas, temple struts, bronze cast deities, windows and woodblocks of traditional design can be bought in the **Patan Industrial Estate** and in **Indrachowk** and **Asan**. Brass and copperware such as water vessels, cooking utensils, butter lamps and candlestick holders — some made for domestic use — make excellent decorative items and are found in the same shopping areas. Images of Hindu and Buddhist deities cast by the rare "lost wax" process are available in varying sizes and quality and can be bought in the **Patan Industrial Estate Cottage Industry** department store at New Rd and Durbar Marg.

Nepali and Tibetan traditional jewellery of silver and old coins, and of turquoise, amber and coral are sold in Thamel, Durbar Marg, Patan and Boudhnath. Precious and semi-precious stones mounted in various designs are best bought in New Rd gem shops and in the shopping arcades of major hotels. Stones include lapis lazuli, moonstone, black-star, agate, garnet, aquamarine, crystal, emerald and sapphire. Other excellent buys are old and new Tibetan carpets, Nepali radi rugs, made of mountain sheep and goats, Nepali and Tibetan thangka paintings, rice-paper paraphenalia, lambs-wool pashmina shawls, hand woollen, sheep-wool sweaters and jackets, Nepali silk and felt slippers.

The main shopping areas are New Rd or Juddha Sadak, Thamel, Patan Industrial Estate, Asan/Indrachowk, Boudhnath, Durbar Marg and the arcades at major hotels. Shops especially worth visiting include **Mandala Boutique, Blue Star Shopping Centres, Mannies Boutique, Nepal Traditional Crafts**, the **Print-shop, Nepal Arts and Handicrafts** and **Curio Shop** at Durbar Marg. **Nanglo Fair Price Shopping Centre** at Ram Shaka Path is also worth a visit.

GEMS AND JEWELLERY

Popular stones available in Nepal are turquoise, lapis lazuli, rubies, garnets, topax and beryl's cats' eyes. The yellow and smokey topaz are available at most of the curio shops in New Rd, Durbar Square and the shops at the deluxe hotels. Hard bargaining is needed to bring down the prices asked by 25-35%, and gems should be bought only on the issue of a guarantee certificate.

INTERNATIONAL CREDIT CARDS

Only American Express and Visa credit cards are accepted by major tourist and deluxe hotels and curio shops in Kathmandu.

Sporting facilities are mainly limited to swimming, tennis, fishing, hiking, cycling, squash and golf. The major hotels have swimming pools and tennis courts (fee about Rs 60). The **Royal Golf Club**, near the airport, has a nine-hole golf course and the **Battisputalli Sports Club** has a squash court for members and guests. There are good billiards tables at the **Annapurna** and **Soaltee** hotels. Cycle hirestands can be found in Asan, Thamel and at the entrances of smaller hotels. Hang-gliding and ballooning can be arranged through **International Trekkers**, but the most attractive sporting activities remain mountaineering and trekking.

Not a week passes without celebration of some festival, whether Hindu or Buddhist, in all or part of the kingdom. Each year most occasions are celebrated on different dates, though birthday celebrations and those commemorating modern political events remain fixed. In addition to the public holidays mentioned (which are the main ones), some other religious festivals are also taken as public holdays.

February-March: Tibetan Lhosar New Year is celebrated at Swayambhu and Baudha Nath on the day of the new moon in February. Shivaratri is celebrated in honour of Lord Shiva, a Hindu god, and there is a great fair with religious observance at the Pashupatinath Temple (public holiday).

Democracy Day commemorates the overthrow of the Rana regime in 1951.

February 18: National-Democracy Day (public holiday).

Mid-April: Navabarsha (Nepalese New Year — public holiday).

April: Baisakh Purnima (triple anniversary of Buddha — public holday).

Ghoda Jatra celebrates the defeat of the demon Tundi; highlights are horseracing, gymnastics and military displays.

May: Rato Machendra Nath Ratha Jatra is celebrated in the town of Patna with the highlight of the month-long observance being the parading of a great decorated chariot.

Golden temple of Lord Shiva

Photo: K. M. Singh

August-September: Gai Jatra honours Yama, Lord of Death. Newars who have had a death in the family parade a cow or its effigy to help the passage of souls and stage a carnival festival.

September-October: Durga Puja (Desain) lasts 15 days and is one of the great festivals of the year. Houses are decorated and people wear their best clothes to worship at the temples.

There are animal sacrifices and various processions (public holiday) for traditional feasts and enjoyment.

A fortnight later the Festival of Light is celebrated for three days by both Hindus and Buddhists. And Indra Jatra pays homage to Indra, King of Gods.

November: Mani Rimdu — Buddhist monks evoke the protector gods with colourful mask dances and chart prayers for prosperity.

December 28: Birthday of King Birendra (public holiday).

Addresses

Nepal Chamber of Commerce, Head Office, Kantipath, GP Box No. 198. (Fax: 977-1-228324; Tlx: 2349 NP; Tel: 213318 and 212005).

Federation of Nepalese Chambers of Commerce and Industry, Tripureswore, Kathmandu. (Tel: 215920; Tlx: 2476 NP).

Publications

There are several excellent guide books for the casual visitor to Nepal, among them the *Insight Guide to Nepal* by Apa (Rs 220); *Nepal; Namaste* by Robert Rieffel (Rs 85); *Kathmandu and the Kingdom of Nepal* by Prakash Raj (Rs 87); *Trekking in the Himalayas* by Stan Armington (Rs 72); *Trekking in the Himalayas* by Tomoya Iozawa (Rs 215), and *The Kathmandu-Nepal Handbook* by Uttara Crees and Kesang Tseten (Rs 25).

Two monthly publications for tourists — *Enjoy Nepal* and *Nepal Traveller* — are available free at the airport and all leading hotels and travel agencies.

The Department of Tourism has also published more than a dozen free brochures for tourists. The department is in Tripureswor (Tel: 211293), with branches at Basantpur at New Rd (220818), the airport and in various towns on the border.

There are also many scholarly, popular and pictorial works on Nepal available in Kathmandu bookshops. They include **Himalayan Booksellers,** Durbar Marg; **Himalayan Book Centre,** Bhotahity; **Ratna Pustak Bhandar,** Bhotahity; **Educational Enterprise,** Kantipath; **Everest Books Service,** Jamal Tole, **Librairie Francaise,** Kantipath and **Mountain Book House,** Kantipath (216913).

Nepal Rastra Bank (Central Bank), Baluwater, Kathmandu. Tel: 4-10158; Tlx: 2207 RABA NP.

Nepal Bank, Dharma Path, Kathmandu. Tel: 2-24337, 2-21185; Tlx: 2220 and 2387 LUXMI NP.

Rastriya Banijya Bank, Tangal, Kathmandu. Tel: 4-13884; Tlx: 2247.

Nepal Arab Bank, Kantipath, Kathmandu. Tel: 222718, 226585; Tlx: 2385.

Nepal Indo-Suez Bank, Tel: 228229; 227228; Tlx: 2435.

Nepal Grindlay Bank, Tel: 212683; Tlx: 2531.

SECURITY EXCHANGE CENTRE
Listed 40 public limited companies as of July 1990 with a total market value of Rs 1.5 billion. Address: Dilli Bazar, GPO Box No. 1550, Kathmandu, Nepal. Tel: 411031.

DISCOVERING NEPAL

THE KATHMANDU VALLEY

The Kathmandu Valley is the most popular place in the kingdom. In addition to the capital city, it contains the ancient towns of Bhadgaon and Patan, mostly built between 6th and 16th century, many temples, 217 monuments and scenic spots.

Kathmandu is said to have been founded in 723 and its **Durbar Square** forms the heart of the city. The square (also called the Hanuman-Dhokha) houses an intriguing collection of temples and palaces and boasts some unexpected erotic wood carvings on the walls of its Hindu temples. Legend has it that the destructive Goddess of Storms is rather prudish and so refrains from hitting these surprising carvings with thunderbolts.

Of note in the square: the famous image of Hanuman (the Monkey God), which guards the entrance to the Royal Palace; the Taleju Temple built by Raja Mahendra Malla; the gigantic figure of Kal Bhairab (God of Terror); the Basantapur Durbar; the Coronation Platform; the Hall of Public Audience; the golden statue of Raja Pratap Malla and his four sons, seated on a stone pillar with a lotus capital; the Big Bell and the Big Drum; Sweta Bhairab's Huge Golden

mask and numismatic collection. There is a Rs 5 charge to enter the Royal Palace.

Near the Durbar Square stands the **House of the Living Goddess** (Kumari Devi), a picturesque building with heavily carved wooden balconies and latticed windows. You may enter the courtyard and see the window of the goddess and you may even be lucky enough to glimpse the young goddess herself, for she reverts to ordinary human form on reaching puberty. The goddess is taken through the city on a special carriage on the third day of the Indra Jatra Festival, celebrated in September. Photography is not allowed, except during the festival.

Also worth seeing is the old house known as **Kastmandup**, built by Raja Laxmi Narsing Malla in 1596 with a single tree. The white **Machendra Nath Temple** is an outstanding example of pagoda-style architecture and is situated off Indra Chowk.

The **Singha Durbar** (now the Secretariat Building) to be found in the southeast of the city was once the official residence of the Rana prime ministers; it is an outstanding piece of architecture set in wide, fountained gardens. It was damaged by fire in 1973 but has been rebuilt in the same style, yet only to one-third the area of the original building.

To the northwest of the city, about 5 km away, lies the **Balaju Water Garden**, an 18th-century design of spouting crocodile heads set in pleasant gardens. There is an Olympic-size swimming pool and an aquarium in the park.

On the banks of the Bagmati River, 5 km to the east of Kathmandu, is the Hindu golden temple **Pashupatinath**, dedicated to Lord Shiva who is worshipped in the form of a lingam. The temple is the centre of an annual pilgrimage on the day of Shivaratri during February or March. Only Hindus are allowed inside the temple but visitors can obtain a good view from the east bank of the river.

On a small hill to the northwest of the city, just past the museum, is the Buddhist sanctuary of **Swayambhunath**. The hill itself is a pleasant spot overlooking the valley and the town and is the home of hordes of small monkeys. The history of Swayambhunath is reputed to stretch back to the time of the Buddha himself. The stupa is daily patronised by adherents who walk around the base of the hill, turn prayer wheels, prostrate themselves and burn butter lamps and incense to accumulate merit from such devotional practices. On such occasions as the Buddha's birthday or Tibetan Losar (New Year), Tibetans throng to the stupa, visiting all the important pilgrimage spots, images and resident lamas. They carry ceremonial scarves (khatag), butter for the butter lamps and small donations.

At the other end of town lies the other important Buddhist stupa in Kathmandu, **Boudhnath**, possibly one of the world's largest stupas. The place now bustles with a large Tibetan population, busy with carpet manufacture, trade and prayers at the several monasteries belonging to different sects of Tibetan Buddhism.

The **Buddhanilkantha** at the base of the **Shivapuri Hill**, 9 km north of Kathmandu, is a stone sculpture of Narayan (Vishnu) lying on a bed formed by the coils of the king serpent Sesha Noga.

Sundari jal, 13 km north of Kathmandu, is famous for waterfalls and mountain scenery. It makes a delightful excursion and picnic spot, especially immediately after the monsoon. **Chovar**, 6 km southwest of Kathmandu, is the site of a gorge where the water drains from the valley (and is said to have been cut by the god Manjushree to drain the lake that supposedly then filled the valley). There is a small pagoda (A dinath) at the top of the gorge, offering a good view. The picnic and pilgrimage spots of **Pharping** and **Dakshinkali** are nearby.

Kirtipur, 6 km west of Kathmandu, is a pictureque Newari village with old lanes and houses and weavers dressed in traditional clothing.

Phulchowki, 16 km southeast of Kathmandu and 3,330 m high, is a noted spot for wild flowers and butterflies. You can go by car some of the way, but it is a three-hour climb on foot to the top of the ridge. The **Nepal Museum**, just beyond the town towards Swayambhunath, possesses a wide range of historical and archaeological objects, including a leather gun allegedly captured in the Tibetan war of 1880.

Patan (Lalitpur), 6 km southeast of Kathmandu across the river, is an interesting town, full of Buddhist monuments, temples and buildings adorned with elaborate wood-carvings and sculptures. It is said to have been founded in 299 AD. Special places of interest in the town include: the **Hiranya Varma Mahavihar**, a 12th-century gilded temple to Lokeswore; **Kumbheshore Temple** (to Shiva), which has a natural spring in its courtyard; **Jagat Narayan Temple** (to Vishnu) near the confluence of the Bagmati and Manahara rivers; **Krishna Temple**, which has some interesting descriptive sculpture from the ancient Hindu religious epics; **Durbar Square**, once the centre of rule for the Malla kings and still a fascinating

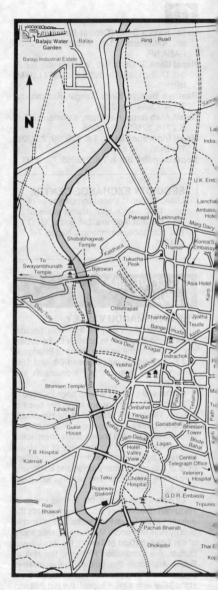

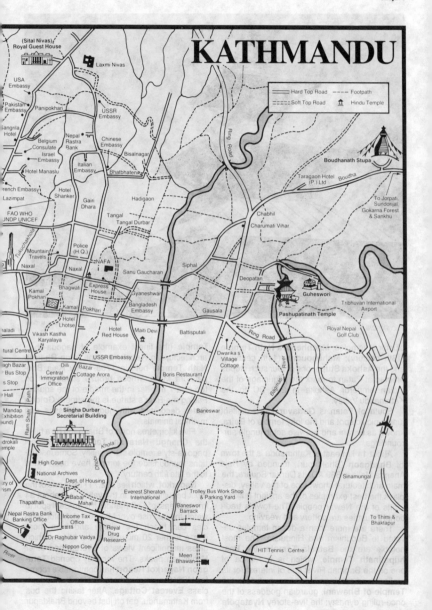

KATHMANDU

Legend	
═══ Hard Top Road	---- Footpath
═══ Soft Top Road	🏛 Hindu Temple

(Sital Nivas)
Royal Guest House

Laxmi Nivas

USA Embassy

Pakistan Embassy

Panipokhari

USSR Embassy

Sangrila Hotel

Belgium Consulate
Israel Embassy

Nepal Rastra Bank

Chinese Embassy

Bisalnagar

Italian Embassy

Bhatbhateni

French Embassy

Hotel Shanker

Lazimpat

Gairi Dhara

Hadigaon

FAO WHO
UNDP UNICEF

Tangal

Tangal Durbar

Chabhil

Charumati Vihar

Boudhanath Stupa

Boudha

Taragaon Hotel (P.) Ltd

To Jorpati,
Sundorijal,
Gokarna Forest
& Sankhu

Tukuchakhola

Mountain Travels

Police (H.Q.)

NAFA

Naxal

Naxal

Sanu Gaucharan

Siphal

Deopatan

Guheswori

Tribhuvan International Airport

Kamal Pokhari

Bhagwati

Express House

Gyaneshwar

Pashupatinath Temple

Royal Nepal Golf Club

Kamal

Pokhari

Bangladesh Embassy

Gausala

Hotel Lhotse

haladi

Vikash Kastha Karyalaya

Hotel Red House

Maiti Devi

Battisputali

tural Centre

USSR Embassy

Dwarika's Village Cottage

Bagmati River

agh Bazar

Bus Stop

s Stop

Dilli Bazar

Central Immigration Office

Cottage Arora

Boris Restaurant

Ring Road

Hall

Ram Shah Path

Mandap (Exhibition ound)

Singha Durbar Secretarial Building

Baneswar

Sinamungal

drokali mple

Dhobi Khola

High Court

National Archives

Dept. of Housing

Everest Sheraton International

Trolley Bus Work Shop & Parking Yard

ry of ism

Thapathali

Babar Mahal

Nepal Rastra Bank Banking Office

Income Tax Office

Baneswor Barrack

To Thim & Bhaktapur

Dr Raghubar Vaidya

Royal Drug Research

Meen Bhawan

HIT Tennis Centre

Nippon Coel

River

197

Machhendra Nath Temple.

Photo: K. M. Singh

cluster of temples; **Machhendra Nath Temple** (13th century); **Mahaboudha** (14th century), and the **Ashoka Stupa**, one of four such stupas erected at Patan to mark the pilgrimage of the Indian emperor Ashoka in 249 BC to the Kathmandu Valley.

South of Patan is **Godavari**, an excellent jungle picnic spot and the lofty temple of **Bajra**, known as Barahi and likewise set in jungle surroundings.

About 14 km east of Kathmandu is the town of **Bhadgaon** (Bhaktapur), founded by Raja Ananda Malla in 889 AD. Its Durbar Square, the main architectural showplace of the valley, displays the best examples of the ancient building crafts of the Newar people. The town's traditional industries are pottery and weaving.

There are more than a dozen temples devoted to Buddhism and Hinduism. The most notable are the **Batsala Temple**; the **Pashupatinath Temple**, which is a replica of one on the Bagmati River and of interest for its erotic wood-carvings and fine pictures; the **Temple of Bhawani**, guardian goddess of the once-ruling dynasty; the five-storey **Nyatapola**

Temple (the finest example of pagoda-style architecture in Nepal), and the huge **Bhairab Nath Temple** built in 1708-18 by Raja Bhupatindra Malla, whose bronze statue sits on top of a 7 m pillar in the middle of the square. Facing the Raja's statue is the superb **Golden Gate**, decorated with gods, goddesses and mythical animals.

Five kilometres north of Bhadgaon on a hill is the **Changu Narayan Temple**, the oldest pagoda-style temple in the valley. Some inscriptions found inside the temple have been dated to the late fifth century.

Nagarkot, which lies at 2,711 m, is one of the most beautiful spots in the valley. It is about 34 km northeast of Kathmandu. It is an ideal spot to watch the sun rise over Mt Everest. Motor vehicles can reach the village and from there it is a further 20 minutes to the hilltop, which gives magnificent views of Everest and other Himalayan peaks. The recently opened **Taragaon Nagarkot Resort** has comfortable rooms for US$18 a single; there is also the budget-class **Everest Cottage**. After taking the bus from Kathmandu, get off just beyond Bhaktapur and hike up to Nagarkot (three hours).

Another excellent spot for mountain views is **Kakani** at an altitude of 2,000 m, about 28 km northwest of Kathmandu. The road to the town takes you out of the valley on a winding drive along its northern rim. Here you can walk and picnic and view the mountains in the middle distance. There is also a tourist bungalow offering accommodation.

Also within easy range of Kathmandu is the ancient and scenic town of **Dhulikhel**, just 32 km to the east along the Arniko Raj Marg road that leads to the Chinese border. From this town the panorama includes the snowy ranges from Makalu in the east to Manaslu in the west. Just 4 km beyond is **Dhulikhel Mountain Resort**, well worth a visit for a meal or an overnight stay (approximately US$45 a single).

UPCOUNTRY
Pokhara, 225 km west of Kathmandu, is the second most popular tourist spot in Nepal (after Kathmandu). Easily accessible by land (six hours) and air (US$60), Pokhara is at a lower elevation than Kathmandu, thus warmer and pleasant in winter, and it has three beautiful lakes with the background of the Annapurna-Dhaulagiri ranges; most conspicuous is the magnificent **Machhapurchare**, or Fish Tail Mountain. Regarded as the lakeside resort valley of Nepal, it offers a whole range of activities — trekking (being the gateway to Annapurna Sanctuary and Jomsom), cycling, swimming, boating and horse-riding. There are some good hotels — the **Fish Tail, New Crystal, Dragon** and **Mount Annapurna** — and plenty of cheap ones around the **Phewatal** (Lake).

On the **Tribhuvan Rajpath** nearly 2,650 m up and 80 km southwest of Kathmandu is **Daman**, which commands a good view of Everest and other great peaks. The **Everest Point Hotel** offers rooms at Rs 95 single and Rs 160 double and there is a viewing tower close by.

Further still to the southwest, some 240 km from the capital, are the **Rapti Valley** and **Chitwan Forest**. Here is the **Royal Chitwan National Park**, the home of the one-horned rhinoceros, elephants, tigers and leopards. **Bharatpur**, the main centre in the Rapti Valley, is connected by road to Kathmandu via Hetaud. From Bharatpur a good road leads to the small but novel bazaar of **Narayangarh**. Nearby is the Narayani River, famous for boating, fishing and crocodile hunting.

Lumbini, the Buddha's birthplace, is accessible by the 32-km motorable road from Naubize on the loop line of Indian Railways (via Gorakhpur). Here in Lumbini Gardens are a broken Ashoka pillar (discovered in 1896) with an inscription commemorating a pilgrimage by the great ruler in the 20th year of his reign, the remnants of a monastery and a holy pond and a stone image of the Buddha's mother, Maya Devi. There is also a tourist hotel, the **Maya Devi** (20 rooms), which charges reasonable prices.

Biratnagar in the southeastern, is Nepal's main industrial centre and the site of the multipurpose Kosi River Valley Project. **Dharan**, 40 km to the north, has some attractive scenic spots. **Dhankuta**, 55 km further east of Dharan, is connected by a British-aided, modern highway connecting British Gurkha villages.

The district of **Helambu**, 80 km northeast of Kathmandu (three days on foot), is a region of Sherpa villages; it also has seven monasteries and the famous lake of **Gosainkunda. Namche Bazaar**, even further to the east in the **Mahalangoor Himalayas**, is the home of the famous Sherpa mountaineers and gives a superb view of Everest and the neighbouring peaks — **Lhotse, Nuptse** and **Ama Dablam**. One can fly there but overland by the bridle path it is a 16-day journey for the adventurous. Note that trekking permits are necessary for this type of journey (see **Immigration**). The celebrated monastery of **Thyangboche** is a one-day walk from Namche.

About 96 km west of Kathmandu is **Gorkha**, the old capital of the Gurkha principality, which is noted for the temples of **Gorhanath** and **Kalika** and for its scenic spots at Bar Park.

TREKKING IN THE HIMALAYAS
Trekking, besides flying, is the only means of seeing the country's central hills and valleys and all the northern highlands. The main trekking areas are in the Everest region, approached via Lukla airstrip (over 3,000 m). From here it is possible to visit Sherpa villages, the monasteries of Thyangboche and Pangboche, the peaks of Kala Pathar (5,045 m) and Gokyo (5,483 m) for the best views, and the Everest Base Camp; the region north of Pokhara, including Jomsom and the Annapurna Sanctuary and the villages of Ghandrung and Landrung; the Helambu-Langtang and Gosainkund Lake area, approached via Sundarijal or Trisuli, and the Jumla and Rara area, approached via Jumla airstrip. RNAC operates scheduled flights to all the trek regions; aircraft can also be chartered if booking is made six months in advance.

HOTEL GUIDE

Hotel address	Phone	Fax	Telex	Cable	≈	🍴	🍷
A (US$90-110) **B** (US$50-70) **C** (US$20-50)							
KATHMANDU AREA							
A							
Hotel de l'Annapurna Durbar Marg, P. O. Box 140	2-21711, 2-21411		NP 2205 AAPU	ANNAPURNA	▲	▲	▲
The Everest Hotel Baneswor, P. O. Box 659	2-20567, 2-20476	977-1-226088	2260 HOTEVS NP		▲	▲	▲
Hotel Soaltee Oberoi Tahachhal, P. O. Box 97	2-72550, 2-72555	977-1-272205	2203 SOALTE NP		▲	▲	▲
Hotel Yak & Yeti Durbar Marg, P. O. Box 1016	2-22635, 4-13999	977-1-227782	2237 YKNYTI NP		▲	▲	▲
Hotel Himalaya Sahid Sukra Marg, P. O. Box 2141	5-23900-9		2566 HOHIL NP	FLORA	▲	▲	▲
Hotel Kathmandu Maharajgunj, P. O. Box 11	4-13082, 4-18494-5		2256 NP	HOKAT	▲	▲	▲
B							
Hotel Malla Lekhnath Marg, P. O. Box 787	4-10320		2238 NP	MALOTWL	▲	▲	▲
Hotel Narayani Pulchowk, Lalitpur, P. O. Box 1357	5-21711, 525015-8		2262 NARANI NP	HONARAYANI	▲	▲	▲
Hotel Shangrila Lazimpat, P. O. Box 655	4-10051		2276 NP	SHANGRILA	▲	▲	▲
Hotel Shanker Lazimpat, P. O. Box 350	4-10151, 4-10152		2230 NP	SHANKER		▲	▲
Hotel Sherpa Durbar Marg, P. O. Box 901	2-28021, 2-28041		2223 NP NEPCOM	SHERPA	▲	▲	▲
Hotel Woodlands Durbar Marg, P. O. Box 760	2-22683, 2-20623		2282 HOWOOD NP	WOODLANDS	▲	▲	▲
Hotel Blue Star Tripureswar, P. O. Box 983	2-11470-74	977-1-226820	2322 BLUESTAR NP	BLUESTAR	▲	▲	▲
C							
Hotel Crystal Sukrapath, P. O. Box 29	2-23636		2290 NPCRYSTAL	CRYSTAL			▲

Hotel address	Phone	Fax	Telex	Cable	〰	🍴	🍽
KATHMANDU AREA – *Cont'd*							
C							
Hotel Yellow Pagoda Kantipath, P. O. Box 373	2-20337, 2-20338		2268 PAGODA NP	YELOPAGODA			▲
Aloha Inn Jawalakhel, Lalitpur, P. O. Box 1562	5-22796		2489 CKCIKT NP				▲
Hotel Ambassador Lazimpat, P. O. Box 2769	4-10432, 4-14432		2321 BASS NP	BASS			▲
Hotel Blue Diamond Jyatha, P. O. Box 2134	2-26320, 2-26392						▲
Hotel Gautam Kantipath, P. O. Box 2757	2-15014		2447 HOGAUT NP				▲
Kathmandu Guest House Thamel, P. O. Box 2769	4-13632, 4-18733		BASS 2321 NP	KATHOUSE			▲
OUTSIDE KATHMANDU AREA							
B							
Dhulikhel Mt Resort C/o Durbar Marg, P. O. Box 3203	2-26779, 2-200316		2415 RESORT NP	RESORT			▲
Dwarika's Hotel Battispatali, P. O. Box 459	4-70770, 4-12328		NP 2239 KTT (DWARIKA)	KATHMANDU			▲
Hotel Flora Hill Nagarkot, Bhaktapur, c/o Chhetrapati	226893						▲
C							
Hotel Sun-n-snow Dhulikhel c/o Kantipath, P. O. Box 1583	225092		2606 MEDREP NP	HORIZON			▲
Taragaon Resort Hotel Boudha, P. O. Box 507	470413, 470409			TARAGAON			▲
Hotel Safari Narayani Bharatpur, Chitwan, P. O. Box 1357 KATH	056-20130	0977-1-521291	2262 NARAYANI NP				▲

PAKISTAN

Pakistan comes as something of a surprise. It has scenery, a long and interesting history and much more. Right now it is a halfway house between Indian culture and that of the Middle East, though it is slowly drifting towards the latter. It has a great deal to offer the tourist but still does not seem to have made up its mind how to do it.

The northern part — Swat, Kaghan, Gilgit, Skardu and Chitral — contains some of the world's most beautiful sights, yet it remains relatively unknown. Three vast mountain ranges, the Himalayas, the Karakorums and the Hindu Kush — meet in this region. Between the mountains lie beautiful unspoiled valleys.

From the north, the Indus River serves in its lower reaches as a neglected communications artery. Pakistan would be a desert without this mighty river and its tributaries.

There are other main communications arteries — the north-south trunk railway and the grand trunk road. The railway has dozens of branches which form a network that straddles the entire country. The trunk road winds down into the plains from the legendary gateway, the Khyber Pass.

Alongside these can be seen evidence of the once great civilisation that shaped this part of the world and set the cultural tone of Pakistan.

Pakistan comprises several regions of different character and peoples: Punjab in the east, Kashmir and the North-West Frontier Province in the north, Sindh in the south and Baluchistan in the west.

Vast and partly arid, with a population of 105 million over its 796,095 km², Pakistan depends upon one of the most extensive irrigation systems in the world to grow wheat, rice, cotton, sugar cane and maize.

Karachi, with a population of more than 7.5 million, is its most populous city and Lahore, with more than 4 million, its next. Other major towns are Faisalabad, Multan, Hyderabad, Peshawar, the twin cities of Islamabad-Rawalpindi and Quetta.

Access has become easy in recent years with the government's desire to boost tourism as a foreign-exchange earner. Karachi in the south and Islamabad, the capital, in the north are on international air routes and both towns have plenty of domestic airline connections to every region.

The Indus civilisation, dated provisionally from about 2,500-1,500 BC, has been identified on more than 60 human settlements grouped into two main regions — one on the central Indus river system near the remains of the city known now as Harappa, and the other on the southern Indus near the remains of Moenjodaro. This significant civilisation, whose written script is yet to be deciphered, ended abruptly around the

middle of the second millennium. The causes are still unexplained.

Northern Pakistan was then the target of a number of invaders and was unwilling host to such diverse people as the Aryans, Persians, Greeks, Scythians, and White Huns, followed later by Arabs, Turks and Afghans. During the following centuries the country was divided into many — often warring — states. It was not until the establishment of the Delhi sultanate by the Muslim Afghan-Turks in 1207 that some sem-

◁ *Lahore street scene.*
Photo: Nancy Nash

203

Pakistan

blance of a centralised government was restored.

The Mogul Dynasty established in 1526 by Emperor Babar ruled much of Pakistan and northern India until the British took over in the 18th century. However, the Mogul emperors were retained as figureheads until 1857 when the British Empire was proclaimed.

Pakistan became independent of Britain on August 14, 1947, and at the same time was partitioned from what was once British India. The idea of a separate state for the Muslims of British India was conceived by the poet-philosopher Sir Muhammad Iqbal in 1930. It was formally adopted by the All-India Muslim League, led by Mohammad Ali Jinnah, generally known in Pakistan as the Quaid-e-Azam (Great Leader), in 1940. Pakistan originally comprised two wings, the one in the west being today's Pakistan. The former eastern wing is now Bangladesh.

The partition gave rise to rioting between Muslims and non-Muslims in Punjab and Bengal which resulted in the migration of several millions of people, with Muslims opting for Pakistan and Hindus and Sikhs for India.

For its first 11 years Pakistan worked under a parliamentary system, though during that period not a single election was held. As governments rose and fell through palace intrigues, army chief Field Marshal Mohammad Ayub Khan seized power through a coup. He enacted some agrarian, administrative and educational reforms that could not stand the test of time. He abolished the adult franchise and introduced an indirect system of elections which restricted the right to vote in presidential and parliamentary elections to only 80,000 members of grassroot municipal groups. The non-party system he introduced was a dismal failure and he had to permit political parties to function once again.

Discontent with Ayub's dictatorial rule and demands for autonomy in East Pakistan led to rioting in 1969. Violating his own constitution, Ayub Khan handed over power to the then army chief Yahya Khan, who declared himself president and annulled Ayub's constitution.

Yahya held the country's first free general elections on December 7, 1970, resulting in a massive victory for the Awami League in East Pakistan and Zulfikar Ali Bhutto's Pakistan People's Party (PPP) in the west. Awami League secured 167 of the 169 seats from the eastern wing and the PPP captured 88 of West Pakistan's 144 seats. The results theoretically allowed Awami League to form a government.

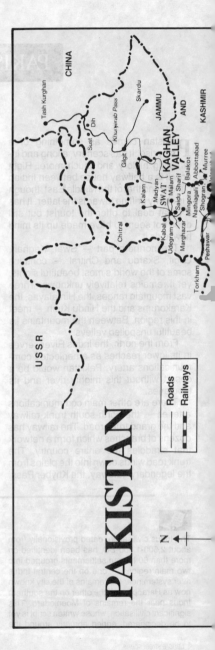

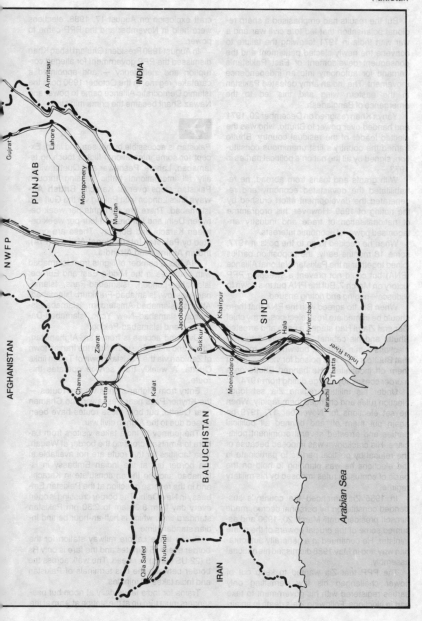

But the results had emphasised a sharp regional polarisation that led to a civil war and a war with India in 1971 following the failure to convene the newly elected parliament and the consequent development of East Pakistan's demand for autonomy into an independence movement. The Indian army defeated Pakistan in the eastern wing and this led to the emergence of Bangladesh.

Yahya Khan resigned on December 20, 1971 and handed over power to Bhutto, who was the elected leader of the residual country. Bhutto framed the country's first unanimous constitution, signed by all the nation's political parties in 1973.

With grants and loans from abroad, he rehabilitated the devastated economy and regenerated the development effort crushed by the rioting of 1969. However, his programme of nationalisation of trade and industry antagonised powerful economic interests.

When he decided to go to the polls in 1977, some 18 months early, the opposition parties joined together in the Pakistan National Alliance (PNA) but could not prevent a sweeping PPP victory on March 7. But the PNA put this down to widescale rigging and rioting ensued.

When Bhutto agreed with the PNA that there should be immediate fresh elections, army chief General Zia-ul Haq staged a coup and arrested Bhutto and his cabinet. Zia promised to hold elections within 90 days, but when he realised that Bhutto's PPP was poised for victory, he put them off indefinitely. He hanged Bhutto on a murder conspiracy charge dating from 1974.

Under his military regime Zia set foggy election rules and changed them rapidly. When he set elections for November 17, 1979 he again put them off and banned all political parties and arrested several prominent politicians. His crackdown was imposed because of the refusal by political parties to participate in the elections he was planning to hold on the basis of confusing rules imposed by his military regime.

In 1985 Zia amended the country's suspended constitution by personal decree, made himself president until March 20, 1990 and assumed some of the crucial powers of the prime minister. He continued in a generally authoritarian way and in May 1988 dismissed his national assembly.

The PPP that Zia wanted to keep out of power challenged his law permitting only parties registered with his government to take part in elections. Following Zia's death in an aircraft explosion on August 17, 1988, elections were held in November and the PPP came to power.

In August 1990 President Ghulam Ishaq Khan dismissed the PPP government for alleged corruption and inefficiency — and appointed a caretaker regime. In the October 1990 polls the Islamic Democratic Alliance came to power and Nawaz Sharif became the prime minister.

Pakistan is accessible by air, sea and land. Except for some international flights touching Islamabad, Lahore, Peshawar and Quetta, virtually all international traffic passing through Pakistan stops over at Karachi. **British Airways** links London with Peking via the Gulf and Islamabad. There are six flights per week between Delhi and Lahore and four per week between Karachi and Bombay. These are operated by **Pakistan International Airlines (PIA)**, **Indian Airlines** and **Air India**.

PIA has a number of flights from Islamabad with countries in the Middle East and Europe: Islamabad-London, Islamabad-Paris, Islamabad-Moscow, Islamabad-Frankfurt, Islamabad-Athens, Islamabad-Amsterdam, Islamabad-Istanbul, Islamabad–New York, Islamabad-Damascus and Islamabad-Peking.

Overland access is from Iran, Afghanistan, China and India. The route from the Iranian town of Zahidan via the Pakistani town of Taftan links Quetta. A weekly train service operates this route.

Entry from Afghanistan is via two routes — the Khyber Pass near Peshawar and Chaman near Quetta, but both these routes have been closed due to the Afghan civil war.

The journey to India takes visitors from Lahore to Amritsar, crossing the border at Wagah. Visa facilities for this route are not available at the border but at the Indian Embassy in Islamabad and the Indian consulate in Karachi, and in the reverse direction at the Pakistan Embassy in New Delhi. The border crossing is open every day from 8:30 am to 2:30 pm Pakistan standard time, which is half-an-hour behind Indian standard time.

Buses leave Lahore railway station for the border every 15 minutes and the fare is only Rs 5 (22 US cents) per head. The walk across the border between the bus terminals of Pakistan and India takes 10 minutes.

Trains for India leave daily at noon but passengers must turn up at the station at 9 am at the

Carpet factory in Lahore. ▷
Photo: Alain Evrard — The Stock House

latest for customs and immigration formalities. The train fare from Lahore to Delhi is Rs 110 for first class and Rs 55 for second class. But the journey is not recommended for those who wish to avoid harassment by customs and immigration staff, who are notorious for extortion. The size of the bribes they sometimes demand can make it more economical to travel by air.

The Pakistan route to China is by the Karakorum Highway across the world's highest mountain range. The border at the 4,876-m-high Khunjerab Pass is open from May 1 to November 30, but for individual travellers it closes on October 31. During this period it is open on all days, including holidays. Valid visas for China and Pakistan are required to cross the border. The Chinese Embassy in Islamabad issues visas for Rs 70. The Pakistan Embassy in Peking and its consulate in Hongkong issue visas for Pakistan. No visa is issued at the border. From the Pakistan side transport is available at Sost. **Pakistan Tours Ltd** runs jeeps and **Northern Areas Transport Service** operates buses between the two countries' border posts. The one-way fare is US$10.

All foreigners entering Pakistan need visas, except nationals of Tanzania, Malaysia, Hongkong, Zambia, Uganda, Trinidad, Tobago, Western Samoa, Nepal, Tonga, Fiji, Singapore, Maldives, Republic of Korea, Philippines and Romania. White South Africans and Israelis may not enter Pakistan. Tourists who are likely to stay for more than 30 days must register at the nearest foreigners' registration office. Failure to do so is against the law and will lead to offenders being refused permission to leave the country and being prosecuted.

A single journey entry visa is valid for a stay of up to three months. Multiple journey visas also are valid for three months at a time. Any number of journeys during the specified period, not exceeding one year, may be allowed on such visas.

Foreigners do not need a visa or permission to cross provincial boundaries within Pakistan. Nationals of India and Bangladesh, unless otherwise stated in their visas, are required to register with the nearest foreigners' registration office, irrespective of the length of their stay. Unless stated otherwise in their visas, Indians are normally allowed to visit only four towns of their choice specifically mentioned in their visas.

A cholera vaccination certificate is required from all travellers arriving from an infected area. A valid yellow fever vaccination certificate is demanded from all travellers arriving from any country where yellow fever is endemic. The exceptions are infants less than six months old, providing the mother holds a vaccination certificate dated prior to the infant's birth. Infants leaving the country for endemic areas have to be vaccinated irrespective of their age.

There are green and red channels at the airports. The red channel is for those with dutiable goods. Visitors can bring in duty free 200 cigarettes or 50 cigars or 220 grams of manufactured tobacco or an assortment of cigarettes and manufactured tobacco not exceeding 220 grams, plus perfumed spirits or toilet-water up to 1/2 a pint and foodstuffs including non-alcoholic beverages of value not exceeding Rs 100.

One camera with five rolls of film and one standard movie or video camera with two rolls of film and one projector, binoculars, portable typewriter or personal computer, portable taperecorder and radio, portable musical instrument, perambulator, toys in reasonable quantity, games and sporting equipment — including sporting firearms and cartridges in reasonable quantity — are also allowed duty free. But no sporting firearm is released by customs unless an arms licence issued by a competent authority is produced. Metal articles, including trophies or prizes, personal jewellery, or immitation jewellery of value not exceeding Rs 1,000, and gifts not more than Rs 500 in value may be brought in duty free.

Duty free entry is allowed for a personal motor vehicle for a tourist with the necessary customs' certificate (*carnet de passage en douane*) for up to three months, provided an undertaking is given to the customs officer at the point of entry that the ownership would not be transferred to anyone during the stay. The vehicle or driver must have a nationality plate, international registration certificate, international driving licence and insurance certificate from a company registered in Pakistan, or which has a guarantor in Pakistan. Car radios are duty free.

The Karachi Automobile Association, Oriental Bldg, McLeod Rd, and the **Automobile Association of Pakistan,** P. O. Box 76, Shadman Market, Lahore, can give useful information for tourists driving into Pakistan.

Visitors are prohibited from bringing alcoholic drinks into Pakistan. Non-Muslims, however, are allowed to buy liquor from authorised hotels — but the prices are steep. Liquor permits for buying drinks at designated stores, where prices are way below those charged by the hotels, can be obtained from the **Excise and Taxation Department**.

The basic unit of currency in Pakistan is the rupee, which is divided into 100 paisas. Coins of 5, 10, 25 and 50 paisa and 1 rupee are in circulation. Currency notes are in the denomination of 1, 2, 5, 10, 50, 500 and 1,000. The Pakistan rupee has a floating exchange rate adjusted against a basket of currencies. The State Bank of Pakistan announces the rates daily. It was Rs 23.1 against the US dollar in April 1991. Tourists may bring in any amount of foreign currency but not more than Rs 100 in Pakistani currency. Visitors are not allowed to take away more than Rs 20 in Pakistani currency. Unspent local currency can be reconverted up to a maximum of Rs 500.

An application has to be made to the State Bank through an exchange bank to reconvert larger amounts. Visitors are therefore advised not to get stuck with more rupees than they need to pay for their taxis to the airports, the airport tax of Rs 370 per head and such other incidentals. The hotels are not allowed by law to accept rupees in settlement of tourists' bills, which must be paid in foreign currency. There are banks at the international airports which display the daily rates announced by the State Bank. It is advisable not to change money at hotels, since they normally offer lower rates than the banks. Changing money with unauthorised persons is a crime and is not worth the risk, for there is too small a difference between the bank's rate and the under-the-counter rate on the streets. Traveller's cheques are converted by banks and hotels at a better rate than they offer for cash.

Urdu is the national language. English is used extensively in all governmental and commercial circles and fairly widely in hotels, airports, railway stations, post offices and large stores. Basic English is taught in all schools and is the medium of instruction for higher education.

Pakistan has extreme temperatures. The areas close to the snow-covered northern mountains are cold. Temperatures on the Baluchistan plateau are high — as they are in the deserts of Thar in Sindh and Cholistan in Punjab. Along the coast the climate is modified by sea breezes, but it is hot and humid. In the rest of the country temperatures rise steeply in summer and hot winds blow across the plains during the day. Dust storms and showers lower the temperature. Winters on the plains are pleasant, with minimum temperatures of 4°C in January. Although the country is in the monsoon belt, it is arid, except for the southern slopes of the Himalayas and the sub-mountainous tract.

There are well defined local seasons. Winter runs from December to February, spring from March to April, summer from May to September and autumn from October to November. In summer the temperatures on the plains may be as high as 45°C or 115°F. June to August is the hottest part of the year. Between July and August the monsoons begin and bring an average of 38-50 cm of rain on the plains and 150-200 inches in the lower Himalayan valleys.

Very light, preferably cotton, clothes are required for summer in the plains. Light woollens are needed in the northern areas in summer and on the plains in winter. In the hills winter temperatures may fall to −10°C. Those going trekking and mountain climbing in the northern areas should have a full clothes kit, even in summer. Night temperatures in winter in the hot deserts of Thar and Cholistan can drop as low as 1°C.

Government offices start and finish work earlier during the hot summer months from April to September — 8 am to 2:30 pm from Sunday to Thursday. Winter hours are from 8:30 am to 3 pm with a 40-minute break from 1:20 pm to 2 pm. The weekly holiday is Friday. The telegraph offices work round the clock seven days a week. The general post offices in all big towns operate normal office hours, with a late evening service until 7:30 pm. Large stores are open between 9 am and 9 pm. Small stores and market stalls remain open longer. Restaurants in major towns are open usually to midnight. Ramadan is the month of fasting and observed according to the Muslim lunar calendar. Office hours during the 30 days of Ramadan are 8 am to 1:30 pm. All restaurants remain closed between dawn and dusk throughout the month, as eating in public is prohibited for Muslims.

FROM KARACHI, LAHORE AND ISLAMABAD AIRPORTS: Buses and taxis are the usual transport available. The normal fare downtown from Karachi Aiport is Rs 100 and from Islamabad Airport Rs 120. The fare from Islamabad Airport to Rawalpindi is Rs 60 and Lahore Airport to downtown costs Rs 70. In the early hours or late at night the charges are increased by 10%. Taxis are available round the clock at the airports. Yellow-top taxis cost less but fares have to be negotiated.

TAXIS: These charge Rs 4 per km by meter, which is likely to be rigged. Therefore fares are negotiable. Hire cars at the front door of tourist hotels are relatively more expensive. It is advisable for tourists to hire the hotel cars if they wish to know in advance how much each trip will cost. The yellow-top taxis may be flagged down on the streets but are hard to find. Drivers usually speak basic English.

MOTORISED RICKSHAWS: For those with steady nerves these offer a cheaper means of travel at Rs 3 per km, though their meters too are faulty.

HORSE-DRAWN CARRIAGES: Two-wheeled vehicles (tongas) and four-wheelers (Victorias) are available for city transport in some neighbourhoods but are not allowed on some roads. Fares are negotiable before the journey and work out at about Rs 10 per km. There are point-to-point regular services of tongas which charge a minimum of Rs 2 per person.

BUSES: City bus fares are cheap, though the buses are overcrowded during rush hours. Fares for most journeys range between Rs 1 and Rs 2 for a journey up to 15 km.

UPCOUNTRY

BUSES: These operate round the clock on all the main highways but are more frequent in the north from Lahore through Islamabad to Peshawar. Private company buses leave Lahore from Badami Bagh bus-stand every 15 minutes for the six-hour journey to Islamabad/ Rawalpindi. The fare is Rs 33. Government transport service (GTS) buses, which are more reliable, leave from opposite the Lahore Railway station. Buses are crowded and seats are not bookable in advance, but advance bookings can be made on what are known as luxury buses of the Punjab tourism department, the GTS and special coaches of private companies. These vehicles are air-conditioned, comfortable and quicker. The charge is Rs 70 Lahore-Islamabad/Rawalpindi and Rs 40 Islamabad-Peshawar. The GTS and Punjab tourism department operate luxury bus services on the Lahore-Multan-Bahawalpur and the direct Lahore-Karachi routes.

Northern Areas Transport Corp. buses operate between Rawalpindi's Pirwadhai bus-stand and Gilgit from where buses leave for Skardu, Hunza and Sost. There is a bus service between Sost and the Chinese border-post of Pirali. There are also daily mini-bus services from Rawalpindi's Kashmiri Bazar bus-stand to Gilgit. Buses leave Pirwadhai bus-stand daily also for Mingora in Swat, Mansehra on the Karakorum highway, Dir and dozens of other destinations.

Fare on the Rawalpindi-Gilgit route is Rs 105, Rawalpindi-Mingora Rs 45, Rawalpindi-Dir Rs 45, Gilgit-Skardu Rs 45, Gilgit-Sost Rs 30 and Sost to Pirali in China US$10 per head. Bus services are available from all major towns to numerous other parts of the country.

TRAINS: An extensive network of railways links the main towns. The trunk line runs from Karachi through Rawalpindi to Peshawar. Services are also available from Karachi through Sukkhur and Quetta to the Iranian town of Zahidan. The railways have several classes. It is essential to reserve seats several days ahead of a journey on the air-conditioned and first-class coaches.

All sleeping accommodation also needs to be reserved in advance. No advance booking is required for the less expensive second-class coaches, but these are less comfortable, especially on long journeys. Advance reservation on these coaches can be made; some trains provide sleeping berths in the second class. Several trains each day operate on the main routes: for instance, twice daily between Quetta and Lahore, three times a day between Lahore and Peshawar via Rawalpindi and twice daily direct between Lahore and Rawalpindi.

Fares were due to be increased at the end of May 1990, but sample fares at that time were: Karachi-Lahore air-conditioned sleeper Rs 775, first-class sleeper Rs 315, first-class seat Rs 190 and second-class seat Rs 98. Karachi-Rawalpindi a/c sleeper Rs 940, a/c seat Rs 540, first-class sleeper Rs 380, first-class seat

Rs 234, second-class seat Rs 121. Karachi-Peshawar a/c sleeper Rs 1,040, a/c seat Rs 600, first-class sleeper Rs 420, first-class seat Rs 261, second-class seat Rs 135. Karachi-Quetta a/c sleeper Rs 575, a/c seat Rs 330, first-class seat Rs 135, first-class sleeper Rs 230 and second-class seat Rs 70.

Pakistan Railways allows a 25% reduction in rail fares to all foreign visitors (except Indian nationals) travelling either in a group or individually, provided their stay does not exceed six months. Foreign students are allowed half-fare concession. These rebates are allowed on production of a certificate from any tourist information centre to the Divisional Superintendent of Pakistan Railways in any major town or to the station masters in small towns.

AIR: Pakistan International Airlines (PIA) is the sole domestic carrier. It has regular services to all main towns and tourist destinations, operating Boeing 707s, 737s, 747s, Airbuses and Fokker Friendships. The most frequent services, operating several times daily, are between Karachi, Lahore, Islamabad, Multan, Faisalabad and Peshawar. There are also daily flights to Quetta, Hyderabad, Sukkhur, Saidu Sharif in the Swat valley, Moenjodaro, Gwadar, Pasni, Chitral (daily from Peshawar and twice a week from Islamabad), Gilgit, Skardu (both twice daily from Islamabad), Bahawalpur, and Muzaffarabad in Azad Kashmir. Sample one-way economy fares at the end of May 1990, including all taxes, were: Islamabad-Gilgit Rs 465, Islamabad-Skardu Rs 560, Peshawar-Chitral Rs 365, Karachi-Islamabad Rs 1,700, Lahore-Islamabad Rs 565. Services to Gilgit, Skardu, Chitral and Swat are subject to weather conditions. Airport tax on tickets bought abroad is Rs 20 on domestic flights and Rs 370 on all international flights.

PIA offers a variety of package tours of special interest which include history and archaeology, mountaineering, trekking and trout-fishing. Inquiries can be made at the nearest PIA office or the tours promotion section of PIA at Karachi Airport. PIA offers discounts ranging from 32.5% for groups of four to 20 visitors from Europe to 40% to those from Japan.

Pakistan Tours Ltd (PTL), a subsidiary of the government-owned Pakistan Tourist Development Corp. (PTDC), offers sight-seeing tours in and around main towns like Karachi, Lahore, Islamabad/Rawalpindi, Peshawar, Quetta, the Swat valley, Gilgit, Hunza, Skardu and Chitral among others. These tours are conducted in air-conditioned coaches, mini-buses, cars and jeeps, which can also be hired by tourists on request. City tours usually cost about Rs 200 per person, provided that at least five visitors are taking the tour. Inquiries can be made at tourist information centres in any major town.

Deep-sea fishing and sea cruises are also arranged on request. Pakistan Tours Ltd also arranges mountaineering/trekking expeditions, adventure tours, jeep safaris, trout fishing, bird-watching tours and overland tours to Kashgar and Urumchi in China. Government-approved guides are available through the tourist information centres and leading tour operators. Mountain trekking trips are arranged in northern areas from April to October.

Some of the leading tour operators are:

Pakistan Tours Ltd, 23/24 Flashmans Hotel, The Mall, Rawalpindi. Tel: 581480/ext 23; Telex: 5620 FH PK (attn PTL).

Sitara Travel Consultants (Pvt) Ltd, 163-A Bank Rd, Rawalpindi. Tel: 64750 and 64751; Telex: 5751 Sitara Pk.

Travel Waljis (Pvt) Ltd, P. O. Box 1088, Waljis Bldg, 10 Khyaban-e-Suhrawardy, Islamabad. Tel: 812151 and 828324 to 26.

Indus Guides, 7-E Shahrah bin Badees (Egerton Rd), Lahore. Tel: 304190 and 304196; Telex: 44344 Deens Pk.

Sehrai Travel and Tours, 6 Sadar Rd, Peshawar. Tel: 72088; Telex: 52369 Pcope Pk.

Polanis (Pvt) Ltd, 46-47 Sind Marsatul Islam, Hasrat Mohani Rd, Karachi. Tel: 226201.

Pakistan for long suffered a serious lack of good hotel accommodation and this still gives leading hoteliers an opportunity to charge unjustifiable rates. But the situation is improving gradually with competition spreading. In addition to **Pearl Continental** hotels in Karachi, Lahore, Rawalpindi, Peshawar and Bhurban in the Murree Hills, there are now **Avari** hotels in Lahore and Karachi. The **Holiday Inn** group is in Karachi and Islamabad and a **Sheraton** is operating in Karachi. Other first-class hotels established in recent years are **Taj Mahal, Plaza International, Mehran** and **Chilton** in Karachi, **Shalimar** and **United** in Rawalpindi, **Islamabad Hotel** in Islamabad. There are **Sarena Lodges** at Gilgit, Faisalabad and Quetta, and **Saidu Sharif** in Swat. A new **Saidu Sharif** is due to be commissioned in Hunza early in 1991. There are also the **Shangrila Resort** at Chilas along the Karakorum Highway, **Greens** hotels at Peshawar, and **Saidu Sharif** and **Nathiagali** in the Murree Hills.

The old Pakistan Tourism Development Corp. hotels, somewhat neglected but still operating, are **Falettis** at Lahore, **Flashmans** at Rawalpindi, **Cecil** at Murree and **Deans** at Peshawar. Most of the popular hotels throughout the country are listed in the easily available hotel guides but there are a great many others that are reasonable with a nightly charge of Rs 150 to Rs 350. All rooms normally have adjoining baths. There are several motels and guesthouses in Islamabad which charge from Rs 350 for a single occupancy to Rs 450 for double occupancy of rooms that have all basic amenities, including bath, air-conditioning, telephone etc.

In places of historic interest like Taxia, Moenjodaro and Katas, there are motels and rest houses run by the PTDC which offer accommodation that can be booked through PTL. PTDC runs motels and resorts at Hunza, Gilgit, Skardu, Chitral, Naran (Kaghan valley), Balakot (Kaghan), Besham (Karakorum Highway), Miandam and Kalam (Swat valley), Ziarat (near Quetta) and Keenjhar Lake. In Thatta region, north of Karachi there are a number of bungalows at Thatta itself, Makli Hill, Haleji and Keenjhar lakes, Bhambore and Jherruck. Normal prices are Rs 50 per person for a room for a day and night. The PTDC lodges usually cost Rs 275 for a single room and Rs 375 for a double.

Accommodation in the beautiful mountain valleys in the north in Swat and Kaghan is available in the PTDC motels and small bungalows of various government departments. There are some small hotels in such towns, but these would attract only those on a very tight budget. Temporary membership of some of the clubs in big towns is possible and, depending upon availability, these clubs will provide accommodation for a three-to-four-day stay. YMCA and YWCA hostels at Lahore, Karachi, Rawalpindi and Peshawar are available to members of affiliated international organisations.

Organisations assisting educational travel include the Pakistan Boy Scouts Association, Amin House, Moulvi Tamizuddin Khan Rd, Karachi, which organises individual and group visits to Pakistan for student members of Scout associations affiliated to the World Scout Bureau. It also organises camps, conferences, hikes, rallies and sight-seeing tours. Accommodation at Amin House (Tel: Karachi 551491, ca-

bles Pakscout) is available on prior request to Scouts and members of the Youth Hostels Association.

The hostel of the Pakistan Girl Guides Association is at sector H-9, Islamabad, with branches at Guide House, 5 Habibullah Rd, off Davis Rd, Lahore, at Streachen Rd Karachi, and Guide House, New Dabgari Gardens, Peshawar. The Pakistan Youth Hostels Association has its headquarters at 110-B, 3 Gulberg-III, Lahore, and maintains hostels at Taxila, Murree, Khanaspur, Balakot, Abbotabad, Sharan, Naran, Batakindi (Kaghan valley), Peshawar, Lahore and Choa Saiden Shah (Jhelum district).

There are a number of good clubs which tourists may use in Karachi, Lahore, Quetta, Islamabad, Rawalpindi, Abbotabad and Peshawar. Most of them have facilities for golf, tennis, squash, cricket and indoor sports. There are also race clubs, boat clubs and flying clubs. Accommodation in public retiring rooms is also available at the major railway stations.

Pakistani food is unexpectedly varied. What is generally known as Moghul cuisine is popular, highly spiced and complex. Curries are widely in vogue, though they are more lightly spiced than is usual in India. Seekh kebabs (minced spiced meat grilled on skewers), shami kebabs (minced meat and chick pea cakes), tikka (barbecued cubes of mutton, beef chicken or fish) and barbecued leg of lamb are delightful gastronomic experiences. Like all dishes they taste better in their place of origin.

Barbecued leg of lamb, called sajji in Baluchistan, has just a touch of spice and can be tried at the **Sarena Hotel** restaurant in Quetta. Relatively more spiced and totally different from the simple Baluch tradition, it is splendidly served at the **Farooq** restaurant in Karachi. Eaten with naan (tasty leavened bread of a wide variety) and green salad, it is a meal fit for a tribal warrior or a ravenously hungry tourist.

The curries come in many combinations of spices known as masalas, which are used in beef, mutton, chicken, fish and egg. Lightly spiced rice dishes with various meats are known as pullao. The more highly spiced dish is called biryani. Desserts are generally very sweet and often flavoured with saffron, rose water and other floral extracts, plus a generous sprinkling of various nuts. Often edible silver foil decorates the dish. Kulfi, a sweet dish similar to ice cream,

Pottery making in Baluchistan.

Photo: UNHCR

is widely available with falooda sprinkled with rose water. Much of the good food in Pakistan is served in small restaurants in the city bazaars and village markets. Follow your nose and eyes.

There are better class restaurants all over the country, though in the large tourist hotels versions of local dishes lack the touch of authenticity. Still they are the best available source of western food for conservative palates. Tuesdays and Wednesdays are meatless and only poultry and fish are served in restaurants.

Those in search of meat dishes in Quetta should try the **Loralai Restaurant's** barbeque section at **Hotel Sarena**, **Lal Kabab** on Prince Rd and **Tabaaq** restaurant, opposite Regal Plaza on the Circular Rd. While in Peshawar try **Usmania** restaurant on University Rd, the **Poolside Barbeque** at **Pearl Continental** and **Jehangir** restaurant on Cinema Rd. In Islamabad the better-known restaurants are **Mr Chips** and **Taj Mahal** restaurant in Jinah supermarket, **Tabbaq** and **Usmania** in Blue Area, **Daman-e-Koh**, perched high on the hill, **Jal Tarang** at Rawal Dam **Islamabad Hotel's** banquet hall for its buffet spread.

In Rawalpindi everyone knows **Shezan** on Kashmir Road and the **Tandoori** at the **Pearl**

Continental in Lahore. Other well-known restaurants are **Tabaq Cuisine** on the main boulevard in Gulberg-III, **Shezan** in Dayal Singh Mansions on The Mall, **Salloos** in the **Wapda House** on The Mall and **Mydaa** on the main boulevard in Gulberg-III. Karachi has the widest variety from **La Rosh** (German), **Le Marquis** (French), **La Mama** (Italian), **Bali** (Indonesian) in the commercial area of the Pechs and **Fujiyama** (Japanese) at Awari Towers.

Local handicraft is among the best buys. This includes gold and silver work, brass and copper vessels and ornaments, leather goods, embroidery (especially the colourful caps in the mountain valleys of the north), cottons, silks, camelskin lamps and vases in Multan and, of course, onyx, which is the best in the world. Pakistan produces some of the best emeralds in the world but the local cutting leaves much to be desired. Carpets are among the world's best and cheapest.

Digging around in the markets and bazaars, such as Kissa Khwani bazaar in Peshawar, can turn up some interesting and traditional pieces, especially in copper and brassware.

Among the main shopping centres in Lahore are Anarkali Bazaar, Liberty Market in Gulberg, The Mall, Shah Alam Market and the old bazaars inside the walled city.

In Karachi, for the cheapest place for shopping, visit Zaibunnisa Street, Abdullah Haroon Rd, Bori Bazaar, M. A. Jinah Rd and the city's many bazaars. The Sindh handicraft shop opposite the Sheraton Hotel has some attractive bargains. As in most other parts of Asia, bargaining is not only in order but a pleasant way of getting to know people. Compare prices before buying and drive a hard bargain, for the shopkeeper is doing his best to get the maximum from you.

Hockey and cricket are the most popular games in Pakistan, which is also one of the leading nations in squash. There are plenty of opportunities for golf, with excellent courses at Lahore, Rawalpindi, Islamabad, Bhurban in Murree Hills, Kabal in the Swat valley and Peshawar. There are tennis and squash courts in the main towns.

Fronting Karachi for 72 km, golden sands are washed by the warm waters of the Arabian Sea and further beaches run for almost 564 km along the Makran coast, most of which is unspoilt. In such surroundings swimming, scuba diving, yachting and deep sea fishing thrive as popular sports. Boats with outboard motors and launches can be hired from the harbour. There are plenty of fish, lobsters, oysters, prawns and crabs in these waters. For sports like yachting and scuba diving, get in touch with Karachi Diving and Salvage Agency (Tel: 224101) and the secretary of Karachi Yachting Club, Grindlays Bldg, Chundrigar Rd (Tel: 232127), the Boat Club, Moulvi Tamizuddin Khan Rd (Tel: 552057) and Sind Club, Abdullah Haroon Rd.

The rivers of the northern areas of Pakistan open for white water rafting and other white water sports are the Indus from Jaglot to Thakot, the Kunhar from Naran to Kaghan, the Swat from Behrain to Saidu Sharif, the Chitral from Dir to Batkhela and the Hunza from Aliabad to Gilgit.

Angling for brown or rainbow trout draws enthusiasts to the Kaghan valley, Swat, Hunza, Baltistan and other areas in the mountains. Major rivers and lakes in other parts of the country are also teaming with a wide variety of fish.

Haleji Lake near Karachi is a bird-watchers

paradise. Birds that can be seen include flamingoes, pelicans, herons, ducks, egrets, purple gallinule, jacanas and kingfishers, many of them coming during the season from as far away as Siberia.

There are ample opportunities for wild boar hunting in the plains of Punjab province. PTL or Sitara Travel consultants will arrange hunting tours.

Hiking trails around Islamabad, Murree Hills, Kaghan and the Swat valley and other areas of the northern part of Pakistan offer excellent facilities for those who like to see the wonders of nature on foot.

There are three skiing resorts in Pakistan, but two of them — Kalabagh in Murree Hills and Nalter, near Gilgit — are not open to the public because they have been taken over by the army and air force. The best equipped, Malam Jabba, which opened to the public and tourists in the winter of 1990, is linked by a 45-km hardtop road with Saidu Sharif. The driving time is about one hour 15 minutes. Saidu Sharif has daily flights from Islamabad and Peshawar. The resort is about 3,000 m above sea level with temperatures during winter hovering between −5°C to 5°C, while summer temperatures are 10°C to 25°C. The skiing season is between December and February-March.

The resort has a 52-room hotel with a 72-line UHF exchange linking it with rest of the world. Fully-equipped family cottages are also available. It has two chair lifts — one for beginners and one for practised skiers — plus stand-by generators in case of power failures. Skiing equipment is available at the resort.

Outdoor activities include skating and trekking. Inquiries should be directed to either Ramada Renaissance Worldwide Reservation system or directly to the Sales and Information Office, Malam Jabba Resort, 1-D Rehmat Plaza, Unit-4, Blue Area, Islamabad. Tel: (051) 819203, 817656; Telex 54476 Avari Park; Fax (051) 828844.

Polo is played in the northern areas of Pakistan — it was invented in this part of the world. Regular matches are held at Gilgit, Hunza, Baltistan and Shandur Pass, near Chitral. A tournament is held on 25 June between teams of the northern areas at Shandur Pass. Polo matches are played at Gilgit on August 14, March 20 to March 23 and other national days. There are polo tournaments between armed forces teams at Rawalpindi, Lahore, Peshawar and other areas.

Some of the highest peaks of the world are in

the Karakorums and Himalayas. The world's second-highest peak, K2, is in Pakistan. Nearly three-quarters of the northern areas of the country is covered by the Karakorum ranges, the southern portion of which face Kashmir and the northern portion Ladakh and Sinkiang province of China. The Hindu Kush ranges lie in the centre of the northern areas, touching Chitral and Gilgit. These provide a wide choice for mountaineers, trekkers and lovers of natural beauty and wildlife.

Dozens of mountain expeditions and trekking parties are given permission each year to climb various peaks, including K2.

Some of the highest peaks in Pakistan are:

- K2 — 8,611m.
- Gasherbrom-I (hidden peak) — 8,068 m.
- Broad Peak 8,048 m.
- Gasherbrom-II — 8,035 m.

Trekking in Pakistan involves walking at heights of up to 6,000 m to places where modern transport is either not available or deliberately not made use of.

No permit is now required to travel on the Karakorum Highway and the border with China across the Khunjrab Pass is open for international traffic during the months of the year when it is passable. Anyone trekking above 6,000 m must have a permit, but no permit is required for trekking in open zones. Trekking permits for restricted zones are issued by the government tourism division, 13-T/U College Road, Commercial Area, Markaz F-7, Islamabad. A list of open and restricted treks and application forms are available at this address.

Mountains are divided into open and restricted zones with permits for the open zones now issued within 24 hours. It takes 14 days from the date of application to secure a permit for climbing peaks in the restricted zone. Pakistani liason officers accompany all mountaineering expeditions. The fee charged for various peaks are:

- K2 (Chogri) peak, Rs 65,000.
- Peaks 8,001 m and higher, Rs 50,000.
- Peaks 7,501 to 8,000 m, Rs 35,000.
- Peaks between 7,001 to 7,500 m, Rs 28,000.
- Peaks between 6,001 and 7,000 m, Rs 20,000.

All mountaineering and trekking parties may bring food and equipment with them duty free.

Pakistan's unique landscape is a delight for trekkers, offering alluring challenges spread over the northern areas, which have the biggest glaciers outside the polar regions.

The PTDC also arranges tours and has marked seven treks, including two medium class and five strenuous treks, taking six to 30 days at different altitudes and covering various distances. The tours are organised in collaboration with British Airways and local tourist authorities. The PTDC provides all equipment, camping gear, guides and food for trekkers and the cost is considerably less than those charged in Nepal.

Pakistan's calendar features several political and religious holidays. The Islamic holidays fall on no fixed date and are observed on a lunar calendar progression.

Last week of February: Sibi festival at Sibi in Baluchistan; Sind Horse and Cattle Show at Jacobabad.

February-March: National Horse and Cattle Show at Fortress Stadium, Lahore.

March 2: Shabe Barat (National holiday).

March 23: Pakistan Day — public holiday to mark 1940 decision to press for a Muslim state independent of India.

Last week of March: Illuminations at Shalimar Gardens of Lahore.

April 17-18: Eid-ul-Fitr (marks the end of the fasting month).

May 1: May Day.

May 14-15: Kalash festival in Chitral Valley.

June 24-25: Eid-ul-Azha — celebration of the Day of Sacrifice during the last month of the Muslim calendar. Those able to do so make a pilgrimage to Mecca.

August 14: Independence Day — commemoration of the nation's founding in August 1947 (public holiday).

September 6: Defence of Pakistan Day — commemoration of the Pakistan-India war over Kashmir.

September 8: Eid-Milad-un-Nabi marks the birthday of the Holy Prophet Mohammad (public holiday).

October: Lok Mela — a folk festival held at Shakarparian Hill in Islamabad.

From October 18-21: The winter festival in Kalash Valley.

November 9: Birthday of national poet Mohammad Iqbal.

December 25: Christmas and birthday of the founder of the nation.

December 31: Bank Holiday (only banks are closed; government offices and businesses stay open).

Kyber Pass.　　　　　　　　　　　　　　　　　　　　　　　Photo: UPI

Addresses

Tourist information centres of the PTDC can be found in the international arrival lounges at Karachi, Lahore, Islamabad and Peshawar airports and at Shafi Chambers and the Metropole Hotel, both on Club Road in Sadar area of Karachi, Falettis Hotel on Egerton Rd in Lahore, 13-T/U College Rd in the commercial area of Islamabad and Deans Hotel on Islamia Rd in Peshawar. They are also at Thatta, Monejodaro, Quetta, Taftan, Bahawalpur, Multan, Rawalpindi, Taxila, Abbotabad, Saidu Sharif in Swat Valley, Skardu and Gilgit.

Pakistani tourist information offices abroad are:

Great Britain, Marketing Services (Tourism and Travel), Suite 433, High Holborn House, 52-54 High Holborn, London C1V 6RL. Tel: 01-2423131, Tlx: 23770 MSTTGPP.

Japan, World Vision Travel Company Ltd, Suite 604/605, Pacific Nogizaka, 9-6-29 Akasaka, Tokyo 107. Tel: 03-5474-4848.

Canada, Bestway Tours and Safaris, Ste. 202-2678, West Broadway, Vancouver, BC, Canada, V 6K 2G3. Tel: (604) 732 4686. Tlx: 0455768 SI BESTWAY VCR.

Denmark, Pakistan Tourism Development Corp., Vester Farimgsade 3, 1606 Copenhagen V. Tel: 01-121188. Tlx: 16307.

Publications

The PTDC, through its various centres, provides free brochures, including maps and the booklet, *Tourist Calendar*, which contains much useful general information. Detailed maps are best brought from abroad, since these are regarded internally as classified information. Other useful publications, which are available at tourist information centres, include a Pakistan tourism directory, trekkers guidebooks and a Pakistan hotel and restaurants guide priced at Rs 50.

DISCOVERING PAKISTAN

ISLAMABAD AND RAWALPINDI

Barely 16 km apart, the twin cities of Islamabad and Rawalpindi lie in the northern reaches of the country on the Potwar Plateau. Islamabad is the capital and though it functions as the administrative heart of Pakistan, because of its very recent origins (it was begun in 1961) it has as yet few of the attributes of a mature city.

An entirely planned city — like Canberra and Brasilia — Islamabad is a fine example of modern-city design. A Greek firm was responsible for the planning and some famous international architects have collaborated on the main buildings.

With the completion of great administrative building complexes over the past few years, the various government offices and associated agencies have been moving up from the old capital, Karachi. The Islamabad Secretariat buildings cover an area of 90,000 m², rising like some massive fortress against the magnificent backdrop of Margala Hills.

Rawalpindi, on the other hand, has a long history. Its location on the Grand Trunk Rd running to the west beyond Peshawar and the Khyber Pass, and to the east beyond Lahore to India, has always made it important to traders and soldiers alike. In recent times it has been a major military cantonment for the British; after independence it became the interim capital from 1959.

Rawalpindi's old buildings, mosques and bazaars are in complete contrast to the hard-edged impression created by the neighbouring capital, though in future years the two cities can be expected to merge; even today they tend to function as one.

In the immediate vicinity of the Islamabad-Rawalpindi complex, places of special interest include: the **National Park**, on the outskirts of Rawalpindi; the **Army Museum** on Church Rd, near The Mall, in Rawalpindi; **Daman-e-koh** and the **Shakar Parian Hills**, two pleasant picnic spots in Islamabad and the nearby **Institute of Folk Art Heritage** which has a permanent exhibition of folk art and collection of folk music; and 25 km from Rawalpindi, the **Margala Hills** overlooking Islamabad and the Rawal Lake.

UPCOUNTRY

Taxila, 32 km north of Rawalpindi, was once a satrapy of the Achaemenian (Persian) Empire, and at the time of Alexander the Great's invasion in 325 BC, a renowned and flourishing city, especially noteworthy for its university. It later came under the sway of Central Asian and Indian dynasties until sacked by the White Huns from the north in AD 455.

Today, the remains of Taxila constitute one of the region's most important **archaeological sites**. There are three distinct city sites within about 5 km of each other: Bhir Mound, the oldest, goes back to the sixth century BC; Sirkap, constructed under Graeco-Bactrian rule in the second century BC, comprises a long street with many buildings including an apsidal temple, a shrine of the double-headed eagle (probably of Scythian inspiration), and a large building be-

lieved to be a palace from which has been recovered a good deal of Western-influenced Gandhara-style sculpture; and Sirsukh, believed to date from the time of Kanishka (a powerful king of the Kushan Dynasty who reigned around AD 130), though only a section of the fortifications has so far been excavated, revealing a wall 5 km long and 5 m thick, with semi-circular bastions 28 m apart.

Besides the three cities, there are the remains of Buddhist monasteries and stupas. A well-kept and interestingly arranged collection of Gandharan art is housed in the nearby museum.

A little more than 160 km northwest of Rawalpindi lies the ancient city of **Peshawar**, the traditional gateway between Central Asia and the Indian peninsula. The heart of the city is the **Qissa Khawani Bazaar** (street of the story-tellers), where over the centuries travellers have met and exchanged stories of places and adventures over endless cups of green tea.

Today one may still enjoy the tea and take a pull on the communal water-cooled pipe, but the conversation doubtless is of politics. Still, the bazaar is no less colourful with its thronging bearded tribesmen resplendent in their bright robes — Afghans, Iranis, Uzbeks, Tadjiks, Afridis and Shinwaris.

Other fascinating bazaars in Peshawar include the **Bazaar Bater Bazen** (just off the Qissa), named for the bird market that once stood there but which in more recent years has become the centre for shops dealing in brass and copper wares; and **Mochilara** — the shoemakers' bazaar also in the same area — which sells exotic slippers and shoes, especially the beautiful Pathan chappal, embroidered in gold, silver or silk.

On the northwestern edge of the city the bastions of the **Bala Hissar Fort** (originally built by the Moghul Emperor Babar in 1519 and reconstructed in its present form by the Sikhs who ruled the Peshawar Valley from 1791 to 1849) give a magnificent view of the city and surrounding areas. The museum on the Grand Trunk Road in the cantonment area houses a rich collection of objects from the Gandharan period. **Mahabat Khan's mosque** in the city is worth seeing.

Shah-Ji-Ki-Dheri, on the southeastern outskirts of the city, comprises the crumbled remains of a huge stupa and monastery built by King Kanishka. Other important archaeological sites in the neighbourhood are **Charsada**, 28 km to the northeast, captured by Alexander the

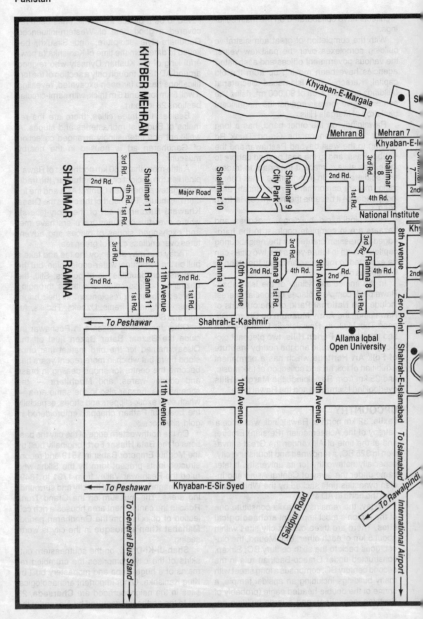

KHYBER MEHRAN

Khyaban-E-Margala

S

Mehran 8

Mehran 7

Khyaban-E-I

SHALIMAR

Shalimar 11

3rd Rd.
2nd Rd.
4th Rd.
1st Rd.

Major Road

Shalimar 10

Shalimar
9
City Park

Shalimar
8

3rd Rd.
2nd Rd.
1st Rd.
4th Rd.

Shalimar
7

3rd

2nd

National Institute

8th Avenue

Zero Point

Kh

Khy

2nd

RAMNA

Ramna 11

3rd Rd.
4th Rd.
2nd Rd.
1st Rd.

11th Avenue

Ramna 10

2nd Rd.
1st Rd.

10th Avenue

Ramna 9

3rd Rd.
4th Rd.
2nd Rd.
1st Rd.

9th Avenue

Ramna 8

3rd
Rd.
4th Rd.
Rd.
2nd
1st Rd.

Shahrah-E-Kashmir

← To Peshawar

Allama Iqbal
Open University

Shahrah-E-Islamabad

11th Avenue

10th Avenue

9th Avenue

To Islamabad

← To Peshawar

Khyaban-E-Sir Syed

To Rawalpindi

To General Bus Stand

Saidpur Road

International Airport

218

ISLAMABAD

Masjid

4th Rd.
School Rd.
Hill Rd.
Shalimar 6
Market Rd.
Aga Khan Rd.
Raza Shah
ritage
Nazimuddin Road
uaid-E-Azam
Kabir Avenue
4th Rd.
Ramna 6
Municipal Road
Cinemas
Ata Turk Avenue
Constitution Avenue
Telegraph Office
Shalimar 5
Nurpur Road
4th Avenue
Old Village of
Nurpur Shahan
3rd Avenue
Khyaban-E-Suhrawardy

Camping Site for Tourists
Murree Road
To Murree →
Rose & Jasmine
Garden
seum
itage)
Islamabad Club/
Golf Course
Sports
Complex
Rawal Lake
Park Road

Islamabad Park

RAWALPINDI

◉ Shopping areas
■ Parliament Building
(Ramna 5)

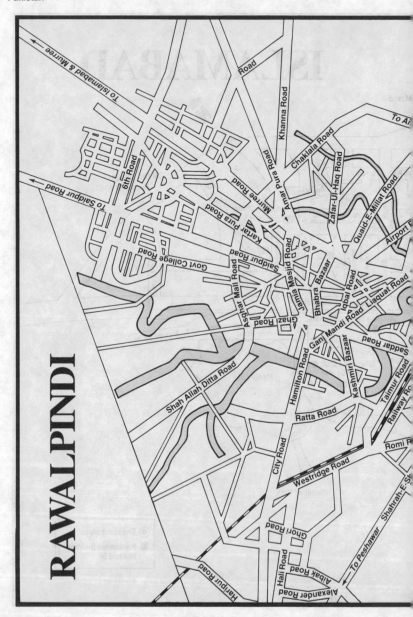

RAWALPINDI

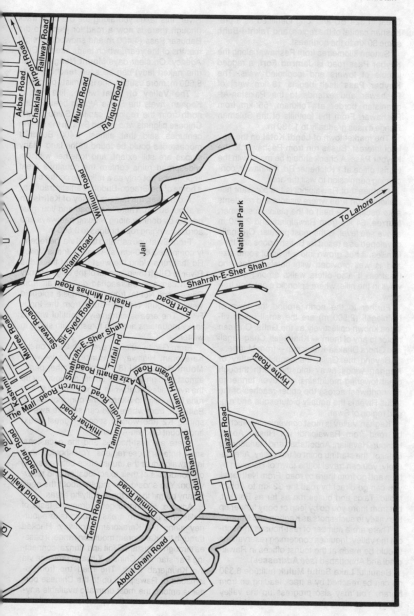

Great in 324 BC and long identified as a pre-Kushan capital of the region, and **Takht-i-Bahi**, some 80 km to the northeast.

Sixteen kilometres from Peshawar along the Khyber Pass road is **Jamrud Fort**, a ragged jumble of towers and loopholed walls. The **Khyber Pass** itself begins 18 km west of Peshawar and extends to the Pakistan-Afghanistan border at Torkham, 55 km from Peshawar. From the foothills of the Suleman Range it rises gradually to 1,130 m.

The market town of **Landi Kotal** on the way is of interest. Buses run from Peshawar to the Khyber Pass. A check should be made with the tourist office at 1 Kitchener Rd. Peshawar, concerning permission to visit the area.

Northeast of Rawalpindi is the pleasant hill-station resort area where visitors and residents alike escape the heat of the plains in summer. **Murree**, 64 km from Rawalpindi and 2,380 m above sea level, is the most popular. Originally developed as a resort for British troops and their families, it has grown into a town of some size and is well provided with hotels, cafes and theatres. It also offers walks among shaded ways in the hills, where splendid giant pine tree grow.

Further to the north around the town of Nathiagali (2,500 m) are the small resort villages known collectively as the **Galis**. One can motor to any of them — Khairagali, Chagalagali and Ghora Dhakka-Khanspur — from Murree.

Beyond the Galis, the beautiful **Valley of Kaghan** winds away into the north through great towering mountains, and even further to the northwest across the upper reaches of the Indus River is the equally picturesque and rugged region of Swat.

Kaghan Valley is most conveniently reached by road from Rawalpindi via Hasan Abdal, Haripur, Havelian, Abbottabad and Mansehra to Balakot, the starting point of the valley. Alternatively, you can travel to the town of Havelian by train and go from there by road. From Nathiagali you can go direct by road the 32 km to Abbottabad. Taxis and buses run as far as Balakot, but from there you go by jeep or pony further up the valley to such spots as Kaghan and Naran.

There are a number of rest-houses throughout the valley. Inquiries concerning reservations should be made at the tourist offices in Rawalpindi and Abbottabad (*see* **Addresses**).

Beautiful **Lake Saiful Muluk** (altitude 3,390 m) can be reached by a track leading up from Naran. You may also progress up the valley from Naran along the course of the Kunhan

River: this takes you along the old mule track (though there is now a road for jeeps) to the Babusar Pass (4,400 m and snowbound eight months of the year), which leads into the Gilgit Agency. On clear days **Mount Nanga Parbat** (the naked lady) can be seen reaching up to 8,500 m; more usually, she is in misty purdah.

The **Valley of Swat** which, like that of Kaghan, rivals the Swiss Alps in beauty, runs north from the regional capital, Saidu Sharif. Chinese pilgrims who visited Swat in the 5th-7th centuries said that almost 1,400 Buddhist monasteries could be found in the land. Many stupas are still extant, and together with the widespread ruins confirm the country's great importance not only as a religious centre but as a home of the Graeco-Buddhist artistic tradition.

From Swat, the famous **Valley of Kafiristan** is about 80 km. There is no road and you must ride up by donkey along winding pathways and across swinging rope bridges to 3,500 m.

From Swat you can also travel via the recently completed 640-km, all-weather Indus Valley Rd that runs along the west bank of the Indus River to **Gilgit** town, capital of the Gilgit Agency which can also be reached daily by air from Rawalpindi. Not far from the town is a splendid view of Mount Nanga Parbat from the Indus River. The area is extremely beautiful with its rocky mountains and rich forests, with skiing in winter.

From Gilgit you can travel by bus/car on the Karakoram Highway to Hunza. The views of **Mount Rakaposhi** (8,368 m) and other peaks almost as high make the precarious journey up the river valley worthwhile. A new road (240 km) runs from Gilgit to **Skardu**, the principal town of Baltistan, from where one can see the awe inspiring **K2** (the world's second-highest peak) and Mount Godwin-Austen.

There are rest-houses and the occasional small hotel in these regions. You should check in Rawalpindi at the tourist office before setting out for details of their exact location and reservation. You should also inquire about the need for any permit to visit these outlying areas.

Anyone wishing to get a dramatic taste of Pakistan's northern areas, should take a journey along the Karakoram Highway. Hacked through the Karakoram mountain range, it passes through Kohistan, Gilgit and Hunza, connecting Pakistan with China's Xinjiang province via the Khunjerab Pass. The road trip from Islamabad or Rawalpindi up to the Chinese border is among the most dramatic available anywhere in the world. Group tours are available from Rawalpindi-Islamabad to the Chinese province of Xingjiang via Khunjerab Pass between May and October, for which PTL, Flashmans Hotel, Rawalpindi and private tour operators can be contacted.

About 275 km southeast of Rawalpindi, almost on the border with India, lies **Lahore**, Pakistan's City of Gardens. Long established, it was noted by the Chinese traveller Hsuan Tsang as a large city in 630. Conquered for Islam by Mahmud of Ghazni in 1021, Lahore enjoyed a golden age during the Moghul Empire from the reign of Humayun (died 1556) to that of Aurangzeb (1707). It later became the capital of the Sikh Empire of Ranjit Singh (1839) and then, with the rest of the Punjab, fell under British rule after the second Sikh War in 1849.

Lahore is Pakistan's second-largest city, with a population of 4 million, and its foremost cultural and educational centre. It owes its distinctive personality to its old walled city and to its many fine buildings and gardens.

Within the old city stands **Lahore Fort**, enlarged and restored by the great Moghul emperor Akbar (reigned 1555-1605). Notable features include the Diwan-i-Am (Hall of Common Audience) with its Jharoka (balcony) on which the emperor was enthroned, the Shish Mahal (Hall of Mirrors) and the Naulakha, a marble pavilion in the form of a Bengali dwelling. Its northern wall displays magnificent kashi tile work, as does the panelling of the walls and minarets of the nearby mosque of Wazir Khan (built in 1634).

Just west of the fort is Aurangzeb's huge **Badshahi Masjid** (mosque). The **Shalimar Gardens**, 9 km east of the city, were laid out by the Emperor Shah Jahan in 1637; they are an outstanding example of Moghul landscaping. In the north of the city is the **tomb of Nur Jahan**, wife of the Emperor Jahangir and the only empress whose name appears on Moghul coins.

The more recent buildings, such as the Punjab University, the railway station and the Supreme Court and High Court buildings, display a fascinating blend of Gothic and Moghul styles. In front of the university building stands the great gun **Zamzama** immortalised in Rudyard Kipling's *Kim*. On the other side stands the excellent **Lahore Museum**, notable for its collection of Moghul paintings and Gandhara-style sculpture; Kipling's father was curator of the museum from 1875-93.

Besides these monuments, there are interesting sights of more recent origin, such as Minar-e-Pakistan (Pakistan Column), and Is-

lamic Summit Column.

The town of **Multan**, well south of Lahore, is noted for its handicrafts — carpets, shoes, glazed pottery and enamel work. Of interest in the town are the Old Fort, the Shrine of Raknud-Din and the **tomb of Shams-i-Tabrez**.

Between Lahore and Multan is the town of Sahiwal, which can be reached either by road or rail; it puts the visitor in reach of the very significant **archaeological site of Harappa**, just 6.4 km away. Harappa, like Moenjodaro, is one of the great cities of the ancient Indus Valley civilisation. At the site there is an interesting museum and a rest-house where visitors with reservations can stay. It is best to visit Harappa in the winter, spring or autumn months when the heat is not a problem.

The **Quetta and Kalat** Division of Baluchistan in the west (formerly called the Baluchistan Agency) is a rugged, sparsely populated land of rocks, hills and mountains, but dotted with fertile valleys and some of Pakistan's finest fruit-growing areas. Its inhabitants are correspondingly tough and belong to a number of tribes, many of which are nomadic. They have a code of honour to which they adhere with almost religious fervour. To be hospitable and to provide for the safety of the person and property of a guest is one of its most important features; to avenge bloodshed is another.

The town of Quetta, Baluchistan's major city, and a place of splendid scenic beauty, is 856 km from Karachi and 1,170 km from Lahore. It derives its name from the Pushtu word kwata — fort. Its summers are pleasant, the winters severe — with abundant snowfall. Considered the cleanest city in Pakistan, Quetta is an important military port well known for its Army Command Staff College. It is reached through the famous **Bolan Pass** which begins at Mach, the railway emerging into the Quetta plain at Kolpur (1,910 m), the highest point on the route.

Less spectacular but equally important is the **Lak Pass**, which connects Quetta with Kalat and the border. Although this pass is rugged and bald, the traveller is well rewarded when he reaches the top at Shelabagh (2,016 m) with a beautiful view of Chaman town, Spin Boldak in Afghanistan and the plains beyond. In winter the high valleys and passes are snowbound for a short period.

Recently, archaeologists have discovered mounds near Quetta which are believed to date back to the Moenjodaro-Harappa period. The Hanna and Urak valleys and the Spin-Karez reservoir and Hanna Lake (12 km from Quetta) are the most popular picnic spots in the area. The most striking and important of all the passes in the area is the **Khojak Pass** linking Quetta with Chaman and ending near the Afghan town.

Pishin Valley, 48 km from Quetta, is surrounded by 4,850 ha of vineyards and orchards. . Its rich harvest of apples, grapes, plums, peaches and apricots is loaded at Yaru Railway Station, 12 km from the small town of Pishin. Thirteen kilometres further on, at **Kushdil Khan**, is a beautiful **artificial lake** which provides good duck shooting. In winter it freezes, offering a skating venue.

Ziarat (also called Kishgi) is a pretty little hill town decorated with abundant wild almond trees and bougainvillea, at 2,480 m amid a large juniper forest. Two motorable roads, the Kach and Kuchlak, link it with the railhead at Quetta, 130 km to the west.

A drive on the Kuchlak Rd provides an opportunity to see mountain sheep and even panthers on the hill slopes. **Sandeman Tangi**, 12 km away, is a valley of towering pale cliffs — like a lost world.

There are government bungalows and a youth hostel at Ziarat.

Karachi, sitting hot and dusty on the edge of the desert, is of little definite tourist interest, though, like all such places, there is much for the connoisseur of the less picturesque aspects of Asian life. The city bazaars are interesting.

Karachi's recorded history goes back only to the 18th century when it was but a fishing village. Once the nation's capital, it still remains the principal commercial and industrial centre. It is the largest city of Pakistan, with a population of more than 7 million.

The crowded **Bohri Bazaar** offers a variety of interesting buys and sights: snake charmers, fortune tellers, pavement dentists and wandering musicians operate side by side with vendors of great piles of spices and sellers of cheap tactic toys. The ginger hair of the more-than-usually-devoted Muslim is a frequent sight.

There are many more bazaars and markets specialising in textiles, silver and gold: Juna Market, Kharadar, Mithadar, Jodia Bazaar and the Empress Market.

Other places of interest in the city include the **Frere Hall** (grandly Victorian) set in the pleasant Bagh-e-Jinnah gardens; the **Quaid-e-Azam Mausoleum** (to the Father of the Nation, Quaid-e-Azam M. A. Jinnah); the **Defence Housing Society Mosque**; the grave of the late prime min ister Liaqat Ali Khan; the **President's House**; the zoo; and the Sindh and Landhi in-

dustrial trading estates where the city's modern factories and mills are located.

The **Karachi Museum** has a collection widely representative of the different regions of the country: ancient sculpture, coins and other relics from the past; especially notable are some exhibits from the archaeological excavations at Moenjodaro. The museum is set in the centre of Burns Garden.

On the northern outskirts of the city lies **Manghopir**, the shrine of a Muslim saint and home for a family of crocodiles.

Clifton, only 5 km south of the city, is a picnic spot with a long promenade pier, bordered by hanging gardens, which leads to the beach. In the vicinity is the **Pidgeon Temple**, a Muslim shrine with a sweet-water spring and the municipal aquarium.

Other **popular bathing beaches** are Sandspit (16 km away), Hawks Bay (18 km), Paradise Point and Baleji. Swimming is enjoyed most of the year with the exception of the monsoon season from about May to August. Keamari, Karachi's harbour, offers boats for those interested in sailing or fishing. Bunder boats (outrigger sailing vessels) can be rented very cheaply, complete with crew.

About 22 km east of Karachi on the road to Thatta are the mysterious **Chaukandi tombs**, whose decorative motives in stone are some of the finest such works in the Subcontinent. Further on (64 km from Karachi) are the recently excavated ruins of the ancient city of **Bhanbore**, once a great port. There is a museum of local discoveries near the site.

Thatta, 103 km from Karachi, is famed for its picturesque Indo-Muslim architecture. Although these particular monuments go back only to the 16th and 17th centuries, the town has a history reaching back much earlier; it was here that Alexander the Great rested his troops after their long march from the north, and his admiral, Nearchus, assembled his fleet before leading it back to the Persian Gulf.

Once the seat of a number of ruling dynasties of Sindh (as this southern area of Pakistan is known), Thatta stands amid the ruins of its ancient glory. The most notable building is a great mosque of the Moghul Emperor Shah Jahan, which has 93 domes, both great and small. Its glazed earthenware tiles and painted stucco decorations rank among the finest.

Years of careful work have gone into the restoration. The mosque is in the outskirts of the present town, a place of narrow lanes and multistorey houses of wood and plaster, with double

Badshahi Mosque, Lahore. Photo: Fialho

windows and horseshoe arches. From the roofs of houses project the wind catchers, which bring the cool breeze down into the otherwise hot rooms.

On the Karachi side, Thatta is dominated by the **Makli Hill**, a vast necropolis extending over an area of 1,540 ha and said to contain some **one million graves**. Most of the remains date back to the dynasty of the Summas, who ruled Sindh from the mid-14th to the early 16th centuries, though the latest monuments were left by Moghul governors of the region.

Perhaps the most notable feature of these remains is the wealth of geometric and floral design carved in the stone. The tomb of Jam Nizamuddin, even though partly despoiled, is the richest of all in this respect. The later Arghun and Moghul tombs are distinguished by brick, enamel and glazed tiles of beautiful colour. The best preserved are the tombs of Mirza Isa Khan, Mirza Jani Beg, Mirza Ghazi Beg, Mirza Tughral Beg, Diwan Shurfa Khan and Amir Khalil.

Pottery of Thatta blue tile is still made today and is available in the area.

Thatta can be reached from Karachi by road (bus, taxi or hire car) and by rail, though the nearest railway station, Jungshahi, is about 20 km from Thatta town; the rest of the journey must be made by road.

Haleji Lake, nearly 90 km from Karachi (but before Thatta), is the main reservoir for Karachi's water supply. There is excellent fishing and some game-bird shooting in season (partridge, quail, duck and snipe). Some 18 km north of Thatta is **Kairi Lake**, which also has fishing, hunting and swimming facilities.

Jherruck, on the banks of the Indus River 56 km from Thatta, is another popular place for aquatic pursuits. The **Shrine of Amirpir** near Jhimpir Railway Station is well worth a special visit.

Some 192 km northwest of Karachi along the National Highway lies the town of **Hyderabad**; with a population of more than 1 million; it, too, was once a capital of Sindh. The city is known for the tombs of the Kalhore and Talpur families who ruled from the mid-18th to the mid–19th centuries — and not least for the fine embroidery work on sale in the city's shops.

There are also **two old forts** worthy of attention, one entirely mud-walled. Close by, Kotri barrage and Ghulam Mohammad barrage supply water through a network of canals to convert the land from desert into fertile fields. Another barrage — said to be the largest irrigation project of its kind in the world — can be found 320 km further north at Sukkur.

But of all the places of interest in Sindh, the excavated remains of the ancient city of **Moenjodaro** (mound of the dead) are by far the most fascinating. Work on the site was begun by the British in 1922, revealing an extremely elaborate urban complex with buildings made of baked bricks, paved and drained streets and what was probably a system of chutes and receptacles for garbage disposal. All this originated as early as the middle of the third millennium BC.

In recent years, owing largely to the rising level of the underground water table (a result of nearby irrigation works), the site was threatened with destruction, but is now safe — thanks to a UNESCO well-pumping project. Moenjodaro — along with the city of Harappa farther north — is believed to have been a major city of a vigorous civilisation that flourished in the Indus Valley from 2500-1500 BC. There is evidence of a sudden termination of activity in the city, but what caused it (invading Aryans or disastrous floodwaters from the river or whatever) has not been determined. Moenjodaro lies 656 km north of Karachi and can be reached either by road, rail or air. Going by train from Karachi, you disembark at Moenjodaro Railway Station (previously called Dokhri) and take a tonga (horse-drawn vehicle) the remaining 13 km to the site. From Lahore, you disembark at Larkana, and the remaining 40 km must be covered by taxi.

The sites and local museum can be covered in a single day. Those interested in making a more thorough inspection can stay overnight in the Archaeological Department's bungalow if a reservation has been made through the tourist office in Karachi. November to March, when temperatures are moderate, is the best period to visit the area.

The remains of the city lie in an irregular series of mounds. They comprise two parts: the upper towards the east and the lower towards the west. The upper city was probably fortified.

The city is well planned and has streets up to 10 m wide, which cross at right angles. Houses of the upper classes seem generally to have comprised a courtyard with access through a side alley, a watchman's room, living rooms of different sizes including a kitchen, a paved bathroom and a well. Bricklined drains opened into the streets and chutes built through the walls for disposal of rubbish opened into rectangular bins, which were probably cleaned regularly by municipal workers.

The citadel or upper city (known as the SD Area) is crowned by a Buddhist stupa with attached monastery, both dating from the Kushan period some 1,700 years after the death of the city proper. From the summit of the stupa mound, one has a fine view of the surrounds including the Indus River.

Immediately to the west of the stupa mound in the old city and across what is called Divinity Street are the remains of a once-imposing structure possessing a spacious hall and a complicated system of apartments. From its general appearance and proximity to the Great Bath — which was probably a sacred bathing pool — it is surmised that this was a building housing a college of priests, in a part of which the chief priest resided.

The Great Bath comprises an open quadrangle with verandahs on its four sides, galleries and rooms at the back, a group of halls on the north and a large bathing pool (12 m long, 7 m wide and more than 2 m deep) in the centre. A flight of steps enters the pool at each end. Great care was taken to ensure the pools' walls were watertight and it was probably filled from a well in a nearby chamber. To the west are the remains of the Great Granary.

Remains of other upper-class houses lie in the so-called HR Area, which is approached by the main road to the east of the stupa mound called East Street and entered by way of First Street. One of the houses in this area contains an interesting pottery kiln. Remains of a well-preserved structure in High Lane represent a typical house of the city. The elaborate drainage system and soak-pits for disposal of sewage are remarkable.

The VS Area also consists of the remains of better-class housing. A room on First Street with conical hollows sunk into its floor was probably used as a shop. In some of these houses drainpipes descending from upper storeys are visible.

Other buildings of interest include a temple, a high official's house and an inn.

HOTEL GUIDE

Hotel address	Phone	Fax	Telex	Cable	〰	🍴	🍷
A (US$90-100) **B** (US$25-50) **C** (US$12-25)							
ABBOTABAD **C**							
Simla Hill Sherwan Rd	5751						▲
Sarban The Mall	4876, 4877, 4888						▲
BALAKOT **C**							
PTDC Motel	8						▲
CHILAS **C**							
Shangrila Midway House	235						▲
CHITRAL **C**							
PTDC Motel	(0533) 683						▲
FAISALABAD **A**							
Faisalabad Sarena Club Rd **C**	(081) 70071-9	(081) 70070	7821 SARENA PK		▲	▲	▲
Rex Satiana Rd	45299, 45922		43353 REX PK				▲

Pakistan

Hotel address	Phone	Fax	Telex	Cable	≈	⫟	☕
HYDERABAD							
C							
City Gate National Highway	611677						▲
Faran Sadar	29993-96						▲
ISLAMABAD							
A							
Holiday Inn Agha Khan Rd	051-826121-15	820648	5470, 5612 HISSD PK				▲
Islamabad Hotel Civic Centre	827311-20	92-51-820763	5643 IHI PK				▲
B							
Lords Inn 18-F-6/2	813582						▲
C							
Capital Inn 18 St-4, E-6/3	815546						▲
Zorez Inn 40, St-30, F-8/1	853404		5552 ZAHUR PK				▲
KARACHI							
A							
Airport Hotel	480141		HOTELIER		▲	▲	▲
Avari Towers Fatima Jinah Rd	525261	(042) 58156	24400 AVARI PK		▲	▲	▲
Holiday Inn Abdullah Haroon Rd	520111		25466 HICK PK		▲	▲	▲
Peral Continental Ziauddin Ahmad Rd	515021		23627 HICK PK		▲	▲	▲
Sheraton Club Rd	521021-60		25255 ASHER PK		▲	▲	▲

Hotel address	Phone	Fax	Telex	Cable	〰	🍴	🍽
KARACHI – *Cont'd* **B**							
Taj Mahal Shahrahe Faisal **C**	520211-50		24267 TAJ PK		▲	▲	▲
Midway House Star Gate Rd, Air Port	480371-5		25860 MHL PK				▲
Plaza International	520351-20		25706 PLAZA PK				▲
Faran	430201-5		256 MAJID PK				▲
Jabees	512011-5		24325 JABIS PK				▲
Mehran Shahrahe Faisal	515061-30		23616 PK				▲
LAHORE **A**							
Avari 87 Shahrahe Qaide Azam	69971	(042) 58156	44678 AVARI PK		▲	▲	▲
Pearl Continental Shahrahe Qaide Azam **C**	69931-20		44877, 44167 PEARL PK		▲	▲	▲
Falettis Egerton Rd	303660-10		44469 FLH PK				▲
Shalimar Liberty Market, Gulberg	870331-33						▲
Service International Upper Mall	870281-87		44230 HINTL PK		▲	▲	▲
MULTAN **C**							
Mangol L. M. Q. Rd	30164-65						▲

Hotel address	Phone	Fax	Telex	Cable	≋	¶¶	⌣
MURREE **C**							
Cecil Imtiaz Sahheed Rd	2247		5620 FH PK				▲
Brightland Imtiaz Shaheed Rd	2270						▲
NATHIAGALI **B**							
Greens Hotel	544						▲
PESHAWAR **B**							
Peral Continental Khyber Rd **C**	76361-9	76465	52389, 52309 PEARL PK		▲	▲	▲
Deans Islamia Rd	79781-3						▲
QUETTA **B**							
Sarena Shahrahe Zarghoon **C**	70071-9	(081) 70070	7821 SARENA PK		▲	▲	▲
Lourdes Staff College Rd	70168-69						▲
RAWALPINDI **A**							
Pearl Continental The Mall	66011-20	63927	54063, 5736 PEARL PK		▲	▲	▲

Pakistan

Hotel address	Phone	Fax	Telex	Cable	≈	¶	◥
RAWALPINDI – *Cont'd*							
C							
Flashmans The Mall	581480-8		5620 FH PK		▲	▲	▲
Kashmir Wala Tourist Inn The Mall	583186-89						▲
SKARDU							
A							
Shangri-La	(0575) 970				▲	▲	▲

SRI LANKA

Sri Lanka entered the 1990s in a climate of uncertainty. This island republic off the southern coast of India, christened as Serendib by the early travellers who marvelled at her natural beauty and serenity, has been gripped by one of the greatest crises it has had to face since her history began to be documented some 2,500 years ago.

A protracted struggle for an independent state by Tamil separatists has led to many communal uprisings over the past three decades, with the movement taking the form of guerilla warfare during the past 10 years and driving the island nation of 16.4 million people deeper into debt and economic crisis. In 1989, the government narrowly escaped being toppled in a leftist youth-instigated rebellion which lasted almost a year and effectively put a stop to tourism — one of the country's major foreign exchange earners.

As Sri Lanka tackles these problems it can partly comfort itself with a literacy rate of 87.2% and a annual per capita income of US$360 (both figures amongst the highest in the region), which demonstrate the nation's growth potential and hold much promise for its future.

Despite internal turmoil over the past decade, the country has demonstrated marked improvements in agriculture, housing, irrigation and living standards. The economy has proved resilient and the problems are now largely confined to northern and eastern districts.

This tropical island of 65,610 km² is inhabited by two major ethnic groups and at least two more sub-groups. The Singalese comprise 74% of the population, Tamils 18.1%, Muslims 7.1% and Burghers (descendants of Dutch and Portuguese colonists) and others 0.8%.

Sixty-nine per cent of the people are Buddhists. Hinduism is the religion of 15%, while Christianity and Islam are practised by 7% each. Sri Lanka has traditionally been an agricultural economy with 46% of the population still making a living from it. However, of late there have been major attempts to industrialise the nation with foreign investments and export-oriented production.

Sri Lanka's traditional major exports of tea, rubber and coconut have today given way to gemstones and garments, symbolising the tilt towards industry and commerce. But the island still produces much of the world's best tea.

The history of Sri Lanka recedes into legend, with some of the earliest references to the island made in the Indian epic *Ramayana*, which describes how the hero Rama conquered most of the island in the process of rescuing his wife Sita, who had been abducted by Ravana, king of Lanka.

From then on, the history of Sri Lanka revolv-

es around the island's struggle with invaders — most of whom came from neighbouring India and towards the 15th century from Europe. All of them left their mark in the contemporary make-up of the nation, its people and their beliefs.

The arrival of North Indian Prince Vijava in Lanka established the Sinhala race here, the first people to indulge in a permanent agro-based industry. Of the original settlements, Anuradhapura grew into a powerful kingdom

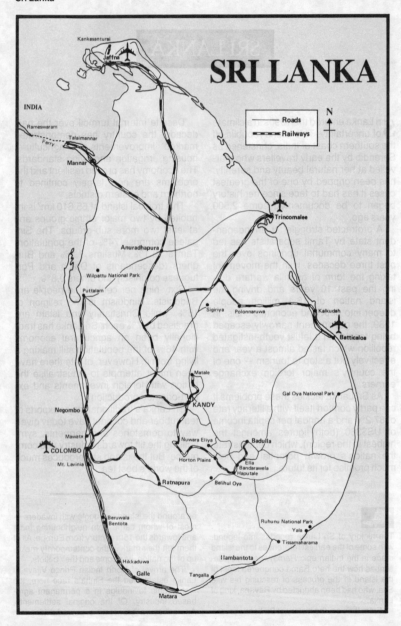

under the rule of King Pandukabhava, to become the governing seat of Lanka for many centuries. In 247 BC the Arahat Mahinda, a disciple of the Lord Buddha and son of Emperor Asoka of India, visited Anuradhapura with an entourage of monks, effectively opening the doors to the Buddhist philosophy.

From time to time the island was partitioned by the rule of invading forces, but there were also periods when a Sinhala king emerged to defeat invaders and rule all Lanka under one banner. King Parakramabahu, who united the country in 1155, was one such monarch who made the country militarily strong and economically prosperous.

Among the European powers that conquered parts of the island were the Portuguese (in the 16th century), the Dutch (in the 17th century) and the British, who in 1815, succeeded in taking the last Inhala Kingdom on the island at Kandy. The British named it Ceylon and ruled until 1948, when it won independence.

Since independence, power has been shared in Sri Lanka by two principal parties, the United National Party and the Sri Lanka Freedom Party, with at least two other minor parties also contesting elections. During this time the electorate brought into power and subsequently removed Sirimavo Bandaranaike, the world's first woman prime minister.

The country experienced its first major internal disturbance of recent times in 1971 when insurgents under a radical leadership rose against government. The revolt was brought under control after considerable damage had been done to property and an unknown number of lives had been lost.

In May 1972 the country became a republic with a new constitution.

This was replaced six years later when a new government proclaimed the country a Democratic Socialist Republic with an executive president. In July 1983 an unprecedented communal conflict broke out, in which Tamils living outside predominantly Tamil areas were subject to a wave of violence.

In 1987 the Indian Peace Keeping Force (IPKF) arrived in the north and east provinces, at the invitation of President J. R. Jayewardene to assist the government in finding solutions to the continuing armed struggle for a separate state. Tabbed as an occupying army, the IPKF was forced to leave after President Jayewardene relinquished office two years later. More than 1,500 IPKF soldiers died in Sri Lanka.

President Jayewardene governed the country from 1977 to 1988. Presidential elections were held at the end of 1988 in the wake of unprecedented turmoil, after rioting and leftist-instigated strikes nearly paralysed the economy. In the ensuing election, Jayewardene's deputy, Ranasinghe Premadasa, succeeded him as president and vowed to tackle the widespread turmoil.

The government succeeded in breaking the back of the leftist rebel movement in November 1989 when security forces killed most of the movement's leaders.

Several attempts to reach a political solution to the conflict of the north and east have been in vain, with fresh fighting raging on in the areas between a Tamil militant group (Liberation Tigers of Tamil Eelam) and the Sri Lankan security forces.

Sri Lanka is an island in the central Indian Ocean off the southern tip of India.

Most visitors arrive by air at Colombo International Airport at Katunayake, 32 km northwest of the city.

As of June 1990, 15 international airlines have been operating scheduled flights in and out of Colombo, with Airlanka, Sri Lanka's national carrier, handling the bulk of the inbound and outbound traffic. Ceylon Tourist Board statistics indicate that approximately 90% of the inbound traffic consists of vacationing tourists, while approximately 8% of the arrivals are for business purposes.

A few visitors still arrive by sea, via the Colombo Harbour, which since 1977 has developed into one of Asia's finest port services. The island has two other harbours — at Trincomalee in the northeast and at Galle in the south, both of which function as cargo inlets. The harbour at Trincomalee was naturally formed and is reported to be one of the deepest in the world.

On entry, tourists will be required to have an immigration landing card duly filled in. Part I will be detached and retained by the immigration officer. The tourist will be required to surrender Part II to the immigration officer on departure after producing it to Customs.

Visitors to Sri Lanka must possess a valid passport. Visas are needed except for nationals of Britain and its colonies, Australia, Austria, Bel-

Sri Lanka

gium, Bangladesh, Canada, Denmark, Finland, France, Germany, Indonesia, Irish Republic, Italy, Japan, Luxembourg, Malaysia, the Netherlands, New Zealand, Norway, Pakistan, the Philippines, Singapore, Sweden, Switzerland, Thailand, Yugoslavia, US, South Korea, Saudi Arabia, Oman, Bahrain, Qatar, United Arab Emirates, Kuwait, Spain and the Maldives. Nationals of these countries are allowed to stay as tourists for one month provided they have outbound tickets or can prove they have means for their onward journey.

Facilities are available for travellers in transit to see parts of the island and visit a few places of interest. Information counters at Colombo International Airport can assist those interested.

Travel within the island is entirely unrestricted, but visitors are advised to check with the Ceylon Tourist Board if they are planning solitary trips to the Northern and Eastern provinces while both regions are in the grip of the protracted separatist war.

A certificate of inoculation against yellow fever is necessary for all visitors arriving from an infected area.

There is no limit to the amount of foreign currency allowed into Sri Lanka, except in the case of Indian and Pakistani rupees, where the maximum permissible is Rs 250.

Visitors must declare the amount of currency they bring into the country on the 'D' form, to be filled by every arriving passenger. On certification by customs, this form should be retained and produced at embarkation. Visitors may not take out of the country a sum of money in excess of what they declared on arrival.

Baggage of the arriving visitor is exempt from import duty if the Collector of Customs is satisfied that the visitor will re-export the same articles. Among personal effects, visitors are allowed bring in 200 cigarettes or 50 cigars or 340 cc of tobacco, 1.5 litres spirits and two bottles of wine, 57 cc perfume and 25 cc of toilet water.

Other personal effects allowed in duty free include two cameras with 24 rolls of film, one cine or video camera with film or tape, a portable radio, portable tape recorder, one typewriter and sporting equipment. Visitors are required to declare items of high value which they bring in, to enable checks to be made to ensure they are

taken out.

Export of antiques is banned. Articles more than 50 years old are considered antiques. Visitors are advised not to buy old statues, ornaments, furniture, palm leaf manuscripts and the like without first checking with the Director of National Archives and the Archeological Commissioner.

A licence is required for the purchase of wild animals, birds or reptiles (dead or alive), their skins, feathers, scales or horns. The exports of certain endangered species of Sri Lankan foliage is banned and visitors are encouraged to make early applications for the export of flora and fauna with the Director, Department of Wild Life Conservation.

Sri Lanka gems, including sapphires, rubies and cat's-eyes of any value, can be exported provided the purchaser declares sufficient currency at the time of entry and can show purchase vouchers. A person may also take out up to 3 kg of Sri Lankan tea duty free.

A visitor will be permitted to import a motor vehicle (which includes a motorised boat) without payment of duty and free of import restrictions, provided he is in possession of a valid carnet de passage. He must, however, re-export the vehicle within six months of the date of import. Third party insurance is compulsory in Sri Lanka.

Any dutiable item imported by a visitor to the country as baggage may be left in bond with the customs authorities pending re-export at the time of departure. Merchandise brought into Sri Lanka for commercial purposes will be liable to forfeiture even if it is in transit if it is not covered by a licence from the relevant authorities.

Visitors have to pay a embarkation tax of Rs 350 at the airport at the time of departure.

The exchange rate for telegraphic transfers is fixed daily by the Central Bank of Sri Lanka. The rate for traveller's cheques is 5-10% better than the rate for currency.

In March 1991 the Sri Lankan rupee was being exchanged at the rate of Rs 40.52 per US$1 and Rs 75 per £1.

What foreign currency is brought in must be declared upon entry, which will help visitors to take out the equivalent, or goods to the equivalent, when they leave. Bank or hotel vouchers must be obtained and safely kept each time foreign currency is converted into local currency.

Hindu temple. ▷

Sri Lanka

These will be demanded when visitors wish to re-convert unspent local currency at time of departure.

No more than US$25 worth of Sri Lankan currency may be taken out of the country.

To obtain the best rates visitors should change currency at banks. Most hotels are authorised money-changers, but they give a poorer rate of exchange. International credit cards are accepted at most hotels, but it is advisable to check on entry whether restaurants will accept them.

A Sri Lankan rupee consists of 100 cents. Coins of 10, 25, 50, 100, 200 and 500 cents are in currency. Notes are in denominations of Rs 5, 10, 20, 50, 100, 500 and 1,000.

Sinhala is the most used language, being the mother tongue of 74% of the population. Both Sinhala and Tamil enjoy the joint status of official languages, while English is recognised as a link language and is widely spoken. Although Sinhala is widely spoken throughout the country, Tamil is the language most commonly used in the north and east. English is spoken by about half the population, while many more understand it but are not fluent in conversation. The high literacy rate makes it easy for a foreign traveller to communicate with Lankans, even if they do not speak the same language. Street signs, shop boards, product names and the like are generally in all three languages.

Sri Lanka is a tropical island, with most of the country's weather hovering around 27°C and rarely rising above 32°C. The central region is hilly and cooler with average temperatures in the region of 16°C. Mountainous areas in the interior, rising up to 2,400 m above sea level, report a temperature in the region of 10°C which occasionally drops to freezing point for a few hours.

The overall climate is generally hot and humid during the day, cooling off in the evenings. Early mornings and late afternoons are ideal times for outdoor exercise and sightseeing.

The southwest monsoon brings rain to the western, southern and central regions from May to July, while the northeastern monsoon occurs in the north and east in December and January.

Light cotton-wear is best for coastal areas, while a light jacket or sweater is advisable for the cooler evenings in the hill country. Slacks, sports shirts and shoes (for ladies casual dresses and skirts) will fit almost any occasion. Coats and ties and business suits are usually not required in restaurants and other places, except for formal functions. For business calls, a shirt and tie are acceptable.

Western fashions are widely acceptable; the Ministry of Tourism encourages foreign guests to dress in accordance with the country's traditions and culture.

Wide-brimmed hats and sunglasses are advisable for those spending long hours outdoors. When visiting places of religious worship, visitors are required to remove their shoes and hats, so it is practical to have a pair of slip-on shoes handy.

All the hotels provide laundry services and all cities and towns advertise such services, but they are much cheaper outside hotels. A visitor could inquire for such services from a room boy, bellboy or taxi driver. Same day or 24-hour service outside hotels may be difficult.

Sri Lanka has a five-day working week, Monday to Friday. Government offices, private businesses, schools and all other services are fully operative during these days.

To ease rush-hour traffic congestion, particularly in Colombo, authorities have recently adopted a staggered working schedule. Under the new schedule all consumer-oriented private businesses (such as department stores and grocery shops) in the city and suburbs, with the exception of petrol stations, pharmacies, restaurants, bakeries, etc. shall open at 10 am and continue till 10 pm.

Government offices will open at 8:30 am and close at 4:30 pm, while post offices will be open from 8:30 am to 5 pm daily and on Saturdays from 8:30 am to 12 noon. Banks will be open from 9 am to 1 pm on Mondays and from Tuesday to Fridays from 9 am to 1:30 pm.

Private-operated post offices (agency post offices) are open 24 hours a day, seven days a week, and offer all postal and telecommunication facilities, including international telephone calls and telexes.

Despite the new operating hours, most shops in the cities will pull down their shutters by

8 pm — earlier in rural areas.

Restaurants are open for breakfast and lunch and in the evening from 7 pm to midnight. Round-the-clock services are available in all the five-star hotels and most of the smaller hotels that cater to tourists.

Sri Lankans also enjoy a variety of public and bank holidays (approximately 30 such days during a calendar year) and tourists are advised to check the local calendar before making important appointments. In keeping with traditional Buddhist customs, every full-moon day of the lunar calendar is observed as a public holiday.

FROM THE AIRPORT: The distance to downtown Colombo from the International Airport is 32 km, 45 minutes by road. Airlines operating into the airport do not provide transport to the downtown area. Visitors on charter flights are usually met on arrival by local travel agents. Approved agents provide a taxi service from the airport to Colombo at Rs 450-500 one way, the best way for independent visitors to get to their hotels. Inquire from airport information counters.

TAXIS: Taxi services are available only in Colombo and a few of the bigger cities. Air-conditioned radio taxi cabs are available in Colombo, by calling the agents. See Yellow Pages for details. Minimum rate is Rs 14 per kilometre. Cabs may be hailed on the road or at central locations such as the Colombo Fort railway station or just outside your hotel. Meters in these cars are often broken, defective or rigged, so it is advisable to negotiate a price before your trip begins. A ride on an auto-rickshaw is a treat and a convenient way of getting about town.

The minimum rate is about Rs 6 a km and these three-wheeler rates are always open for negotiation.

BUSES: The Sri Lanka Transport Board maintains an island-wide network of what is considered to be one of the most comprehensive and least expensive bus services in the world. But buses are very crowded much of the time. Express bus services operate between major towns. The Central Bus Station in Colombo's Pettah area has buses leaving for many destinations every hour. Privately operated minibuses also ply the roads on most of the routes at a slightly higher fare than those of the government buses. All buses are very crowded during rush hour.

MAJOR AIRLINES

Airlanka, 14 Sir Baron Jayatilake Mawatha, Colombo 1, or 55 Janadhipathy Mawatha, Colombo 1. Tel: 421161, 27735, 548242-3, 548148, 25369.

Aeroflot, Hemas Bldg, 79-81 York St, Colombo 1. Tel: 25580, 433062.

Balkan Bulgarian Airlines, 6 York St, Colombo 1. Tel: 548235.

Balair (Charter), Walkers Tours Ltd. 130 Glennie St, Colombo 2.

Condor (Charter), 57A, Dharmapala Mawatha, Colombo 3. Tel: 548167, 24532, 29804, 548541.

Emirates, Hotel Galadari Meridien, 64 Lotus Rd, Colombo 1. Tel: 544544, 540709, 541362.

Indian Airlines, 95 Sir Baron Jayatilaka Mawatha, Colombo 1. Tel: 29838, 23987.

KLM Royal Dutch Airlines, 61 Janadhipathi Mawatha, Colombo 1. Tel: 26359, 25984-6.

Kuwait Airways, Ceylinco House, 69 Janadhipathi Mawatha, Colombo 1. Tel:

547828.

LTS & ITU International Airways (Charter), 281 Union Place, Colombo 2. Tel: 27244, 435597, 422875.

Pakistan International Airlines, 432 Galle Rd, Colombo 3. Tel: 575052, 573475.

Saudi Arabian Airlines, Mercantile House, G1 Janadhipathi Mawatha, Colombo 1. Tel: 27911, 27506, 436725.

Singapore Airlines, 30 Sir Baron Jayatilake Mawatha, Colombo 1. Tel: 422711-9.

Thai Airways International, 16 Janadhipathi Mawatha, Colombo 1. Tel: 436201-5.

UTA French Airlines, 5 York St, Mackinnon Mackenzie Bldg, Colombo 1. Tel: 27605-6, 436026.

The following airlines have representative offices in Sri Lanka: Air France, Air India, Alitalia, British Airways, Cathay Pacific, China Airlines, Garuda, Japan Airlines, Korean Air, Lufthansa, Malaysian Airline System, Pan American, Scandinavian Airline System, Swissair and TWA.

TRAINS: Trains are available from the Colombo Fort station to many places of interest. Trains, too, are very crowded during rush hour, but for long-distance travel to the hill country, the north or down south, seats can be reserved in advance via the Colombo Fort station. First-class carriages with air-conditioning, sleeping berths and observation cars are also available. For those willing to meet locals and mingle with the ordinary people, a trip by train can be a pleasant experience. There is also a luxury Hitachi tourist train, a modified steam train (the Viceroy Special) and a luxury rail car plying the southern line.

HIRE CARS: Chauffeur-driven vehicles are available for day hires and for island-wide trips. Follow the recommendations of the information counter staff at your hotel. Rent-a-car services are available through Avis, Hertz, Europcar and a number of other companies listed in the Yellow Pages.

INLAND AIR TRANSPORT: The Sri Lanka Air Force operates internal commercial flights between Colombo and Jaffna, Trincomalee, Ampara, Batticaloa and Vavuniya and has aircraft and helicopters available for charter. Helicopters and small aircraft for travel to any part of the island are available for charter from several private companies that advertise through hotels and travel agents. Rates are negotiable, depending upon the number of passengers.

When travelling on public transport, travellers are advised to keep their money in a safe place. Pickpockets often operate in buses and trains. Most people visitors meet on the roads are friendly, speak good or passable English and will be helpful with directions. Comprehensive road maps of Sri Lanka are available at city book shops.

Tours of Colombo city by day and night, boat cruises on the Indian Ocean and guided bus tours to places of interest in the outstations originate from the capital every day.

Local travel agents can arrange a tour for any visitor in keeping with his or her interests and needs.

Tourists visiting and photographing the ancient monuments must get a ticket from the Cultural Triangle Office, Ministry of Cultural Affairs, 221 Bauddhaloka Ave, Colombo 7 (Tel: 587-912). Tourists are advised to buy a single round ticket for one month for US$12 per adult and half that rate per child. This will permit the

holder to view and photograph monuments in all parts of Sri Lanka (where photography is permitted) without having to pay at each site upon entry.

The Ceylon Tourist Board (CTB) publishes a comprehensive accommodation guide which is supplied free of charge by the travel information counters at the airport and the CTB headquarters at 321, Galle Rd, Colombo 3. This contains full details on accommodation and restaurants which have been inspected and found suitable for visiting foreign guests.

Sri Lanka offers a wide range of accommodation, from international chain hotels to informal guesthouses and unique 'rest houses.' For the visitor who wishes to become acquainted with the Sri Lankan way of life, rooms (with or without food) are also available in private homes, especially in resort areas.

Due to the drop in tourist arrivals during the times of ethnic unrest, Sri Lanka's hotel rooms became amongst the world's cheapest, with a five-star hotel room-rate dropping to US$20 a night. As the situation improves, tourism authorities have insisted that hotels maintain competitive prices in keeping with similar destinations in the Asian region and the rate rose to US$45-50 — still an excellent bargain in view of the quality of service available. Accommodation at other hotels and guesthouses ranges from US$10 to US$45, but is rising. Special suites, conference facilities and business facilities are available in most of the better hotels in Colombo.

COLOMBO

Colombo is home to the country's six five-star class hotels, all affiliated with an international hotel chain of repute. They are **Hotel Ceylon Intercontinental**, **The Hotel Lanka Oberoi**, **Ramada Renaissance Hotel**, **Taj Samudra Hotel**, **Le Galadari Meridien** and the **Colombo Hilton**.

Among the other well-regarded hotels in Colombo are the 125-year-old **Galle Face Hotel**, the **Hotel Taprobane** in the heart of the old Front, and Colombo's only beach resort hotel, the elegant **Mount Lavinia Hotel**.

UPCOUNTRY

Most of the hotels in the hill country still maintain traces of the grandeur of the British Raj, since the colonialists frequented the salubrious hills often to get away from the humidity of Colombo. Worth a visit are **The Grand Hotel** in Nuwara Eliya, **Queen's Hotel** in Kandy (the grand old lady of the hill capital) and honeymooners' paradise, **Hunas Falls Hotel** on the foothills of the Hunnassiriya mountain range. There is a number of government-approved rest houses, which offer clean and comfortable accommodation, in picturesque spots throughout the hill country. These are a good place to stop for breakfast or lunch while on the road, since most of the rural towns lack restaurants of good standard. Bookings for most rest houses can be made from the **Travel Bureau of the Sri Lanka Hotels Corp.** at 63 Janadhipathi Mawatha, Colombo 1.

RESORTS

Spreadings south from Colombo along the Indian Ocean and extending 108 km to Galle are many of Sri Lanka's beach resorts. Among the bigger resort hotels along this strip are **Bentota Beach Hotel** at Bentota, **Coral Gardens Hotel** at Hikkaduwa and the **Neptune Hotel** at Beruwela. There is a number of other hotels, guesthouses and rooming houses along the stretch. These beach communities cater exclusively to the sun-seeking vacationers and offer wind surfing, water skiing, snorkelling, skin diving, deep diving, deep sea fishing and boating. Night life is geared to entertain the vacationer with many open-air restaurants, calypso bands and fresh seafood buffets.

The old Dutch town of **Negombo**, 40 km north of Colombo offers a second beach resort with a number of well-established hotels which cater to beach-bound tourists.

Trincomalee and **Batticaloa** used to be the resorts of the Eastern Province, but the ethnic troubles of the past decade have virtually put a stop to tourism in the area and most of the hotels have closed. Nevertheless, the potential for excellent watersport still exist in this region, with Trincomalee considered as one of the world's finest locations for deep diving.

WILDLIFE AND NATIONAL PARKS

Sri Lanka has a rich and exotic variety of wildlife and a long tradition of conservation. Places to visit include **Yala National Park** and **Kumana Bird Sanctuary** in the far south, **Wilpattu National Park** in the north, **Gal Oya** and **Maduru Oya National Parks** in the east, the **Elephant Orphanage** in Kegalle and the **Botanical Gardens** in Kandy and Nuwara Eliya.

Accommodation within wildlife sanctuaries is provided by the Department of Wild Life Conservation, which maintains bungalows for overnight visitors. Geared to cater to the outdoor types, these rustic bungalows offer essential services only for nature lovers. The bungalows are in heavy demand and bookings must be made in advance at the **Department of Wild Life Conservation**, 54 Chatham St, Colombo 1 (Tel: 24208).

Sri Lankan food is spicy, colourful and a treat to the adventurous palate. Rice plays a major role in the diet, with most people consuming either rice, or a by-product of rice, with all their meals. Rice and curry is the local staple diet and is served in all restaurants. Meals usually consist of a large plate of rice, accompanied by five or six meat, fish and vegetable curries, which the consumer will mix together with his fingers while eating.

Sri Lanka curries consist of a ground chilli and coconut milk base, mixed with a variety of fresh spices, cooked well done and served hot. Any food can be made into a curry and having rice and curry every day is not boring at all, because each curry tastes different.

Restaurants that cater to foreign tourists prepare a tame rice and curry in keeping with the sensitive palates and digestive systems of Westerners; but for a real taste of Sri Lanka one must venture out and experience a real rice and curry meal, even if it is necessary to have a big glass of water, or better still some ripe bananas, to cool off.

Among the exotic curries that are likely to awaken a connoisseur's taste-buds are prawn curry, fresh seafood curry of any sort, mutton and potato curry, egg curry, banana flower curry, jak fruit with coconut sambol (scraped gound coconut with hot, red chilli), curried lotus roots, curried eggplant and chicken curry. There are also numerous varieties of fresh vegetables, most of which are healthy and tasty when cooked in curry form.

Two typically Lankan dishes that visitors must try are egg-hoppers and string-hoppers. The first is a thin, crisp bowl–shaped pancake made of rice flour with an egg baked on top. It is eaten with curry or sambol. Hoppers without eggs are also made and visitors enjoy eating them crisp and hot, straight from the pan, with curry or jam and butter. String-hoppers are nests of thin rice noodles; steamed and lighter than rice, they are popular on dinner and break-

Fishing boats at Negombo.

Photo: Vijitha Yapa

fast tables and go well with kiri-hodi, a very mild coconut milk gravy. Other tasty and uniquely Lankan foods are pittu, roti, milk rice, achchar (pickled onions and green chillies), breadfruit and a variety of local yams.

Sri Lanka boasts of an abundance of fresh fruit, available at every street corner at reasonable prices. Don't forget to sink your teeth into a fresh pineapple, mango or an avacado. Hundreds of other varieties of exotic fruits are also available, among them rambutan, mangosteen, durian and close to 50 varieties of bananas, referred to locally as plantains.

Another pleasant Sri Lankan experience is to drink a king coconut on a hot day. These orange-coloured coconuts are sold at the side of the road and are consumed by making a hole in the fruit and placing it directly over the upturned mouth and letting the sweet water slide down the throat.

Wayside boutiques and restaurants may not be up to standards, though most of them will dish out tasty food at value for money. Local restaurants will not have any cutlery prepared, due to the acceptable local custom of eating with fingers, but you can request cutlery if you feel you need it.

Most of the larger cities will have restaurants that serve Western meals only on order. Colombo has many fine ethnic restaurants — among them restaurants that specialise in Chinese, German, French, Indian, Moghul, Italian, Japanese, Korean, Mexican and Oriental food.

All the five-star hotels have exclusive restaurants, bars, nightclubs and coffee shops open round the clock. Most bars serve foreign liquor, though it is expensive. Locally prodcued liquor includes coconut arrack, rum, gin, brandy and beer.

A 10% service charge is added on to the bill at established restaurants, but most local eateries are so informal that they may not even give you a formal bill.

Most big hotels have floor shows and provide music for dancing late into the night. Gambling has also become one of Sri Lanka's major tourist attractions with licensed casinos being operated in quite a few of the bigger hotels in Colombo and the resort towns.

Among the better known night spots are **The Supper Club** at the Hotel Lanka Oberoi, the **Colombo 2000** and **Le Casino** at Le Galadari Meridien Hotel, **Ritz Casino** at the Ramada Renaissance Hotel, **My Kind of Place** discotheque at the Taj Samudra Hotel, the **Blue Elephant** nightclub at the Colombo Hilton, **Rooftop Casino** at the Hotel Ceylon Intercontinental, the **Blue Leopard** at the Hotel Taprobane, the **Star Dust Club** 15th Lane, Galle Rd, Colombo 3, **Little Hut** at Mt Lavinia Hotel and the **Coral Club Casino** at the Coral Gardens Hotel in Hikkaduwa.

Colombo has several excellent air-conditioned cinemas which screen British, American, and Hindi films. Check morning newspapers for current attractions. English and Sinhala language plays and Sinhala translations of Western plays are staged frequently in Colombo. Popular theatres are **The Lionel Wendt Theatre**, Guildford Crescent, Colombo 7, **YMBA**, Borella, Colombo 8, **Tower Hall**, Maraddana, Colombo 10, and **John de Silva Memorial Theatre**, Ananda Coomarawamy Rd, Colombo 7.

In the resort areas, especially during the tourist season, there are organised outdoor cultural performances, which include traditional dances from the ancient times.

Gems and precious stones are Sri Lanka's most celebrated exports and visitors can buy blue sapphires, cat's-eyes, rubies, amethysts, etc., for personal use and take them out of the country duty free. The export of gems is allowed up to any value so long as the buyer shows that sufficient foreign exchange was brought into the country to cover the purchases.

The State Gem Corp. guarantees the stones it sells and also tests all outside purchases free of charge at its commercial branch office at York St in the Colombo Fort (Tel: 23075). Valuable information on Lanka gems can be obtained from the corporation's headquarters at 25 Galle Face Terrace, Colombo 3 (Tel: 29295). Reputed private dealers in Colombo also sell precious stones. They are listed in numerous shopping guides issued free of charge by the trade. Guarantees are issued for stones. Receipts should be retained for presentation at customs on departure.

Visitors will also find a wide range of exotic and interesting items for sale — among them handicrafts, ceramics, batiks, brassware, caneware, leather products and ready-made garments. Check local shopping guides for details.

Places shoppers will find attractive include **Laksala** on York St, Colombo 1; **Lakmedura** at 26 Rotunda Gardens, Colombo 3, **Lakpahana** on Colombo 3, **Dankotuwa Porcelain**, Laklain Showrooms, 293 Galle Rd, Colombo 3; **Salu Sala**, Vilasitha Niwasa, Havelock Rd, Colombo 5; **Viskam Nivasa**, Thunmulla Junction, Colombo 5, **Mariposa**, 61 Dharmapala Mawatha, Colombo 7, and **Arcadia**, 450 Galle Rd, Colombo 3.

Among the main shopping centres of Colombo are **World Market** in the Pettah, **Liberty Plaza** on Duplication Rd, Colombo 3, **Unity Plaza**, Galle Rd, Colombo 4, **Cornels Super-**

markets in Colombo 4, 5 and 6, and **Galle Face Shopping Arcade** at the Galle Face Hotel. Most of the bigger hotels have their own shopping arcades, but for the real bargains visitors should walk about town.

Duty-free shopping is available at the Colombo International Airport, where purchases have to be made in foreign currency. Although the range of duty-free goods available are good, prices are not as low as in Dubai or Singapore.

A gold purchase facility, run by the Central Bank, operates at the airport.

Being an island country, water sports are Sri Lanka's major attraction. All the resort areas offer professional lessons and equipment for yachting, canoeing, deep-sea fishing, diving, snorkelling, skiing, surfing, wind surfing, etc. Serious fishermen should contact the **Ceylon Anglers Club** in Colombo (Tel: 421752). For fishing in inland lakes, contact the Department of Wildlife Conservation.

Tennis, squash and fitness programmes are available at the leading hotels. There are two 18-hole golf courses in Sri Lanka — one in Colombo and the other in Nuwara Eliya. Golfers regard these courses as excellent.

Sri Lanka is a cricket-mad country. On any given day, visitors can catch a game to watch in most of the city cricket grounds. Rugby is also popular from May to September.

Most of Sri Lanka's festivals date back many centuries, having been born of the religious, superstitious and agricultural traditions that have persisted through the years. One of the noteworthy aspects of these festivities is that prominence is given to all four of the country's major religions — Buddhism, Christianity, Hinduism and Islam. Similarly, holidays have taken into account all the major communities that inhabit the island — the Sinhalese, Tamils, Muslims and Burghers.

Major festivals are observed as holidays, as are full-moon (poya) days. All places of entertainment are closed and no liquor is sold during these days. Participation in functions and events that mark the festivities are encouraged. Here is a sample of Sri Lanka's festival calendar:

January: Full-moon of this month revolves around the colourful Duruthu Perahera, the procession of elephants and lights originating from the Kelaniva Temple in the outskirts of Colombo. Tamils celebrate Thai Pongal day.

February 4: Independence Day, parades and cultural shows, largely in Colombo; Full-moon days' Navam Perahera in Colombo, which proceeds along the Beira Lake.

March: Easter is celebrated throughout the country.

April: Singhala and Tamil New Year, the festive season for most Lankans. Visiting relatives, lighting firecrackers, observing auspicious times and giving gifts.

May: May Day observed in Colombo; Vesak, the Buddhist festival of lanterns to mark the birth, enlightenment and parinibbhana (death) of the Lord Buddha; Ramazan observed by Muslims.

June: Poson, the commemoration of the arrival of Buddhism to the island; celebrations in the ancient capital of Anuradhapura.

July-August: Esala Perahera in Kandy, the reknowned parade of the sacred tooth relic in the hill capital lasts for 10 days; Hindu Vel festival in Colombo and the Kataragama festival, in homage to the god Skanda, held at Kataragama, 280 km south of Colombo.

October-November: Prophet Muhammad's birthday; Deepavali Hindu festival.

December: Christmas celebrations and end-of-year parties.

Addresses

Accident Service, Ward Place, Colombo 7. Tel: 693184, 693185. Ambulance. Tel: 22222.

Emergency, Tel: 433333.

Hospital Durdans, 3 Alfred Place, Colombo 3. Tel: 575205-7.

Hospital Nawaloka, 23 Sri Sugathodaya Mawatha, Colombo 3. Tel: 544444-7.

Ceylon Tourist Board, Steuart Place (opposite the Hotel Oberoi), Colombo 3. Tel: 437059, 437060.

Central Telegraph Office, Duke St, Colombo 1. Tel: 24340, 27167, 27187, 25799.

Railway Tourist Information Centre, Fort Railway Station, Colombo 1. Tel: 435838.

Ceylon Transport Board (Inquiries), Central Bus Station, Olcott Mawatha, Colombo 1. Tel: 28081.

Colombo Airport Katunayake, Tel: 45-2861-5 (Exchange); **Assistant Airport Manager**, Tel: 45-2344; **Tourist Information Centre**, Tel: 45-2411.

Greater Colombo Economic Commission, Investment Promotion Department, P. O. Box 1767, 14 Sir Baron Jayatilake Mawatha, Colombo 1. Tel: 548880, 548105, 22447; Tlx: 21332 ECONOM CE; 21428 DGGCEC CE; Fax: 547995.

Airlanka, 37 York St, P. O. Box 670, Colombo 1. Tel: 421291.

Ceylon Chamber of Commerce, 50 Nawam Mawatha, Colombo 2. Tel: 21745-7.

Automobile Association of Ceylon, 40 Sir Macan Markar Mawatha, Galle Face, Colombo 3. Tel: 421528.

Department of Archaeology, Sir Marcus Fernando Mawatha, Colombo 7. Tel: 694727.

Publications

This Month in Sri Lanka is published by the travel trade and is available for sale at all tourist information counters. *Explore Sri Lanka* is a complimentary monthly trade magazine, available at the Explore Sri Lanka counter at the Colombo International Airport and hotels. Both magazines are updated every month and contain comprehensive cuisine guides, shopping guides, information on nightlife and other activities in the country during the month.

Publications by the Ceylon Tourist Board, such as the *Accommodation Guidebook* and *Sri Lanka Official Tourist Handbook* are available at information centres.

Ample publications on the country's history, traditions, politics, civic life and the economy are available at Colombo bookshops. Two well-known bookshops in Colombo are Lake House Book Shop, 100 Sir Chittampalam Gardiner Mawatha, Colombo 2, and K. V. G. de Silva & Sons, 415 Galle Rd, Colombo 4.

DISCOVERING SRI LANKA

Colombo, a city of open spaces and balmy breezes has grown over the past 10 years to become a thriving metropolis and a regional nerve-centre for South Asian economic activity. Buoyed by the government's liberal open economic policies, Colombo has grown from a gracious colonial showpiece to a crowded and busy business centre, catering to the needs of about 4 million people. Such a large population brings with it the attendant urban evils of pollution, traffic jams and noise.

Although newer and taller structures have

Tea picking in southern Sri Lanka. ▷
Photo: Marcel Barang

Mosque and Colombo City Hall.

Photo: Ellen Rudolph

come up (tallest building is the 38-storey Bank of Ceylon headquarters), Colombo still maintains some of her ancient charm in the turn-of-the-century architecture in the city's **Old Fort**. East of the Fort is the bazaar area **Pettah**, the nation's bargain basement and the receiving and the distribution point of most of the country's produce. Spreading south of the Fort are the newly developed industrial areas, namely Colombo 2, 3, 4 and 5. On the outskirts of the city, in Ratmalana to the south, Kelaniya to the east and in Katunayake to the north, are some of the nation's largest industries. Most of the government and administrative machinery is concentrated in the city boundaries, prompting the daily arrival of large numbers of people from the rest of the country for business purposes.

An attempt is now being made to take administration to the outstations, and the development of industry and other economic activity away from Colombo is well under way.

The governing capital has also been shifted from Colombo to the city of **Sri Jayewardenepura**, a new suburban development 15 minutes away from the city. Parliament and some of the major government-owned ventures have already shifted their headquarters there.

ANCIENT CITIES

Anuradhapura, the besk known of Sri Lanka's ancient cities, was the capital of the island for more than 1,000 years from the 5th century BC. A number of Buddhist monuments and royal ruins dating back 2,000 years prove there was a thriving civilisation here long before many others. The better known of these ruins are the Thuparama Dagaba (3rd century BC); Ruvanveliseya (2nd century BC); the Sri Maha Bodhi (the oldest historically documented tree in the world); the seven-storey Lovamahapaya (also known as the Brazen Place); the Abhayagiri Dagaba (the precincts of which are now being excavated under a special UNESCO project); and the Jetawana Dagaba.

Anuradhapura also has several large irrigation reservoirs — monuments to ancient Sri Lankan engineering ingenuity — more than 1,000 years old. Mihintale, the gateway to Buddhism in Sri Lanka, is 13 km north of Anuradhapura.

Polonnaruwa, Sri Lanka's capital from the 11th to the 13th Century, has at its centre the **Terrace of the Tooth Relic**. The quadrangle here is a group of 12 magnificent buildings. The most popular sites include The Vatadage, a circular relic chamber; the Thuparama, with its ancient stonework roof still intact; and the Galpotha — the stone book with medieval inscriptions. Best examples of sculpture of the Polonnaruwa reign are seen at the Gal Viharaya, a monument with beautifully carved images of the Buddha. Visitors should also visit the site of the

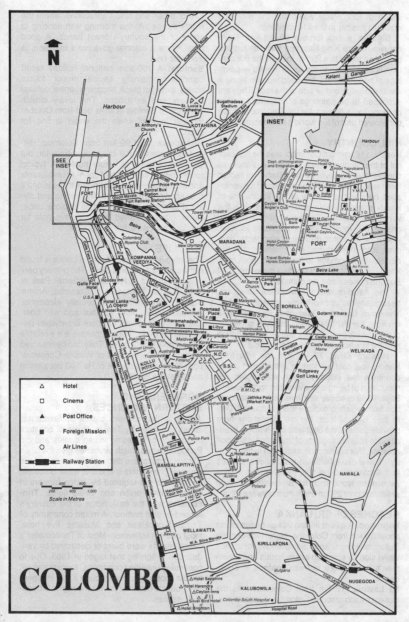

COLOMBO

Legend:

△	Hotel
□	Cinema
▲	Post Office
■	Foreign Mission
○	Air Lines
▬	Railway Station

Scale in Metres
200 400 600 800 1,000

INSET

statue of King Parakramabahu, the monarch who built this city in the 11th century.

Sigiriya, a rock fortress 66 km from Polnnaruwa, where King Kasyapa built his fortified palace on top of this 200-m rock, in the 6th century, is best known today for its murals — paintings of beautiful bare-breasted women along a sheltered ledge on the side of the rock. They are supposed to be paintings of the king's harem plucking lotus flowers for the Buddha and are considered part of the world's art treasures.

HILL COUNTRY

Kandy, 116 km from Colombo, was the last capital of the Singhala kings before the island was completely taken over by the British. The sacred tooth relic of the Buddha is preserved for veneration here at the Temple of the Tooth, one of Kandy's unmistakable landmarks. Kandy is the venue of the annual Esala Perahera in August, one of the most colourful pageants in Asia, where for 10 nights decorated elephants, dancers, torch-bearers and drummers parade the city steets in homage to the sacred tooth relic. Kandy is also home of the two major sects of Buddhist priesthood predominant in Sri Lanka — the Assiriya and the Malwatte Chapters, headquartered in two lovely ancient temples. The Royal Botanical Gardens at Peradeniya (8 km from Kandy) has a wide and rare collection of tropical indigenous flora and an orchid house with the largest known collection in Asia.

Nuwara Eliya, 77 km into the hills from Kandy, is a cool hill station in the heart of the country's tea industry which still enjoys the reputation of being a fine vacation spot. Nuwara Eliya, 1989 m above sea level, is the ideal location from which to explore the tea country. Due to their high altitude, the tea plantations here provide some of the best teas in the world. In addition to maintaining one of the island's two golf courses, this scenic mountain town is the country's flower capital with many varieties of flowers in full bloom round the year. Horton Plains (where the world ends for Sri Lankans) nature reserve is only 29 km away from Nuwara Eliya.

BEACHES OF SRI LANKA

Negombo: A quaint fishing village beach resort about 35 km from Colombo. Here 17th-century Dutch buildings and old Catholic churches stand side by side with luxury hotels and fishermen's huts. There is fresh seafood in abundance.

Mt Lavinia: 12 km from Colombo, it is the closest beach resort to Colombo. A unique mixture of urban and resort attractions, where the nights merge into the morning with dancing to some of the country's finest bands. A good hotel, once a colonial governor's mansion, is available here.

Bentota: A 100-acre national holiday resort complex containing several major tourist hotels, a market place, shopping centre, cultural displays and exhibitions. The lovely stretch of beach at Bentota is at its best from October through to April when the water is fine for sport.

Hikkaduwa: Just 99 km from Colombo, Hikkaduwa caters to the low-budget traveller, but also has some fine luxury hotels. A typical tourist town, it has plenty of open-air restaurants and beach parties. It is also home to the island's best known coral gardens, snorkelling and diving. For those not inclined to explore under water, glass-bottomed boats are available for hire for a glimpse of the sea-bottom.

WILDLIFE

The majority of the wildlife in Sri Lanka is found in the country's national parks. The primary park open to visitors is **Ruhuna National Park** at Yala, 305 km southeast of Colombo. Animal sightings are frequent, especially elephants, leopards, deer, bear, sambur and wild boar. The best time to visit the park is between December and May. Two bungalows are available for rent on a nightly basis. They can be reserved through the Department of Wildlife Conservation. There is a park fee of Rs 100 per person and a vehicle fee of Rs 10.

NORTHERN AND EASTERN PROVINCES

Jaffna is the northern capital of Sri Lanka, largely inhabited by Tamils. Ruins of constant occupation by invading Indian armies and old Portuguese and Dutch structures give the city a cultural atmosphere distinct from the rest of the country. The climate is arid and water is scarce, so hard work is required by Jaffna farmers to maintain their onion and chillie fields. **Trincomalee** is in the east, home of the country's second-largest harbour. A mixed community of Tamil, Singhalese and Muslims live here, most of them fishermen. Most of Trincomalee's beach resorts were burnt or destroyed by vandals during fighting that raged in 1983. Due to continuing unsettled conditions, tourism has yet to take root again, even though a few independent tourists continue to visit the region's beautiful beaches.